Publications of the Committee on
Taxation, Resources and Economic Development

9

Proceedings of a Symposium Sponsored by the
Committee on Taxation, Resources and
Economic Development (TRED)
At the University of Wisconsin—Madison, 1974

Other TRED Publications

Metropolitan Financing and Growth Management Policies

Principles and Practice

Edited by
George F. Break

Published for the Committee on
Taxation, Resources and
Economic Development by
THE UNIVERSITY OF WISCONSIN PRESS

Published 1978
The University of Wisconsin Press
Box 1379, Madison, Wisconsin 53701
The University of Wisconsin Press, Ltd.
70 Great Russell Street, London

First printing
Printed in the United States of America

For LC CIP information see the colophon
ISBN 0-299-06920-6

Publication of this book was made possible in part
by support from the Schalkenbach and the Lincoln foundations

Contributors

Roy W. Bahl

Professor of Economics and Director, Metropolitan Studies Program,
The Maxwell School, Syracuse University

Arthur P. Becker

Professor of Economics, University of Wisconsin—Milwaukee

George F. Break

Professor of Economics, University of California, Berkeley

Gail C. A. Cook

Executive Vice President, C. D. Howe Research Institute, Montreal

Daniel M. Holland

Professor of Finance, Alfred P. Sloan School of Management,
Massachusetts Institute of Technology

Hans R. Isakson

Assistant Professor of Real Estate and Urban Economics, University of Georgia

Richard W. Lindholm

Professor of Finance, University of Oregon, Eugene

Peter Mieszkowski

Professor of Economics, University of Houston

William H. Oakland

Professor of Economics, The Ohio State University

Oliver Oldman

Professor of Law and Director of the International Tax Program,
Harvard Law School

George E. Peterson

Director of Public Finance, The Urban Institute

Henry O. Pollakowski

Assistant Professor of Economics, University of Washington

Larry D. Schroeder

Associate Professor of Public Administration, The Maxwell School,
Syracuse University

Donald C. Shoup

Associate Professor of Urban Planning, University of California,
Los Angeles

David L. Sjoquist

Associate Professor of Economics, Georgia State University

Contents

vii

List of Tables and Figures

Tables

Figures

Metropolitan Financing and
Growth Management Policies
Principles and Practice

George F. Break

Introduction

Planning the program for the Thirteenth Annual Conference of the Committee on Taxation, Resources and Economic Development (held on October 25-27, 1974) on such a vast and intractable theme as the fiscal problems besetting our nation's cities—a theme already well worked over and incapable of comprehensive treatment, even by highly accomplished experts—meant taking the plunge into some rather arbitrary choices. One option was to select some single aspect of the urban fiscal scene narrow enough to be coped with in a three-day discussion. Another was to follow the more free-form route of fashioning the program around the current research interests of a number of leading specialists in the field. Each of these approaches—the one directing the attention of experts to a single topic, the other following the experts into the areas currently engrossing them—offers comparative advantages and disadvantages. In the end the second of the alternatives was chosen, primarily because it seemed the better way to capitalize on the special quality of TRED meetings. These annual events are closely knit professional and social gatherings providing the participants with unusual opportunities to exchange ideas, obtain candid appraisals of developing research studies, and hammer out together some of the ambiguities and complexities that impede the development of effective urban fiscal policies. Focusing the program on the working research of the participants, it was felt, would lead to more productive discussion than would concentration upon some predetermined issue.

This format produced a spirited and fruitful discussion of a wide variety of urban policy questions. What, if anything, should be done to control the rate of urban growth or to direct it into particular activities? How should zoning laws be changed to achieve the most efficient patterns of urban land use? How great is the risk that a move toward areawide metropolitan government would increase local government expenditures and tax burdens? How real are the fears that higher local taxes will repel business enterprises and thereby frustrate the efforts of hard-pressed city governments to raise more money? How can the property tax be improved and what will be the effects of different measures designed to do so? How would different families be affected by a shift from local property to local income taxation or by the assumption of more state responsibility for the financing of particular local government programs? How much and in what ways would a shift from property to land value taxation affect the capital intensity of urban land development? What impact does the federal individual income tax have on local land use and development and which federal tax reforms should local officials especially push for? What other factors determine the timing of land conversion sales at the urban fringe, and what, if anything, can policy makers do to alter that timing when it threatens to produce chaotic land development patterns?

The chapters dealing with these questions may be divided into three broad groups. The first group discusses some important aspects of the economic and fiscal environment in which local governments operate. From the point of view of households living in any community the nature of that environment is determined by three main outside influences: business enterprises, state governments, and the federal government. In his survey of the effects of local taxes on intraurban industrial location, William H. Oakland deals with the first of these outside groups. One of the dilemmas of local public finance has always been that economists typically regard local tax burdens as a minor factor in most business decisions to locate new plants, while politicians look on them as major determinants. Focusing on intraurban property tax differentials because they are the most likely source of tax-induced business relocations, Oakland demonstrates that they are frequently a high enough fraction of profits to be important, and that federal deductibility does not diminish that importance. He notes that widespread capitalization of intercommunity property tax differentials into higher and lower land values would eliminate their impact on business locational decisions but concludes that this is an empirical question requiring further study. His search of the literature, however, turned up only three such studies, and none of these, after critical examination, yielded reliable results. What is needed, in Oakland's view, is the development of a general equilibrium model of industrial location that analyzes jointly the behavior of business firms and their host communities in urban areas. The last part of his chapter deals with some important building blocks for that model which will be of interest not only to economic researchers but to local government policy makers as well.

Perhaps no state has publicized as well as has Oregon its deep concern over the potential environmental costs of mismanaged growth. In any case, in 1973 Oregon did become the first state to adopt statewide regulations on land use, and these are discussed in the first part of Richard W. Lindholm's chapter on property taxation and growth management in Oregon. He then surveys similar state activities elsewhere in the nation and concludes with a discussion of Oregon's special property tax treatment of farmland, forest land, open-space land, and federally owned lands. The result has been the establishment in Oregon of a formidable group of bureaucratic controls and economic inducements to nonintensive use of nonurban land and natural resources that other parts of the country will watch with interest. At first glance, so bucolic a topic may seem far removed from the treatment of this country's urban ills. Growth and land use management, however, is a policy area of increasing importance to metropolitan governments and one, moreover, that faces some of the same problems either dealt with, or created by, Oregon's pioneering legislative efforts. Urban experts need make no apologies for studying that state's leadership efforts to optimize rates of regional growth and the structure of land use patterns.

The other two important actors in the current urban fiscal drama are the owners of land on the urban-rural fringe and the federal government itself. Both of these are dealt with in George E. Peterson's land conversion and development model, presented in the first section of his chapter on federal tax policy and land conversion at the urban fringe. Having thus specified the interacting factors determining bid prices for land in both developed and undeveloped uses, Peterson goes on to discuss the effects on the timing of land sales of estate taxation, capital gains tax rules, and preferential property tax assessment laws. Several empirical tests of the land conversion model, using 1971-73 data for the Baltimore metropolitan area, were made, and their results compared to those from other studies. Peterson concludes that federal tax laws are not an important determinant of the timing of land sales and conversion at the urban fringe but that the life-cycle stage of the landowner is. In Baltimore County, he notes, the overwhelming majority of the land converted to subdivision use came onto the market in the period between the owner's retirement and death.

The second group of chapters deals with the theory and practice of metropolitan finance both here and abroad. Peter Mieszkowski leads off with a theoretical discussion on three aspects of urban land-use regulation. The first aspect involves ways and means of achieving maximum economic efficiency in urban land markets and contains a number of guidelines for the development of better zoning laws. The second is one all too frequently neglected by urban planners and fiscal policy makers. This is the complex set of capitalization effects by which private land markets adjust to intercommunity differentials in tax rates and government service levels. Failure to take account of these effects means both that policy changes will be proposed when none is needed and that those changes actually enacted will generate unintended windfall gains and losses. Another result, as Mieszkowski stresses, is that relative land prices may be an incorrect guide to land use planning both at the local (municipal) level and at the metropolitan level. The third aspect of urban land-use regulation involves the case for, or against, government intervention in order to change the allocation of population among metropolitan regions. This leads immediately to such highly controversial policies as curbs on growth in some areas and subsidies to growth in others. These issues, which are likely to be much in the public eye in future years, can benefit greatly from theoretical analyses of the type Mieszkowski provides here.

The second theoretical chapter in this group deals with the effect of property taxes on the capital intensity of urban land development. Critics of the present property tax, and particularly those favoring land value taxation as an alternative, have long stressed the deleterious effects they believe property taxation has on the development of urban land, and supporters of the property tax have vigorously disputed these contentions. What this debate has most lacked is a comprehensive theoretical framework that could serve as the basis for empirical estimation of the importance of the different disputed effects. It is that kind of base that Donald C. Shoup seeks to provide in his essay. Having identified the key structural parameters that need to be estimated, he concludes by discussing two examples of the kind of empirical research needed to resolve the dispute between land-value and property tax advocates. Though these provide no definitive answers, they do strike an optimistic tone about future research prospects and suggest some directions that designers of such projects might fruitfully take.

The next two chapters shift the focus from general theoretical considerations to some of the practices of metropolitan finance in other countries. Both present and discuss some of the results of large, ongoing research projects, Gail C. A. Cook dealing with her studies of metropolitan Toronto and Roy W. Bahl reporting on his detailed case studies of metropolitan governments in less developed countries. Cook first discusses the history and objectives of governmental reorganization in the Toronto urban area and then turns her attention to three propositions that will be of interest to all fiscal experts: (1) that centralizing the financing of a government function formerly characterized by significant interlocal expenditure level differentials will increase total expenditures on that function; (2) that total education expenditures of the different boroughs in a metropolitan area are a positive function of the net subsidy received from the metropolitan government for educational purposes; and (3) that the tax differentials that were eliminated by the 1967 consolidation of Toronto governments tended to be capitalized into higher and lower residential property values.

Systematic empirical testing of these three hypotheses yielded a mixture of conclusive and inconclusive results. The first hypothesis, dealing with the "equalizing-up" pressures thought to characterize any systematic elimination of interlocal expenditure differentials, was confirmed solidly for education, and somewhat less so for fire expenditures. Police expenditures provided a convenient control group for this analysis since they, unlike education and fire programs, were not affected by the 1967 consolidations. Consistent with the first hypothesis under test, no significant "before and after" change in police expenditures was found. Consistent with the second tested hypothesis, local expenditures on education were also found to be consistently higher, the higher the net subsidy received by the school district from the metropolitan government. The evidence on capitalization effects, on the other hand, was sometimes indicative of their occurrence and sometimes inconclusive.

Bahl presents a wealth of information about urban property taxation in less developed countries. While some cities apply a single tax rate to all taxable property, for example, others apply a progressive rate structure to different assessment value classes (Ahmedabad, Kingston, and Cartegena), while still others differentiate their rates by location of property (Bogotá, Bombay, Singapore, Kingston, and Hong Kong), or by type of property taxed (Lusaka and Seoul). Property taxes as a percentage of income in 1971-72 ranged from a high of 6.4 percent in Lusaka to a low of 0.2 percent in Jakarta. Three examples of the use of property taxation to finance and guide urban development are discussed: the rehabilitation of core city housing in Bombay after 1969, the land adjustment scheme in Seoul, and the Colombian valorization scheme in Bogotá and Cartegena. The chapter closes with a short evaluation of the performance of urban property taxation in developing countries. Lack of systematic data precludes the kind of analysis that is possible for this country, but Bahl's studies do indicate the widespread existence of weak assessment and policy planning practices, a relatively low income elasticity of property tax revenues in most areas, and a much more active use of property taxation to change the nature of urban development in less developed countries than has been the practice in the United States.

The last three chapters deal with various aspects of property tax reform and test their consequences for three of the major metropolitan areas in the country. Larry D. Schroeder and David L. Sjoquist take the Atlanta SMSA for a case study of the incidence and economic effects of the homestead property tax exemption. They begin by developing a modified general equilibrium model based on previous work by Arnold C. Harberger, Mieszkowski, and Charles E. McLure, Jr., and then proceed to estimate empirically the key structural parameters in that model. These results are then used to determine the differential incidence, by family income class, of a tax policy that increased the size of the homestead exemption for homeowner-occupants and recouped the resulting revenue losses by an increase in the tax rate on all taxable property. This is an undertaking of considerable complexity both theoretically and empirically. On the theoretical side the main problem is to determine the extent to which the burdens of property taxes levied in the city of Atlanta are likely to be exported to persons living outside that area. The authors deal deftly both with the many analytical uncertainties and with the widespread data inadequacies that characterize this kind of fiscal research. Their final set of alternative burden distribution estimates, shown separately for renters and homeowners, provides not only a better basis on which to judge the equity and economic efficiency of changes in the property tax homestead exemption in Atlanta but also a useful model for future policy analysts to follow.

In their chapter on estimating the impact of full value assessment on taxes and value of real estate in Boston, Daniel M. Holland and Oliver Oldman deal with a policy change that soon may be ordered by the courts in different parts of the country. Though Massachusetts law requires taxable property to be assessed at full market value, experts have long known that actual assessments depart significantly, and what is worse nonuniformly, from that standard. The first task of the Holland-Oldman study was to document these assessment variations by developing, for broad categories of taxable property in 1972, measures of both their full market and their current assessed values. This is a major research undertaking, fraught with pitfalls and booby traps that the authors adroitly avoid or defuse. The result, of course, is not a nice neat set of definitive estimates, but rather one, in the authors' words, "based on fragmentary data and numerous assumptions, many of them questionable." That, however, is the nature of research in this area, and the estimates obtained do indeed appear to be sufficiently accurate to suggest the orders of magnitude of the redistribution of tax liabilities attendant on changing the basis of property valuation for tax purposes.

Having established that large variations in assessment ratios do exist—whereas residential property had an average assessment-to-full-market-value ratio of 27 percent, commercial property had an average ratio of 18 to 52 percent depending on whether it was built after or before 1960—Holland and Oldman proceed to simulate the effects on different tax-payer groups of moving to full market value assessments on all properties, while keeping total property tax revenues constant. This, too, is a difficult exercise. Account must especially be taken of the shifting of tax burden changes into higher or lower property values in Boston. This set of interactions is particularly bothersome because property values cannot be determined until tax liabilities are known and tax liabilities cannot be determined until property values are known. Holland and Oldman provide an especially illuminating analysis of this complex, but unavoidable, phenomenon. The final results show a rather massive redistribution of property tax burdens that few politicians could contemplate with equanimity or with much expectation of electoral appeal. Quite appropriately, the final part of the Holland-Oldman chapter is devoted to a discussion of ways and means of dealing with this difficult fiscal dilemma.

The final essay deals with the burden on the city of Milwaukee and its residents of the real property tax compared with the individual income tax. Using expenditure and revenue data for 1970, Arthur P. Becker and Hans R. Isakson simulate the effects on Milwaukee residents of two major changes in the financing of local government services: (1) a state-wide shift of financing responsibility for certain services from the local to the state level and in particular from the local property tax to the state individual income tax; and (2) a shift in Milwaukee only from the property tax to a local income tax levied as a flat percentage of each resident's state income tax liability. Both are policies of high current interest, and a major contribution of the authors is to show that the effects of these policies are by no means obvious or unambiguous. Each interested locality will have to make its own calculations, and each will have to deal with the uncertainties of property tax incidence which, unfortunately, have an important bearing on the results to be obtained from these simulation exercises. Becker and Isakson move a long way toward an answer for Milwaukee and in the process illuminate the way for other researchers. As with the other essays in this volume the message to policy makers is clear: look before you leap and be guided by what you find here.

I. GROWTH MANAGEMENT

1 *William H. Oakland*

Local Taxes and Intraurban Industrial Location: A Survey

There are few issues in public finance which arouse as much controversy as the impact of jurisdictional tax differentials upon the location of industry. Controversies exist only when there is conflicting evidence or when there is no evidence. In this case, it is much more the latter than the former which is true: to date, economists have provided little evidence one way or the other. Three interrelated factors account for this: (1) we do not yet fully understand the processes which influence industry intrametropolitan location; (2) there is a general lack of necessary data; and (3) few researchers have attempted to study the issue. Indeed, other than a few none-too-informative questionnaire studies, I have been able to identify only three serious efforts to isolate the impact of fiscal variables upon intrametropolitan industrial location. If we are to make progress with respect to this important issue, we simply need to devote more resources to the subject. The difficulties posed by (1) and (2) above, in my view, are not insurmountable.

The debate over the issue of tax differentials and industrial location has been spawned by a considerable body of evidence that activity in our large urban areas is becoming increasingly suburbanized (see, for example, Goldstein and Moses, 1973; Mills, 1974; and Muth, 1969). Suburbanization has not been confined to housing but has characterized employment as well. This process has been held to have an adverse

13

impact upon the urban poor. Since the poor are concentrated in our central cities, their access to employment is diminished. Furthermore, decentralization has eroded the tax base used to support redistributive fiscal activities.

There is also a considerable body of evidence showing that fiscal conditions in central cities have deteriorated and are continuing to deteriorate relative to their suburbs (for example, ACIR, 1967a; Netzer, 1966; and Oakland, 1973). This deterioration has been manifested in substantially higher property tax rates in central cities than in their suburbs. Since central cities rely much more heavily upon nonresidential property taxes as a source of local revenue, some observers have alleged that central cities are caught in a vicious spiral (among the studies emphasizing such a process are Oates et al., 1971; and Rothenberg, 1970). The suburbanization of employment has placed heavy upward pressure on city tax rates, and the tax rates, in turn, are alleged to provide further impetus for industrial outmigration. It is this latter effect which is at issue: to what extent does the higher central city tax rate lead to a relocation of industry? Few observers have argued that the major thrust for employment suburbanization stems from fiscal forces. Rather, there appears to be a broad consensus that the principal causes of decentralization have been transport cost reductions and the growth of urban population and real income. The area of controversy surrounds the extent to which this process has been exacerbated by fiscal considerations.

While the plight of our central cities has occupied a major place in the debate, the question of industrial location is also important with respect to the suburban site to which industry is attracted. To the extent that the choice of a particular suburban community reflects tax rate differentials, fiscal neutrality is violated.[1] Even if it should be demonstrated that the suburbanization of employment is not reinforced by city-suburban fiscal differentials, it is important to determine whether such differentials among suburban jurisdictions have an impact upon industrial location.

Earlier Surveys

Due (1961) and the Advisory Commission on Intergovernmental Relations (1967b) have surveyed the evidence concerning the impact of interjurisdictional tax differentials upon industrial location. It seems fair

---

1. This assumes that tax differentials are not accompanied by expenditure differentials. For a somewhat different view of the problem posed by industrial mobility, see Rinehart and Laird (1972).

to assert, however, that the major focus of these surveys was on the impact of interstate differentials upon industry's choice among states or urban areas. Neither survey found convincing evidence that such a relationship exists. To quote Due: "On the basis of all available studies, it is obvious that relatively high business tax levels do not have the disastrous effects often claimed for them. While the statistical analysis and study of location factors are by no means conclusive, they suggest very strongly that the tax effects cannot be of major importance" (1961, p. 71). Underlying these findings is the judgment that tax differentials are insignificant relative to other regional cost differences. That this is generally felt to be the case is reflected by the total absence of fiscal considerations in recent comprehensive econometric models of the regional distribution of industry within the United States (Burrows and Metcalf, 1971).

The significance of these findings for this study is that the supply of industrial firms to a particular metropolitan area can be assumed independent of the fiscal environment in the area. Thus the problem reduces to one of determining whether fiscal factors influence the spatial distribution of this stock of firms within the urban area.

Despite his negative findings with respect to interstate tax differentials, Due conceded that taxes may play a more significant role in the intraurban location decision. At this level, factors affecting regional choice are neutralized—hence, taxes may play a decisive role. Due argued, however, that local taxes represent too small a portion of total cost to be controlling in a significant number of cases.

In its study, the ACIR arrived at a similar result. Because the non-fiscal forces underlying the decentralization of urban employment are very strong, intraurban tax differentials may not exert a significant influence. Nevertheless, the ACIR was less confident than Due about its conclusions. It pointed to the existence of industrial tax havens in some of our major urban areas as evidence that tax factors can and do matter.

That taxes become more important as the region of search narrows has intuitive appeal. This hypothesis has been given support by McMillan (1965), who re-examined questionnaires which were sometimes used to deemphasize the importance of taxes. He found that if factors which do not significantly vary within an urban area are eliminated taxes rank high among those location factors mentioned by businessmen.

Whether intrametropolitan tax cost differentials are too small to be of major consequence, as alleged by Due and to a lesser extent by the ACIR, is not clear. Due seemed to base his conclusions upon three considerations: (1) that local business taxes amount to a small fraction of total cost; (2) that local taxes are deductible under the federal income tax; and (3) that businesses may be in a position to shift the burden of what tax cost differentials remain. We shall treat these in turn.

That local taxes comprise a small part of total cost does not mean that they constitute an insignificant part of total profits. Consider the property tax. Effective rates of 3 percent or more are not uncommon in urban areas. Stigler (1963) has found that the average rate of return in manufacturing to be 14 percent. Hence, a 3 percent property tax amounts to more than 20 percent of total profit for manufacturing firms—not an insignificant amount. The appropriate computation relates to tax *differentials* among urban units, however, not to the level of urban property tax rates. Nevertheless, there is good reason to believe that suburban-central city property tax rate differentials are substantial—often differing by as much as a factor of two (see ACIR, 1967b). This would imply a cost differential of approximately 10 percent of profits. Hamer (1972) also arrived at such a figure in his study of the Boston area, in which he compared the costs of a typical firm operating in the central city or suburbs. Taken alone, therefore, differential local tax costs constitute a nontrivial locational incentive. This is given added weight when it is realized that comparisons of *average* suburban rates with the central city rate may considerably understate the *range* of tax cost differentials existing in many urban areas. For example, Beck (in ACIR, 1967a, pp. 170-76) found that effective rates in the Jersey City area varied from 8.07 percent to 2.27 percent, while the difference between the central city and average suburban rate was only 1.5 percent.

As far as federal income tax deductibility of state and local taxes is concerned, this is somewhat of a red herring. If gross tax costs amount to 10 percent or more of preincome tax profits, net tax costs also amount to the same percentage of after-tax profits.

Finally, we must consider the possibility that tax rate differentials may be shifted from business firms to other units. For example, it is conceivable that land costs will fully reflect tax rate differentials, thereby negating any locational incentive that may exist.[2] There are, however, also conditions under which land prices will not adjust at all to industry tax differentials. This issue cannot be settled a priori; it can only be resolved by empirical study. Neither Due nor the ACIR, however, offered any evidence regarding this important issue.

Thus, it would appear that the conclusions of Due and the ACIR were based upon introspection or casual empiricism rather than upon careful empirical analysis. Acceptance or rejection of their positions must await further empirical analysis. It is to such studies that I now turn.

---

2. For a discussion of backward shifting, see Brazer (1961).

Table 1.1. Summary of Multiple Regression Models on the Relationship of Local Taxes and Industrial Location[a]

	Beaton and Joun (1968)	Fox (1973)	Schmenner (1973)
Dependent variables	Percentage increase in manufacturing employment, 1958–65 (Y)	Per capita increase in industrial tax base, 1964–69 (Y)	(a) Percentage of SMSA manufacturing employment (establishments), 1967–69, 1969–71 (Y) (b) Percentage increase in SMSA manufacturing employment (establishments), 1967–69, 1969–71 (Y)
Independent variables			
Tax	(a) Effective property tax rate (PT) (b) Recent percentage changes in property tax rate (ΔPT)	Statuatory property tax rate (PT)	(a) Effective property tax rate as a fraction of central city's rate (t'') (b) Same as (a) but for income tax (t') (c) Number of years income tax in effect (Du)
Access	(a) Proximity to railroad (R) (b) Proximity to freeway (F)	(a) Access to interstate highway (F) (b) Population density (D) (c) Distance to city center (u) (d) Percentage of real property base industrial (I)	(a) Access to railroad (R) (b) Number of freeway interchanges (F) (c) Population density (D) (d) Distance to city centers (u)
Land market	(a) Price of land (P) (b) Percentage of industrially zoned land vacant (V)	(a) Price of land (P) (b) Percentage of land which is vacant (V)	
Scale factor			Percentage of SMSA population or land (%)
Amenities		Safety expenditures per capita (S)	Per pupil expenditure as a fraction of central city level (e)
Other	Capital assets per unit of industrial land (K)		
Simultaneous variables	Price of land	(a) Price of land (b) Property tax rate	Percentage of SMSA population
Regions studied	Orange Co., Calif.	Cleveland, Cincinnati	Cleveland, Cincinnati, Minneapolis-St. Paul, Kansas City

[a] Letters in parentheses represent the notation used when presenting results.

Statistical Studies

Let me begin this section with the observation that my literature search turned up only a single study which has been reported in the usual outlets—scientific books and journals. And the one study I did uncover consisted of a six-page dissertation abstract (Schmenner, 1974). Fortunately, however, I was able to procure a copy of the dissertation (Schmenner, 1973).

Continuing my search, however, I was able to identify two additional studies (Beaton and Joun, 1968; Fox, 1973). The first was a monograph published as a report by a California state college and the other an unpublished study financed by the Ohio Department of Economic and Community Development. Undoubtedly other studies exist—sponsored perhaps by state and local agencies, chambers of commerce, or bureaus

Table 1.2. Regression Results[a]

Beaton and Joun (1968)
Orange County, California

$$Y = -35.08 - 86.84PT - 2.06(\Delta PT) + 3.73P - 48.96K - 1.16R + 1.74F - .54V$$
$$\quad\quad (34.06) \quad (6.45) \quad\quad (.75) \quad (9.94) \quad (1.31) \quad (1.06) \quad (.42)$$

(Figures in parentheses are standard errors; R^2 not applicable)

Fox (1973)
Cleveland

$$Y = 3.46 - .066PT - .021P + .531u - .051F + .028I - 1.29V + .022S$$
$$\quad (2.24) \quad (3.52) \quad (1.64) \quad (2.09) \quad (2.39) \quad (2.42) \quad (1.73) \quad (2.37)$$

Cincinnati

$$Y = -.168 + .003PT + .0005P + .010u - .004D - .0009S$$
$$\quad\quad (1.41) \quad (1.49) \quad\quad (.198) \quad\quad (.414) \quad (2.06) \quad (9.48)$$

(Figures in parentheses are t values; R^2 not applicable)

Schmenner (1973)
Percentage of SMSA employment, 1969–71 (all areas)

$$Y = .029 + .00165t^p + .0045t^t - .00104Du + .00612R + .00235e - .483\% \text{ Land}$$
$$\quad (.98) \quad (.08) \quad\quad (.52) \quad\quad (2.06) \quad\quad (.86) \quad\quad (1.45) \quad\quad (3.73)$$

$$-.00104U + 1.50F + .00000124D$$
$$\quad (1.93) \quad\quad (11.10) \quad (1.34)$$

($R^2 = .56$; figures in parentheses are t values)

Percentage of SMSA new establishments, 1969–71 (all areas)

$$Y = .0231 + .00244t^p - .01154t^t - .00103Du - .39\% \text{ Land} - .00177e + .00682R$$
$$\quad (1.19) \quad (.19) \quad\quad (3.03) \quad\quad (3.10) \quad\quad (4.61) \quad\quad\quad (.11) \quad\quad (1.47)$$

$$-.00277U + .170F - .00000071D$$
$$\quad (.79) \quad\quad (1.93) \quad (1.17)$$

($R^2 = .21$; figures in parentheses are t values)

[a]Symbols are explained in table 1.1.

of business research at state universities. Time and resources precluded me, however, from carrying out a more thorough search. Nevertheless, it is my view that if significant progress had been made on this important issue, it would, in time, appear in one of the traditional outlets. Furthermore, the two studies on which I report can be assumed to be representative of the type of results obtained in such studies.

Each of the studies I am about to summarize uses the technique of multiple regression analysis to isolate the effect of tax rate differentials upon the distribution of industry within an urban area. To be successful, the multiple regression technique requires that all determinants, tax as well as nontax, be included in the analysis. To do so generally requires an underlying theoretical framework. While the studies differ with respect to the attention given theoretical considerations, none develops a theoretical model of industrial location. Rather, the choice of nontax determinants is approached in an ad hoc fashion.

Given the preceding remarks, it is rather surprising that the set of nontax determinants employed in the several studies is remarkably similar (see table 1.1). For example, each study employs one or more measures of access to transportation facilities. Two of them employ other access measures: to labor supply; and to urban markets. Two of them allow for supply conditions in the market for land. Finally, two of them employ measures of government expenditures. Despite these similarities, the various authors often offer a completely different rationale for the inclusion of a variable; not infrequently, their sign expectations are opposite. In all cases, the authors recognize the possibility of simultaneous equations bias; hence, simultaneous equation estimating techniques are employed.

Beaton and Joun (1968)

Let me begin with the study done of the twenty cities in Orange County, California. Here the authors simultaneously estimated two equations: one for manufacturing employment growth; the other for the price of land. The authors reasoned (correctly in my view) that the price of land could not be treated as independent of other variables in the regression equation. The estimates for manufacturing employment are shown in table 1.2.

It would appear that the property tax rate retards economic development; its sign is negative and is statistically significant. In fact, however, Beaton and Joun found the reverse to be true—high property tax rates encourage industry! Notice that the price of land has a large positive coefficient (itself a highly suspicious result). Also, recall that the price of land was simultaneously estimated. In this equation, employment growth had a large, positive, significant coefficient. In addition, the coefficient of the tax rate was positive and significant. If we substitute from the land price equation into the employment growth equation, most of the coefficients of the latter change sign—including that of the tax rate. Given the unreasonableness of the signs of the price of land in the employment equation, and of the tax rate in the land price equation, such an incredible result cannot be accepted.

Fox (1973)

Let me turn next to the Fox study of the Cleveland and Cincinnati areas. Separate estimates were obtained for the two areas. The Cleveland results are the more interesting so I shall discuss them first. Like the Orange County study, industrial investment was simultaneously estimated with the price of land. But Fox went one step further: he also estimated the property tax rate itself. His reasoning was that areas which have high industrial investment would, ceteris paribus, tend to enjoy lower property tax rates.

Fox's estimate of the structural investment equation is shown in table 1.2. It will be noted that the tax rate coefficient is negative and is statistically significant. Evaluated at the mean, the elasticity of investment to the tax rate is 4.4—which suggests that industrial investments is highly sensitive to changes in tax rate. Furthermore, the coefficients of land price, degree of industrialization, and safety expenditures have the expected sign. The positive coefficient on distance from the city center reflects the other forces which underlie urban decentralization. The coefficients of vacant land and highway accessibility, however, run counter to one's intuition. Fox's explanation of these perverse signs is suggestive of an underlying weakness in the model. He argued that the negative sign of the highway proximity variable is a statistical artifact, simply reflecting the way in which the dependent variable is scaled. From table 1.1 it is seen that industrial investment is expressed in per capita terms. Fox interpreted the coefficient of highway accessibility as simply reflecting that people are more attracted to highways than is industry. He pointed out that when the equation was estimated with the *level* of investment as the dependent variable, the sign of the highway variable was positive.

If we accept Fox's logic, his estimate says nothing about the sensitivity of investment *levels* to property tax rate changes. For one could argue that his results simply reflect that people respond more to tax rate differentials than does industry. Indeed, his results are consistent with the premise that investment responds positively to tax rate increases.

Putting the matter differently, there is no reason to suppose that industrial investment would be proportional to population if tax rate differentials did not exist. Unfortunately, Fox did not present the results of estimating the *levels* of industrial investment.

That Fox's results for Cleveland are suspect is further confirmed by the inability of the model to work in the Cincinnati area. Here we find that tax rates are positively related to industrial investment. This confirms my suspicion that the model, as formulated, is compatible with any response to property tax changes. The poor performance of the other independent variables also supports my contention that the model is inappropriately specified. Nevertheless, there are several additional reasons why the model does poorly in the Cincinnati area. For one thing, Fox's sample did not include the Kentucky portion of the SMSA. For another, property tax differentials are much narrower in Cincinnati than in Cleveland. This is because the income tax differentials are more pronounced in the former than in the latter. Strangely, Fox did not include income tax differentials in the investment equation. He did, however, include it in the property tax equation. If one calculates the reduced form for industrial investment, it turns out that income taxes adversely affect investment. Interestingly enough, this result was obtained by the next work I shall discuss.

Although Fox did find strong negative impacts of the property tax on industrial investment for the Cleveland area, the normalization of investment by population and the weak performance of the model in the Cincinnati area substantially weaken his results. At best, his results are suggestive that local taxes are important in the location decision.

Schmenner (1973)

The last empirical study is that of Roger W. Schmenner. Compared to the other two studies, his work is considerably more exhaustive. Schmenner not only examined the impact of intraurban property tax differentials but analyzed local income tax differentials as well. Furthermore, he examined tax impacts upon the intraurban distribution of manufacturing employment *levels* as well as upon their change. He also considered the distribution of manufacturing *establishments* and their change within the urban area. Finally, he estimated relationships for two separate time periods and for four metropolitan areas. While his focus was upon behavior in all areas taken together, he provided separate estimates for each of the SMSAs.

In general, his results for the distribution of employment and establishment levels failed to show a significant tax association. The results, shown in table 1.2, are representative of his findings. Tax differential variables often had the wrong sign and were statistically insignificant. The one exception is for Cleveland, where the income tax differential showed a significant effect upon the distribution of employment. This result is extremely surprising since income tax differentials in Cleveland are virtually nonexistent. Indeed, by 1970, Cleveland and its surrounding municipalities had *identical* local income tax rates (Ohio Municipal League, 1970).[3] What this suggests is that the Cleveland results with respect to the income tax are a computer artifact—probably reflecting rounding errors.

Turning to his estimates for *changes* in industrial activity, one characteristic of the estimating model immediately stands out. The specification of independent variables is exactly the same as for the level regressions. One would not ordinarily expect to find a model which is equally applicable to stocks as to flows. It is not surprising, therefore, that the performance of the model differs considerably with respect to changes as opposed to levels.

Schmenner's results for changes in establishments (see table 1.2) indicate that, while property tax differentials are unimportant, income tax differentials are important. This is advanced by the author as one of the principal findings of his study. Closer scrutiny of his results reveals, however, that the evidence for this proposition is very weak. For one thing, the fit of the regressions is quite poor—seldom does R^2 exceed .25. More important, the result shows up only when the SMSAs are aggregated into a single sample. As was mentioned above, the Cleveland area does not exhibit significant income tax differentials. Minneapolis-St. Paul did not have local income taxes during the period. In Kansas City only the central city levied an income tax. The only significant variation in local income taxes occurred in the Cincinnati area. Thus, the income tax variable took the following form: ones for all Cleveland and Minneapolis-St. Paul observations; zeros for all Kansas City suburbs; intermediate values in the Cincinnati area. The income tax variable, then, is nearly a dummy variable for the Cleveland and Minneapolis-St. Paul areas. If establishment decentralization is proceeding less rapidly in these areas, the calculated coefficient can be anticipated. Unfortunately, Schmenner did not provide the information directly to test this hypothesis.

Another test, however, is available. If the income tax is important, we would expect it to be significant in the Cincinnati area regressions. But this is not the case. While the coefficient is negative, it is statistically

---

3. In 1967 only seventeen of fifty-seven municipalities had a tax rate different than for Cleveland.

insignificant. This suggests that the result shown in table 1.2 does not accurately reflect tax effects.

This conclusion is reinforced when we consider Schmenner's results for employment changes. In all cases, the income tax is statistically insignificant. Interestingly enough, for the 1969-71 period, the property tax emerges as statistically significant. The property tax, however, is not significant when the model is tested on the individual SMSAs. This suggests that, in the aggregate sample, the property tax reflects regional differences not accounted for in the model.

It appears, therefore, that Schmenner's work provides little evidence that tax considerations are important in intrametropolitan industrial location decisions.

Evaluation

The preceding review, I believe, indicates the limitations of ad hoc statistical studies in identifying local tax influences upon industrial location. Given the enormous investment required for securing adequate data, I would not encourage others to replicate existing approaches to other urban areas. Before undertaking further tests, it seems imperative to make further progress in model specification. This will not be a simple task. Urban theorists have made very little headway with regard to models of intraurban industrial location. As one leading scholar in the area has recently put it: "I have spent considerable time and effort on such models [of the intra-urban distribution of employment], but have obtained almost no results" (Mills, 1974, p. 140).

Admittedly, the prospect of developing a truly general equilibrium model of industrial location in the reasonably near future is bleak. Yet this does not mean that our understanding cannot be enhanced by more comprehensive partial equilibrium models. One major advance over present models would be to incorporate the fact that industrial location is *jointly* determined by the behavior of firms and host communities. Existing studies are implicitly based upon the assumption that locational decisions are solely in the domain of firms. Hence, the emphasis in such models is upon variables which reflect costs of production and distribution. This totally ignores the fact that communities have a strong interest in the locational choice of firms. And they have policy tools at their disposal such as business services, tax rates, and *zoning* to influence such choices. That such tools are available to communities and are effectively employed is evidenced by the existence of purely bedroom communities and industrial enclaves. Such communities are not the exception. Out of forty-four municipalities in Cuyahoga County, Ohio, thirteen have no industry whatever. Clearly, such situations are not entirely attributable to the locational decisions of industry. More likely, they represent a conscious policy of keeping industry out.

If the only effect of industry upon a community were to serve as a free source of tax revenues, it would be difficult to explain the existence of bedroom communities. This suggests that the tax benefits of industry are not a free good. Rather, the following considerations may be relevant: (1) the taxes paid by industry may in part be shifted to local residents; (2) industry imposes costs upon a community; and (3) in order to reap whatever fiscal benefits may be available from industry, residents may have to tax themselves as well.

The first proposition has been discussed in depth in the property tax literature. It is now widely accepted that differential property taxes may be borne by immobile local factors of production (Aaron, 1974; Mieszkowski, 1972). The most immobile local factor is land, and ownership of land, in turn, is highly localized. The second proposition has also been recognized in the literature. It is clear that the presence of industry will require additional government outlays. It is generally felt, however, that such outlays are small relative to tax payments. Not so widely recognized is that industry gives rise to environmental costs—pollution, congestion, and crime are examples. The level of such costs is likely to rise with the average income level of the community and may actually swamp government outlays in terms of magnitude. The third proposition is based upon the fact that the major tax instrument of local governments is the property tax. Generally, state constitutions prohibit differential property tax rates upon different classes of property. This means that if a community wishes to extract a greater subsidy from industry, it must tax itself as well. Any community which, because of environmental factors, chooses to restrict its industrial base below the market clearing level may find itself in this position. It may be unwilling to tax the rent its zoning power has created because to do so would require greater tax payments by its own residents.

Further Consideration

Fischel (1974) has recently incorporated many of the preceding considerations into a model of community behavior. A rough sketch of his model is as follows. Communities seek to maximize an objective function which depends upon their constitutents' consumption of private goods, locally provided public goods, and the quality of community environment. While business firms are assumed to make a net contribution to a locality's consumption of public goods via property tax payments, they also generate environmental costs. The supply of business firms to a locality is perfectly elastic at some maximum property tax rate which is established through intercommunity competition. A community whose property tax rate is below or equal to the maximum limits the number of business firms through zoning action. The optimum level of business is determined by balancing environmental costs against net fiscal benefits. The latter, in turn, will depend upon a community's tastes for public as opposed to private goods. Hence, a community's demand for business firms is jointly determined with its demand for other goods—public, private, and environmental.

For present purposes, the importance of Fischel's work lies in the development of the *supply* side of the industrial location market. In other words, through its demand behavior for public, private, and environmental goods a community gives rise to a supply of industrial sites. This supply must then be matched with the demand by business firms in order to determine the actual location pattern. It follows that, to be successful, empirical tests of the importance of fiscal variables in industrial location decisions must simultaneously estimate the supply and demand relationships. Unfortunately, Fischel did not attempt such an undertaking. Instead, he confined his empirical work to several indirect tests, two of which I shall summarize briefly.

The first test concerned whether business firms do indeed provide net fiscal benefits. If not, the model loses its logical basis. Fiscal benefits were defined as a decrease in residential property taxes or an increase in educational expenditure. To estimate these effects, Fischel regressed each variable against industrial tax base and commercial tax base (suitably normalized) and other controls for suburban communities in northern New Jersey.[4] While he found that both commercial and industrial property decreased taxes, the effects were small—$8.60 and $10.40 per $1000 valuation, respectively, compared with an average tax payment of $678.[5] Turning to education expenditures, he found that only

4. Residential property taxes were regressed on commercial tax base, property tax base, public school pupils, median income, and miscellaneous local revenue; variables were normalized by households, where appropriate. Locally financed expenditure upon education per pupil was regressed upon the same set of independent variables. The model was estimated for Bergen County, N.J., for 1970.

5. William Vickrey pointed out at the TRED conference that whether tax impacts of business are small cannot be deduced from this line of reasoning. To do so involves the comparison of a tax *rate* (i.e., $8.60 and $10.40) with a tax *payment* (i.e., $678). A tax impact of approximately 1 percent cannot be said to be *small,* in absolute terms. Nevertheless, as is indicated below, it is small *relative* to average tax rates.

commercial property tended to increase education expenditures, industrial property being statistically insignificant. Furthermore, the effect
of commercial property was small—$12.10 per $1000 of valuation compared with an average outlay of $929. Thus, it would appear that fiscal
benefits arising from the presence of business are insignificant, and
hardly worthy of the attention given them. Before this conclusion is
accepted, however, it is necessary to discuss a second test.

Fischel also estimated the impact of business property upon the level
of local expenditure for business-related expenditure.[6] This can be interpreted as the fiscal cost associated with business. He found that business
had a small impact upon such expenditure—$2.10 and $3.30 per $1000
valuation of commercial and industrial property, respectively.

If we compare fiscal benefits with fiscal costs, we see that business
property provides a small net fiscal gain to a community. More important, however, a comparison of the estimates raises the question of
where business tax receipts are spent! By the budget identity, receipts
must equal outgo. If the tax levy is fifty mills (a conservative estimate for
northern New Jersey, where Fischel made his study), a $1000 increase in
business property produces an added $50 in tax revenue. Yet, Fischel's
estimates provide for scarcely 25 percent of this figure. One possibility is
that the funds are absorbed by the state's education equalization
formula. But Fischel indicated that state grants to education amounted
to only 12 percent of education outlays in the sample area, so this
appears unlikely. Being unable to account for the discrepancy, my
intuition suggests that Fischel's estimates of fiscal benefits of business
are much too low. This position is given support by the results of Ladd
(1974), to whom I now turn.

While it does not directly address the question of industrial location,
Ladd's study of the demand for public services in the Boston SMSA
provides some indirect evidence on the sensitivity of business location to
intraarea tax differentials and the net fiscal benefits accruing from a
business tax base. Ladd's hypothesis was that business firms affect a
community's demand for public services in two ways: (1) by reducing the
"price" of public services to local residents; and (2) by expenditures
which are necessary to service the needs of business *and* to mitigate the
environmental damage business creates.

To test her hypothesis, Ladd estimated separate demand functions for

6. Municipal expenditures (defined as outlays for police, fire, street, sewers, garbage,
environmental protection, and public buildings and grounds) were regressed on median income, commercial tax base, industrial tax base, miscellaneous revenue, and distance from
the George Washington Bridge; variables were normalized by households, where appropriate.

educational and noneducational services, respectively.[7] The former is designed to capture the tax price effects, while the latter attempts to isolate the costs associated with business.

As her measure of tax price, Ladd employed the expression $(1 - \alpha C - \beta I)$, where C and I correspond to the commercial and industrial portion of a community's tax base, respectively. The parameters α and β measure the community's perception of the marginal fiscal benefit associated with commercial and industrial property. If $\alpha = \beta = 1$, the community perceives that it will have to "pay" only $R \; (= 1 - C - I)$ percent of the cost of an additional dollar of expenditure, where R is the residential portion of the tax base. In other words, the increased commercial and industrial taxes are fully exported to nonresidents. Similarly $\alpha < 1$ and/or $\beta < 1$ means that a portion of the additional tax is borne by local residents. This would be the case if: (1) the tax is shifted to local residents; and/or (2) the tax gives rise to business relocation resulting in lower business tax receipts in the future. Ladd advanced the hypothesis that $\alpha > \beta$ implies (2) and $\alpha < \beta$ implies (1). Her reasoning was that commercial taxes are more easily shifted and commercial firms less mobile.

Her results for educational expenditures indicate that $\alpha > \beta$, with α in the range of .8 and β approximately .45. If one accepts her logic that relocation considerations are dominant, $(1 - \alpha)$ and $(1 - \beta)$ can be interpreted as the elasticities of commercial and industrial tax bases with respect to the property tax rate.[8] The elasticity implied for the industrial tax base is large—in excess of $1/2$. It must be kept in mind, however, that these are *perceived* elasticities which may bear no relation to objective reality. Furthermore, to the extent that α and β reflect shifting effects, the elasticities are overstated. Indeed, to the

---

7. Educational expenditures per pupil were regressed upon tax price, state and federal block grants per pupil, public and private pupils per capita, and incidence of poverty. In addition, the variables professional workers per capita and blue collar workers per capita were sometimes added.

Noneducational expenditures were regressed on tax price, commercial tax base, industrial tax base, incidence of poverty, fraction of households who rent, and blue collar workers; where appropriate, variables were normalized by population.

8. The direct cost to residents of a \$1 increase in education expenditure is r, where r is the residential share of the tax base. The indirect cost is $\Delta B . t$, where ΔB represents the loss in business tax base and t stands for the tax rate. By definition $\Delta B = \frac{\epsilon B}{t} . \Delta t$, where ϵ is the elasticity of business tax base, B, with respect to the tax rate. To raise one dollar of revenue, $\Delta t = \frac{1}{A}$, where A is the aggregate tax base. Hence $\tau \Delta B = \epsilon \cdot b$, where $b = B/A$. Adding direct and indirect costs yields: $1 - b - \epsilon b = 1 - b(1 + \epsilon)$.

extent that α and β are elasticities, the estimates are subject to simultaneous equations bias.

Turning to Ladd's estimates of noneducational expenditure, we find that industrial property has little direct impact. Commercial property, on the other hand, has a significant positive impact. The expenditure elasticity is in the range of .13. Nevertheless, when we allow for the fact that noneducational expenditures are less than one-half of local expenditure, revenues from commercial property considerably outweigh the expenditures associated with such property.[9] Together with the estimates of exported business taxes, therefore, these results suggest that business firms, commercial and industrial, give rise to substantial fiscal benefits to a community.

Whereas Ladd's work is suggestive, her approach is best characterized as tangential to the major issues addressed by this essay. While a study of the determinants of a community's demand for public services is important in its own right, it cannot be expected to provide definitive evidence concerning the locational pattern of business activity. Such an approach, however, is an essential ingredient to a complete model for this purpose.

Conclusion

My search of the literature has failed to uncover any solid evidence for or against the proposition that intraurban location decisions of business firms are significantly affected by fiscal considerations. Part of the reason for this is the paucity of empirical work on the question. Another is that the work that has been done has completely neglected the supply side of the question. The recent work of Fischel and Ladd, however, provides a framework through which supply decisions can be incorporated into a more complete model of locational choice. I eagerly await the construction and testing of such a model.

References

Aaron, Henry. 1974. "A New View of Property Tax Incidence." *American Economic Review Papers and Proceedings* 64, no. 2: 212-29.

Advisory Commission on Intergovernmental Relations (ACIR). 1967a. *Fiscal Balance in the American Federal System.* Vol. 2, *Metropolitan Fiscal Disparities.* Report A-31. Washington, D.C.: The commission.

---

9. The elasticity of nonschool expenditure with respect to the commercial base is .13. Nonschool expenditures, however, usually represent less than one-half of total expenditure. Hence the elasticity of total expenditure with respect to the commercial base is less than .07. On the other hand, the elasticity of total revenue with respect to commercial base is roughly .11. Hence the elasticity of net fiscal benefits is .04.

Advisory Commission on Intergovernmental Relations (ACIR). 1967b. *State-Local Taxation and Industrial Location.* Report A-30. Washington, D.C.: The commission.

Beaton, Charles R., and Young P. Joun. 1968. *The Effect of the Property Tax on Manufacturing Location.* Fullerton, Calif.: California State College.

Brazer, Harvey E. 1961. "The Value of Industrial Property as a Subject of Taxation." *Canadian Public Administration* 4, no. 2: 137-47.

Burrows, James C., Charles E. Metcalf, and John B. Kaler. 1971. *Industrial Location in the United States.* Lexington, Ky.: D. C. Heath.

Cameron, Helen A. 1969. "Property Taxation as a Location Factor." *Bulletin of Business Research* 44, no. 4: 1-3.

Due, John F. 1961. "Studies of State and Local Tax Influences on Location of Industry." *National Tax Journal* 14: 163-73.

Fischel, William A. 1974. "Fiscal and Environmental Considerations in the Location of Firms in Suburban Communities." Ph.D. diss., Princeton University.

Fox, William F. 1973. "Property Tax Influences on Industrial Location within a Metropolitan Area: A report for the Department of Economics and Community Development." Columbus: State of Ohio.

Goldstein, Gerald S., and Leon N. Moses. 1973. "A Survey of Urban Economics." *Journal of Economic Literature* 11, no. 2: 471-515.

Hamer, Andrew N. 1972. "The Comparative Costs of Location of Manufacturing Firms in Urban Areas: A Boston Case Study." *Review of Regional Studies* 2, no. 2: 95-134.

Ladd, Helen F. 1974. "Local Public Expenditures and the Composition of the Property Tax Base." Ph.D. diss., Yale University.

McMillan, T. E., Jr. 1965. "Why Manufacturers Choose Plant Locations vs. Determinants of Plant Locations." *Land Economics* 41, no. 3: 239-46.

Mills, Edwin S. 1974. *Studies in the Structure of the Urban Economy.* Baltimore, Md.: The Johns Hopkins University Press.

Mieszkowski, Peter. 1972. "The Property Tax: An Excise Tax or a profits Tax?" *Journal of Public Economics* 1, no. 1: 73-96.

Morgan, William E. 1967. "Taxes and the Location of Industry." *University of Colorado Studies.* Series in Economics no. 4. Boulder: University of Colorado Press.

Moses, Leon, and Harold F. Williamson, Jr. 1967. "The Location of Economic Activity in Cities." *American Economic Review Papers and Proceedings* 57, no. 2: 211-22.

Mueller, Eva, and James N. Morgan. 1962. "Location Decisions of Manufacturers." *American Economic Review Papers and Proceedings* 52, no. 2: 204-17.

Muth, Richard F. 1969. *Cities and Housing.* Chicago: University of Chicago Press.

Netzer, Dick. 1966. *Economics of the Property Tax.* Washington, D.C.: Brookings Institution.

Oakland, William H. 1973. "Using the Property Tax to Pay for City Government: A Case Study of Baltimore." In *Property Tax Reform,* ed. George E. Peterson, pp. 141-74. Washington, D.C.: Urban Institute.

Oates, W. E., E. P. Howrey, and W. J. Baumol. 1971. "The Analysis of Public Policy in Dynamic Urban Models." *Journal of Political Economy* 79, no. 1: 142-53.

Rinehart, James R., and William E. Laird. 1972. "Community Inducements to Industry and the Zero-Sum Game." *Scottish Journal of Political Economy* 19: 73-90.

Rothenberg, Jerome. 1970. "Local Decentralization and the Theory of Optimal Government." In *The Analysis of Public Output,* ed. Julius Margolis, pp. 31-64. New York: National Bureau of Economic Research.

Schmenner, Roger W. 1973. "City Taxes and Industry Location." Ph.D. diss., Yale University.

Schmenner, Roger W. 1974. "City Taxes and Industry Location." *1973 Proceedings National Tax Association-Tax Institute of America.* Columbus, Ohio: NTA-TIA.

Stigler, George. 1963. *Capital and Rates of Return in Manufacturing Industries.* New York: National Bureau of Economic Research.

Richard W. Lindholm

Property Taxation
and Land Use Control
Policies in Oregon

Oregon's Land Use Planning

In 1973 Oregon, with a population of 2.3 million and a land area of 96,931 square miles, became the first area to adopt statewide regulations on land use administered by a state commission that designates and regulates through a permit system the planning and siting of public transportation facilities, public sewerage systems, water supply systems, solid waste disposal sites and facilities, and public schools (section 25 of S.B. 100, chapter 80, Oregon Laws, 1973).[1]

The legislation for these controls and a considerable list of other innovations is called the Oregon Land Use Law. Administration is provided through the seven-member Oregon Land Conservation and Development Commission (LCDC) appointed by the governor and approved by the Senate. The legislation also provided for a state Department of Land Conservation and Development and established the only committee of the legislature that remains in session between the biennial regular sessions of the Oregon Legislative Assembly. The law provides (section

1. Discussions of legislation in this chapter are largely based on State of Oregon, Local Government Relations Division, Executive Department, and the Oregon State University Extension Service, 1974. Legislation similar to S.B. 100 but applicable only to cities with a population over 300,000, e.g., Portland, was provided in S.B. 769. New basic legislation was not adopted in 1975, and none is expected in 1977 (as of May 1977).

55) that the Department of Land Conservation and Development must report monthly to the legislative committee and a written report (section 51) is required at the end of each even-numbered year. The first report was prepared for submission at the end of 1974.

LCDC decisions can be appealed to the courts by anyone whose interests are substantially affected by the action. These appeals must be filed not later than sixty days after date of final action. By the end of 1977 two appeals had been filed, but no court decisions had been handed down.

The activity of the department until recently was largely involved with the planning and development of public hearings around the state and through these hearings the preparation and adoption of goals that would guide state and local agencies in comprehensive land use and planning through 1977. Fourteen goals were adopted on December 27, 1974 (see *The Oregonian*, December 28, 1974, p. A23). This goal-development method arose from section 11 of the law, which provides that "pursuant to the provisions of this act the Commission shall insure widespread citizen involvement and impact in all phases of the process."

S.B. 100 provides in Section 33 that "not later than January 1, 1975 the department shall prepare and the Commission shall adopt statewide planning goals and guidelines for use by state agencies, cities, counties, and special districts in preparing, adopting, revising and implementing existing and future comprehensive plans." This deadline was met but only after giving in to the mayor of Portland and adopting an energy conservation goal that had not undergone a lengthy review by citizens and specialists as had the other goals and after failing to adopt a goal on shorelands, leaving control in the hands of the Oregon Coastal Conservation and Development Commission (OCCDC) established in 1971. This shortcoming was largely remedied when an OCCDC member was made an adviser to the LCDC and the OCCDC became a regional advisory body, with the staffs of the two groups merged under the direction of the LCDC.

The LCDC goals for recommendation to the department were developed out of the completed questionnaires and discussions of citizens attending the local meetings called and staffed by volunteers as well as by LCDC personnel. The final public hearing was carried out by the department before adoption of the final revisions of land use goals and guidelines. The preliminary and introductory hearings and all previous sessions were held in different places around the state but the final public hearing was at the state capitol.

Although S.B. 100 includes a number of vital provisions, it is section 19 that is of most immediate interest. It provides for bringing all planning agencies of an area under the control of the county planning authority.

For this purpose Portland is considered to be a county. In addition, the planning programs and enforcement record of each county are subject to a review by the LCDC aimed at the initiating of action to correct short-comings.[2]

Section 11, in addition to providing for widespread citizen involvement, requires the LCDC to do the following: review and recommend to the Legislative Assembly the designation of areas of critical state concern; prepare inventories of land uses; establish statewide planning goals consistent with regional, county, and city concerns; prepare statewide planning guidelines; review comprehensive plans for conformance with statewide planning goals; coordinate planning efforts of state agencies to assure conformance with statewide planning goals and compatibility with city and county comprehensive plans; prepare model zoning, subdivision, and other ordinances and regulations; and report periodically to the Legislative Assembly and to the committee.

Legislative provision was made for a single coordinated state planning program for identifying land use problem areas that are of general state concern and for establishing procedures to meet the need as seen by the LCDC after carrying out procedures provided for in S.B. 100. The coverage, however, left out one area of statewide interest, land along the Pacific Coast. Here conservation responsibility continues to be carried out by the OCCDC (ORS 111.120). The new legislation providing for the LCDC delegated to the OCCDC any of the functions the LCDC considers appropriate to delegate. Even after delegation, however, the LCDC remains responsible for reviewing actions taken by the OCCDC. The OCCDC was expected to be terminated in February 1975 but instead it continued as a planning group under the LCDC (see p. 37).

As was mentioned above, the principal activity, in addition to getting organized, of the department established by S.B. 100 has been to carry out meetings with citizens around the state. These sessions were aimed at developing the program to be implemented through the powers granted by the legislation and to learn the attitudes of the citizens around the state. The first round of these "people and the land" public workshops was carried out during April and May of 1974, and the second series between September 16 and October 7 of 1974. The final public hearing was held on December 13, 1974, on the revised draft of statewide land use. "Goals, Guidelines, and the Columbia River Gorge as a Critical Area" was adopted by the LCDC on November 30, 1974.

2. Section 19 of S.B. 100 states "each county, through its governing body, shall be responsible for coordinating all planning activities affecting land uses within the county including those of the county, cities, special districts and state agencies, to assure an integrated comprehensive plan for the entire area of the county."

First Round of Public Meetings

The first series of meetings was aimed at getting an expression of attitude toward a wide variety of position statements, and a statewide
opinion poll was published and distributed to those who attended the
first sessions and prior to the second session. The questions asked and the
responses given are not included in this essay. A few examples, however,
can give the flavor of the questions and reactions.

Participants were asked to agree or disagree with the statement,
"Oregon is losing too much of its farm land." The response was 78 percent
agreed, 7 percent disagreed, and 14 percent had no opinion. There was a
total of forty questions in the questionnaire completed by the participants in the first series of sessions.

In addition, group discussions were carried out around the following
six questions: (1) what do you like most about living and working in your
area? (2) what should be done for the future to insure that you and
future generations of Oregonians will be able to enjoy living and working
in this area? (3) what specific geographic areas or places in this area of
Oregon do you think should be a concern of Oregonians and receive
special attention by the LCDC? (4) what specific geographic places in
other areas of Oregon do you think should be a concern of Oregonians
and receive special attention by the LCDC? (5) S.B. 100, which created
the LCDC, identifies five areas with which it will be concerned (see above).
Is this an adequate list? and (6) are there other activities which should be
added to the list (State of Oregon, Department of Land Conservation
and Development, 1974)?

It was only in the responses to (1) and (5) that the "development"
portion of the title of the legislation was given some economic content.
The section titled "general economic base" included the following items
(the number after each item is total including it in answering question
[1]; to give an idea of relative importance, the item mentioned most
frequently was "recreational opportunities," with 224 designations):
general economic base (26); diverse economy (22); balanced economy (7);
development opportunity (19); stable economy (41); room for growth
(11); managed growth (3); employment opportunities (67); low cost of
living (12); low taxes/good tax base (8); acceptable power rates (2);
renewable resources (3); no sales tax (1); and slow growth (2).

Fifteen percent of those attending enjoyed a total before-tax family
income of over $25,000, and another 31 percent enjoyed incomes
between $15,000 and $24,999. About 50 percent of the sixty-seven listing
"employment opportunities" were from the Portland suburbs. It is of
interest that over 50 percent of the forty-one listing "stable economy"
came from eastern Oregon.

In answering question (5) the greatest interest was in adding to the legislative list of areas of land use to be controlled by the LCDC power production sites. Under "other," however, there were seven who listed taxation affecting land use and another one who listed property tax reform.

It is quite obvious from the provisions of S.B. 100 and the summary of the questions and discussions of the first series of meetings that the economic impact of what was being advocated possessed little attraction. Also, practically no appreciation was evidenced of the impact of the property tax on land use decisions.

Second Round of Public Meetings

As a result of the first series of meetings, the LCDC came up with eleven possible statewide land use goals. These goals formed the basis for the discussions of the second round of meetings.

The second series of meetings developed fifteen goals. These goals were included in the final LCDC report. The goals were: (1) air, water, and land resources quality; (2) carrying capacity (eliminated as a separate goal and added as an aspect of each goal); (3) economy of the state; (4) recreation needs; (5) areas subject to natural disasters and hazards; (6) public facilities and services; (7) transportation; (8) open spaces, scenic and historic areas, and natural resources; (9) transition from rural to urban land use; (10) agricultural lands; (11) forest lands; (12) shorelands; (13) citizen involvement; (14) land use planning; and (15) housing.

Participation in the second series of sessions was down by a third from that of the first series. Fifty percent of those attending the second series, however, had not attended the first. One of the reasons new participants surfaced was that people had begun to realize that a fairly good answer to any later criticism of the goals and procedures adopted to implement S.B. 100 consisted of the reply, "You had a chance to participate in establishing policy, but you didn't carry on" (State of Oregon, LCDC, 1974).

Economy of the State

The second series of sessions was attended by more people interested in urban and economic considerations and was not entirely dominated by those largely interested in lakes and streams and what the LCDC would do to preserve outdoor recreation in Oregon as had been true of the first series. This meant that it was goals 3, 7, 11, and 15 that came up for additional consideration in the second series of hearings. It also became apparent that the legislation adopted and the administrative procedures followed, including the required substantial citizen participation, were less suited to dealing with economic problems than with those associated with estuary and scenic site preservation.[3]

What is involved here becomes apparent when the overall goal "economy of the state" is considered. The goal as stated in the guidebook prepared for the second series of sessions by the staff of the LCDC as a result of their consideration of the discussion of the first series of sessions is as follows:

Land conservation and development activities shall provide for and contribute to increased employment, stable growth and broader geographic distribution of economic activity in coordination with state and local economic development, energy, and environmental quality programs; comprehensive plans shall provide for such economic and employment considerations and for the management of growth based upon the capacity of the various areas of the state.

This is quite a paragraph and certainly attributes to policies in the land conservation and development area a potential for creation of the good economy that is not generally accepted. The question that was apparently being asked most frequently in 1974 and 1975 was not "How can conservation be economically helpful?," but "How can employment opportunities be expanded in my community?" When the second question is considered, the answer is seldom "through improved land conservation and development activities." At the same time, because more people mean sharing "my fishing hole," a strong resistance exists to proposals that would attract new people to Oregon while in the process of providing jobs for those already in Oregon.

The urban portion of LCDC goals is defined as "those conditions and activities which lead to the creation and growth of urban areas." The urban land use problem is set down in six points. Each of them is considered a problem that must be addressed. The six are: insufficient land use controls to direct development to suitable areas; continuing population growth in urban areas; personal preference for single-family homes in the suburbs and for the use of the automobile; transportation systems, urban services, and facilities uncoordinated with desired land use patterns; property tax and assessment policies encouraging scattered developments; and scattered development resulting in expensive and inefficient urban services. Those attending the first round of sessions, however, when asked to identify areas of action "to insure that you and

3. Also the sharp reduction in housing construction throughout the nation caused Oregon's principal industry—lumber and plywood—to suffer a severe recession. As a result, unemployment increased to 8 percent. One effect of this economic decline was a reduced interest in ecology and an increased interest in jobs. See Williams (1974).

future generations of Oregonians will be able to enjoy living and working in this area," came down heavily on the side of preservation and protection of prime agricultural and ranch lands; such urban problems as public transportation and limited commercial development were given only token support.

The general impression of knowledgeable people is that potentially the LCDC can become the state's most powerful agency. It is also generally acknowledged that the budget made available is quite inadequate to carry out the legislative mandates of S.B. 100. The very substantial progress that has been made since mid-1973 has been due to a most enthusiastic staff and an abundance of experienced volunteer workers. In fact, considerable planning effort is currently going into the development of procedures for the use of volunteers to gather and evaluate data needed in carrying out LCDC enforcement and recommendation responsibilities.[4] The shortage of budgetary funds and the federal government's support of coastal planning has been an element in the push of the LCDC to incorporate the OCCDC and not to be satisfied with only the power of review. The LCDC-proposed budget for the 1975-77 biennium was $6.5 million, with most funds allocated for use by local governments to carry out their planning obligations as established by S.B. 100. The new governor promised to protect this budget request (Eugene, Oregon, *Register-Guard,* January 9, 1975, p. 3A). In 1975 the legislature eliminated the OCCDC. The coastal governments organized a new group called Oregon Coastal Zone Management Association. The funds used are largely provided by the LCDC.

One provision of S.B. 100 requires the LCDC oversight joint committee of the Legislative Assembly to make recommendations to the legislature on "the implementation of a program of compensation" whenever "zoning ordinance or similar regulation prohibits reasonable use of property or results in economic loss to landowner." A procedure for working out compensation procedures in this area when the action is judged to be of "statewide significance" was provided for in S.B. 849 (1973) but the bill was not adopted.

The provisions of S.B. 849 contain no reference to increases in property values due to zoning activity. Also, no discussion was carried out of general zoning financing and enforcement through this type of special assessment.

4. Gassaway (1974). Gassaway considers the background of S.B. 100 and the Oregon Supreme Court Decision of March 1973 (Fassano decision) that ruled planning committee decisions were quasijudicial in nature. In addition, she gives considerable attention to Oregon boundary commissions. See also Little (1974).

Subdivision Control

Another piece of Oregon legislation adopted by the 1973 Legislative Assembly to buttress and complement S.B. 100 is the subdivision act (S.B. 487) which became effective on October 5, 1973 (chapter 696, Oregon Laws, 1973). This legislation requires: regulation of all subdivisions having four or more lots; regulation of all partitions involving creation of a street or road; optional power to regulate subdivisions of less than four lots not involving creation of a street; each city and county to adopt a subdivision ordinance and to adopt a hearing procedure; ordinances and regulations to comply with comprehensive plans (this provision of this subdivision regulation directly ties into the LCDC power provided under S.B. 100); and builders to submit tentative plans and to develop plots meeting water and sewer availability standards.

S.B. 190, with an effective date of July 20, 1973, provides regulation of subdivisions in special districts, for example, those in which irrigation is necessary, and is therefore basically an extension of S.B. 487 (chapter 351, Oregon Laws, 1973).

A few months after S.B. 487 became effective it was amended and clarified by S.B. 1011, which became effective March 19, 1974 (chapter 74, Oregon Laws, 1974). The impact of the new legislation was basically to reduce the discretionary power of city and county government and to increase state regulation authority. The new requirement that a city or county make certain through bond or contract that adequate water and sewerage facilities are available, for example, also provides that the state real estate commissioner include a disclosure statement on the availability of water and sewerage facilities. Some easing in the planning of subdivisions is also provided. For example, tentative plans need not be demonstrated to comply with the comprehensive plan. Also, the city or county must accept a certification of a private or public utility system of the availability of water and sewerage.[5]

County Authority

Throughout the discussion of the Oregon land use and growth management legislation, reference has been made to actions required of county and city governments. The basic legislation establishing the county as the principal governmental level for controlling land use is the County Planning Commission Act (H.B. 2548), which became effective on October 5, 1973 (chapter 552, Oregon Laws, 1973). The highlights of

5. "Where public sewers are necessary for development, the sewer agency may be the real planning body" (Clawson and Hall, 1973, p. 23).

this legislation are of interest as they developed out of considerable Oregon experience with government action in this area (Gassaway, 1974).

In order to reduce the influence of real estate people, for example, section 2 requires that no more than two voting members may be engaged in the same kind of business. Also, to avoid having the governing body absolve itself of direct responsibility for work of the planning commission, it is required to hire the planning director and his staff.

Section 15(3) requires that proposed land uses be in compliance with the county's comprehensive plan. Again the tie-in of the comprehensive plan with day-to-day decisions causes the LCDC to be directly associated with whatever land use proposals are accepted and rejected at the county level. Appeal by any aggrieved person is provided for in section 15(4), and a second hearing is required when an appeal is made to the governing body. If the aggrieved party is still unsatisfied, a judicial review can be requested from an inferior court, officer, or tribunal. Only the record is reviewed, however, and the court does not retry the case.

City Authority

Major amendments were also adopted by Oregon's 1973 Legislative Assembly in the legislation providing for city planning commissions. These changes were incorporated in H.B. 2965 (chapter 739, Oregon Laws, 1973). Again, considerable concern is demonstrated with the problem of avoiding having the commission controlled by those who would benefit or be harmed directly by decisions of the planning commission.

Section 2(3) provides that "no more than two voting members shall be engaged principally in the buying, selling or developing of real estate for profit as individuals, or be members of any partnership, or officers or employees of any corporation that is engaged principally in the buying, selling or developing of real estate for profit." Also, no more than two voting members shall be engaged in the same kind of business, trade, or profession (section 2[3]). Because the legislation does not specify the number of members, the two from real estate could conceivably amount to two votes out of three (section 2[1]). This is not possible in the county planning commissions for the law requires the commission to consist of five, seven, or nine members (H.B. 2548, section 2[1]).

There are several other interesting new features in the Oregon city planning commission legislation. For example, city officers (only two) may be only nonvoting members of the commission; joint and intergovernmental planning commissions are encouraged; the city council appoints and removes the members of the commission and conducts hearings;[6] and the role of the hearings officer is expanded and assignment of discretionary land use permit responsibility is encouraged, but appeal to the city council is always available.

Oregon's H.B. 2086 of 1973 established conditions under which subdivisions can be considered to be developed and procedures to vacate an undeveloped subdivision by the owner (chapter 569, Oregon Laws, 1973). The main substantive purpose of the legislation is to provide for a continuing periodic review and updating of undeveloped subdivisions by local government.

Another portion of the legislation of importance within the context of this study is its reference to the LCDC. Section 6 requires the LCDC to review activities of agencies or bodies and to report on the progress of the review activities of such agencies or bodies to the 1975 Legislative Assembly. The LCDC is authorized in this instance to carry out activities of a legislative investigative nature.

Conclusion

The Oregon legislative package adopted in 1973 was the culmination of efforts to use state powers to preserve a generally accepted desirable level of livability. The strong leadership Tom McCall provided as governor came to an end in January 1975. Also, as is clear in the above discussions, many tough problems relating to guiding economic activity and growth so that the environment is improved remain unsolved.[7]

National State Planning

Hawaii

Although Oregon's statewide land use control and planning legislation is similar in many respects to Hawaiian legislation of 1961, the difference in the geographical characteristics, land ownership, and citizen participation traditions have combined to make the two approaches quite different. For example, the great emphasis in the Oregon legislation in developing citizen participation and county-developed and enforced

6. The provision that the city council conducts hearings has caused difficulties because under the Oregon Supreme Court decision in the Fasano decision of March 1973 (*Fasano* v. *Board of County Commissioners of Washington County* [489 Pac 2nd 693] confirmed 507 Pac 2nd 23) the land planning decision hearings are quasijudicial and therefore council members involved must not be privy to information not generally available. Also, the hearings have absorbed much time and a hearing officer procedure has been recommended.

7. To continue his efforts Governor McCall established a citizens' group to defend land use laws. The original budget was $50,000, collected from five hundred people (*Register-Guard,* Eugene, Oregon, January 9, 1975, p. 3C).

comprehensive plans is not found in the Hawaiian law (Lindholm, 1973a, pp. 223-42). Also, tax encouragement of underdevelopment of privately owned lands is great in Oregon, while in Hawaii the pressure is toward more complete development of the potential of land (Done, 1962; see also Mack, 1974). Finally, Hawaii has not developed specific legislative criteria or guidelines, while the Oregon legislation provides an elaborate machinery for the development of legislative guidelines in 1975 out of citizen grass-roots action.[8] These meetings resulted in planning programs for every city and county government by the fall of 1977. Each of these programs is in compliance with statewide planning goals.

Other States

The Pennsylvania Land Policy Project includes a review of state and local land use laws of the nation as an element in its preparation of information in this area for the Commonwealth of Pennsylvania.[9] The project has released a summary first draft of the basic land use planning existing in the fifty states. The study lists only ten states that have entered into this type of action. Only two, Hawaii and Oregon, have legislated a statewide program. The other eight states (Delaware, 1971; California, 1972; New Jersey, 1973; North Carolina, 1974; Vermont, 1970; Maine, 1971; Colorado, 1971; Florida, 1972) have legislated state control over land use in only particular areas; for example, certain coastal areas or certain large industrial developments.

The State of Vermont seemed to be moving along with Oregon when it adopted Act 250 in 1970. But additional legislative progress has not been made since.[10]

In addition to the ten-state program analyzed by the Pennsylvania Land Policy Project, the project listed and briefly described seven other examples of state land-use related legislation: these are the Massachusetts Wetlands Program (1965), the Wisconsin Water Resources Act

8. The citizen groups of Oregon have not seriously considered land banking in land use planning. The potential here is considerable. See Harriss (1974, esp. pp. 134-54, 31-66).

9. The project is under the directorship of Arthur A. Davis, and is an activity of the Western Pennsylvania Conservancy. See also Levin, Rose, and Slavet (1974).This study describes the Wisconsin scenic easement program, the Puerto Rico land banking effort, and San Francisco's incentive zoning.

10. In 1973 Vermont initiated a land capital gains tax, using the federal basis. The rates increase with the percentage of the gain and the shortness of the period for which the land is held. For example, if the gain is 200 percent or over and the holding period less than one year, the rate is 50 percent. On the other hand, if the holding period was five years or more and the percentage gain 0-99 percent, the rate is 5 percent. Collections have been running at an annual rate of $1 million. It had been expected that annual collections would be at the $3 million level.

(1965), the Hackensack (New Jersey) Meadowlands Reclamation and Development Act (1968), the Maine Mandatory Shoreline Zoning Act (1970), the Washington Shoreline Management Act (1972), the Nevada Land Use Planning Act (1973) (for details on Nevada development, see Lindholm, 1974), and the Maryland Land Use Law (1974). Wetlands and coastal zone legislation of an even more limited nature also exists. Among these acts are the Rhode Island Coastal Wetlands Act (1965), the Connecticut Wetlands Act (1969), the Georgia Coastal Marshland Protection Act (1970), the Maryland Wetlands Act (1970), the Michigan Shorelands Protection and Management Act (1970), and the North Carolina Wetlands Protection Act (1971).

Conclusion

The state legislation around the country in this area is largely very new and basically untested. The effectiveness of efforts will in the long run depend on public support, for it is only if this support exists that legislative loophole filling and expansion of coverage activity plus budgetary support actions can be expected.

Perhaps achievement can only be expected in states and areas that are basically middle class. The entire process of preservation through keeping things as they are and forbidding activities that are environmentally destructive is conservative and somewhat selfish. It also has within it, however, the development of pressures to examine if all economic goods are really worthwhile when all production costs (externalities) are taken into consideration.

Oregon Land Taxation Legislation

Oregon's exclusive farm use zoning and special assessment legislation has been amended through the years in a fashion that can be generally characterized as moving toward a stricter stance. In 1973 S.B. 101 made major changes to previous Oregon law.[11]

Exclusive Farm Use (EFU) Benefits

A new general policy section 1 was added. The section in the first three paragraphs states the belief that to use land for agriculture "is an efficient means of conserving natural resources." These paragraphs go on to state that preservation of the limited supply of agricultural land is necessary and, in addition, that urban expansion into rural areas "is a

---

11. Land used exclusively for farming in an area not zoned exclusive farm use (EFU) may also benefit from farm assessment.

matter of public concern because of the unnecessary increases in costs of community services." Paragraph 4 states that for these reasons the state is justified in its policy of offering "incentive and privileges" to "owners of rural land to hold such lands in exclusive farm use zones."

Section 2 was amended to place under local zoning restrictions land previously benefiting from lower tax liabilities under EFU. This is aimed primarily at placing farming under local environmental laws and regulations.

The amendments to section 3, paragraph 2, have caused considerable problems to county assessors. This is the portion of EFU that defines farm use. The definition is "current employment of land including the portion of such land under building (homesite is excluded) supporting accepted farming practices for the purpose of obtaining a profit in money." The previous law had set $500 gross income from farming as qualifying for farm use. Also, the 1973 legislation deleted "farm wood lots of less than 20 acres appurtenant to farm use land" from the benefits of the legislation.[12]

In order to administer this provision properly, provision needs to be made for taxpayers' appeal before a board of agriculture specialists; perhaps from the state college of agriculture. Under the current procedure the assessor is operating somewhat outside his area of competence, and he hesitates to place the land in the nonfarm-use category. Certainly after the first full year of applicability the judgment is that the new provisions have not made a difference.

Also, section 4 has been loosened somewhat to make EFU benefits available if the county governing body grants permission. This is in addition to nonfarm uses permitted outright in an EFU zone. The outright grants are for: (1) public and private schools; (2) churches; (3) propagation or harvesting of a forest product (new in 1973); and (4) necessary utility services except generation of power for public sale (new in 1973). (4), however, does not apply to nuclear and thermal generating facilities under the authority of the Nuclear and Thermal Energy Council.

The conditional nonfarm uses permitted in EFU with county governing body approval are listed in S.B. 101. Golf courses and other non-profit recreational uses have been moved from outright grant of EFU benefits to the new conditional category. Single-family residential dwellings is an addition to the list of nonfarm activities permitted in an EFU area. The grant is conditional on county governing body approval, and this approval must be based on four conditions newly legislated in 1973.

---

12. It is estimated that EFU-assessed valuations on the 1973-74 tax rolls were decreased by $713 million.

They are: that it does not seriously interfere with accepted farming practices, does not materially alter stability of land use, is situated on land generally unsuitable for farm crops and livestock, and complies with other conditions set by the county.

Section 9 sets down for the first time provisions governing land division in EFU areas. The law requires approval by the county if parcels of less than ten acres are set up, and the county may require approval of other divisions of land; this approval must be appropriate under provisions of section 1 of S.B. 101 and legislative intent as given in section 1 of S.B. 100. Undoubtedly, legal cases will be arising and decided under these provisions, but none were decided during the first year of the legislation. Since 1976 statewide planning and zoning have reduced county discretion and therefore the possibility of appeals from decisions made.

Section 5 makes clearer the requirement to assess EFU land on basis of true cash value for farm use and not true cash value if used for other purposes. The assessor is specifically put on notice that he should remove land from EFU treatment if farm use standards as established in section 3 are not being followed.

Assessment Practices

Paragraph 308.345 of Oregon Laws and Administrative Rules relating to property assessment and taxation provides for use of both the sale and income approach in setting *farm use valuation*. The assessor is admonished to consider land sales figures to determine if uses other than for farming affected the value. When other possible uses are reflected in the land sales prices, the assessor is required to use the income approach and to capitalize the average annual return of similar lands at the current rate of interest charged by the Federal Land Bank. In calculating the average annual return, the cost total to be deducted from receipts includes the cost of land. Individual assessors recognize that land costs are increased by low tax costs and that this practice involves circuitous reasoning, since higher taxes would reduce land costs as an item in calculating net income and also land value based on sales. Undoubtedly all income is not included in the income approach, for sales prices in areas that could only be used for agriculture are much higher than land values obtained from the application of the income approach. As long as Oregon does not have a state land tax, however, the valuation below sales price only affects relative tax payments within the county, and even here the valuation difference is only important economically if a countywide school district is used.

Section 6 of S.B. 101 provides for the payback of taxes if land is removed from EFU zone. Up to ten years the payback penalty is equal to taxes saved. After ten years the penalty is taxes saved during the ten years only. No provision, however, is made for the payment of interest.

Section 10 provides for penalties if the landowner fails to report non-EFU use. Again, the payback period may be as long as ten years. The payment is the amount that would have been paid if properly reported during the ten-year or less period. In addition, a 6 percent interest rate on the delayed payments and a 20 percent penalty based only on taxes unpaid are charged (interest due is not in penalty base).[13]

Upon request by the owner to the county assessor Oregon land can be given a value corresponding to highest and best use as *forest land*. The form that must be completed in making the request is provided by the State Department of Revenue. The questions are aimed at restricting forest valuation to land that is being managed in a commercially acceptable manner, and the applicant must sign an affirmation that the statements made are true. It is assumed that land is not being managed primarily for commercial forestry if the land is subject to a plot filed under Oregon requirements (ORS 92.120).

When the land is removed from a primary use that consists predominantly of "growing and harvesting trees of marketable species," taxes saved through the forest use classification become payable. The amount of back taxes due is limited to five years plus simple 6 percent interest on the amount of taxes that were not paid because the land was classified as forest land (ORS 321.815).

The legislation currently applicable was the result of substantial amendments in 1971. New and tougher legislation was not adopted in 1973 when farm use valuation favors were reduced.[14]

The Oregon property tax legislation includes provision for valuation of land at its highest and best use as *open-space land* as defined by the law (ORS 308.740). This legislation was adopted in 1971 and was not amended in 1973 except to the extent that S.B. 100 will affect land use through actions of county and municipal zoning and land planning commissions under the general statewide supervision of the LCDC. Application is made to the county assessor upon forms prepared by the State Department of Revenue.

Open-space lands are assessed at highest and best use value for the use accepted when application to be under the provision of the law is made. If the land is later put to a use not acceptable under the open-space land use legislation, the owner is liable for the amount of taxes he would have

13. As of July 1, 1976, twenty states had legislation providing for differential assessment of farmland, eighteen states had legislation providing for deferred taxation, and nine states use contracts and agreements agreed upon between government and landowner to restrict land use in exchange for lower property taxes (ACIR, 1977, p. 126).

14. An estimate of land value assessment reductions has not been made.

paid if he had not benefited from an open-space land use classification. In addition, the owner must "pay interest at the rate of two-thirds of one percent a month, or fraction of a month, from the dates on which such additional taxes would have been payable . . . ." But the amount of taxes and interest payable are not to be greater than "the dollar difference in the value of the land as open-space land for the last year of classification and the market value under ORS 308.205 (true cash value) for the year of withdrawal" (ORS 308.770[3]).[15]

The open-space land tax provisions do not limit the number of years over which taxes and interest must be paid if the full productivity of the land is later utilized. Rather, the limit is set by the difference in the market price with unrestricted use of the land and open-space use.

Open-space taxation treatment is available to land that if left undeveloped to its highest use will: (1) conserve or enhance natural or scenic resources; (2) protect air or streams or water supplies; (3) promote conservation of soils, wetlands, beaches, or tidal marshes; (4) conserve landscaped areas, such as public and private golf courses, which enhance the value of neighborhood property; (5) enhance the value to the public of neighborhood parks, forests, wildlife preserves, nature reservations, sanctuaries, or other open spaces; (6) enhance recreation opportunities; (7) preserve historic sites; (8) promote orderly urban or suburban development; or (9) affect any other factors relevant to the general welfare or preserving the current use of property.

It is specifically provided that the granting authority may not deny open-space classification simply because "of the potential loss of revenue" (ORS 308.755[2][i]). Also, provision is made for gathering of information by the assessor as to change in the use of land and the immediate application of penalties (ORS 308.785).

Circuit Breaker

Oregon's 1973 "circuit breaker" law provides for homestead property tax relief based on the amount the property tax portion of rent or property taxes paid, if owner-occupied, exceeds established percentages of a broadly defined household income. Taxpayers under the law may claim state income tax reduction, or a payment from the Department of Revenue, if income tax liability is less than the amount of property tax relief to which they are entitled under the law. The legislation is very expensive and will cost $77 million in fiscal year 1977.[16]

15. The legislation has not been used extensively and assessment reductions are now estimated at less than $1 million.

16. Out of a total state tax revenue prior to the allocation of about $760 million in fiscal year 1977. Because the program has not been adjusted for inflation the real burden has declined since 1974.

The major impact of the law seems to have been to keep Oregon the lowest or next to lowest state in terms of portion of school financing provided by state revenues. As a result, local school financing continues to be a very major expenditure, with some 72 percent of costs coming from local property tax collections. Therefore, to a considerable extent, the Oregon circuit breaker has acted to increase property taxes paid by the users of modest homesteads relative to incomes and by owners of commercial industrial and natural resource property in areas with many children. The general impact must be to discourage productive investment and to provide inequality in the allocation of school costs, while encouraging expenditures for housing by those with considerable liquid wealth but low incomes as defined by the legislation.

Federally Owned Land

Over 50 percent of the land area of Oregon is owned by the federal government. About two-thirds of the timber reserves of the state are included in national forests, and some mineral resources of commercial value are also located in these areas. Full development of both resources has been retarded through activities of the Oregon delegation to Congress, who are responding to the desires of the electorate as they see them.

The national forests include large quantities of timber possessing the maturity which gives it great value as lumber and plywood. The value of timber held in national forests is nearly three times that held by the private forest industry (Lindholm, 1973b, table 3, p. 41).

Management standards for these huge productive tracts permit the occupation of space by old and unproductive trees that annually add very little, if anything, to the production of usable wood fiber. Economic pressure to speed up the cutting and replanting of forests developed during the 1973 housing boom in the United States and Japan and the resulting timber shortage. The solution to the shortage found to be most acceptable to Oregonians was to cut off the exports of logs to Japan and other markets rather than to allow more rapid cutting of mature trees on government land.

Economic Impact

The management of economic growth through control of the use of land has developed very substantial political support in Oregon. The Association of Oregon Industries, a business organization, has not felt it to be expedient to do much more than cite duplication of responsibilities that they perceive in the land use legislation and to exploit the 1975 shortage of employment opportunities.

It is also true that jobs for the young people of Oregon require the use of economic bases in addition to the traditional beef, wheat, and timber. The three additional industries that appear to best fit in with Oregon's high local property and income taxes, no sales tax, and land use management policy are tourism, retirement facilities, and retail merchandising.

These industries find Oregon's parks and relatively unpolluted landscapes plus the general environment stimulating. They are also industries that live off high annual incomes earned currently or previously outside the state in "dirty" industries. Also, these industries fit in well with the very popular slogan of Oregon's outstanding governor during the past eight years—"Come visit us but don't stay." He might have added "and particularly don't place upon us the responsibility of educating and finding jobs for your children."

The population and economic data demonstrate that the Oregon proenvironment and prounderutilization of land tax policy has had some influence. Per capita personal income is lower than in any other Far West state, and the percentage increase of personal per capita income between 1950 and 1969 was slower than that of California and Washington, but more rapid than that experienced by Nevada and Alaska. The forecasted rate of increase of Oregon's per capita personal income from 1969 to 1990 is set at 94 percent of the national growth rate. It is the only Far West state with a forecasted growth less than the national average (*Survey of Current Business,* April 1974, p. 33).

The portion of the population over sixty-five years of age was 10.9 percent in Oregon in 1971—the only western state having over 10 percent of the population in excess of that age (*Statistical Abstract of the United States,* 1973, p. 32). During the period 1960-70 Oregon experienced an estimated net migration of 9 percent, but a population growth at about the national average. Estimates of the past several years place Oregon's net population growth above the national average.

Summary

Oregon's effort to preserve a low level of utilization of its land through management practices set at the state level has been at least partially successful. The provisions of S.B. 100 and the many ancillary measures, including the tax treatment of farm, forest, and open-space lands, combine to form a formidable group of bureaucratic controls and economic inducements to nonintensive use of nonurban land and natural resources. The procedures to assure intensive use of urban land are somewhat less impressive, but perhaps they need not be if the basically rural-oriented programs succeed.

References

Advisory Commission on Intergovernmental Relations (ACIR). 1977. *Federal-State-Local Finances: Significant Features of Fiscal Federalism.* Washington, D.C.: The commission.

Clawson, Marion, and Peter Hall. 1973. *Planning and Urban Growth.* Baltimore, Md.: The Johns Hopkins University Press.

Done, Stephen M. 1962. *Some Questions and Answers on Act 187 or the State Zoning Law.* Public Affairs Series no. 9. Honolulu: Cooperative Extension Service, University of Hawaii.

Gassaway, Carolyn. 1974. *Oregon Plans the Land.* Portland, Oreg.: League of Women Voters.

Harriss, C. Lowell, ed. 1974. *The Good Earth of America: Planning Our Land.* New York: Prentice-Hall.

Levin, Melvin R., Jerome G. Rose, and Joseph S. Slavet. 1974. *New Approaches to State Land-Use Policies.* New York: Lexington Books.

Lindholm, Richard W. 1973a. "Taxation of Land with Emphasis on Site Value Taxation in Hawaii and Oregon." In Advisory Commission on Intergovernmental Relations, *Financing Schools and Property Tax Relief—A State Responsibility,* appendix H, pp. 223-42. Washington, D.C.: The commission.

Lindholm, Richard W. 1973b. *Taxation of Timber Resources* (Oregon Case Study). Eugene: Bureau of Business and Economic Research, College of Business Administration, University of Oregon.

Lindholm, Richard W. 1974. "Taxation and Assessment of Rural and Fringe Area Lands in Nevada." In *Final Report, Assessment and Tax Equity Committee,* ed. Glen W. Atkinson. Reno: Department of Economics, University of Nevada.

Little, Charles E. 1974. *The New Oregon Trail.* Washington, D.C.: Conservation Foundation.

Mack, Pamela C. 1974. "Piecemeal Approach Dilutes Federal Environmental Laws." *The Mortgage Banker,* pp. 6-17.

State of Oregon, Department of Land Conservation and Development. 1974. *A Report on "People and the Land" Public Workshops.* Salem, Oreg.: The department.

State of Oregon, Land Conservation and Development Commission (LCDC). 1974. *Workbook for Public Workshops, September 16-October 7, 1974* (Possible Statewide Land Goals). Salem, Oreg.: The commission.

State of Oregon, Local Government Relations Division, Executive Department, and the Oregon State University Extension Service. 1974. *Oregon Land Use Legislation, Vol. I, Analysis, and Vol. II, Enacted Bills.* Salem: State of Oregon.

Williams, Roger M. 1974. "Oregon: The Fight for Survival." *Saturday Review World,* pp. 10-15.

3 *George E. Peterson*

Federal Tax Policy
and Land Conversion
at the Urban Fringe

Over the years the role of tax policy in land-use decisions has proved to be the source of much controversy. Most recently this controversy has touched the structure of federal taxation. The Tax Reform Act of 1976 represented the culmination of several years of lobbying by farm owners in opposition to the federal estate tax, on the grounds that the tax forced the premature conversion to developed use of farmland at the metropolitan fringe. Similar charges have been brought against the structure of federal capital gains taxation.

What one senator termed "federally compelled destruction of farmland and open space"[1] in turn has been lamented both for the inroads it is thought to make on the nation's agricultural capacity and for its distortion of urban development patterns. If anything, the latter concern seems to be more powerful. As the *New York Times* editorialized on May 10, 1976: "The needs of the environment . . . argue in favor of estate tax reform. As farmlands go on the market and become converted to non-farm uses, the open space that once surrounded cities, large and small,

I gratefully acknowledge research support from the Council on Environmental Quality and the National Science Foundation. This essay was prepared as part of a larger study reported in George E. Peterson, *Federal Tax Policy and Urban Development* (Washington, D.C.: The Urban Institute, 1977). Research assistance was provided by Prudence Larocca.

1. Press release issued by Senator Mathias (R-Md.) and Maryland Environmental Trust, Inc., on May 28, 1974.

disappears. It is replaced by mile after dreary mile of low density, semi-suburban fringe development—a disaster in terms of ecological balance and human recreation and refreshment." Though the *Times*'s critique emphasizes the aesthetic and environmental damage done by prematurely converting farmland to residential uses, other writings have stressed the public sector capital costs inflicted by leapfrog development of new land beyond the urban fringe (Downs, 1970; Gaffney, 1969; Real Estate Research Corporation, 1974).

This essay seeks to evaluate the role of federal tax policy in rural-urban land conversion. The first section will sketch a model of the land conversion process and will review the public's stake in the sequencing of residential development. The second section will consider the manner in which federal tax laws can influence suppliers' decisions on the urban land market. The timing of land sales may be sensitive not only to federal estate tax regulations, but to capital gains tax laws that make the period between retirement and death a propitious one for land disposition. Both sets of tax effects, however, may be overwhelmed by other life-cycle considerations, as well as by ordinary profit comparisons. Accordingly, the third and fourth sections of the essay will turn to an empirical examination of the timing of farmland sales and the sequencing of land conversion. A large number of land transactions in the Baltimore metropolitan area will be examined for the evidence they provide as to the importance of federal tax effects in the timing and location of new development. Other empirical evidence also will be reviewed. The final section of the chapter will then turn to an evaluation of the recent estate tax reform.

In general, it appears that the link between federal estate taxation and urban development patterns is a red herring. Many farmland sales (and subsequent conversions of farmland to developed uses) do take place during the period between the original owner's retirement and the transmission of his estate to his heirs. This life-cycle timing lends a random, or hopscotch, element to land conversion. It also suggests the possibility of an important role in the land conversion process for the estate tax. A case-by-case examination of the reasons for land sales and land conversions, however, shows federal tax policy to be of only minor significance. Urban planners and federal tax reformers alike would do well to shift their attention to more important concerns.[2]

If the empirical evidence dictates skepticism about the power of federal tax laws to shape land development at the urban fringe, it

2. This essay, first presented to the Committee on Taxation, Resources and Economic Development in the fall of 1974, subsequently was used in the congressional debate over federal estate tax reform. As the reader will see, the ultimate legislation was in no respect influenced by its analysis.

confirms the importance of other life-cycle considerations in the timing of land sales. The pattern of fringe development proves to be extremely sensitive to the personal characteristics of the owners of undeveloped land—an element that traditionally has been ignored in economic models of urban land conversion. Landowner characteristics are especially decisive in explaining the apparently random components of urban growth. Demonstration of this linkage provides the positive side of the present essay.

The Land Conversion Process

We may visualize urban land conversion as the outcome of competitive bidding for land between current developers, on the one hand, and speculators and farmers (these often are the same people), on the other.

Given the overall demand for new housing in a metropolitan area, the relative demand for particular parcels of land for housing construction (or for other developmental purposes) can be represented by an inverted demand function, where the bid price for land is:[3]

$$(1) \qquad P_D = f[D, F, S, N, Z],$$

where P_D is the bid price for land in developed use; D, the distance of the land from the metropolitan center or, more generally, the accessibility of the land to centers of economic activity; F, the availability of public facilities (major access roads, sewer and water, utilities); S, the site characteristics (slope, extent of ground cover, etc.); N, the neighborhood characteristics (average value of housing in the area, racial character of neighborhood, etc.); and Z, the zoning and other rules limiting development.

At the same time, there will be demand for farmers and speculators to maintain the land, at least temporarily, in undeveloped uses. The demand for undeveloped land can be represented, also in inverted form, as[4]

$$(2) \qquad P_U = g[A, C, \Delta P_D, X],$$

where P_U is the bid price for land in undeveloped use; A, the annual income from the land in agricultural use; C, the annual carrying costs of

3. The parameters in equation 1 will differ by type of development demand. That is, developers' bid prices for land in commercial or industrial use generally will differ from developers' bid prices for land in residential use.

4. Note that the demand function for undeveloped land is the complement of the land supply function for the development market.

the land; ΔP_D, the projected future change in developers' bid prices; and X, owner-specific factors that incline the owner to sell or to withhold his land from the market during the current period.

In the simplest possible case, where there are no owner-specific considerations to take into account, where undeveloped land is being held primarily for speculative purposes, and where it is possible to abstract from the risk involved in predicting future price changes, the bid price for land in an undeveloped state will equal the net present value of the income that can be earned from developing the parcel in the future, where this annual net income is equal to $\Delta P_D + A - C$. This is to say, the speculative price of undeveloped land will adjust so that, after taking into account the risks involved, landowners, on the average, will earn the standard rate of return by withholding their land for development in the future, rather than offering it for development in the current period.

The rate of appreciation anticipated in developers' bid prices for land, ΔP_D will be a function largely of projected population growth for the metropolitan area as a whole. The sequencing of land development, however, will depend upon *relative* bid-price changes. Relative changes in P_D will be determined by anticipated changes in the variables on the right-hand side of the developers' bid-price function as given by equation 1. If water and sewer lines are to be brought into an area, if the probability of rezoning for more intensive residential use is high, if metropolitan growth is occurring in a way that will make the parcel more accessible to economic activity in the future, then developers' future bid prices can be predicted to rise at a faster-than-average rate. Conversely, if water and sewer services already are available, if zoning regulations already permit intensive development, and if the land is located in close proximity to existing job centers, then developers' *current* bid prices will be high, and the prospect for future bid-price increases will be relatively weak.

The owner-specific factors, X, in equation 2 are explored in more detail in the next section. In general, these are factors—such as the owner's place in the life-cycle—that make him especially willing to sell his parcel in the present period or that make him likely to hold onto his land until a more advantageous selling point is reached from his personal point of view.

The market price for undeveloped land at any given point in time will be the higher of the two bid prices, P_D or P_U. At the moment of sale, of course, it may not be clear to an outsider whether he is observing a bid price for current development or a bid price for undeveloped land. Thus, an empirical estimate of the determinants of land prices generally will have to combine the variables in the right-hand sides of both bid-price functions into a single estimating equation.

Land Conversion

In the foregoing model, land will be converted from an undeveloped to a developed state if, and only if, current developers can outbid farmers and speculators, or if $P_D \geq P_U$. The probability that $P_D \geq P_U$ is a function of the right-hand variables in both bid-price functions. Any characteristics of a parcel that enhance its present development value relative to its anticipated future increase in development value will increase the probability of land conversion. Conversely, any characteristics that are likely to produce above-average future increases in development value or that depress the land's current value for development will tend to cause land to be withheld from development in the present period.

Note that the private market must resolve two types of competition for land use—that between development and agricultural use and that between current development and future development. The many trade-offs involved in these markets imply that the sequence of land development never will appear optimal by any single criterion alone. Even though, *ceteris paribus,* poor agricultural land will be converted to developed uses before prime agricultural land, *some* good-quality farmland will succumb to development, simply because it also possesses features (such as a close-in location or a gentle slope) that make it valuable in residential use. Even the most orderly development pattern will leave pockets of undeveloped land—either because the jumped-over parcels are especially valuable in farm use or because it pays to leave a few gaps in the settlement pattern to accommodate future demand for new development. Obvious as these trade-offs may seem, they often are overlooked in policy debates wherein the sequence of development tends to be evaluated in terms of its success at prime farmland preservation or some other single criterion.

What, then, is the public's stake in the pattern of land conversion? Why should the private market's allocation of land sites be a source of concern to public policy makers? The public's interest may enter from several directions. First, there is the possibility of production externalities. A particular land use may generate externalities that make it difficult to conduct other economic activities at adjoining sites. For example, there is evidence that the productivity of metropolitan farms is often impaired by the pollution generated by commercial, industrial, and transportation uses and by laws passed by suburban communities re-

stricting machinery and other farm operatons (see Peterson and Yampolsky, 1975; and Waddell, 1974). In this case, the market allocation of
land may be inefficient because the private advantages of developing a
particular site do not take into account the externalities resulting from
an unplanned juxtaposition of land uses. If open space or agricultural
land can be rendered unproductive by adjoining development, it may
make sense to preserve large stretches of land as agricultural districts
rather than entrust the sequencing of land conversion to the market
(Conklin et al., 1972; U.S. Department of Agriculture, 1976).[5] In
general, where external effects of this type occur, the public interest may
require segregation of land uses or channeling of development in a way
that makes different activities more compatible with one another. This
was the original rationale for zoning regulations.

A possibly more important source of inefficiency is the failure of the
local tax and public service pricing system to recover the full public costs
of developing certain sites. If developers and/or homebuyers are not
charged the full cost of installing roads, sewers, and other items of
capital infrastructure, but these are financed from general tax revenues,
local citizens will find it in their interest to channel growth into areas
where it can be accommodated at least cost. As a rule, it costs more to
provide capital facilities to far-flung residential developments than to
compactly developed areas. Hopscotch development patterns thus may
impose tax costs on the public at large—though, strictly speaking, the
inefficiencies are more properly attributable to the pricing system than to
the pattern of land conversion. If all land development were forced to
bear directly the full burden of the public costs it created, hopscotch
development would be no more expensive to the public at large than any
other form of growth. Any extra capital expense involved in development
at the far fringe would be borne by the homebuyers who chose to live in
out-of-the-way locations. Where capital infrastructure costs are still paid
for out of general tax revenues, however, planners may be able to reduce
the public's tax bill by guiding growth into areas where capital facilities
are already available or planned.

Finally, the efficient sequencing of land conversion may be upset by
the fact that landowners often dispose of their properties according to
private incentives, peculiar to the owner, rather than by balancing the
economic value that land has in alternative uses. These are the X factors
in equation 2. The federal income tax system, for example, is arranged
so that landowning families benefit by realizing capital gains at certain

5. Several states are now using some variant of agricultural districting; the State of
California has pending legislation that would require urban areas to designate urban
development zones and (with a few strictly defined exceptions) prohibit conversion of prime
agricultural land outside these zones.

periods in their life histories—such as at retirement or at the time of estate transfer—when capital gains tax liability is lowest. Even though the pretax rate of return to land conversion would be greater at some other point in time, a landowner may delay or accelerate his land sales so as to take maximum advantage of the private timing incentives incorporated into federal tax laws. Other private considerations may likewise prompt owners to place their land parcels on the development market at a particular time or to withhold them from the market. Foremost among these considerations is the owner's stage in the life cycle. The owner of a moderate-sized farm who retires or who is struck by ill health will generally want to dispose of his land as soon as possible, since he no longer is able to work it himself. Even more selling urgency is likely to be felt by heirs who have inherited farmland as part of an estate but have no intention of farming it.

These factors introduce an element of apparent inefficiency into the timing of land conversion. At least in part, sites will be targeted for development at a certain time because of the historical accident of who the owners are and where they stand in the life cycle, rather than by a balancing of the productive value of the land in alternative uses.[6] Since the original distribution of landownership by the age and personal characteristics of owners is nearly random, land conversion induced by life-cycle considerations is likely to possess a wide geographic scatter. Any public costs associated with hopscotch development thus will be exacerbated by the influence of X factors on land sales and land conversion.

The Role of Tax Policies in Land Conversion

The tax considerations that may affect the timing of land sales fall into two categories: liquidity or income effects that "force" farmers to sell their land to pay off the tax bill, and price effects that make it more profitable to consummate a sale at one point in time rather than another.

Estate Taxation

When a farm owner dies, his heirs must pay estate taxes on the net worth of the farm property they inherit. For tax purposes a farm tra-

6. In a broader sense, of course, such sales and land conversions may be economically efficient. If landownership imposes great inconvenience or psychological stress, it is perfectly rational for the owner to dispose of his property, even at below-market prices. The transaction costs may be large enough to make it unprofitable for another farmer or speculator to buy the parcel and preserve it in an undeveloped state until the originally optimal moment for land conversion. The only pure inefficiencies arise when (1) the X factors precipitating sale are arbitrary products of the tax structure or other public policy, or (2) the hopscotch character of land conversion introduces external costs not borne by the buyer or seller.

ditionally was assessed at its market value, which in urban areas generally exceeds by a large amount its use value as a farm. It is popularly believed that the cash burden posed by estate tax liability created a liquidity squeeze which often forced farmowning families to sell their land for development. In presenting the Ford administration's reform proposals, the assistant secretary of the treasury for tax policy, Charles M. Walker, stated flatly: "Inflation has had a particularly serious impact upon the family farm. . . . Property values have risen dramatically with the result that owners have been faced with higher estate taxes. This has created a greater need for liquidity. . . . Therefore, many families have found it necessary to sell the family farm."[7] The liquidity squeeze, if present, forces those who inherit farmland to place more land on the market than they would in the absence of tax pressure.

One does not have to accept the full claims as to the severity of the estate tax's liquidity squeeze to acknowledge that estate tax burdens can influence the timing of land sales. Perhaps a more likely explanation is the income effect of estate taxation. The investment portfolios of farm families, naturally, are strongly skewed in favor of landholdings. The need to pay upwards of $120,000 in estate taxes on a $400,000 farm, though it may not have "forced" farm households to sell their property, in the literal sense that households were unable to come up with the cash to meet their tax obligations, did at the least require liquidation of some of the family's nonfarm assets, and may have necessitated fresh borrowing. As a result, the family's net worth would have become even more concentrated in land. As a simple matter of portfolio balance, it would then become advantageous for the heirs to try to dispose of some of their landholdings.

Capital Gains Tax Effects

Besides the "stick" of a liquidity squeeze, federal tax policy contains several "carrots" that make the period between retirement and death an attractive one for liquidating asset holdings. Under the Internal Revenue Code, as it existed until 1976, property that was transferred to heirs as part of an estate escaped all capital gains tax liability on the appreciation in value that occurred before the original owner's death. The basis for computing capital gains for tax purposes was automatically adjusted to the property's value at the time of inheritance. Given the sizable capital gains that exist on most farms located within metropolitan boundaries, families have had a strong tax incentive to hold onto property until the

7. Testimony delivered to the House Ways and Means Committee, March 22, 1976.

original owner dies and the property is transferred to heirs. They then could escape all capital gains tax liability.[8]

Retirement is another moment with important capital gains tax consequences. For a family that will move into a sharply lower tax bracket when its head retires (as is generally true of farmers who have no special pension benefits), there are significant tax advantages to be gained from postponing land sales until retirement and then spreading the sale proceeds over several years. Also, after the age of sixty-five, families whose farms have served as their homesteads are granted partial tax exemption on capital gains realized when their farms are sold. This provides another (albeit minor) reason for postponing sale until retirement age.

State Preferential Assessment of Farmland

State tax policy, too, acts to reinforce the life-cycle timing of land sales and land conversion. Forty-one states now have differential assessment laws that assess farm property for property tax purposes at its use value in farming rather than at its market value in development.[9] This differential assessment policy drastically lowers property taxes and hence total carrying costs on farmland at the metropolitan fringe. In Bucks County, Pennsylvania, Montgomery County, Maryland, and other suburban locations, it is not unusual for property taxes to be reduced by 90 percent or more through use-value assessment. The reduction in property tax burdens, in turn, raises the value of land as a speculative or agricultural holding. As indicated by equations 1 and 2, the bid price for the land in an undeveloped state will rise relative to the bid price for its development, thus tending to postpone farmland conversion for a period of time.

One of the indirect effects of preferential assessment laws has been to make it feasible for families to avail themselves more fully of private timing incentives. Under normal market conditions, many families could not afford to postpone land sales until the period between retirement and death. The property taxes paid on the true market value of favorably situated land would greatly exceed the ultimate savings in federal tax liability. Once the property tax burden has been slashed to a fraction of its normal level, however, landowners are able to give much greater

8. The Tax Reform Act of 1976 established property values as of January 1, 1977, as the basis for computing future capital gains tax liability on property transferred at death. Capital appreciation accumulated prior to that time will continue to escape capital gains taxation; capital appreciation attributable to subsequent years will be subject to taxation. This change in the law has the effect of reducing future timing incentives for land sales.

9. For a recent review of state differential assessment programs, see Regional Science Research Institute (1976).

weight to the timing incentives built into federal tax laws and to timing preferences based on their personal circumstances.

Empirical Evidence on Land Conversion

The hypothesis I will investigate in this section holds that the pattern and timing of land conversion near the urban fringe is determined in large part by the life-cycle circumstances of rural landowners rather than by the economic characteristics of the land itself. In the terminology used

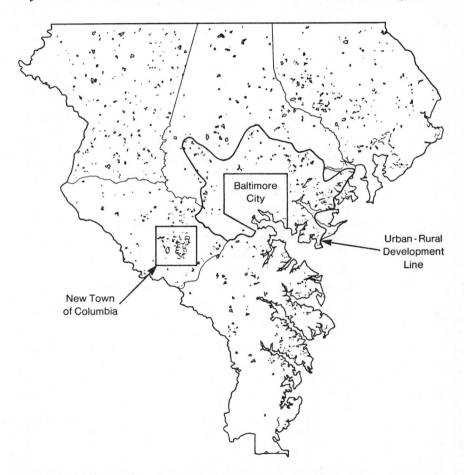

Figure 3.1. Spatial pattern of recorded subdivision plats. Black dots indicate subdivision locations. *Source:* Subdivision map prepared by the Baltimore Regional Planning Council; Urban-Rural Development Line superimposed from a map prepared by the Baltimore County Planning Office.

earlier, the hypothesis holds that the X factors of equation 2 loom large in the land-conversion process. The testing of this hypothesis is an empirical matter. This section reports the results of an analysis of land sales and land conversion in the Baltimore metropolitan area.[10] The results are presented first in simple tabular form, then as a more formal test of the land conversion model developed at the beginning of the chapter.

Figure 3.1 illustrates the pattern of recent residential development in the Baltimore metropolitan area. The map shows the location of new residential subdivisions built during the period 1970-73. The black dots indicating subdivision locations offer a graphic portrayal of the scattered character of metropolitan growth. The Urban-Rural Development Line (URDL), which was devised by planners to guide urban growth in the Baltimore area, is also indicated on the map. According to the Baltimore County master plan, the bulk of new growth should be accommodated *inside* the URDL, where the availability of public infrastructure can sustain it at least cost. The county's master plan places particular emphasis on discouraging leapfrog development because of the "costly extensions of sewerage, water lines, schools, roads and other facilities and services" it would require (Baltimore County, Maryland, 1972, p. 4).

Table 3.1. Reasons for Farm Sales

Reason	Percentage of acreage sold
Life-cycle considerations	55.4%
Retired or moved (includes ill health)	33.8
Death	21.0
Other (divorce)	0.6
Economic considerations	31.0
Good price	24.9
No farm labor available	3.7
Unproductive farmland/more efficient to farm elsewhere	2.4
Other	13.6
Title change within family	10.7
No reason given	2.9

10. Four separate samples are used in the analysis which follows. The first is a random sample and interviewing of forty current farmland owners. The second is a "sample" of 135 farmland sales (the total number of farm sales in Baltimore County between 1971 and 1973). Basic information (such as selling price and age of owner) was obtained for all 135 sales; personal interviews regarding the reasons for sale were carried out for 84 of the sales, where representatives of the buyers and sellers could be located. The third sample is a random sample of 27 large subdivision developments with 5143 housing units. For these developments, land transfers were traced backward to determine the reasons that the original landowners placed their land on the development market. The final sample consisted of 185 land parcels identified as operating farms in 1966. Sale and development histories were constructed for these parcels for the period 1966-73, inclusive.

The map of subdivision locations makes clear that Baltimore County's development plan, like many a land use plan before it, has been honored mainly in the breach. Whatever else may determine the location and timing of development in the Baltimore metropolitan area, it is not the planners' conception of where growth can be accommodated most efficiently.

Table 3.1 presents basic information relevant to the testing of the life-cycle hypothesis. From 1971 to 1973 135 sales of farmland were recorded in Baltimore County. Representatives of the selling parties for eighty-four of these transactions were located and interviewed. The reasons for sale, as given by the owners, are shown in the table. Well over half of the farms offered for sale during this period reached the market because the owner died, retired, or moved from the area (usually in conjunction with retirement). The median age of all farmers selling land was just under seventy.

Table 3.2 examines the development process from a different perspective. It starts with a random sample of twenty-seven of the large new subdivisions illustrated in the map in figure 3.1. The land on which these subdivisions were located was traced backwards to determine the timing and conditions of its conversion from rural use. Together, the subdivisions in the sample accounted for the construction of 5143 housing units, or approximately one-eighth of total Baltimore County growth

Table 3.2. Reasons for Sale of Land Subsequently Developed into Tracts

Reason for selling	Acres		Housing units	
	Number	Percentage of total	Number	Percentage of total
Death	1267.7	58.3	1265	24.6
Retirement	796.2	36.6	3105	60.4
Good price	112.2	5.2	773	15.0
Total	2176.1	100.1[a]	5143[b]	100.0

[a] Due to rounding errors.
[b] Total new housing construction for Baltimore County in this period was 41,529 units.

Table 3.3. Reasons Given for "Premature" Land Conversion[a]

Reason for selling	Acres		Housing units	
	Number	Percentage of total	Number	Percentage of total
Death	1110.4	74.5	263	74.1
Retirement	344.7	23.1	72	20.3
Good price	35.0	2.4	20	5.6
Total	1490.1	100.0	355	100.0

[a] "Premature" land conversion refers to housing built on land outside the Urban-Rural Development Line.

between 1971 and 1973. Among these subdivision sites, life-cycle considerations were a still more dominant factor in the original selling decision. Approximately 95 percent of the rural land developed into these housing tracts was sold because of the death or retirement of the original owner. The contrast, evident in the table, between acreage and housing unit shares attributable to different selling motivations also is instructive. Farmland sold at retirement was developed at almost four times the density of farmland sold at death; farmland sold because of "good price" was still more intensively developed. The average price received per acre for land in the latter two categories was also much higher. Such a relationship is consistent with the hypothesis that economic considerations are a more important factor in land sales made at the prime of life or at retirement, when the typical landholder is in no rush to sell, than at death, when heirs normally want to dispose of property without awaiting zoning changes, sewer installation, or other measures that would enhance the value of their land. As implied by table 3.2, a joint mapping of subdivisions and "reason for sale" shows that estate transfers were particularly important in bringing remote land, at or beyond the urban fringe, onto the development market.

A classification of land sales by the "cause" of sale, of course, runs the risk of oversimplification. Although respondents may give their reasons for selling farm property as "retirement" rather than "good price," this does not mean that the receipt of an adequate price is not a consideration in the sale. If farmland could be disposed of only at a much lower price, farmers might well postpone disposition of their property. Indeed, in many cases it is the possibility of reaping large capital gains from the sale of land which makes it *possible* for a farm family to retire. The figures in tables 3.1 and 3.2 reflect the reasons cited by rural landowners for timing their land sales as they did. Only if the price offered by a developer was unexpectedly high or unlikely to be repeated was a respondent likely to cite "good price" as the reason for sale. As long as the price received for land conformed roughly to the usual market level and reflected what the owner thought he could receive whenever he decided to sell, the reason given for sale tended to be the reason for disposing of the land *at that particular time,* however important the high price offered by developers may have been as a general background consideration inducing sale. Every farm in a metropolitan area is no doubt "on the market" in the sense that it can be acquired by developers for some price. But the decision to sell a land parcel at the price offered appears to be extremely sensitive to the personal circumstances of the owner.

Perhaps the most revealing data gathered from the Baltimore survey are those in table 3.3. From the standpoint of efficient growth, it matters much less why farmland in general is sold for development than why apparent inefficiencies emerge in the growth process. Slightly more than half the subdivisions covered in table 3.2 were built outside the URDL planning boundary. Although counties in the Baltimore metropolitan area try to recover from developers many of the costs of extending sewer and water lines to new developments, there remains a presumption (as indicated in the master plan) that development outside of the service boundary imposes a net cost on the public at large and is inefficient in this sense. Table 3.3 shows that almost 98 percent of the land converted for residential use beyond the Urban-Rural Development Line was sold by the rural owners because of death or retirement. (Note that the very low density of development of this land meant that, though it accounted for more than two-thirds of all the converted acreage in our sample, it provided less than 6 percent of the new housing units.) From the developers' perspective, the favorable terms on which heirs and retirees were willing to sell their land parcels apparently more than compensated for the relatively unattractive locations of the land offered for sale.

Premature land development is one type of inefficiency in the metropolitan growth process. At the opposite extreme, orderly metropolitan development may be impeded by withholding land from the market in areas that are ripe for housing growth. Of the twenty-three landowners interviewed in depth who reported no present intention to offer their land for sale, in all but four cases the owners stated that they would not place their parcels on the market until they reached retirement age. Six of these owners were holding undeveloped blocks of land within the Urban-Rural Development Line and—from the planners' perspective—were responsible for promoting disorderly development by requiring urban expansion to jump over their farms. Three of these holdouts were family farmers who stated that they intended to hold on to their land until retirement, while the other three owners were acting primarily as speculators. The sample here is thin enough to dictate extreme caution, but the general picture of the reasons for withholding land from development is consistent with the reasons former owners cited for *selling* their properties. Households that have reached retirement age are likely to sell their properties to developers; younger farm households are likely to plan to wait for retirement before selling. Life-cycle reasons overwhelmingly dominate selling decisions at the far fringe of the urban area; speculative considerations become more important at close-in locations. It seems safe to conclude, however, that, at least in Baltimore County, life-cycle factors have played an important role in determining where and when large tracts of land reach the development market.

Testing the Model of Land Conversion

It is possible to use the data collected in our Baltimore study to carry out a more formal test of the land conversion model sketched at the beginning of this chapter. The essence of that model is that site characteristics which raise a land parcel's current development value,

Table 3.4. Empirical Estimates of Determinants of Land Prices and Probability of Land Conversion, Baltimore Metropolitan Area (*t*-statistics in parentheses)

Variable	Contribution to market price per acre ($)	Contribution to probability of sale[a]	Contribution to probability of land conversion[a]
Developers' bid factors			
Distance of parcel from	− 49.0	− .011	− .018
metropolitan center (miles)	(9.1)	(1.5)	(2.7)
Water and sewer available	+434.0	+ .056	+ .077
(yes/no)	(11.0)	(3.2)	(5.8)
Access to main road	+315.0	+ .042	+ .064
(yes/no)	(6.6)	(1.8)	(3.7)
Front interstate highway	+920.0	+ .013	+ .039
(yes/no)	(14.8)	(0.6)	(2.8)
Average value of housing	+ .027	− $.3 \times 10^{-6}$	+ $.2 \times 10^{-6}$
in area[b] (dollars)	(7.5)	(1.2)	(1.9)
Zoned for ≤ one-half acre	+557.0	+ .061	+ .085
development[c] (yes/no)	(8.0)	(3.7)	(7.1)
Zoned for ≥ five-acre	−406.0	+ .033	− .166
development[c] (yes/no)	(5.5)	(2.0)	(12.2)
Supply factors			
Value of land in agricul-	+ .21	− $.5 \times 10^{-4}$	− 1.1×10^{-4}
tural use[d] (dollars)	(4.4)	(0.8)	(4.7)
Area designated for sewer in-	+232.0	+ .071	− .098
stallation before 1980[e] (yes/no)	(5.1)	(3.3)	(4.1)
Owner reached age seventy	−160.0	+ .28	+ .19
during period[f] (yes/no)	(3.0)	(18.5)	(12.9)
Owner died	−245.0	+ .47	+ .16
(yes/no)	(3.8)	(25.0)	(10.1)
Adjusted R^2	.68	.59	.54

[a] Sales and land conversions were those observed during the period 1966-73.

[b] "Area" was defined as a two-mile radius around the land parcel. Average housing value was estimated from the assessed value of single-family homes, converted to market value.

[c] Other zoning categories are implicit in the constant terms of the equations.

[d] The use-valuation of farmland under Maryland's preferential assessment law, measured as of 1972.

[e] By local master plans.

[f] This dummy variable was set equal to zero if the owner also died during the period of observation.

relative to its potential for future appreciation, will increase the probability of land sale and the probability of land conversion in the present period. But it is hypothesized that other considerations—such as the owner's place in the life cycle and the agricultural value of the land—also will influence both land prices and the probability of conversion.

For empirical purposes the variables on the right-hand side of equations 1 and 2 were combined to estimate land prices, sale probabilities, and land conversion probabilities. Although the resulting equations are literally reduced forms, the fact that the variables in the bid functions for land in developed and undeveloped uses are different from each other makes it possible to partition the variable set into two groups, simplifying greatly the interpretation of the results. The bid function for land in undeveloped use determines the supply of land to the development market. That is, the price required by present farm owners (or offered by other bidders for land in an undeveloped state) establishes the price at which land is made available, or "supplied," to the development market. Thus the variables in equation 2 have been referred to in table 3.4 as "supply" variables.

For the model of land-price determination and land conversion sketched in the first section to receive its fullest confirmation, all of the variables in table 3.4 should influence land prices. Developer-demand variables should have the same signs in all three equations, indicating that as developer-bid prices rise, other things being equal, the probability that an undeveloped parcel will be sold for development also rises. "Supply" variables, or variables that affect bid prices for land in an undeveloped state, in contrast, should have opposite signs in the sale and conversion equations from their signs in the price equations. That is, farm owners' willingness to sell their parcels at below-market prices should enhance the probability of sale and development. These effects are predicted most clearly for the price- and land-conversion equations. The determinants of sales probability are much less clearly implied by the model, although owner-specific factors are hypothesized to be important both in depressing land prices and in promoting sales.

To test and quantify this model of the land conversion process, histories were developed for 185 land parcels identified as operating farms in the Baltimore metropolitan area in 1966. Public records and telephone interviews were employed to determine whether each of these parcels was sold and/or developed during the eight years 1966-73. Information on the age of each original owner was also collected, as was information on deaths during the period. This sample forms the basis of the land sale and land conversion equations reported in the last two columns of table 3.4. In these equations the proportion of 1966 farmland in each parcel that was sold or developed during the period 1966-73 is made a function of the independent variables listed. For the most part, farms were either sold for development in their entirety or maintained in an undeveloped state. For these observations the dependent variable takes on values of 0 or 1 only. But some of the owners in the sample sold off parts of their farms; in these cases, the dependent variable assumes fractional values between 0 and 1. The equations in the last two columns thus can be interpreted as linear probability functions; they indicate the probability of a parcel's sale and development, respectively.

The first column of the table reports the effects that the same independent variables have on land values. This market-value equation was estimated from a separate sample of 135 actual land sales during the 1971-73 period.

Table 3.4 bears out our general model of land conversion and fills in many of the quantitative details. The factors that contribute most heavily to developers' bid prices for land, and to observed market prices, also raise the probability that land will be converted to developed uses. Proximity to the metropolitan center, the presence of water and sewer lines, availability of road access, and intensive zoning authorization all contribute both to land values and to the probability of land conversion. The empirical estimates imply that many of the traditional planning devices for phasing development, such as zoning regulations and the timing of infrastructure construction, have been successful in sequencing land conversion. (The association of these variables with land sales is much less systematic.)

Life-cycle considerations play a statistically significant role in all three equations. They are, however, much more important in selling and development decisions than in price determination.

From the empirical estimates of table 3.4 we can infer a good deal about the operation of the market in land at the urban fringe. Prices appear to be determined primarily by developer-demand factors. As is evident from the first column of table 3.4, developer-bid variables have far greater impact on the market prices of undeveloped land than do the factors in the lower part of the table, which are hypothesized to influence bid prices for land in an undeveloped state. The model adopted implies that individual landowners operate as price takers. The aggregate amount of land in the hands of owners of given characteristics—for example, the total amount of land owned by elderly landowners—may affect the overall level of land prices by making it more or less likely that this land will be offered for sale and hence shifting upward or downward the aggregate land supply curve, but for individual landowners selling prices are relatively fixed. The modestly lower prices realized by retirees and heirs probably reflect the lesser time they are willing to invest in the search for buyers.

Given the market price for land, the location and timing of land sales appears to be determined primarily by "supply" factors—in particular, by the personal characteristics of landowners. The age of the owner and whether or not the owner died during the period completely dominate the sale-probability function. Part of this sale activity, of course, occurs between farmers or between farmers and speculators. It does not necessarily lead to land conversion. On balance, however, there is also a much greater probability of development on land originally owned by owners who reach retirement age or die. This is indicated in the last column of table 3.4. Both developer-bid factors and owner-supply characteristics influence the probability of land development, but owner-specific characteristics appear to be dominant.

In diagrammatic form the relationship summarized in table 3.4 can be represented as shown in figure 3.2, which shows the demand for and supply of land for development within a particular planning grid. The developer-bid-price curve for land in any given grid is highly elastic, since developers can choose to develop any of several comparable sites and because, at existing price levels, even dissimilar sites become approximate substitutes for one another. Because the bid-price curve is highly elastic, any change in local landowners' willingness to place land on the market, such as occurs when owners reach retirement age or die, has its primary impact on the quantity of land in the grid that is sold and developed. This can be seen from the outward shift of the "supply-price" curve in figure 3.2. Local landholders' supply decisions have only a small effect on the price at which their land sells.

Developer-bid factors are much more decisive in determining the probability of conversion of different types of land. Figure 3.3 illustrates developer-bid prices at two different locations, where the higher, dotted

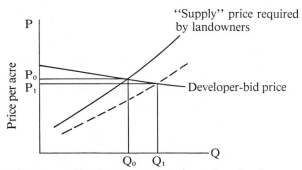

Figure 3.2. Development market in a single planning grid: effect of change in landowner characteristics

curve represents developer demand at more centrally located sites or at sites that otherwise enjoy an advantage in homebuyers' eyes. If the alternative use value of land in farming, landowner characteristics, and other supply factors are similar at the two locations, supply conditions at the two locations can be represented by a single supply-price curve. As is apparent, both the price of land and the quantity of land developed then are sensitive to developer-demand factors. This corresponds to the empirical findings in table 3.4. It is the systematic pattern of developer demand that imposes orderly gradients on both land prices and conversion probabilities, despite the "random" influence of owner characteristics.

Evidence from Other Studies

Relatively few empirical studies of the reasons for rural/urban land conversion have been carried out. The scattering of other evidence that is available, however, seems to confirm the importance of life-cycle considerations in the timing of land sales at the urban fringe.

In one of the most extensive studies Massie (1968) examined decade-long histories of two hundred rural land parcels outside of each of three North Carolina cities. He found that retirees were more likely to sell than other owners. There also was a lower probability of sale by owner-occupants than by absentee owners of land parcels. Massie found that landowners' characteristics exerted more influence over the probability of sale as one moved outward from the urbanized center. This would suggest that strict market calculations are more significant determinants of selling activity at close-in sites, where land prices are highest and the frequency of parcel turnover greatest. As in our Baltimore study, land sales and land conversion at the far fringe seem to be most sensitive to

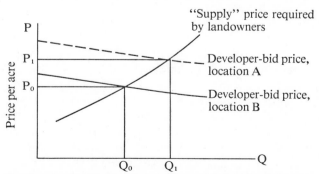

Figure 3.3. Development market in two different planning grids: effect of developer-bid factors

owner characteristics. One drawback to Massie's analysis is that he investigated only the probability of sale, not the probability of land conversion.

An analysis of rural land in New Castle County, Delaware (outside of Wilmington), concluded that "retirement or death of the owner generally results in transfer of the property involved. Thus, an area with a large proportion of elderly landowners may reasonably expect frequent ownership changes" (Crosswhite and Vaughan, 1962, p. 17). Like several other studies, this one emphasizes the large share of undeveloped fringe land that is in the hands of elderly households. In northern New Castle County at least one-third of the land lying outside of subdivisions and incorporated municipalities was owned by individuals sixty years of age or older. Despite the strong element of randomness imparted to sale activity by owner characteristics, the aggregate pattern of land conversion in New Castle County displays a systematic response to the variables determining developer-bid prices. For example, the share of land converted to residential use declines regularly with distance from the urban center (Vaughan and Moore, 1963).

In her study of the expansion of the Philadelphia metropolitan area, Milgram (1967) stressed the interplay between individual landowners' selling decisions and developer-demand factors in fixing the pattern of development. *Ceteris paribus,* the sequence of development was sensitive to characteristics such as the land's access to the central city, its location in relation to older towns at the urban fringe, the presence of sewer networks, and favorable zoning regulations; but the "accidental" factor of the location of a willing seller seemed to be of at least equal significance in deciding the specific locations of developments. Milgram found, however, that the practice of inventorying land for future development kept the location of current sellers from influencing development locations as strongly as it might otherwise do. Less than half the land in the sample was developed during or in the year following its acquisition by the ultimate developer; almost a quarter of the land was held four years or more before development. This landbanking by developers in anticipation of future demand makes it possible to smooth over some of the random shocks provided by life-cycle selling decisions.

Two other statistical tests of a model like that presented in the current paper have been carried out. In an analysis of land conversion in Fairfax County, Virginia (outside of Washington, D.C.), Peterson (1974) demonstrated that when the county was divided into uniformly sized grids both the total shares of land in developed use and the shares of land converted to development in a given period were systematically related to developer-bid variables of the type included in table 3.4, which also largely determined land prices. No information was secured on owner characteristics, however. Church and Sander (1976) have shown that variations in the rate of development in uniform land grids of the Albuquerque, New Mexico, region also can be explained by the competition between current developers' bid prices and speculators' bid prices, although again no information was collected on owner characteristics.

In summary, the available data seem to bear out the broad lines of the land conversion model sketched earlier in this chapter. Systematic influences are apparent in the land conversion process. Other things being equal, land close to the urban center commands a higher market price and is more likely to be converted to developed uses than land at more distant locations. Poor quality farmland, *ceteris paribus,* will be converted to alternative uses before top quality farmland. The completion of access roads, installation of sewers, or rezoning for high density use will enhance the value of land *for present development* and increase the likelihood of land conversion.

Nonetheless, when all is said, there remains a sizable element of apparent randomness in decisions as to where and when development will take place. This chapter has traced this nonsystematic component of development timing to landowner characteristics. The considerations that induce particular landowners to offer their parcels for sale at particular times greatly influence the pattern of metropolitan growth—in particular the "hopscotch" element of development at the urban fringe.

The Role of Tax Considerations in Life-Cycle Sales

It is difficult to establish the exact importance of tax considerations in life-cycle sales of rural property. On the one hand, the timing of most farmland sales coincides with moments that have been advantageous from the tax perspective. Farm families display a surprising awareness of some of the lesser known provisions of the Internal Revenue Code. In the Baltimore County sample it was common for farmers selling their land to demand 29 percent down payments from developers in order to spread the recognition of capital gains over a number of separate years after retirement rather than bunch their capital gains into a single year when they would be subject to a higher tax rate.[11] Several respondents were actively considering subdividing land on their own and were aware of the Internal Revenue Code limitations on the number of lots they could sell

11. If less than 30 percent of the value of an asset is received at the time of sale, the seller can pro-rate his capital gain according to the share of principal received in each year.

before being considered "dealers" in land and thus having their profits treated for tax purposes as ordinary income rather than capital gains.

In direct interviews, however, all of the farmers citing life-cycle reasons for land sales held that the timing of their sales was determined primarily by personal events rather than by the prospect of tax savings. Many older farmers remain committed to agriculture as a way of life, despite the fact that they may not be able to squeeze top dollar out of their land by using it for farm purposes. As long as the economic returns to farming and landholding are adequate, they are willing to remain in farming until retirement. The children of the current generation of metropolitan farmers, however, are much less ready to make an economic sacrifice to keep favorably located land in agricultural production. Farming as a life style does not hold the same attraction for rural sons and daughters that it does for their parents. Consequently, metropolitan farmland that is passed on to children as part of an estate is likely to be sold, regardless of tax considerations. The prospect that no family member will carry on the farm also makes owners more ready to offer their land for sale at the time of their retirement. At least in the rural landowner's eyes, the income tax breaks incorporated into the federal tax code are something to be taken advantage of, wherever possible, but they are not an important determinant of the timing of land sales.

In contrast, virtually all of the farmers interviewed, as well as the representatives of farm organizations, were convinced that the federal estate tax is responsible for a large share of the farmland conversion taking place in Baltimore County. In the words of one of the farmers interviewed, "since the estate tax appraises the land at market value, it in effect forces a family to buy back their own land, which is impossible. Farmers just don't have that kind of cash lying around."

In view of the strong feeling expressed about the effects of the estate tax, a special effort was made in the Baltimore study to locate families who had been directly affected by it. This proved much more difficult than expected. Although respondent after respondent seemed convinced that many farmland owners had been forced to sell by estate tax burdens, very few could suggest names of those affected; in fact, only nine specific references were gathered during the course of more than two hundred interviews. Of these nine, five reported no hardship at all in paying the estate tax and had continued their farm operations. Of the remaining four, only one family had actually been forced to sell its property because of the amount of the estate tax. This particular property went into development, and because of its size and favorable location, it accounted for more than five hundred housing units. In two other cases families were forced to go into debt to pay the estate taxes on their land. There remains a possibility that some acreage from these farms will be sold to cancel the families' indebtedness. In the fourth case three of the four heirs wished to liquidate their shares of the estate, and the remaining one could not afford to buy out his fellow inheritors; the necessity of paying the estate tax contributed in some degree to the desire for liquidity.

In a purely statistical sense it is clear that the liquidity squeeze posed by the estate tax is not a major cause of land conversion, at least in the Baltimore area. Only 1 of the 135 farmland sales in our sample could be traced explicitly to the estate tax burden. No other studies have produced empirical evidence that estate taxation plays a larger role than this in the sale or conversion of farmland.

Most popular discussions seem to exaggerate the liquidity squeeze created by estate taxation. It must be kept in mind that the estate tax in the United States is imposed on the net worth of a decedent. Though it is common to speak of the "heavily mortgaged" farmer as unable to meet his estate tax bill, tax liability is computed only after all outstanding debts have been subtracted from the market value of farm assets. Moreover, sizable adjustments in net worth were allowed in computing the "taxable estate" under the law as it existed prior to 1976. An unrestricted or specific deduction of $60,000 was allowed on all estates. Further deductions were permitted to cover funeral expenses, expenses of administering the estate, and donations to approved, tax-exempt charities. Up to half of an estate could be left tax free to a surviving spouse. In addition, each spouse was able to give away $30,000 tax free while he or she was alive and to make an unlimited number of further gifts of up to $3,000 per year without tax obligations.

An examination of the estates transmitted to heirs reveals that it has been relatively rare for farm households to face a literal shortage of cash. In recent years more than 90 percent of farm estates contained, *as part of the estate,* more liquid assets than were needed to cover the full estate tax liability (Smith, 1976). (Liquid assets were defined as cash, savings deposits, and marketable securities.) Coupled with the liquid assets possessed by the heirs, this wealth was sufficient to avoid a true liquidity squeeze.

Finally, if a family so desired, it could generally mortgage its property to raise the cash necessary to meet its tax obligations. Any family that possesses unencumbered property of significant value will find it relatively easy to persuade a bank to make a loan to cover its taxes. In cases where a lump-sum payment would impose economic hardship, federal estate tax law authorized the commissioner of the Internal Revenue Service to permit estate tax payments to be spread over as many as ten years. In view of these facts, it seems doubtful that the cash flow burden literally "forced" ordinary farm families to dispose of their properties in order to pay their tax bills.

This is not to deny that the estate tax burden could make it extremely difficult to preserve intact truly valuable estates. Many a prized land-holding, art collection, or stock portfolio has had to be broken up by heirs looking for cash. In fact, it is one of the purposes of estate taxation to place some limits on the ability of families to accumulate vast wealth over successive generations. Only in instances of substantial wealth, however, do estate taxes rise to a rate where they literally compel dismantling of assets. Otherwise, they prod heirs toward liquidation by leaving them "land-rich" in comparison with their current income. Other studies of the impact of estate taxation on the disposition of farmland have come to the same conclusion. For example, after a thorough review of the economic impact of federal and state death taxes, Thomas F. Hady of the United States Department of Agriculture concluded that "death taxes are not a major problem for the typical American farmer" (1963, p. 23).

Federal Estate Tax Reform

Despite the scant empirical evidence that federal estate tax liability has "forced" farm families to sell their land for development, reform of the estate tax, as it applies to farmland, became a popular cause in Congress, issuing eventually in the estate tax provisions of the Tax Reform Act of 1976. Proponents of reform insisted that the estate tax in its previous form left metropolitan farmers no choice but to sell out to developers and therefore "flout[ed] the first principle of sound land use planning which calls for a mix of uses in urban areas."[12] Some consideration of the likely effect of estate tax reform on the suburban land market therefore seems in order.

The Tax Reform Act both raises the value of estates exempt from taxation and introduces provisions specifically favorable to the owners of farm property. The previous $60,000 specific deduction has been replaced by a tax credit, which by 1981 will have the effect of eliminating tax liability on the first $175,000 of all estates. Marital deductions also have been made far more generous. At the owner's option, farm property may be valued for estate tax purposes at its *use* value rather than at its market value.[13] The taxable value of inherited farm property may be

12. Wills (1974). See also remarks entered in the *Congressional Record* for the 93d Congress, Tuesday, May 28, 1974, by Senator Mathias.
13. According to the law, the following method is to be used in establishing the use value of farms: the annual gross cash rental for comparable land used for farming purposes, after subtraction of average state and local property taxes, is capitalized by the average annual effective interest rate for all new Federal Land Bank loans.

reduced by a maximum of $500,000 under this provision. To enjoy the full benefits of lessened tax liability, the heirs of farm property must retain it in that use for fifteen years. If the property is sold, or converted to other uses, in the first ten years the full tax liability based on market value must be paid. The excess liability based on market rather than use value is gradually phased out for property held between ten and fifteen years.

The most important of these special provisions is the application of the principle of use-value assessment. This device has been widely used to lower local property tax burdens on farmland. Its extension to federal estate taxation was proposed in no fewer than thirteen separate bills introduced in the 93d Congress. Preferential valuation of farmland, of course, has its most pronounced impact on farmland in the vicinity of large urban centers, where the market and use values of farm property diverge most significantly. Use valuation provides relatively few benefits to owners of farmland in the country's agricultural heartland, since the market value of land there *is* its value in agricultural production rather than its value in alternative uses. Formal valuation of such farm property according to agricultural use has little effect on tax liability.

In evaluating the recent shift in the estate tax structure, it is fitting to ask three questions: Would the objective of farmland preservation be desirable if achieved? Is the tax reform enacted likely to preserve land in farm use? How much will the tax savings granted to farmers cost other taxpayers?

The adoption of use-value assessments of farmland, whether for property tax or estate tax purposes, implies that it is desirable to preserve land in agricultural or open-space uses, regardless of its location. Such programs reduce the tax burdens on all metropolitan farmland; in fact, they grant the largest tax savings to farmland located near the urban core. As was noted in the first part of this chapter, the preservation of good-quality farmland must always be balanced against other metropolitan development objectives. Farms typically are scattered throughout an urbanized area, and random preservation of them is likely to fly in the face of orderly urban expansion. In the few areas where the effect of preferential property tax assessments on metropolitan growth has been evaluated in detail, it was found that the use of assessment differentials to preserve close-in farming caused urban expansion to jump over farm parcels in ways that increased the cost of public service provision and complicated planning arrangements (see, for example, California State Assembly, Select Committee on Open Space Land, 1973; and Gustafson and Wallace, 1975). This experience carries the clear lesson that tax subsidies should be granted for the preservation of farmland, or for the preservation of land in other open-space uses, only when these uses conform to an area's long-range development plans.

Apart from questions about the desirability of randomly preserving farmland in urban environs, the feasibility of achieving this objective through federal tax reform must be judged doubtful. Advocacy of use-value assessment for estate tax purposes was based on the presumption that many farm families will persist in farming, even if they can earn higher rates of return from employing the land in alternative uses, if only they are freed from the liquidity squeeze created by estate taxation. This premise has been shown to be of doubtful validity. There is no empirical evidence showing that estate tax liability is a major cause of the sale or conversion of farmland at the urban fringe, and my own empirical work indicates that estate tax considerations are of minor importance.

Moreover, the Tax Reform Act of 1976 substitutes for the "stick" of liquidity and income effects a new "carrot" that is likely to exert even stronger effects on the timing of farmland sales and development. In effect, the law grants very large tax reductions to heirs who are willing to postpone the sale or development of their land for ten to fifteen years. If the law has any important effect on land use at the suburban fringe, it will be to delay development on randomly selected farm parcels by this period of time. Conceivably, such postponement will serve local development objectives, but it seems more likely that its effect will be to create haphazard shifts in development sites.

The costs involved in use-value assessment of farm property are rather modest. The Library of Congress Research Service estimated that a predecessor use-value bill, introduced by Senator Mathias, would cost about $20 million per year in reduced tax yield. Presumably, the net cost was reduced further by the other changes in the estate tax structure, which had the effect of lessening the tax due even on fully taxable estates.

Summary and Conclusion

This chapter set out to examine the urban land market. It began with the hypothesis that personal considerations in the life histories of land-owners help determine when land parcels come onto the development market and thus indirectly help to fix the pattern of metropolitan sub-division location. Tax factors are among the personal considerations that potentially affect land supply. The structure of capital gains taxation in the United States had made the period following retirement an opportune time for realizing capital appreciation. The burden of federal estate taxation is commonly thought to have forced farm families in metropolitan areas to liquidate their landholdings in order to meet their tax bills. Both of these federal taxes could be instrumental in influencing "hopscotch" or "leapfrog" development at the urban fringe, since the timing and location of residential development would be sensitive to the distribution of landowner characteristics rather than to the economic characteristics of the land itself.

The investigation of land sales and land conversion in Baltimore County strongly substantiates the life-cycle hypothesis. In this sample the overwhelming majority of the land converted to subdivision use came onto the market in the period between the owner's retirement and death. This finding is supported by other empirical studies; all report a greater probability of sale and use conversion among properties held by elderly owners than among other properties having similar characteristics but held by different types of owners. The apparently random element in land conversion resulting from owner characteristics is imposed on a more systematic pattern of urban development, in which land located close to work centers, within sewer districts, and in areas possessing favorable zoning rules, tends to be converted to development before land lacking these characteristics.

In contrast to the support found for the general life-cycle hypothesis, no convincing evidence was found that federal tax laws have figured importantly in the timing of land sales or land conversion. Though rural landowners are generally aware of the tax advantages of realizing capital gains at certain periods in the life cycle, they are of the opinion that tax advantages have not been decisive, or strongly influential, in their timing decisions. Federal estate tax laws did arouse considerable concern among farmers and farm organizations, who believed that they greatly influenced farm land sales. The search for empirical support for this view, however, was unproductive. No doubt some farmers have been forced to sell their lands by estate tax liability. Many more farm families have been inconvenienced by the estate tax obligation. But we must conclude that federal estate tax burdens have been of only marginal significance in shaping the pattern of metropolitan development.

References

Baltimore County, Maryland. 1972. *1980 Guideplan.* Baltimore: The county.
California State Assembly, Select Committee on Open Space Lands. 1973. *Special Hearings on Suggested Remedial Approaches to the California Land Conversion Act of 1965.* Sacramento, Calif.: The assembly.
Church, Albert M., and Barbara A. Sander. 1976. "Using Local Policy Instruments to Adjust Environmental Quality: The Albuquerque Case." Paper presented to the Committee on Urban Economics Conference, Albuquerque, N.M.
Conklin, Howard E., et al. 1972. *Maintaining Viable Agriculture in Areas of Urban Expansion.* Albany, N.Y.: State Office of Planning Services.

Crosswhite, William, and Gerald Vaughn. 1962. *Land Use in the Rural-Urban Fringe: A Case Study of New Castle County, Delaware.* Agricultural Experimental Station, Bulletin no. 340. Newark: University of Delaware.

Downs, Anthony. 1970. "Alternative Forms of Future Urban Growth in the United States." *Journal of the American Institute of Planners* 36: 3-11.

Gaffney, Mason. 1969. "Land Planning and the Property Tax." *Journal of the American Institute of Planners* 35: 178-83.

Gustafson, Gregory C., and L. T. Wallace. 1975. "Differential Assessment as Land Use Policy: The California Case." *Journal of the American Institute of Planners* 41: 379-89.

Hady, Thomas F. 1963. "The Impact of Estate and Inheritance Taxes on Farm Enterprise." *Agricultural Finance Review* 24: 20-23.

Massie, Ronald W. 1968. *Landowner Behavior: Factors Influencing the Propensities to Sell Land on the Urban Fringe.* Chapel Hill: University of North Carolina, Center for Urban and Regional Studies.

Milgram, Grace. 1967. *The City Expands.* Washington, D.C.: Department of Housing and Urban Development.

Peterson, George E. 1974. *Land Values and the Sequence of Land Conversion.* Washington, D.C.: The Urban Institute.

Peterson, George E., and Harvey Yampolsky. 1975. *Urban Development and the Protection of Metropolitan Farmland.* Washington, D.C.: The Urban Institute.

Real Estate Research Corporation. 1974. *The Costs of Sprawl.* Report prepared for the Council on Environmental Quality, Department of Housing and Urban Development, and Environmental Protection Agency. Washington, D.C.: U.S. Government Printing Office.

Regional Science Research Institute. 1976. *Untaxing Open Space.* Washington, D.C.: Council on Environmental Quality.

Smith, James D. 1976. "The Impact of the Estate Tax: Only the Wealthy Feel Its Bite." *Tax Notes,* pp. 18-22.

United States Department of Agriculture. 1976. *Dynamics of Land Use in Fast Growth Areas.* Agricultural Economics Report no. 325. Washington, D.C.: The department.

Vaughn, Gerald, and Edward Moore. 1963. *Idle Land in an Urbanizing Area: The Delaware Experience.* Newark: University of Delaware, Division of Urban Affairs.

Waddell, Thomas E. 1974. *The Economic Damage of Air Pollution.* Washington, D.C.: Environmental Protection Agency.

Wills, George S. 1974. "An Example of How Government Tax Policy Fosters the Destruction of Farmland." Baltimore: Maryland Historical Trust.

II. METROPOLITAN FINANCE

4 *Peter Mieszkowski*

Three Aspects of Urban Land Use Regulation

Externalities and Land Use Regulation

Despite the widespread use of zoning and other forms of development control by city governments, economists have not analyzed land use regulation until relatively recently. Bailey (1959), Crecine, Davis, and Jackson (1967), Davis (1963), and Stull (1974) have made the most notable contributions to such an analysis. The main thrust of their studies has been to emphasize the incompatibility of various activities in urban land markets. Industrial and commercial activity may diminish the value of neighboring residential property, while zoning is used to "protect" residences and to minimize the incompatibility of different activities. As owners of residential property are typically averse to taking risks and do not like the uncertainty associated with undeveloped land in their areas, they use zoning as a form of collective insurance in order to minimize the possibility of any capital losses which might be associated with incompatible development.[1] The existence of possible incompatibilities between different land uses suggests that different sections in urban areas should be zoned for homogeneous, or compatible, uses and also that the standard efficiency rule that the return to a factor of production

1. This view of the social value of zoning has been developed by Breton (1973). My colleague, Richard Bean, tells me that in the unzoned city of Houston his house, which is located next to a large undeveloped tract of land, sells at a discount as a result of the uncertainty regarding the future development of the adjacent area.

(urban land) should be, at the margin, equal in all alternative uses must be qualified. Bailey (1959) was the first to argue that if two zones (activities) co-exist side by side, and one of these, say high density apartments, detracts from the amenity values of the second, say single-family homes, then *decentralized* market decisions will lead to an *over-supply* of high density use. Under decentralized decisions land use conversions will take place so that land values are equalized at the border of the two activities. Since the "shadows" associated with apartments, however, detract from neighboring low density land use, Bailey argued that a coordinated or centralized system of ownership would maximize profits by equating land prices in the interiors of the two zones, where the effects of the shadows are no longer felt. This rule, recently derived more formally by Stull (1974), implies that at the border of the noncompatible properties the value of single-family homes will be worth less than the value of land used (zoned) for apartments.

The example of coordinated land ownership, as a device to internalize an externality in urban land markets, or equivalently to maximize total land values, is an example of the asset-utilization approach first presented by Knight (1922) in his famous two-road example. Knight argued that two roads which are close substitutes for traffic would be optimally utilized under a single or coordinated ownership. As is well known from the literature on the economics of natural resources, for example, fishing effort will be set at the optimal level only if the stock of fish, which is typically a free common property resource, is under the control of a single party. Also, Mohring and Boyd (1971) have recently extended the asset-utilization approach to the utilization of the atmosphere or water resources. Under coordinated ownership the conflict between alternative conflicting uses of an asset will be mediated through appropriate pricing rules designed to maximize the value of the asset.

An alternative to the internalization of externalities is the direct interaction approach Ronald Coase first developed. In a famous essay (1960) Coase argued that when transaction (bargaining) costs are small, incompatibility between different parties can be resolved through bargaining and compensation between individuals. This hypothesis has been supported in the context of land use regulation by Crecine, Davis, and Jackson (1967), who in an empirical study found little if any discount of properties located in heterogeneous neighborhoods and concluded that the effects of nonconforming land uses are probably quite small or are highly localized spatially. The small number of parties involved in a localized interaction would enhance the likely success of bargaining and conflict resolution.

It seems quite clear, however, that conflict in urban land markets will not be solved spontaneously through bargaining without the prior determination of "initial conditions" or property rights. Typically, one of the two conflicting parties will feel wronged by the other and will seek compensation and/or restriction on the activities of the other through the judicial system. One reason why the courts may be asked to intervene is that the assignment of a property right carries with it a distributive or income effect. Being protected from the intrusion of factory activity is clearly worth something to the homeowner. On the other hand, if industrial areas are allowed to expand wherever they wish, the homeowner will be worse off as he runs the risk of suffering a capital loss or incurring expenses through land purchase or compensation designed to stop industrial expansion.

If conflicts are typically resolved through court action, the question naturally arises whether the assignment of property rights is likely to lead to an efficient allocation of land among alternative uses. Coase argued that liability rules or property rights are irrelevant for resource allocation, for regardless of the property right, bargaining among conflicting parties will lead to efficient resource allocation.

Mohring and Boyd (1971), however, have persuasively argued that Coase's proposition is incorrect except in the very special case in which the supply of a particular activity is not responsive to the assignment of the property right. Their basic point is that the assignment of a property right in a particular dispute is likely to act as a precedent in further court decisions. Thus, if homeowners are assigned the right to protection from industrial noise they will treat that protection as a free good and will disregard the possible costs which they impose on the industrial activity. The property right of freedom from industrial encroachment will result in an overexpansion of residential activity or at least will lead to location of residential activity in areas which would not be used in the absence of the property right assigned to them. Mohring and Boyd's important proposition has a number of implications for land use policy. It suggests that a particular activity should not have a prior claim to protection from other activities *in all circumstances and under all conditions.* In other words the principle that there is a "higher" land use which always deserves protection from an incompatible lower use will result in a misallocation of land because the "higher use" will disregard the intrinsic imcompatibility between the two activities.

Since the degree of incompatibility is most frequently a function of location and proximity there is good reason for the setting up of homogeneous zones that will separate urban activities. The separation, however, should not be absolute; there is no reason why residential or commercial activities should not be set up in industrial areas as long as the developers or purchasers of the properties developed there are not entitled to, and do not expect, compensation or protection for disamenities associated with the industrial activity. As long as the prior claim of industry in an industrial zone is established the residential activities set up in industrial zones will be set up at the developer's risk.

The asset-utilization approach to land use allocation also suggests that broad development under a single developer or group of developers should be promoted. A profit-maximizing developer will promote a heterogeneous community if the advantages of mixture outweigh the possible costs of friction or incompatibility between uses. Also the use of restrictive deeds or covenants written by the developer will protect the purchasers of various properties from modification and change.

The most controversial disputes occur when change is proposed or is introduced; when commercial zones are extended, high rise apartments are built in previously low density residential neighborhoods, and so forth. It is quite natural that changes in the urban landscape will occur. The establishment of relative supply of land for different types of land is bound to be imperfect; cities will grow and this growth will necessitate transformation of low density areas into high density uses.

The basic principle which should guide rezoning and conversion decisions is simple and is implicit in what has been said above. Does the conversion increase overall land values or, equivalently, can those who gain from the conversion compensate those who lose? I shall be concerned here with whether it is possible to determine how much compensation should be paid.

The empirical work on urban land values lends itself directly to determining the level of compensation. While it is very difficult to estimate the real income loss associated with uniform air pollution covering an *entire* metropolitan area, in principle it is a relatively straightforward matter to determine what disamenities are associated with high density developments, industrial areas, highways, airports, and so on. All we have to do is to control for housing characteristics and measure house values in relationship to their proximity to the objectionable nonconformities. This experiment requires the existence of heterogeneous development; but if it exists, the results derived from these estimates can be used as compensation for proposed rezoning changes.

It is sometimes argued by its opponents that zoning infringes on property rights since landowners are prevented from using their property freely. But as discussed above there are perfectly valid reasons for imposing land use regulation. In my opinion the main shortcomings of zoning are probably due to regulation officials not allowing market principles to dictate appropriate zoning and rezoning decisions. Protest is cheap and public opinion is easily swayed in favor of homeowners protecting their cul-de-sacs against apartments and shopping centers. Although appropriate compensation for losses would unquestionably moderate protest, it is important to recognize that overall efficiency in land use allocation requires the maximization of land values. Consequently it will often be appropriate to grant homeowners their right to peace and quiet and absence of traffic only if they are willing to "pay" for it. Otherwise the prior claims by some activities will result in serious misallocation of land and will impose losses on those who consume the services of the activities whose levels are constrained and restricted by zoning.

Zoning and "Fiscal" Externalities

In the previous section on nonconformities and land use regulation I suggested only minor qualifications to the conventional proposition that efficiency in urban land markets requires land to be allocated so that its value in alternative uses is equalized. The basic conclusion is that if a rezoning proposal increases *overall* land values, it should be undertaken.

The situation becomes somewhat more complicated when fiscal differences between various activities are introduced. For example, suppose there are three activities, A (high rise apartments), B (industry), and C (single-family homes), and that a partially developed municipality recognizes that at the prevailing tax rate, C will generate sufficient taxes to pay for the additional public expenditures required to service this activity. Activity A will yield, on a per acre basis, taxes less than marginal public expenditure (a fiscal deficit), while activity B will yield a fiscal surplus. Under these circumstances it will clearly be to the self-interest of the existing residents in the community to discriminate between different activities, to favor activities B over C and A, and C over A. If the undeveloped land in the community is publicly owned by the existing residents it can be argued that the public land authority will price discriminate between activities and that in equilibrium land prices "zoned" for the three different activities will perfectly reflect the fiscal externalities associated with each. This argument in favor of public ownership of land, or centralized development (the asset-utilization approach with a different label), also suggests that fiscal advantages will be capitalized in land values in a decentralized market situation.

Our understanding of the effects of zoning and capitalization in fragmentally owned urban land markets has been significantly enhanced by the work of Hamilton (1976).[2] Hamilton put forth a number of provocative propositions. Foremost among them is the hypothesis that under certain conditions the *overall* (total) value of a community will be independent of its composition among different types of activities. In particular, in the special case of two activities, high income housing, *H,* and low income housing, *L,* Hamilton argued that the fiscal *disadvantages* for *H* households of living in heterogeneous communities will be reflected in the lower value of *H* houses in the mixed communities, while the fiscal advantages for *L* households living in mixed income communities will be reflected in the high value of *L*-type homes in high income communities.

To demonstrate the conditions under which this proposition is correct, I shall use a rather contrived example of a steak house where there are only two inputs, the rental cost of chairs, which is fixed, and the cost of the meat. The owner of the steak house is constrained to follow an indirect pricing policy. The patrons are not charged a fixed price for the steak but are charged on the basis of the amount of a property tax. Also, the tax rate must be the same for persons at a given table, and the amount of revenue collected at each table must cover total costs. The owner of the steak house must decide whether he should stratify the tables in his establishment by income class or whether his business will be enhanced by having mixed tables. He chooses each table composition by placing *H* and *L* labels at each table setting. Dinner is served only when every table is fully occupied, and so each customer knows exactly how much he will have to pay for his dinner before he sits down. Finally, it is assumed that each customer who enters the restaurant wishes to purchase the same steak exactly, which costs the owner $5.00.

Assume initially that tables are completely stratified by *H* and *L* groups. Each person at these tables pays a rental fee to cover the cost of providing chairs, tables, and so on of $2.00 and then is assessed a tax to cover the cost of the steak. Members of the high income group, all of whom live in $50,000 houses, each pay a mill rate of 10, while the *L* income group, who live in $25,000 homes, pay a unit rate of 20. Now suppose that some of the tables are "mixed" and are equally divided between *H* and *L* houses. Although the seat rental (entrance) charge remains fixed at $2.00 at stratified (homogeneous) tables, the rental charges for the seats at the heterogeneous tables are determined through competitive bidding.

It follows from the assumptions made above that the rental on the

2. Although Hamilton and I may disagree on detail and emphasis, I would like to acknowledge his work as being fundamental to my understanding of the issues discussed in this section of the chapter.

mixed tables will average out at $2.00 a seat. When there are two seats at a mixed table the H person will pay $6.67 for his steak while the L person will pay $3.33. (The ratio of tax paid, H/L, is by assumption $2:1$.) A tax rate is imposed to finance per capita expenditures of $5.00. Consequently, there is a transfer of $1.67 from the H household to the L household. In order for the rich person to "sit down" at the mixed table, however, he must somehow be compensated for the fiscal disadvantage of eating there. This compensation will take the form of a lower entrance fee which will be $2.00 $-1.67 = $.33. The L income person, however, will pay up to $3.67 for a seat at the mixed table, as his alternative is to sit at a homogeneous L table and pay $5.00 for his steak rather than the $3.33 he pays by sharing a seat at a mixed table. Consequently, the total seat rents which are collected on the mixed table are $3.67 from the L household and $.33 from the H household. This works out to $2.00 a seat, which is the same price which is collected in the perfectly stratified H and L tables. In short (putting this example in terms of housing), as long as both groups have the alternative of residing in perfectly stratified communities, the formation of heterogeneous communities will *not* change total or average land values in the mixed communities. It also appears that both groups pay for what they get. High income groups pay higher taxes in mixed communities, but they recapture these higher taxes by paying lower prices for land. On the other hand low income groups, if they reside in a community in which they pay lower taxes, will be willing to pay higher prices for land for this fiscal advantage, and under the rather strong assumption that they wish to purchase the same amount of the collective good as the H group they will fully pay for the fiscal advantage. It would appear, therefore, that the concern with the distributive aspects of zoning and the formation of stratified communities is inappropriate; for if *some* communities are opened up to low income groups, these groups will have to pay for the fiscal world characterized by the simple steak house example is a characterization of a Tiebout world in which the redistribution of income through the public sector at the local level is kept at a minimum through the capitalization of fiscal advantages and disadvantages.

In examining these propositions it is necessary to examine the key assumptions of the model, in particular the assumption of identical preferences for the "jointly consumed," publicly financed good. As might be expected when one allows for differences in demand for public goods by different groups the strong capitalization results no longer hold. Before turning to this complication, however, I would like to reinterpret the Hamilton propositions in a somewhat broader perspective.

Another key assumption in the derivation of the strong propositions on fiscal capitalization is existence of perfectly stratified H and L communities and the assumption that land prices are equalized at the replacement cost of the housing sites (the opportunity cost of land in agriculture plus locational advantages plus various improvement costs). These assumptions "anchor the model" and allow one to calculate absolute land prices, as well as relative land values. To see that this assumption is the likely outcome of competitive markets, consider two extreme development patterns for a metropolitan area.

The first is a situation wherein there is a single metropolitan government that provides an equal amount of the publicly financed good for each household and finances the cost by means of a property tax. If the ratio of property owned by the two groups is 2 : 1 and there are an *equal* number of H and L households, the H group pays for two-thirds of the total budget.

The second case occurs when urban development takes place through a number of fully stratified H and L communities, which are fiscally independent of each other. For simplicity we assume that the per-household public expenditures are the same in all communities. The relative tax burdens for the two groups will be quite different than in the case of a single metropolitan government since both groups will each pay fully for what they receive. In the stratified situation there is no transfer of tax revenue from the H to the L group.

Although it should be clear that the redistribution of income differs between the single government and the system of individual governments, the *overall* value of land in the metropolitan area and the structure of land prices should be identical in both cases. If it is assumed that the overall population is given, land values and location of individuals in both situations will depend solely on locational considerations. If the H group has a strong preference for land they will live farther out in both situations. In effect, fiscal considerations are irrelevant in the determination of location, for in one case there is only one government and in the second "fiscal externalities" are fully internalized by means of stratification. Exclusionary zoning can have a very significant impact on the distribution of income between different groups if it has a marked effect on the typical pattern of development in a metropolitan area.

To introduce the possibility of mixed patterns of development, consider the situation in which originally there exists a single governmental unit, the central city (*CC*). H housing and L housing are located in different parts of the *CC*, but there is a common tax base and income is redistributed from H households to L households. Such a redistribution would not take place if stratified communities were located in the land area occupied by the *CC*. Next, assume that new *H* households enter the metropolitan area (*MA*) while the population of *L* households remains unchanged. If the new *H* housing units, constructed on the fringes of the *CC*, are annexed by the *CC*, both *L* and *H* households in the older parts of the *CC* will benefit from an increase in the tax base per capita. Land values will not change, however, except for the rent increases associated with the larger population. Now, if the new *H* houses are constructed in an independent fiscal community, the price of *H* houses located in the suburbs must rise relative to the *H* units in the *CC*. When the original development of the stratified *H* communities is partial, the price of the *H* units will rise above their replacement costs. These profits should induce further development of *H* houses in other stratified *H* communities so that in the long run the price of *H* houses in the suburbs will fall toward their replacement costs.

When this competitive price is achieved the value of *H* houses in the central city will fall by the amount of the fiscal disadvantage of residing in the *CC*. From this point on Hamilton's proposition on tax capitalization will apply; "new" *H* households which enter the metropolitan area will have a choice of buying in the *CC* or in the suburbs. Relative land prices should reflect the relative fiscal advantages of the two areas for *H*-type housing. The redistribution of income from *H* to *L* household continues to take place in the central city. But now that *H* households have an alternative residential choice in the suburbs the fiscal redistribution will be reflected in *CC* land values.

It is clear that the *H* newcomers to the metropolitan area, if they settle in the suburbs or if they purchase *H*-type housing in the central city, benefit from the creation of independent, *H*-stratified suburbs. The older residents in the metropolitan areas, however, would clearly gain from an annexation or extension of the fiscal boundaries of the older fiscal jurisdiction. The *H* households located in the *CC* suffer a capital loss as a result of fragmented fiscal development, while the *L* households pay higher taxes as a result of the formation of independent suburbs.

Next, we introduce growth in the number of *L* households, either through natural population growth or through in-migration. This group has a large stake in the extension of the fiscal boundaries of the central city. If the boundaries are extended, the growth in the *H* and *L* populations is such that the ratio of *H/L* remains unchanged; if this is the case, the extended central city will be, *from a fiscal standpoint*, an enlarged version of the original central city. But if new *L* neighborhoods can be constructed only in new homogeneous *L*-type suburbs, fiscal redistribution from *H* to *L* will be less than it would be in an extended

CC. In long-run equilibrium, *L*-type suburbs will be produced at their replacement cost, and the value of *L* houses in the central city will rise. For the same reason, if the price of *H* houses in the *CC* falls relative to *H* houses in the suburbs, the price of *L* houses will rise relative to *L* houses in stratified suburbs.

Although it is quite reasonable to assume that *H* households typically own their homes, a substantial number of *L* households will be renters of small houses or will live in apartments. Consequently the capitalization effects on the welfare of *L* households are ambiguous. The *L* households in the *CC* who own their homes will experience a capital gain. On the other hand the increase in land values on rental housing in the *CC* will accrue to landlords. As we continue to assume that the level of per-household public expenditures are the same in all parts of the *MA*, the rents on *L* rental housing will be the same throughout the *MA*, apart from locational considerations, and the lower taxes on *L* housing the *CC* will result in higher profits on these units.

While most construction of *H* housing occurs in the suburbs there are a number of reasons for believing that *L*-type suburbs will be difficult to form. First, large-lot zoning in the areas surrounding the *CC* will preclude the development of modest single-family homes and higher density development tracts. It will be difficult for developers to finance public improvement, roads, sewers, and so on for *L*-type construction in the suburbs, especially since social overhead capital already exists in the *CC* and the prices of *H*-type developments are depressed in the *CC*. Also, *H*-type housing will be converted to *L*-type housing there, and any undeveloped land in the central city will be developed as *L*-type housing.

The existence of *L*-type housing in the suburbs also has an important bearing on the effects of various policy measures. Consider first the effects of fiscal aid to the central city. Taking the level of public expenditures as predetermined, the fiscal aid provided by state and federal governments will provide tax relief to *H* income groups located in the central city and should promote *H*-type development there. Whether the fiscal relief will be translated into benefits for *L* households will depend on the possibility of further *L*-type developments in the central city and on the existence of *L* housing in the suburbs. On the one extreme we have a situation wherein it is not possible to expand *L*-type housing in the *CC* (the land is completely filled in, and the possibility of conversations is limited) and so all new *L*-type development will take place in the suburbs. Under these conditions the fiscal relief in the *CC* will accrue to the owners of *L*-type housing located in the *CC*, and rents on *L*-type housing will remain unchanged in the *CC* and in the suburbs.

The other extreme possibility is that L-type development is zoned out of the suburbs, L-type development is restricted to the CC, and the quantity and quality of this housing is responsive to the property tax rate. Under these conditions any fiscal aid to the central city will decrease house rents there.

Any policy which opens up the suburbs to L-type development will naturally lower the rent on L housing in the metropolitan area. For example, state or federal assistance for the development of public facilities in L-type suburban communities will lower the cost of L-type housing in the suburbs, and, as the CC and suburban housing are close substitutes, this will lead to a decrease in the rent on L housing in the whole metropolitan area.

A "narrow" reading of Hamilton's capitalization results will suggest that a weakening of various zoning restrictions in the suburbs will not have a significant impact on the rents on L-type housing and that the basic effect of the rezoning restrictions will be to change relative land values in different communities.

Consider the case where stratified H and L communities are being formed in the suburbs and where zoning restrictions in a partially developed H-type community are struck down by the courts. If the removal of the restriction on L-type construction is partial and applies to only one community, the owners of undeveloped land in the H community will receive a capital gains windfall at the expense of owners of H-type housing located in this community because purchasers of L-type housing will pay a premium for land in the rezoned community. Since the rezoning is partial (limited to one community), the construction of other L-type suburban communities will continue, and rents on L-type housing will not fall. But because of the lower taxes paid on L housing in the new heterogeneous suburbs, profits will be larger on L-type housing, and these excess profits can be expected to be capitalized in land values.

On the other hand if the weakening of the zoning restrictions are more general so that a significant number of H communities are opened for L-type housing, the excess profits will be squeezed out by competitive building. Construction of stratified L communities will cease, and the value of the houses in these communities will fall below their cost of reproduction. The L housing constructed in the heterogeneous suburbs will be sold (rented) at competitive prices (their cost of reproduction). Whether H-type housing continues to be constructed in the heterogeneous suburbs depends on whether some H suburbs remain stratified. If such communities continue to be developed it is quite possible that H-type development in the heterogeneous suburbs will cease. After the change in rezoning, relative house prices will change in the manner predicted by Hamilton. The price of H housing will fall in the communities where the rezoning has occurred, and if the increase in the supply of land for L housing in the heterogeneous areas is sufficiently large the price of L houses in perfectly stratified communities will fall below their replacement cost. These revaluations do *not,* however, rule out the possibility of real benefits to low income groups. By being able to move into heterogeneous communities at the same capital cost they would have had to pay in the completely stratified communities, they end up paying a lower overall rent, as taxes are lower in the heterogeneous communities. *In short, real changes in rental rates over broad segments of the* L-*type housing stock are perfectly consistent with changes in relative values of housing capital resulting from changes in the relative fiscal advantage of different communities.*

One of the main contributions of Hamilton's analysis of capitalization of fiscal differences between communities is that it brings out the complexity of making decisions on land use allocation on the basis of land price differentials. It is quite likely that the combination of zoning restrictions and fragmented land markets will lead to the misallocation of land within metropolitan areas. Consider a situation in which an industry has to make a locational decision between the central city and a low-tax industrial enclave in the suburbs. As the result of higher taxes on industrial capital in the central city, the price of industrial land in this location will be depressed relative to its value as L-type housing.

The price of L-type housing will be higher than its value in the stratified suburbs because of the fiscal advantages of being located in a fiscal jurisdiction with industry and H-type housing. As the price of the undeveloped land is higher as L-type housing it will be developed as housing instead of as industry. Yet its social value may be considerably higher as industrial land, and this difference may be considerably larger than the price differential between industrial land and housing land in the central city.

The maximum price industry will be willing to pay for land in the central city is the price of land in the industrial enclave in the suburbs plus any natural advantages of locating in the central city such as savings in transportation costs of product delivery, proximity to labor, and related economies of scale of locating in the central city *minus* the difference in the taxes between the central city and the suburbs. If the tax difference is large enough it will wipe out the natural advantages of locating in the central city, and industry will not be able to compete for land in the central location. The loss of this natural advantage will represent a real loss of output, and so there is an efficiency basis for not paying heed to the "dictates of the market" and for restricting the use of an undeveloped plot of land in the central city for industrial use.

In taking account of "fiscal externalities" a land use planner who considers the welfare of the metropolitan area *as a whole* would compare the land price differential with the *net* fiscal dividend associated with the central city location. This net fiscal dividend would be equal to the difference between the taxes paid by industry in the central city and the suburbs *minus* the higher taxes the residents of L-type housing would have to pay if they were forced to locate in stratified L-type suburbs. On the other hand the fiscal authority of the central city would not account for the higher taxes paid by the persons excluded from the central city and would compare land price differences with fiscal differences that would be generated on the land in an alternative use in the central city.

The fact that alternative developments have very different fiscal implications for individual jurisdictions coupled with the fact that land is privately owned by very large numbers of uncoordinated individuals implies that it is highly likely that land will be misallocated between different activities. It is only when undeveloped land is jointly owned by the existing residents of a community, who will control the zoning authority, that the loss of land value will be equally weighed with fiscal considerations. Thus, even if the present value of the fiscal differential between industrial use and residential use is $100,000, while residential land is selling for $200,000 an acre more, the zoning authority may ignore the high value of land in residential use, since in the absence of side payments the profits resulting from an industrial to a residential conversion will accrue to the owner of the specific piece of land. On the other hand, the fiscal advantages accrue to the public in general, in proportion to their tax liabilities.

Again a coordinated policy implied by the asset-utilization approach to externalities is called for. There are a number of ways in which this approach might be approximated. One would be to encourage public ownership of undeveloped land. Alternatively, developers of residential land might be allowed to pay development taxes that would offset the fiscal disadvantages of residential development. Finally, a land value tax or a special tax on capital gains earned through zoning changes might be used indirectly to increase the degree of public ownership of undeveloped land in a community.

It should be noted, however, that all these proposals tend to violate the principle of equal treatment of equals (horizontal equity). Under the development grant proposal the "new residents" will be admitted into the community at a price approximating marginal cost. Any advantages of fiscal redistribution in the community will under these arrangements accrue to the owners of the existing house stock.

Nevertheless, whatever the inequities, these arrangements should be an improvement on the existing situation wherein zoning promotes further redistribution toward the existing residents at the expense of industrial land users and the owners of land zoned for industrial use. In effect the use of zoning to encourage industrial development in a community means that the owners of specific pieces of land will be providing subsidies for the benefit of the rest of the community. Certainly on considerations of equity industrial subsidies should be paid out of

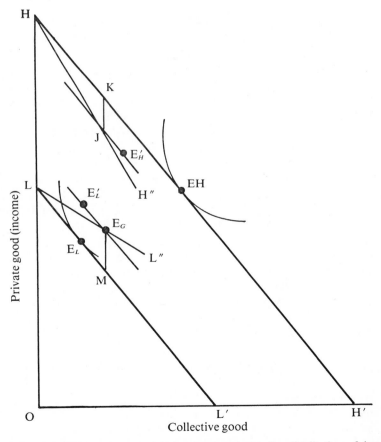

Figure 4.1. The effects of various fiscal arrangements on the distribution of income between low and high income groups

general tax revenues rather than by means of lower land prices achieved through zoning.

One possible compromise that would strike a balance between consideration of equity and efficiency would be to require that a residential development could not be blocked if the taxes levied on it would pay for the cost of providing the required public services for the development. If the taxes are not made lump sum and if the existing residents living in comparable housing have to pay an equivalent tax, the fiscal system would move closer to a system of benefit taxation in which the amount of fiscal redistribution would be minimized.

The dilemma posed by such a move is that efficiency in intrametropolitan development and location would be promoted at the expense of redistribution for some members of the low income population of metropolitan areas. It is worth developing this point further, especially since the above analysis has been based on the highly unrealistic assumption that H- and L-type households have the same taste (demand) for the collective good. This is equivalent to assuming that the income elasticity of demand for the public good is equal to zero.

More realistically, assume that the H group will wish to spend more on the collective good than the L group. Figure 4.1 shows the isolated equilibrium for the two households, H and L, that would exist if the two groups resided in perfectly stratified communities. OH and OL measure the incomes of groups H and L, respectively, and HH' and LL' depict the transformation schedule between private goods for the two groups. In an isolated (perfectly stratified) situation the equilibrium for H and L would be E_H and E_L, respectively.

Consider next the situation wherein the H and L households live in a mixed community and have to decide on a common expenditure level for each and on a common property tax rate. Assume that the collective equilibrium has to be agreed upon unanimously by both parties. Due to their differences in income levels the two individuals will originally be far apart on their choice of a common expenditure level. To increase their expenditures on the collectively provided good, group L has to be subsidized by H. The price line for the public good for L is tilted up from LL' to LL'', while for H, because of the subsidy paid to L, the price line shrinks inwards to HH''.

One of the characteristics of the agreed-upon collective equilibrium, E_G, is that the subsidy paid by H, KJ, is exactly equal to the subsidy received by L, E_GM. For this equilibrium, wherein each household consumes (receives) the same amount of the collectively provided good, the marginal rate of substitution between private and public goods is not the same for the two individuals (groups) and the equilibrium E_G is inefficient. It would be possible for group H to transfer an amount, KJ, in exchange for the possibility of independently increasing its consumption of the collective good. Freed of the constraint of having to consume the same amount of the collectively provided good, H would move to a new equilibrium E'_H while group L would decrease their consumption of the collective good to E'_L. By assumption, the collective good is divisible, so the difference in consumption levels could be effected by permitting a varying amount of education in the same school district and varying the quality of police and fire protection in different neighborhoods and so forth.

The above analysis repeats one of the propositions recently put forth by McGuire (1974)—namely, that stratification is efficient and that income redistribution should be implemented by income transfers rather than by mixing various income groups together and choosing a common level of the collectively provided good. The intuitive explanation of the excess burden is that low income households receive the income transfer in the form of subsidized public services rather than in the form of an income transfer that they are free to spend as they wish. On the other hand, higher income groups not only have to provide tax subsidies to lower income groups but are also constrained to consume a suboptimal level of the collectively provided good.

The differences in the demand for public goods by different income groups destroys the exact relationships between land values for H-and-L-lot mixed communities, and the total value of each community is *not* independent of its composition between H and L houses. But the general conclusion of previous models, that what households receive in the way of public services is what they pay for in the way of property taxes, remains approximately correct. The principal qualification to this conclusion is that capitalization in mixed communities is incomplete and that low income groups do not pay fully for (in the form of taxes and higher land values) the higher level of public services they receive in mixed communities. On the other hand the lower value of H houses in mixed communities will reflect the higher taxes they pay there, relative to taxes in perfectly stratified high income communities, and will also reflect the unsatisfactory level of public services they are "forced" to consume there. All this is roughly in accord with the empirical work of Oates (1969) and others in which property values are postulated to be a function of taxes and benefits levels. Note, however, that the above analysis implies that the absolute effect of benefit levels will vary across house types and that the capitalization effects are likely to be highly nonlinear.

The "excess burden" reflected in the lower, overall value of land resulting from the formation of heterogeneous communities will fall on the owners of land in these communities. As most communities are developed over a long period these landowners will be difficult to identify in any precise way.

In large measure the equilibrium results Hamilton put forth are correct. I believe, however, that unless the analysis is put into a somewhat broader framework, one which would also take into consideration the overall development of a metropolitan area, the capitalization results, which are essentially equilibrium conditions, may be misleading on the redistributive aspects of alternative forms of fiscal development. In particular one has to distinguish between the rezoning of a single piece of land, or even one small community, and a more dramatic change (a break in structure) wherein the supply of L-type land in previously stratified suburbs is substantially increased.

Other implications of the capitalization analysis are that fiscal capitalization effects will distort the patterns of development within metropolitan areas. The simple decision rule that land should be allocated to the highest bidder has to be modified to account for fiscal distortions and capitalization. Relative land prices may be an incorrect guide to land use planning both at the local (municipal) level and at the metropolitan level. In a sense the false signals provided by fiscally distorted land prices are a reflection of the excess burden associated with tax rate differentials that exist in fiscally fragmented metropolitan areas.

Optimum City Size and the Allocation of Population among Cities

In the first two sections of this essay we discussed the externalities associated with nonconformities between alternative land uses and discussed some aspects of fiscal externalities. This section deals with another basis for land use regulation and city planning, namely, the possible inefficiencies associated with decentralized investment and locational cities *across* different metropolitan areas in the nation. If intervention on this level is called for it would have to be carried out by the federal government or by a regional authority.

As the issues discussed here are closely related to earlier discussions of regional subsidies it is useful to briefly review this literature. Buchanan (1952a, 1952b) argued, in the context of the relative underdevelopment of the American South, that federal subsidies should be provided to this region to overcome some of the disadvantages that it was experiencing vis-à-vis the North and West. Buchanan was concerned with the effects of the quality of public services on the locational decisions of managers and professionals and of capital. If the North was better endowed with natural resources and "environment," the population it could support would be larger and the economies of scale in the provision of public services and other collectively consumed goods would distort the locational decisions of managers between the North and the South. Consequently, as a result of fiscal distortion, the population of the nation would be misallocated in the absence of federal intervention.

This point of view was challenged by Scott (1950, 1952a, 1952b) on the grounds that these subsidies would artificially bolster unproductive regions and would inhibit the migration of resources (primarily unskilled labor) to the regions better endowed with resources and with a more productive environment. In retrospect it seems that the impasse of this earlier discussion was over the definition of environment—and which aspects of environment were natural and should be respected and which aspects merited modification through taxes and subsidies.

More recently Buchanan and Wagner (1970), Buchanan and Goetz (1972), and Flatters, Henderson, and Mieszkowski (1974) analyzed more formally the effects of public goods on location choice and the resulting implications for an efficient distribution of the nation's population between regions. This work is based on a Ricardian model in which two regions have different resource endowments and each produces a pure, Samuelson-type public good as well as private goods. The varying resource endowments result in different population levels between regions, and the heavily populated region will have a comparative advantage in the production of the public good as there are more people to pay for each unit of the public good. The existence of the pure public good represents an economy of scale in consumption. On the other hand, diminishing returns set in as the population grows because of the fixed amount of land (natural resources) in each region. The general conclusion which emerges from this model is that it will be in only very special circumstances that the free migration of labor results in an efficient (Pareto-optimal) allocation of population between regions. So in general there exists an efficiency basis for federalism. A higher level of government, or coordination between governments, should redirect population through appropriate taxes and subsidies in order to increase the welfare of all members of the federation (nation).

More recently Henderson (1974) published a paper on the determinants of city size. I shall use his model as the basis of the optimal allocation of population between cities. In Henderson's formulation each city produces an export good χ_1, and there exist economies of agglomeration in the production of this export good.

For simplicity the industry production function is written

$$(1) \qquad\qquad \chi_1^{1-S} = L_1^{a_1} K_1^{b_1} N_1^{c_1},$$

where $a_1 + b_1 + c_1 = 1$ and $OL < SL < 1$. The variable, S, represents the increasing returns to scale, and L_1, N_1, and K_1 are inputs of land sites, labor, and capital, respectively.

The economy of scale is external to each firm, though internal to the industry (city). So each firm pays labor the value of its private marginal product, $c_1 \dfrac{\chi_1}{N_1}$, rather than the social marginal product, $\dfrac{c_1}{(1-S)} \dfrac{\chi_1}{N_1}$. This preserves exhaustion of firm revenue by factor payments.

The second good produced, Z, in the city is housing (home goods), χ_2, with a production function

$$(2) \qquad \chi_2 = L_2^{a_2} K_2^{b_2} N_2^{c_2},$$

where $a_2 + b_2 + c_2 \leqq 1$. One can assume decreasing returns to scale in the production of housing or follow Henderson by assuming constant returns to scale and introducing a third activity, the production of land sites, which are "produced" through travel, under conditions of decreasing returns to scale.

$$(3) \qquad (L_1 + L_2)^{1-Z} = L^{1-Z} = N_0,$$

where L and N_0 are sites and labor inputs in the production of sites. Whatever the form of the specification, the important assumption is that one of the activities is produced under conditions of decreasing returns to scale.

There are two essential production activities: one is characterized by increasing returns to scale, the other by decreasing returns to scale. For small values of populations an increase in the population will increase utility (real income), while beyond a certain level of population the diseconomies of commuting, congestion, pollution, and so on will dominate the increasing return in the production of the manufactured good.

A hypothetical path of per capita utility is given in figure 4.2. P_0 is the population level at which per capita utility is maximized.

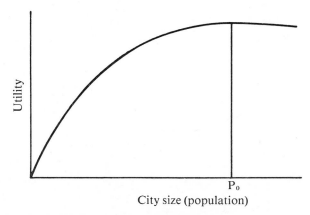

City size (population)

Figure 4.2. Relationship between utility and population size

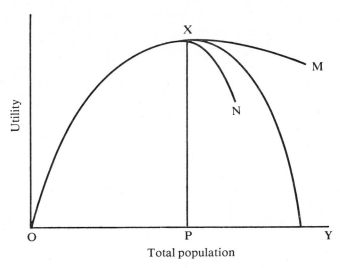

Figure 4.3. A system of two optimally sized cities

It will be a rare occurrence when the population level for the nation will permit the formation of a number of optimally sized cities; also there is no guarantee that with even a total population of ideal size that an optimal system of cities will be stable under decentralized market decisions.

The possibility of instability and inefficient city size is illustrated in figure 4.3. This figure is drawn on the assumption that the nation's population is equal to twice the population of an optimally sized city OY = $2OP$. Ideally two optimally sized cities would form. Whether decentralized population movement will produce such a system seems to depend on the shape of the utility path in the neighborhood of the optimum. The segment XY is systematic with OX. If XM, the downward portion of the utility path for a hypothetical very large city lies above XY, however, a tendency toward instability will exist. Assume that the optimal population for a city is 3,000,000 and the total population is 6,000,000. Then if per capita utility is larger for a 3.5 million population than for a 2.5 million city, the larger city will tend to grow and the smaller city will decline. On the other hand if the utility path is OXN the system will tend to converge toward a system of two cities consisting of two populations of three million each.

Even if a system of two or more cities is stable, there remains the question of whether a decentralized equilibrium, where per capita utilities are equalized, is efficient. For the special case in which the total population permits the formation of optimally sized cities and the cities are exact replicas of each other, a stable equilibrium will be efficient.

Once these assumptions are dropped, however, there is no guarantee that decentralized locational and investment decisions will result in an efficient equilibrium. Although it is a rather straightforward matter to derive the necessary conditions for a social optimum, these conditions are not very helpful beyond raising the strong possibility that some sort of intervention will typically be required. On the other hand, I do not have, at present, the specific results that would come out of a more specialized, explicit solution. So while the formal analysis remains quite sketchy, the analysis is suggestive in a number of respects.

First, it provides a rationale for the restriction of population growth in some cities and subsidies to others. In a general way, the analysis is very similar to the growth pole theories put forth by various European writers. The above analysis also serves to explain the antigrowth or antidevelopment views of some city and state (provincial) governments. Although in the United States outright restrictions seem to be limited to selected suburbs and some smaller cities in resort states, in Canada three major cities, Toronto, Vancouver, and Ottawa, appear to be adopting a policy of restriction and strict population planning.

The analysis presented here can be used as a justification of these restrictions. At the same time the rather significant distributive implications of such a restrictive policy should be apparent. For my taste, population restrictions in the highest income urban areas in a nation are justifiable only when the restrictions are made in a comprehensive urban and regional plan, so that the benefits of the restrictions can accrue to all citizens rather than just to the existing residents of a city. Otherwise, not only may overall output be decreased as a result of the restrictions but some groups will gain large windfalls at the expense of the persons who are excluded.

Suppose the population of Toronto or San Francisco is stabilized at some level. If per capita utility and wages are higher in these highly productive urban areas than in alternative areas (smaller cities and rural areas), large rents will accrue to the existing owners of property. Homeowners and owners of rental property will be able to extract the difference in real income that may arise between the areas which restrict development and the rest of the nation. The cost of the restrictions to those who are excluded depends on their alternatives and on whether the restrictions in some areas stimulate development of other urban areas. Restrictions in New York, Chicago, Los Angeles, and San Francisco may stimulate growth of metropolitan areas in the South and Southwest and in satellite cities such as San José. But another possible implication of the restrictions is that the opportunities of persons will be highly limited and they will be forced to remain in unproductive small towns and cities and in the rural sector.

As in all "externality problems" a policy of restriction must face up to the question of property rights and entitlements. Do the existing residents have the right to protect themselves from a deterioration in their real incomes at the expense of excluded groups and individuals?

One can conjecture that a more systematic analysis of the optimal structure of cities will yield solutions in which the optimal policy will be to restrict growth (output) of certain areas so that in absence of transfer payments the level of real incomes will vary between cities. An egalitarian ethic implies that subsidies and income transfers be made to the lower income areas. A part of the subsidy funds will be used as a device to stimulate development of the smaller urban cities, the other part to redistribute the benefits of a coordinated national urban policy.

The types of policies sketched above present a number of practical difficulties. Information will have to be obtained on economies of scale for various types of activities. Certain industries should be concentrated in a few large urban areas. Others might be decentralized without significant loss of output. The effects of "scale" may be nonlinear in that they may be unimportant over low population levels, say up to 500,000 persons, then become important over a range of two or three million, and then drop off.

A coordinated policy which determines national urban policy implies a centralized form of government and may be unrealistic in a highly fragmented federal state such as the United States, with its varied sectional interests, or in an even looser federation such as Canada. It seems that coordination will also greatly increase the involvement of the public authority in influencing intercity distributions of income. The inefficiencies connected with economies and diseconomies of scale relate to intercity migration. The promotion of urban growth necessitates the choice of specific cities as growth poles and these decisions carry with them significant effects on the level of land rents in various urban areas. A system of coordinated urban development is more likely to have broadly based support in a situation in which capital gains and losses, arising from public action, are spread across the public as a whole. This implies public interest or even ownership in (of) urban land.

Although national coordination of urban development is unlikely to occur in North American countries, state and provincial involvement in planning urban growth over a smaller region will be necessary. In a smaller area there is the difficulty of establishing the rights of state citizens vis-à-vis out-of-state residents who may seek entry to the state. But in general the rationale for restricting the growth of some cities and restricting development elsewhere applies at the state as well as the national level.

Conclusion

In this essay I have tried to distinguish between three different rationales for public intervention in urban land markets. Special emphasis has been placed on the fiscal aspects of zoning in the context of a single metropolitan area and on the restriction of the development of certain cities and the promotion of the development of others. These two aspects of land use and city planning have not received much attention in the economics literature in the United States.

The general thrust of my argument is favorable to greater coordination of regulation at the metropolitan and the national (state) level. But I am fully aware of the pitfalls of increased public intervention and regulation. The inefficiencies arising out of governmental intervention in transportation, communication, and agriculture do not bode well for strict public controls that will be frequently dictated by political rather than economic considerations. Nevertheless, what concerns me most are the implications of a fragmented regulation by local governments, which by following self-interests narrowly defined over fiscal considerations, may misallocate land within metropolitan areas. And for distributive and allocative reasons, the restriction of entry into specific cities or regions without national coordination and compensating subsidies and the taxation of capital gains on land goes against the logic of basic considerations of equal protection (opportunity) and may greatly restrict the opportunity of many low and moderate income groups to improve their material status by entering the most productive cities and regions of our country.

References

Bailey, M. J. 1959. "Note on the Economics of Residential Zoning and Urban Renewal." *Land Economics* 35: 288-90.

Breton, Albert. 1973. "Towards a Theory of Land-Use Regulation." In *Issues in Urban Public Finance,* pp. 241-51. Saarbrücken: International Institute of Public Finance.

Buchanan, James M. 1952a. "Federal Grants and Resource Allocation." *Journal of Political Economy* 60: 201-17.

Buchanan, James M. 1952b. "Reply." *Journal of Political Economy* 60: 536-38.

Buchanan, James M., and Charles J. Goetz. 1972. "Efficiency Limits of Fiscal Mobility: An Assessment of the Tiebout Model." *Journal of Public Economics* 1: 25-44.

Buchanan, James M., and Richard E. Wagner. 1970. "An Efficiency Basis for Federal Fiscal Equalization." In *The Analysis of Public Output,* ed. Julius Margolis, pp. 139-58. New York: National Bureau of Economic Research.

Coase, Ronald H. 1960. "The Problem of Social Costs." *Journal of Law and Economics* 3: 1-44.

Crecine, J., O. Davis, and R. Jackson. 1967. "Urban Property Markets: Some Empirical Results and Their Implications for Municipal Zoning." *Journal of Law and Economics* 10: 79-99.

Davis, O. 1963. "Economic Elements in Municipal Zoning Decision." *Land Economics* 39: 375-86.

Davis, O., and A. Whinston. 1961. "The Economics of Urban Renewal." *Law and Contemporary Problems* 26: 105-17.

Davis, O., and A. Whinston. 1964. "The Economics of Complex Systems: The Case of Municipal Zoning." *Kyklos* 17: 419-46.

Flatters, F., V. Henderson, and P. Mieszkowski. 1974. "Public Goods, Efficiency and Regional Fiscal Equalization." *Journal of Public Economics* 3: 99-112.

Hamilton, Bruce. 1976. "Capitalization of Intra-Jurisdictional Difference in Local Tax Prices." *American Economic Review* 66: 743-54.

Henderson, J. V. 1974. "The Sizes and Types of Cities." *American Economic Review* 64: 640-56.

Knight, Frank H. 1922. "Some Fallacies in the Interpretation of Social Cost." *Quarterly Journal of Economics* 38: 582-606.

McGuire, Martin. 1974. "Group Segregation and Optimal Jurisdiction." *Journal of Political Economy* 82: 112-32.

Mohring, Herb, and J. H. Boyd. 1971. "Analysing Externalities: Direct Interaction vs. Asset Utilization Framework," *Economica,* n.s., 38: 347-61.

Oates, W. E. 1969. "The Effects of Property Taxes and Local Public Spending on Property Taxes: An Empirical Study of Tax Capitalization and the Tiebout Hypothesis." *Journal of Political Economy* 72: 957-71.

Scott, Anthony D. 1950. "A Note on Grants in Federal Countries." *Economica,* n.s., 17: 416-22.

Scott, Anthony D. 1952a. "Evaluation of Federal Grants." *Economica,* n.s. 19: 377-94.

Scott, Anthony D. 1952b. "Federal Grants and Resource Allocation." *Journal of Political Economy* 60: 534-36.

Stull, W. J. 1974. "Land Use and Zoning in an Urban Economy." *American Economic Review* 64: 337-47.

5 *Donald C. Shoup*

The Effect of Property Taxes
on the Capital Intensity
of Urban Land Development

Introduction

From many sources there is increasing interest in finding substitutes for the local property tax. A major objection to the existing general property tax is that it is a disincentive to both the quantity and quality of new construction and to maintenance of existing structures. By decreasing the supply of improvements to land, property taxes raise the price of real estate services. Since the property tax rate is relatively high in many areas, the effect of the tax in reducing the supply of improvements and thus raising the price of real estate services may be significant. Netzer (1968, p. 13) estimated that property taxes accounted for 19 percent of total annual housing costs in the United States in 1962 and that, if it can be considered as an excise tax, the tax on real property is higher than any other excise tax except those on liquor, tobacco, and gasoline. In some particularly hard-pressed cities this "excise" tax rate on housing is much higher than the national average. In remarkable contrast to, and perhaps partly necessitated by, this heavy tax on the

I would like to thank Harvey Brazer, David Kiefer, William Neenan, Richard Pollock, Louis Rose, Daniel Rubinfeld, Jay Stein, Phillip Vincent, and Gary Williams for their very generous advice and assistance during the long gestation of this essay. Research support was provided by the Pacific Urban Studies and Planning Program at the University of Hawaii and the Institute of Public Policy Studies at the University of Michigan.

105

services of housing are numerous federal and local aid programs in-tended to increase the supply of housing.[1]

The property tax is also the most important source of local government revenue, providing $40,876,000,000 or 84 percent of local tax revenue in 1971-72 (U.S. Bureau of the Census, 1973, p. 20). Thus, any proposal to reduce property taxes implies that there is an alternative tax which is preferred—one that produces comparable revenues. An alternative form of local property tax, often recommended on theoretical grounds, is a tax on unimproved land value, or "site value." The major theoretical advantage of the land value tax is that, as a tax on pure economic rent of land, it should be neutral in its effect on incentives to supply improve-ments to land. To the investor the land tax is a lump-sum tax that does not affect his decisions at the margin. Another theoretical advantage of the land tax is that if the benefits of some public services are capitalized in higher land values the land tax closely resembles a benefit tax for those services.

The theoretical advantages of the neutrality of the land value tax are generally conceded, but to many observers it is not clear that the advantages associated with a full or even partial shift of property taxation from improvement values to land values are sufficient to out-weigh the disadvantages, which include the inevitable distribution of windfall gains and losses associated with the shift of the tax base. It seems clear that a shift of taxation from building to land value would increase the incentive to invest in greater quality, durability, and height of all improvements to land and would decrease the incentives for urban sprawl. The *direction* of the change in incentives is clear, but the *mag-nitude* of resulting changes in urban form is unknown. For instance, just how much more new housing would be built in response to a shift of taxation from building to land value? How much change in urban density gradients would result? Would the impact be small or large? Unfortunately, few empirical studies have measured these effects of land value taxation in jurisdictions that now practice it, nor has it been

---

1. When the impact of the entire national, state, and local tax system is considered, it is possible to demonstrate that owner-occupied housing is taxed at a lower average rate than is nonhousing capital because the corporate income tax and sales tax exclude the housing sector, and because owner-occupiers are granted favorable income tax provisions (Ladd, 1973, p. 40). But, rental housing and nonresidential real property are subject to a higher tax rate than is owner-occupied housing, especially if they are included in the corporate sector. In any case, the property tax does operate at cross-purposes with many housing programs, especially in areas where property tax rates are high relative to the national average.

possible to predict quantitative effects for jurisdictions that might introduce it.

Netzer believes that "the case for site value taxation is a good one," and that "in theory, there are few if any legitimate economic arguments against site value taxation," but he also says that "one may doubt the actual strength of the positive tendencies associated with a switch to site value taxation. It is, after all, a major institutional change, and major institutional changes should not be pressed unless their positive effects are also expected to be major in extent. But it should be noted that effective property tax rates in most American metropolitan areas are high and rising. The negative land use effects of the present tax are likely to become increasingly apparent in time, and the likely benefits from a change in the basis of taxation will correspondingly increase" (1968, pp. 41-42). In a study of Pittsburgh's graded property tax, which has a higher tax rate on land than on buildings, Richman concluded that "there is little evidence that the graded tax has been a significant stimulus to property improvement in Pittsburgh, or to urban renewal and re-development in particular," but noted that one of the reasons for this is that the tax rate on buildings was only about 30 percent less than that on land (1965, p. 270). In a study of the effect of property taxes on land use patterns in Australia and New Zealand, Woodruff and Ecker-Racz concluded that "at tax rate levels now prevailing in Australia and New Zealand, the economic and social impact of property taxation based on unimproved capital value is minor. No differences are perceptible between communities that use unimproved capital value rating and those with other taxation systems" (1969, p. 184). In a study of Auckland, New Zealand, where three different property taxation systems (taxation based on unimproved land value, on capital value of the improved property, and on annual rental value) exist side by side within separate parts of the same city, Clark concluded that "the taxing system has no identifiable impact on urban development" (1974, p. 110). Thus, although the theoretical advantages of site value taxation have been persuasively demonstrated by many authors, there is apparently a place for further empirical study of the probable size of the effects of a change from general property taxation to site value taxation.

The purpose of this essay is to estimate empirically the effect of property taxes on the capital intensity of land use in an urban area. First, a theoretical model for determining the profit-maximizing investment in improvements to an urban site is presented. Then the effects of land and improvement taxes on investment in construction are examined in a comparative static analysis. The parameters of the model are estimated in two ways: from hypothetical data on a planned building and from actual data on a sample of newly constructed buildings. Finally, two partial-equilibrium case studies are used to estimate the increase in investment in improvements which would follow from eliminating the property tax rate on improvements, with property tax revenue maintained by an increase in the tax rate on land value. The focus is not on the incidence or the progressivity of the property tax, but rather on its effect on the supply of improvements. Obviously, however, the effect of the tax on the supply of improvements has implications for each of these other issues.

The Optimal Capital Intensity of Urban Land Development

When considering land as a factor of production in an urban area, it is important to note that, unlike other factors of production, entrepreneurs usually cannot obtain as much land as they would like at a constant marginal cost. In urban areas land ownership is divided among a large number of separate owners, and many or all sites are already developed. The typical development decision concerns a specific site that the developer already owns or can buy, but the developer cannot increase the size of his site at a constant marginal cost per square foot; rather he must usually pay successively higher prices for discontinuous additions to the site. The discrete nature of the supply curve of urban land to a developer is caused by the need to demolish existing structures on adjacent land and to bargain with its owners and/or leaseholders. Because of the "holdout" problem, the price of contiguous land for expansion of a site can rise very sharply. Therefore, the development decision often involves determining the profit-maximizing capital input in improvements to a constrained amount of land.

On the constrained site the developer can, in his initial development decision, continuously vary the amount of capital applied in the form of improvements to land. In the planning stage both the type of use (residential, commercial, and so on) and the capital intensity of use (low-rise, high-rise) are variable within bounds legally permitted by zoning regulations and building codes. But once the building is constructed, it is relatively costly to change the type or intensity of land use because of the extreme durability of most improvements. If land and capital are the only two factors of production, diminishing returns will be associated with adding capital to a given amount of land, and the profit-maximizing outlay on improvements to the site will occur where the discounted marginal revenue product of an increment in building size equals the marginal cost of the increment in size. The classic example of calculating the marginal revenue product of improvements to land is the determination of the optimal economic height of a skyscraper. As building height increases, nonrentable space devoted to structural elements, mechanical equipment, and elevators increases as a proportion of total floor space, and this causes the construction cost per square foot of net rentable space to increase.[2] As the cost per square foot increases with height, there comes a point where the cost of additional space is just equal to the discounted value of its future rental returns. Alternatively stated, the profit-maximizing outlay on improvements occurs where the marginal rate of return on capital investment in construction equals the interest rate. Though the example is most obvious in relation to building height, the method also applies to any sort of capital expenditure for quantity or quality of improvements to land.

In addition to capital improvements and land, the third major factor in the production of real estate services is operating and maintenance inputs. Unlike land and capital, operating and maintenance inputs are easily varied after the planning stage, but the initial construction decision has obvious implications for subsequent operating and maintenance expenditures. For instance, in the planning stage, there is a trade-off between capital expenditures on durable construction materials versus subsequent expenditures on building maintenance inputs. In the planning stage, for every level of capital investment, there is an associated profit-maximizing level of operating and maintenance expenditures. In terms of annual revenues and cost, this occurs at the point where the marginal revenue product of operating and maintenance inputs equals their marginal cost. Since our emphasis here is on ascertaining the optimal capital intensity of development, it is convenient to assume that, for each amount of capital applied to a given site, the entrepreneur adjusts the level of subsequent operating and maintenance inputs to the point where their marginal revenue product equals marginal cost. Then, by deducting the annual cost of operating and maintenance inputs from annual total revenues of the developed property, we find the annual net revenue after operating and maintenance expenses. The annual net revenue is a quasi-rent for the life of the building, and includes all factor payments to capital and land.

With the above definition of annual net revenue and given both the

---

2. In a study of thirty-six post-World War II high-rise office buildings in Los Angeles County, Berger (1968, pp. 11-14) found that building efficiency (the ratio of net rentable area to gross building area) declines by approximately 0.5 percent for each additional story when average floor area is held constant.

demand and production functions for real estate services, it is possible to derive the optimal capital intensity of development for a specific site. Let:

K = capital (in dollars) invested in improvements to a site;
L = land area (in square feet) of the site;
M = annual operating and maintenance inputs;
w = price of operating and maintenance inputs;
q = total annual output of real estate services;
$p = p(q)$ = price per unit of output of real estate services, which is a function of q;
$A = q[p(q)] = A(q)$ = total annual revenue, which is a function of q;
$q = q(K,L,M)$, the production function for real estate services;
$R = A - wM^*$ = annual net revenue after operating and maintenance expenditures;
M^* = level of M for which the marginal revenue product of M = the marginal cost of M, for each pair of K and L;
T_k = annual tax on improvement value;
T_l = annual tax on land value;
t_k = tax rate on improvement value; and
t_l = tax rate on land value.

In the planning stage for a new building, the annual net revenue can be expressed as $R = A[q(K,L,M^*)] - wM^*(K,L) = R(K,L)$. On a given site, $\bar{L}$, annual net revenue can then be expressed as a function of the capital investment in improvements to the site, $R = R(K,\bar{L})$, as illustrated in the top panel of figure 5.1. The $R(K,\bar{L})$ curve is the envelope of a series of separate $R(K,\bar{L},M)$ curves for all separate possible fixed levels of M. The shape of the $R(K,\bar{L})$ curve depends on (1) the physical production functon, $q = a(K,L,M)$; (2) the revenue function, $A = A(q)$; and (3) the price of operating and maintenance inputs, w, assumed to be fixed. If both the production and revenue functions are continuous, the revenue production function, $R(K,\bar{L})$, is also continuous. Annual net revenue is assumed here to be constant stream of payments for the life of the improvement. From this $R(K,\bar{L})$ function can be derived two related functions, the marginal net revenue product of capital $(\partial R/\partial K)$ and the average net revenue product of capital (R/K).[3] The marginal net revenue product of capital $(MNRPK)$ and average net revenue product of

---

3. These definitions were first proposed by Robinson (1933, pp. 235-412) and were further developed by Bishop (1967). The concept used here corresponds to Bishop's long-run $MNRP$ and $ANRP$.

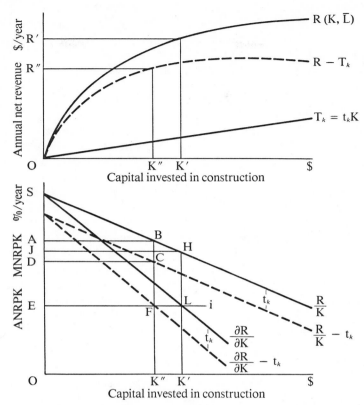

Figure 5.1. Total, average, and marginal net revenue with a tax on improvements

capital (*ANRPK*) are shown as solid lines in the bottom panel of figure 5.1.[4]

The construction of any improvement is in theory part of a dynamic choice of a sequence of successive improvements on the same site. But the development process usually involves commitment of both land and capital to a very long-lived combination, especially when high-rise con-

4. The negative slope of the *MNRPK* curve may be caused by any or all of three separate phenomena: (1) diminishing marginal returns associated with combining two variable factors (*K* and *M*) with a fixed factor (*L*); (2) an imperfectly elastic demand for real estate services at the site; and (3) an imperfectly elastic supply of construction, operating, and maintenance inputs. If tenants are willing to pay higher rents for upper story locations, the marginal net revenue product of capital will be less negatively sloped than in the absence of such a height premium, or may even have a positive slope within some range. Beyond some height, however, the *MNRPK* must decline for there to be an economic limit to height.

struction is involved. Thus, a developer may well not explicitly consider the remote time when redevelopment will take place.[5] If the annual net revenue of the improved property is assumed to be a level stream continuing infinitely far into the future, or at least beyond the "planning horizon" of the entrepreneur, the profit-maximizing outlay on construction occurs where the *MNRPK* equals the interest rate on borrowed funds, or the opportunity cost of equity capital.[6] In figure 5.1 this occurs where the capital investment in improvements is K'. For any investment in size or quality of building below K', the marginal rate of return on further investment exceeds the interest cost, and the reverse is true for any investment above K'.[7] The resulting annual net revenue is R' in the top panel, or the rectangle $OK'HJ$ in the lower panel of figure 5.1. This revenue must be divided among land rent for the site, interest on the capital invested in the improvement, entrepreneur's profit, and property taxes (which are assumed initially to be zero).

The interest on capital invested in improvements to land is given by the rectangle $OK'LE$ (the interest rate times the capital invested). If there is perfect competition in the bidding for vacant sites, entrepreneurs will bid up to an amount equal to the rectangle $ELHJ$ (which is equal to the triangle ELS) in terms of annual rental payments for the right to use the site.[8] Different types of land use (for example, commercial versus residential) will result in different annual net revenue curves, and the land use which produces the largest annual rent payment in terms of the rectangle $ELHJ$ will be the "highest and best" use of the land.[9] The

5. Some buildings are even built with the explicit intention of being potentially permanent. As an example when the Singer Building in New York, once the tallest building in the world and still the tallest ever to be demolished, was pulled down in 1967, it was recalled that its architect, Ernest Flagg, once stated that the building was "as solid and lasting as the Pyramids."

6. If the interest rate on borrowed funds is an increasing function of the amount borrowed, the relevant capital cost is the *marginal* rate of interest (the increase in total yearly interest payments divided by the increase in borrowed funds).

7. Quality and quantity of improvements to land are not measured separately here. Rather, the total amount spent on construction is taken as the market estimate of the two combined.

8. If there is competition among developers, all above-normal profits of development will tend to be passed on to landowners. But better informed or more optimistic entrepreneurs may often recognize demand for new real estate services where all others fail to see it, and thereby be able to capture some of the potential land rent as part of their profit of development. Of course, if the developer overestimates the demand for real estate services he may overbid for land and overinvest in construction and thereby lose money. In an uncertain world, variations among developers in estimates of demand must account for part of the observed variation in the capital intensity of contiguous land uses.

9. This normative term refers to private profit maximization and neglects positive or negative external effects of the alternative land uses. Land use regulations, which are in

market value of the land will be the capitalized value of the expected future rent payments.

In this formulation of the profit-maximizing capital intensity of land development, all revenues, costs, and taxes have been measured on an annual basis, with the assumption that they continue as level streams infinitely far into the future. As an alternative way to formulate the problem, all revenues, costs, and taxes could be measured in terms of their present discounted values at the time the construction decision is made. For instance, R could be redefined as the present value of the net revenue for the life of the building, plus the present value of the land at the end of the building life. There is then no need to assume that the annual net revenue is a perpetual level stream and it is also possible to take into account the tax advantages of real estate investment (principally the use of the depreciation allowance as an income tax shelter in the early years of the building). It is also possible to take into account the fact that the construction cost is not expended at a single point in time; the construction of a building takes time, and the cost of the capital investment, K, can also be converted to a present value at the time of the decision to begin construction.

When all revenue and cost flows are converted to their respective present values, the curves in figure 5.1 would be expected to have roughly the same shapes, but the condition for the profit-maximizing amount of capital would then be found at the point where $\partial R/\partial K = 1$; that is, at the point where an additional dollar of capital investment in construction increases the present value of the net revenue from the building by one dollar. The rectangle *ELHJ* would then represent the market value of the site rather than its annual rent. When property taxes are introduced into the model, the conclusions to be drawn are unaffected by whether the annual value or present value version of revenues, costs, and taxes is used, and the analysis is carried out below in terms of annual values. In the subsequent empirical estimation, both forms of the model are used.

The Effect of Property Taxes on Land Development Decisions

Within the framework of this static Ricardian model, consider the effects of the two major types of property taxes: on land value and on improvement value. The general property tax is usually levied as an annual tax on the total assessed value of the property or on the combined

---

part intended to correct for these externalities, alter the revenue function by imposing various prohibitions and requirements on the developer, and may in some cases produce a coincidence between privately calculated and socially calculated highest and best use.

value of the building and of the land, separately assessed. When the tax rate on land and improvements is the same, however, the assessor has little incentive to divide total property value accurately between building value and land value.[10] Assuming it possible to assess land value and building value separately, we can consider the effect of each tax in isolation. In the following analysis I will ignore the effects on the demand for real estate services of the expenditure side of the government budget. This procedure is justified by the concentration on the effects of shifting the tax base from building value to site value, with government revenues and expenditures held constant.

A Tax on Improvement Value

First, consider the introduction of an annual tax on the capital value of improvements to a site ($T_k = t_k K$), where t_k = the property tax rate on the improvement value.[11] In figure 5.1 the tax as a function of capital invested in improvements to the site is a ray from the origin. Deducting this tax from R, we obtain annual net revenue after property taxes ($R - t_k K$) shown as the dashed line in the top panel of figure 5.1. Since this after-tax revenue is the relevant one for investors, we calculate the marginal and average net product of capital *after* property taxes, $\partial(R - t_k K)/\partial K$ and $(R - t_k K)/K$. These are shown as the dashed lines in the lower panel of figure 5.2. These after-tax functions are obtained by a simple downward shift of the before-tax functions, because $\partial(R - t_k K)/\partial K = (\partial R/\partial K) - t_k$ and $(R - t_k K)/K = (R/K) - t_k$.

The profit-maximizing outlay on capital improvements now occurs when the after-tax *MNRPK* is equal to the interest rate.[12] This point is shown as K'' in figure 5.1. The resulting annual revenue after operating and maintenance expenses ($R'' = OK'' BA$) is divided among interest payments ($iK'' = OK'' FE$), tax payments ($t_k K'' = ABCD$), and land

10. The problems of defining and separately measuring land value for taxation purposes are discussed by Hicks (1970), Turvey (1957), and Vickrey (1970). It is interesting to note that in New Zealand, which permits local governments to tax either unimproved land value or the capital value of land and improvements, one study found the relative cost of the two types of assessment to be ($NZ) 0.6 per assessment for unimproved land value and ($NZ) 4.00 per assessment for land and improvement value (Brown, 1968).

11. The analysis has been cast in terms of a tax on improvement value alone, whereas the usual property tax is based on the total market value of real property (land and building value). In the appendix it is shown that a property tax has the same effect on incentives regardless of whether it is applied to the total market value of the property or only to the value of the building.

12. In a model very similar to the one presented here, Becker (1969) shows the equivalent result that the profit-maximizing outlay on capital improvements occurs where the before-tax *MNRPK* is equal to the interest rate plus the tax rate.

rent (*EFCD*).[13] From this it can be seen that the capital improvements tax (1) reduces the optimal investment in real estate construction from K' to K''; and (2) reduces land rent of the site from *ELHJ* to *EFCD*. The first result confirms that a tax on improvements reduces investment in construction and thus reduces both the quantity and quality of improvements supplied.[14] The second result demonstrates that part of the tax on improvement value is incident on land rent and therefore on land value.[15]

This reduction of capital investment from K' to K'' is a maximum estimate: the actual reduction in capital improvements to a site will be less than this maximum estimate of K' to K'' depending on the extent to which the property tax is shifted forward to the users of real estate services or back to the factors that enter into the production of real estate services. Three possibilities should be noted.

First, if *all* buildings are subject to the same tax rate, the reduction in new construction on all vacant sites would decrease the output of real estate services and would therefore raise the price of these services if demand is not perfectly elastic. Some of the tax burden would thus be shifted forward to the consumers of real estate services. This would have the effect of increasing net revenue as a function of capital and would shift the *MNRPK* and *ANRPK* curves upward; thus the intersection of the new *MNRPK* curve with the interest rate would occur somewhat to the right of K'' when we recognize that the tax also decreases the supply of real estate services on competing sites. If we are considering a change in the tax rate for one small local jurisdiction in a large metropolitan

13. From this diagram it can be seen that, beyond some point, an increase in the property tax rate on buildings may reduce the total property tax revenue. A higher t_k reduces K, so that $t_k K''$ may either increase or decrease as t_k increases.

14. The disincentive effect of property taxes on the elusive "quality" dimension of new construction is magnified when the tax assessment is based on construction cost rather than on the capitalized rental income or sale value of a building. For example, because of its unusual design and large landscaped plaza, the construction cost of the Seagram Building in New York City exceeded the capitalized value of its expected rental income (i.e., in figure 5.1 the builder was operating either in a region below the revenue production function or somewhere to the right of the optimum point). The New York State Court of Appeals upheld New York City in its decision to use the high construction cost figure as evidence to justify assessing the building at a value greater than the estimate of its capitalized rental income. This is a clear fiscal disincentive to construction expenditures for external amenities that produce no income (*New York Times*, June 11, 1964, pp. 35-38). This is not meant to imply that every building whose construction cost exceeds its capitalized rental income is necessarily good architecture or provides external amenities.

15. If the demand for the services of real estate were perfectly elastic, and if the supply of capital and construction services were also perfectly elastic, *all* of the tax on improvements would be incident on land rent.

area with a competitive real estate market, however, the effect of the tax on each new building in the small jurisdiction may be similar to that pictured above because the price of real estate services in the entire metropolitan area will be only slightly affected.[16]

A second reason to expect that the reduction in building size to K'' is an overestimate of the actual effect is related to the elasticity of supply of capital funds to the construction industry within the taxing jurisdiction. If capital is in less than perfectly elastic supply to the local real estate sector, the interest rate would decline when investment in construction declines, and the intersection of the $MNRPK$ curve with the lowered interest rate would occur to the right of K''. Some of the tax burden would thus be shifted back to the suppliers of capital funds. This consideration is particularly relevant at the national level, where it is usually assumed that the supply of savings is interest inelastic. To the extent that there is a perfectly elastic supply of capital to one local jurisdiction in an open national economy, however, the interest rate would decline very little in response to reduced construction activity.

A third possibility that may mitigate the impact of an improvements tax on building size is the elasticity of supply of construction services. If construction services are in less than perfectly elastic supply, their price would decline if new construction contracted in response to a tax. Some of the tax burden would thus be shifted back to the suppliers of construction services, and this would raise the $MNRPK$ curve. Again, the elasticity of supply of construction services depends on the openness of the taxing jurisdiction to flows of construction industry inputs across its borders.

Because of the above three tax-shifting possibilities, the reduction in construction investment from K' to K'' in response to a capital improvements tax is a maximum estimate. The magnitude of this estimated reduction depends on the values of i, t_k, and on the shape of the $MNRPK$ curve, which in turn depends on the price elasticity of demand for real estate services, on the elasticity of supply of construction services, and on the elasticity of substitution between L and K in the production of real estate services. Either an inelastic demand for real estate services, an inelastic supply of construction services, or an inelasticity of substitution between L and K would lead to an inelasticity of $MNRPK$ with respect to K. If the $MNRPK$ curve is very inelastic with respect to K, the investment in improvements to the site is insensitive to changes in t_k; if

16. Mieszkowski (1972) emphasizes the open economy aspect of any one local government jurisdiction's decision about property tax rates and argues that the tax rate *differential* between one jurisdiction and all other relevant jurisdictions results in an excise tax effect of the sort we are discussing.

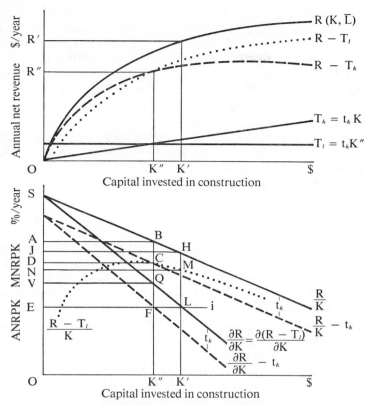

Figure 5.2. Total, average, and marginal net revenue with a tax on land

the *MNRPK* curve is very elastic within the relevant range, however, the reduction in investment from K' to K'' may be quite large, and there would be a significant reduction in intensity of development. Before turning to the evidence on this point suggested by the two case studies, I will first complete the theoretical analysis by briefly showing the effect on investment incentives of a tax on land value only, and in particular the effect of shifting the basis of taxation from improvement value to land value.

A Tax on Land Value

The improvement tax yields a revenue of $T_k = t_k K''$. A tax on site value, T_l, that raises the same revenue from the site and that does not vary with the value of the improvement to the site would therefore be represented by a horizontal line equal in value to $t_k K''$, as shown in the top panel of figure 5.2. Annual net revenue minus T_l would be represented by a simple downward shift (dotted line) of the $R(K,\bar{L})$ curve, with the slope of the curve everywhere unchanged. Since T_l is not a function of K, $\partial(R - T_l)/\partial K = \partial R/\partial K$, and the *MNRPK* curve is unchanged from the no-tax situation. The *ANRPK* will be changed by the land tax; $(R - T_l)/K$ is very low for small values of K and asymptotically approaches the no-tax *ANRPK* for larger values of K as shown by the dotted line in the lower panel of figure 5.2. Since the *MNRPK* is unaffected by the land tax, the optimal capital investment in improvements is K', the same as without the tax, and is greater than the optimal investment, K'', that results from the equal-yield improvements tax.[17] The resulting annual net revenue ($R' = OK'HJ$) is divided among interest payments ($iK' = OK'LE$), tax payments ($T_l = HJNM$), and after-tax rent ($ELMN$).

We have assumed that the switch in tax base produces a land tax revenue T_l equal to the alternative improvements tax revenue t_kK''. Thus we are applying the assumption of equal yield to a particular *site,* while the common use of the term refers to equal yield for a particular taxing *jurisdiction.* In any tax jurisdiction the ratio of improvement value to site value varies among sites and thus with uniform tax rates, an equal-jurisdiction-yield shift of the tax base from improvements to land will in general not produce equal site yields. But the incentive to invest in improvements is independent of the magnitude of the land tax. Therefore, a change in tax base from improvement value to land value produces the same effect on incentives to invest in improvements to a site *regardless* of whether the new equal-jurisdiction-yield land tax rate produces a land tax yield from the particular site greater or less than the alternative improvement tax yield.[18] If the total tax yield from a particular site *is* the same under either tax base, the after-tax land rent with the land tax is greater than the after-tax land rent with the improvements tax. This can be seen in figure 5.2. With the improvements tax, the site owner will invest K'' and the after-tax rent is the triangle QSV. With the land tax, the site owner will invest K' and the after-tax rent is the triangle ELS (the before-tax land rent) minus the rectangle $EFQV$

17. In the comparative static model I have concentrated on the effect of property taxes on the optimal capital intensity of new construction; in a dynamic model, property taxes may also have an effect on the *timing* of new construction. For a discussion of the effect of property taxes on the timing of development, see Gaffney (1973b), Neutze (1968), and Shoup (1970).

18. Although decisions concerning optimal investment in improvements are *at the margin* unaffected by a land value tax, the change from improvement value to land value taxation may, by reducing the wealth of owners of land devoted to low capital intensity uses, cause additional land to be released for development. Gaffney (1973b, pp. 81-82) believes that, in terms of stimulating development, this wealth effect accompanying a change of tax base would be at least as important as the effect on decisions at the margin.

(the improvements tax, $t_k K''$, which by assumption is equal to the land tax). Thus, the after-tax rent with the land tax is greater by an amount equal to QFL. But when we recognize that the optimal improvement value to land value ratios do vary considerably within a jurisdiction, it is obvious that some sites with low improvement value to land value ratios would experience a decrease in after-tax land rent and windfall losses in land value if the general property tax were replaced by a site value tax. Also, the incidence of a tax change may in the short run be quite different from that in the long run. Land uses existing at the time of the tax change will in general not be at the capital intensity that would be optimal after the land tax is instituted. Only after land uses have been adapted to the new tax incentives will the change in incidence be as described above.[19]

The redistribution of tax burden is of course one of the factors that may arouse opposition to a change from the general property tax to a site value tax. The only state that has in recent years moved toward site value taxation is unique in this respect. In 1964 the State of Hawaii adopted a graded real property tax law which in gradual stages will increase the tax rate on land to as high as 2.5 times the tax rate on improvements. One explanation of the political feasibility for such a change may lie in the fact that land ownership in Hawaii is unusually concentrated among a few large owners. In 1960 approximately 84 percent of all privately owned land in Hawaii, and 70 percent of all privately owned land on the highly urbanized island of Oahu, was in holdings of 5000 or more acres (Baker, 1961, p. 8). By 1962 more than two-thirds of new residential development land on Oahu was available only with leasehold tenure, and seventeen landowners accounted for 99.8 percent of all residential leaseholds on Oahu (Vargha, 1964, pp. 10-12). Thus, if the shift in tax base does cause windfall losses to some landowners, in Hawaii the losers may be relatively few compared to the number who might gain if the reduction in the tax on improvements had any effect in lowering the price of housing (or moderating its rate of price increase).[20]

19. The problems of transition from a general property tax to a site value tax are discussed by Harriss (1970). The theory of land tax capitalization is discussed in Jensen (1931, pp. 63-75) and Gaffney (1970, pp. 189-90).

20. This view corresponds to Woodruff's and Ecker-Racz's findings: "The fact that a number of Australian and New Zealand communities have been voting to change to unimproved capital value basis for property taxation has less implication for the inherent superiority of that system over others, as it generally reflects taxpayer desire to minimize tax bills. Communities vote to shift to unimproved capital value when they are on the outskirts of a developing metropolis and a majority of homeowners stand to benefit at the expense of a few. The reverse is true in older prosperous sections of metropolitan areas where the shift would be in the opposite direction and store and factory owners would benefit at the expense of the more numerous homeowners" (1969, pp. 185-86).

As noted above, the optimal investment in improvements to land is unaffected by a tax on land value because it has no effect on an investor's decisions at the margin. This neutrality in its effect on the incentive to improve land is usually cited as an advantage of land value taxation. It is sometimes also stated, however, that the *non*neutrality of a tax on improvement value is actually an advantage in that it discourages "too intense" development of urban areas. Certainly, if land value taxation were instituted, some low intensity uses of land might thereby become unprofitable and yet deserve preservation on the basis of their external benefits. For instance, some historic single-family residential areas which have a low building value to land value ratio might experience an increase in taxes if site value taxation were introduced, and this tax increase might lead to a replacement of the older buildings by new and larger structures. In this sense the general property tax may "preserve" some desirable low intensity uses. Not *all* low intensity uses deserve such preservation (some may have net external costs), however, nor should *all* urban renewal be discouraged, and the current general property tax makes no distinction between "good" and "bad" low capital intensity uses in conferring a low property tax. Taxation of the market value of improvements is in general not the best way to handle the external costs and benefits associated with improvements to land. User charges for specific municipally supplied building-related services combined with appropriate land use planning and building regulations would seem preferable to the general property tax as methods of accounting for externality problems.[21] This is especially evident when it is noted that the improvement value component of the general property tax base refers to quality as well as quantity of improvements.

Estimation of the Impact of Taxes: Two Examples

As noted above, the magnitude of effect of the general property tax on the supply of improvements depends crucially on the elasticity of the *MNRPK* curve. Thus, in order to estimate the impact of the property tax it is important to have an estimate of the revenue production function $R(K,L)$, and its derivative with respect to capital investment in construction. There is, however, no reason to believe that the function relating yearly net revenue to the capital and land inputs is the same for

---

21. Land use regulations could take the form of taxes on specific features of improvements that are thought to produce external costs. For instance, if building height or site coverage is per se thought to be undesirable, there could be a tax on these features.

all types of real estate, and therefore one would not expect the effect of a property tax on the supply of improvements to be the same in all uses. For instance, one would expect that real estate services with a low price elasticity of demand would also have an inelastic *MNRPK* schedule, and therefore a property tax would have little effect on the quantity supplied; for those services with a greater price elasticity of demand, the effect of a tax on the quantity supplied should be greater. Thus, the impact of a property tax on the supply of improvements to land will vary according to type of property use, and in the framework of our model it is difficult to make a single overall estimate of the effect of a property tax on the supply of improvements. Within more narrowly defined categories of real estate, however, it should be possible to estimate the relevant revenue production functions and from these predict the effect of a property tax on the supply of improvements within each category.

An Example Using Ex Ante Data

One method of estimating a real estate revenue production function is to use the actual ex ante calculations made by a developer. By using architectural and engineering data to make estimates of the construction costs of several alternative quantities of rental space on a given site, and then using market research data to make estimates of the resulting alternative rental revenues, it should be possible to quantify the functional relationships that are implied by the schedules drawn in figure 5.1. Such data are unfortunately difficult to obtain and when available are necessarily specific to a particular project and site. This method does have the important advantage of concentrating directly on the decisions of individual entrepreneurs, however, and on the way property taxes enter into these decisions.

Partly as a matter of historical interest, the early research of Clark and Kingston (1930) on the economic (that is, profit-maximizing) height of skyscrapers provides an example of the way property taxes affect ex ante profitability calculations in the framework of our model. Clark (an economist) and Kingston (an architect) collaborated in an examination of the rate of return to capital invested in the construction of eight hypothetical sizes of office buildings on a one-block site in the Grand Central Terminal area of New York City in the late 1920s. Their investigation resulted in the design of "eight different buildings, varying in height from 8 to 75 stories, each designed as an effective architectural solution, under the assumed building height limitations, of the problem of developing a large site in the Grand Central Zone of New York City" (Clark and Kingston, 1930, p. 11). New York zoning regulations, construction

Table 5.1. Summary of Investment Cost, Gross and Net Income, and Return upon Investment (assuming land value at $200 per square foot) (in thousands of dollars)

	8-story building	15-story building	22-story building	30-story building	37-story building	50-story building	63-story building	75-story building
Investment								
Land (81,000 sq. ft. @ $200)	$16,200	$16,200	$16,200	$16,200	$16,200	$16,200	$16,200	$16,200
Building	4,769	7,307	9,310	11,775	13,808	16,537	19,390	22,558
Carrying charges:								
Interest during construction								
Land (6% on cost for full period)	810	972	1,134	1,296	1,458	1,620	1,780	1,944
Building (6% on cost for half period)	119	219	326	471	622	826	1,065	1,353
Taxes during construction—land	292	350	408	466	524	584	642	700
Insurance during construction	3	5	8	12	21	35	65	95
Total carrying charges	1,224	1,546	1,876	2,245	2,625	3,065	3,552	4,092
Grand total cost	22,193	25,053	27,386	30,220	32,633	35,802	39,142	42,850
Total assignable to land	17,302	17,522	17,742	17,962	18,182	18,404	18,622	18,844
Total assignable to building	4,891	7,531	9,644	12,258	14,451	17,398	20,520	24,006
Income								
Gross income	1,819	2,780	3,483	4,181	4,755	5,581	6,302	6,901
Expenses:								
Operating	311	482	592	723	814	942	1,058	1,213
Taxes	479	541	591	653	705	774	846	926
Depreciation	95	146	186	235	276	331	388	451
Total expenses	885	1,169	1,369	1,611	1,795	2,047	2,292	2,590
Net income								
Gross of property taxes	1,413	2,152	2,705	3,223	3,665	4,308	4,856	5,237
Net of property taxes	934	1,611	2,114	2,570	2,960	3,534	4,010	4,311
Net return on total investment								
Gross of property taxes	6.37%	8.59%	9.88%	10.66%	11.23%	12.03%	12.41%	12.22%
Net of property taxes	4.22%	6.44%	7.73%	8.50%	9.07%	9.87%	10.25%	10.06%
Increase in investment from last addition of stories	—	2,860	2,333	2,834	2,413	3,169	3,340	3,708
Increase in net income resulting therefrom								
Gross of property taxes	—	739	553	518	442	643	548	381
Net of property taxes	—	677	503	456	390	574	476	301
Net return on increase in investment								
Gross of property taxes	—	25.84%	23.70%	18.27%	18.32%	20.29%	16.40%	10.27%
Net of property taxes	—	23.69%	21.51%	16.09%	16.16%	18.11%	14.25%	8.12%

Source: Reproduced with additions and corrections from Clark and Kingston (1930), by courtesy of the American Institute of Steel Construction, Inc.

and maintenance costs, rental levels, and tax rates of the period were assumed as the basic governing conditions. Then, using very detailed estimates of the cost and expected rental returns for each hypothetical building, they calculated the expected average and marginal rates of return on investment of each height. Although Clark and Kingston were not concerned with the effect of taxes on the economic height of buildings, their original data can be manipulated to show this effect. Table 5.1 is a presentation of the Clark and Kingston data, with modifications to show the effect of property taxes on the *MNRPK*, which is calculated both before and after deduction of property taxes (shown in the last two rows of the table). The assumed property tax rate, expressed as a percentage of the total cost of land and building, is the then-current 2.16 percent per annum.

The *MNRPK* declines for increments in size to fifteen-, twenty-two-, and thirty-story buildings, but increases for increments to thirty-seven and fifty stories before declining again thereafter. The increasing marginal returns between thirty and fifty stories in height are attributed by Clark and Kingston to the complicated set-back restrictions contained in the New York City zoning code which produced the familiar zoning-induced ziggurat structures of the period.[22]

From the data in table 5.1, the before-tax *MNRPK* is computed to be 16.40 percent per year at sixty-three stories and 10.27 percent per year at seventy-five stories.[23] Thus, if there were no property taxes and if the required rate of return on additional investment were 10 percent per year, the profit-maximizing height on this site would be approximately seventy-five stories. Given the then-existing 2.16 percent effective property tax rate, the after-tax *MNRPK* would decline to 8.1 percent at seventy-five stories and therefore the profit-maximizing height would also decline, but it would still be greater than sixty-three stories, at which

22. For lower floors of high-rise buildings, the zoning code required additional set-backs from the street line to compensate for increases in building height. Once the required set-backs had reduced the floor area of the building such that above a given level it covered not more than 25 percent of the area of the site, no further set-backs were required regardless of further increases in height. Above the thirty-seven-story height, the set-back regulations had little effect on floor areas and therefore no further zoning-induced tapering of the building with additional height was required (Clark and Kingston, 1930, pp. 13, 23). Many of the buildings built under this New York City code are convincing evidence of the maxim that "form follows money."

23. The *MNPRK* shown in the column for each height is actually the rate of return on investment in an increment from the height of the next lower design, rather than the rate of return on investment in a small further increment in height. Thus, if the *MNRPK* is declining as height increases, the actual *MNRPK* at each height is somewhat less than the marginal rate of return figure shown in the column for that height. This small discrepancy is not considered in our discussion.

height the after-tax *MNRPK* is 14.25 percent.[24] Since the before-tax *MNRPK* at sixty-three stories is 16.40 percent, if the after-tax required rate of return were 10 percent, it would take an effective property tax rate of 6.40 percent to reduce the profit-maximizing height from a no-tax seventy-five stories to the with-tax sixty-three stories; the corresponding reduction in total rentable space would be from 1,791,924 to 1,653,342 square feet, or 7.7 percent (Clark and Kingston, 1930, p. 40). Thus, if the cost and revenue data provided by Clark and Kingston are accurate, the effect of raising the property tax on this building from zero to 6.41 percent would have reduced the profit-maximizing quantity of rental space supplied on this site by only 7.7 percent, and rarely are effective property tax rates that high.[25]

The reason that even a relatively high property tax has a surprisingly small effect on building height in this particular case study is, of course, the rather sharp decline in *MNRPK* above a sixty-three-story building height. One of the most important technological factors explaining the declining *MNRPK* in high-rise construction is the increasing amount of space on lower floors that must be devoted to elevator shafts as building height increases, and this is illustrated by the Clark and Kingston data; in the eight-story design, elevators absorbed 1.9 percent of the gross floor area, while in the seventy-five-story building elevators absorbed 9.78 percent of gross floor area (Clark and Kingston, 1930, p. 66). In addition to the loss of rentable space to elevator shafts, there is also the direct monetary cost of installing and operating the elevators. Another important factor affecting the *MNRPK* schedule is the restriction on building size imposed by zoning; in this case, the zoning regulation which limited the area of the higher floors to 25 percent of the site area has an obvious influence in shifting the *MNRPK* schedule downward and thus in reducing economic height—an impact that in this particular case may be more important than that of property taxation. It should also be

24. Clark and Kingston themselves concluded that the optimum economic height was sixty-three stories on the basis that the "maximum economic return" (i.e., the highest *average* rate of return) occurred at this height (1930, p. 20). Despite calculating the marginal rate of return ("the increase in investment required to produce the last addition of stories"), they ignored it in favor of the average return on total investment criterion; the highest after-tax average rate of return on total investment is 10.25 percent for the sixty-three-story building. They chose this as the optimum height despite the fact that the net return on investment in twelve additional stories is 8.12 percent compared to their own assumed 6 percent interest cost.

25. As was mentioned above, if there is less than perfectly elastic demand for rental space, and/or less than perfectly elastic supply of capital and of construction services, this 7.7 percent figure is an overestimate of the reduction in the quantity of space supplied. The reduction in height also depends on the assumed after-property-tax required rate of return.

noted that the data in this example permit an estimate of the effect of property taxes only on the quantity of space provided on a site; there is no way to examine the possibly important effect of taxes on the harder to measure quality aspect of the improvements supplied.[26]

Of course the estimated impact of property taxes in the Clark and Kingston study is very much dependent on the assumed site, zoning regulations, building technology, and input and output prices of the time.[27] Other examples might well show much greater sensitivity of height to the tax rate. Because of the difficulty of obtaining other examples of ex ante estimates, we turn now to the study of revenue production functions estimated from cross-section analysis of ex post data.

An Example Using Ex Post Data

In the work of Clark and Kingston the relationship between building height and building cost was estimated from engineering data. In two recent studies Berger (1967, 1968) used cross-section data to estimate by ordinary least-squares regression equations the effect of building height on several building characteristics: building efficiency, construction cost per square foot of gross building area, and the length of the construction period. The data were obtained for twenty-seven post-World War II high-rise (eight or more stories) apartment buildings and thirty-six post-World War II high-rise office buildings in Los Angeles County. He then used these estimated relationships to provide the cost and revenue data necessary to determine the optimal height of a hypothetical high-rise office building. Berger assumed that in the construction decision the entrepreneur seeks to maximize the present value of profits over the life of the building and that optimum height thus occurs where the present discounted value of the annual net revenue from an additional story equals the construction cost of the additional story. The present discounted value of annual net revenue is equal to the present discounted value of the annual total revenue, minus total annual operating expenses, property taxes, and corporation income taxes, plus the present value of the land and building residual at the end of the economic life of the building. This formulation of the optimum height determination in terms of the present discounted value of net revenue has several advan-

26. Kingston did not, however, set out to design an early Seagram Building. "No money was to be wasted in needless ornamentation or in immoderate striving for grandeur or aesthetic effect but short of such extremes, the utmost endeavor was to be made to secure the maximum rental appeal . . ." (1930, p. 11).

27. The 1930 publication date of Clark and Kingston's research indicates that any entrepreneur who had actually relied on the ex ante data was in for a very big surprise.

Table 5.2. Investment Characteristics of Hypothetical High-Rise Office Buildings of Varying Height: The Effect of a 2 Percent Property Tax on Building Value

Height in stories (1)	Total investment (2)	Total net cash flow (no tax) (3)	Total net cash flow (2% tax) (4)	Marginal investment (5)	Marginal net cash flow (no tax) (6)	Marginal net cash flow (2% tax) (7)	Net present value (no tax) (8)[a]	Net present value (2% tax) (9)[b]
8	$3,641,460	$4,144,758	$3,875,755	$ —	$ —	$ —	$503,298	$234,295
9	4,070,415	4,655,199	4,345,400	428,955	510,441	469,645	584,784	274,985
10	4,516,599	5,164,505	4,812,277	446,184	509,306	466,877	647,906	295,678
11	4,979,810	5,672,533	5,276,246	463,211	508,028	463,969	692,723	296,436
12	5,460,198	6,179,334	5,737,358	480,388	506,801	461,112	719,136	277,160
13	5,957,993	6,685,017	6,195,698	497,795	505,683	458,340	727,024	237,705
14	6,472,286	7,189,392	6,651,161	514,293	504,375	455,463	717,106	178,875
15	7,003,954	7,692,627	7,103,830	531,668	503,235	452,669	688,673	99,876
16	7,552,834	8,194,639	7,553,640	548,880	502,012	449,810	641,805	806
17	8,118,554	8,695,357	8,000,599	565,720	500,718	446,959	576,803	−117,995

Source: Reproduced with additions from Berger (1968, p. 36).

[a] Equal to column 3 minus column 2.

[b] Equal to column 4 minus column 2.

tages over the Clark and Kingston method: (1) when there is a corporation income tax, the effect of depreciation on after-tax income can be taken into account; and (2) the effect of assuming a finite lifetime for the building can be shown.

With an assumed 15,410 square foot average floor area (the mean for post-World War II Los Angeles high-rise office buildings) and with an assumed annual rental value of $5.81 and operating cost of $2.04 per square foot of net rentable space (the means for the sample of high-rise office buildings), Berger calculated the initial construction cost and the annual revenues and costs for buildings of height varying between eight and thirty-two stories (Berger, 1968, pp. 262-64). Depreciation was calculated by the sum-of-the-years' digits method, with an expected usable building life of forty-five years. A corporation income tax rate of 50 percent and a property tax rate of 2 percent (approximately equal to the 1964 Los Angeles tax rate) were assumed, and the net cash flow (annual net revenue) for the life of the building was discounted to the date of construction with an interest rate of 4.15 percent, which was the 1964 average yield on U.S. government bonds. Berger did not intend to show the effect of property taxation on the optimal height of high-rise buildings, but his data can be extended to show this effect. Table 5.2 is an adaptation of Berger's original data.[28] This table displays the construction cost for each building height (in column 2), and the present discounted value of net cash flow, both without (in column 3) and with (in column 4) the 2 percent property tax. In column 5 is shown, for each height, the increase in construction cost (marginal investment) from the next lower height, and in columns 6 and 7 are shown the increase in the present discounted value of net cash flow (marginal net cash flow) from the next lower height, both without and with the 2 percent property tax. Marginal investment increases with building height because both construction cost per square foot of gross building area and the length of the construction period increase with height. Marginal net cash flow declines as building height increases because building efficiency declines with height. Finally, in columns 8 and 9 are shown the differences between the present discounted value of the net cash flow and the construction cost, both without and with the property tax; it is this difference that the entrepreneur is assumed to maximize. In columns 8 and 9 it can be seen that the optimal height in the absence of the property tax is thirteen stories, and that when the 2 percent annual property tax is introduced the optimal height falls to eleven stories. This corresponds to a reduction

28. I am grateful to Jay Berger for permission to use his data, and for his generous advice in making additional computations. For details of the calculations see Berger (1967, 1968).

of net rentable space from 155,095 square feet to 132,828 square feet, a reduction of 14 percent.

This 14 percent reduction in rentable space in response to a 2 percent property tax is, as mentioned in the second section of this chapter, a maximum estimate which depends on specific assumptions concerning the incidence of the property tax. These assumptions were that the demand for rentable space is perfectly price elastic, that the supply of capital funds is perfectly interest elastic, and that the supply of construction services is perfectly price elastic. Other more plausible and conventional shifting assumptions would reduce the estimated impact of the tax on the supply of rentable space.

The estimate of the impact of property taxes also depends on the assumption that investors in their construction decision employ marginal analysis to determine the profit-maximizing outlay on building construction. In interviews with a sample of twenty-eight investors in high-rise buildings in Los Angeles County, Berger did not find evidence that investors explicitly utilized marginal analysis of the sort that underlies the model of optimal investment in construction, at least as far as the decision on height is concerned (Berger, 1967, pp. 156-64). A major reason is that the information and information processing requirements for accurate estimation of the revenue production function greatly exceed the typical real estate investor's capabilities. Thus, the true impact of taxes on Berger's sample of buildings may well be quite different from what the model predicts.[29] This finding concerning the limited applicability of marginal analysis in practice may provide some support for Gaffney's statement that "wealth effects [of changing from a general property tax to a land tax] are at least as important as the marginal trade-off effects" (1937a, p. 82). It is difficult, however, to make estimates of the response to property taxes when profit-maximizing behavior is not assumed. Within the framework of a profit-maximization model, Berger's data do have advantages over the Clark and Kingston data since the effects of both the corporation income tax and depreciation allow-

---

29. Although the net present value of the building is maximized at a height of thirteen stories without a property tax, and at a height of eleven stories with a 2 percent property tax, the net present value of several alternative heights is also very close to the maximum in each case. Since a failure to choose exactly the correct profit-maximizing height may not greatly reduce profits, Darwinian "survival of the maximizers" may not weed out entrepreneurs who fail to select the exact optimum height. Thus, a model that assumes perfect profit maximization may not accurately predict the height that a "satisficing" entrepreneur will choose or the effect of a property tax on that choice. Furthermore, in any field of investment where the product is so heterogeneous and where major decisions by any one developer are relatively infrequent, economic "natural selection" may fail to eliminate non-maximizing entrepreneurs (Winter, 1964).

ances are included. The major limitations of both sets of data are the assumption of constant rental values per square foot for the life of the building (investors may expect increasing rent) and the assumption that the investment is financed entirely with equity funds, with no mortgage debt. These assumptions represent further qualifications to the empirical results in both examples.

Conclusion

It is tempting to draw conclusions from these two case studies about the impact that a change from general property taxation to site value taxation would have on land development decisions. A surprising finding was that a complete elimination of taxes on improvements would have, at most, resulted in an 8 percent larger building in the first case and a 17 percent larger building in the second. But the temptation to make any general statement from this finding should be resisted, for the cases are very limited approximations to reality. Both cases referred only to the effect of property taxes on the supply by profit-maximizing entrepreneurs of office space in high-rise buildings. Even if the estimates are accurate for the type of use assumed, the effect of a tax base change on the supply of office space in other locations might be quite different, and the effect on the supply of other types of land uses, such as residential or industrial uses, might be even more different.[30] Thus any general statement about the magnitude of the effects that would accompany a change of property tax base from improvement value to land value is also subject to qualification regarding the mix of affected land uses. One way to obtain a better idea of the impact of such a tax change on various land uses might be to conduct more studies with a micro-data basis, perhaps working more closely with land developers to see how capital-intensive decisions are made in practice and how taxes enter into these decisions.

Appendix

It can be shown that a property tax rate has the same effect on incentives regardless of whether it is applied to total market value of improved property (land value plus building value) or to the value of the

---

30. Richard Pollock and I (1977) estimated a revenue production function, using data on capital input, land input, and annual revenue collected for a sample of twenty-eight hotels recently built in Honolulu. The results indicate that the *MNRPK* schedule estimated from this sample is quite elastic and that the optimal investment in hotel construction, if based on marginal analysis, appears quite sensitive to the tax rate and interest rate, much more so than in the two case studies reported here.

building alone. Let: $R = R(K,\bar{L})$ = annual net revenue after operating and maintenance expenditures; T_p = property tax on market value of improved property (land and building); t_p = property tax rate on market value of improved property (land and building); and $R_n = R(K,\bar{L}) - T_p$ = annual net revenues after property taxes.

The market value of improved property is the capitalized value of after-tax annual net revenues. For a constant stream of revenue and a constant interest rate, this is R_n/i. Hence,

$$T_p = t_p\left(\frac{R_n}{i}\right) \quad \text{and} \quad R_n = R(K,\bar{L}) - t_p\left(\frac{R_n}{i}\right).$$

The after-tax $MNRPK = \dfrac{\partial R_n}{\partial K} = \dfrac{\partial R}{\partial K} - \left(\dfrac{t_p}{i}\right)\left(\dfrac{\partial R_n}{\partial K}\right).$ Therefore,

$$\left(1 + \frac{t_p}{i}\right)\left(\frac{\partial R_n}{\partial K}\right) = \frac{\partial R}{\partial K}, \text{ and } \frac{\partial R_n}{\partial K} = \frac{\dfrac{\partial R_n}{\partial K}}{1 + \dfrac{t_p}{i}} = \left(\frac{i}{i + t_p}\right)\left(\frac{\partial R}{\partial K}\right).$$

The profit-maximizing capital investment in construction occurs where the after-tax $MNRPK$ is equal to the interest rate, $\partial R_n/\partial K = i$. Therefore,

$$\left(\frac{i}{i + t_p}\right)\left(\frac{\partial R}{\partial K}\right) = i \quad \text{and} \quad \frac{\partial R}{\partial K} = i + t_p.$$

Thus, in the presence of a general property tax on land and building value, the profit-maximizing investment in construction occurs where the before-tax $MNRPK$ is equal to the interest rate plus the tax rate. This is the same result that was found in the presence of the tax rate applied to building value alone. This result seems reasonable, since the general property tax is, conceptually, two separate taxes: a tax on land value and a tax on building value. If the land value component of the general property tax has no effect on incentives, the total effect on incentives of the general property tax is the same as that of a tax of the same rate on building value alone. Of course, the same tax rate on the two different bases would not produce the same tax yield. If a tax on building value alone is to raise the same revenue as a general property tax, the tax rate on building value alone would have to be higher than the equal-yield general property tax rate.

References

Baker, Harold L. 1961. *The Land Situation in the State of Hawaii.* Land Study Bureau Circular no. 13. Honolulu: University of Hawaii.

Becker, Arthur P. 1969. "Principles of Taxing Land and Buildings for Economic Development." In *Land and Building Taxes, Their Effect on Economic Development,* ed. Becker, pp. 11-47. Madison: The University of Wisconsin Press.

Berger, Jay S. 1967. "Determination of the Economic Height of High-Rise Buildings." Ph.D diss., University of California, Los Angeles.

Berger, Jay S. 1968. *The Determination of the Economic Height of High-Rise Buildings.* Occasional Paper no. 3. Los Angeles: Housing, Real Estate & Urban Land Studies Program, Graduate School of Business Administration, University of California, Los Angeles.

Bishop, Robert L. 1967. "A Firm's Short-Run and Long-Run Demands for a Factor." *Western Economic Journal* 5, no. 2: 122-40.

Brown, J. Bruce. 1968. "The Incidence of Property Taxes Under Three Alternative Systems in Urban Areas in New Zealand." *National Tax Journal* 21, no. 3: 237-52.

Clark, W. A. V. 1974. *The Impact of Property Taxation on Urban Spatial Development.* Report no. 187. Los Angeles: Institute of Government and Public Affairs, University of California, Los Angeles.

Clark, W. C., and J. L. Kingston. 1930. *The Skyscraper, A Study in the Economic Height of Modern Office Buildings.* New York: American Institute of Steel Construction, Inc.

Gaffney, Mason. 1970. "Adequacy of Land as a Tax Base." In *The Assessment of Land Value,* ed. Daniel M. Holland, pp. 157-212. Madison: University of Wisconsin Press.

Gaffney, Mason. 1973a. "An Agenda for Strengthening the Property Tax." In *Property Tax Reform,* ed. George E. Peterson, pp. 65-84. Washington, D.C.: The Urban Institute.

Gaffney, Mason, 1973b. "Tax Reform to Release Land." In *Modernizing Urban Land Policy,* ed. Marion Clawson. Baltimore, Md.: The Johns Hopkins University Press.

Harriss, C. Lowell. 1970. "Transition to Land Value Taxation: Some Major Problems." In *The Assessment of Land Value,* ed. Daniel M. Holland, pp. 213-51. Madison: University of Wisconsin Press.

Hicks, Ursula K. 1970. "Can Land be Assessed for Purposes of Site Value Taxation?" In *The Assessment of Land Value,* ed. Daniel M. Holland, pp. 9-36. Madison: University of Wisconsin Press.

Jensen, Jens Peter. 1931. *Property Taxation in the United States.* Chicago: University of Chicago Press.

Ladd, Helen F. 1973. "The Role of the Property Tax: A Reassessment," In *Broad-Based Taxes: New Options and Sources,* ed. Richard A. Musgrave, pp. 39-86. Baltimore, Md.: The Johns Hopkins University Press.

Mieszkowski, Peter. 1972. "The Property Tax: An Excise or a Profits Tax?" *Journal of Public Economics* 1, no. 1: 73-96.

Netzer, Dick. 1968. *Impact of the Property Tax: Its Economic Implicatons for Urban Problems.* Supplied by the National Commission on Urban Problems to the Joint Economic Committee, Congress of the United States. Washington, D.C.: U.S. Government Printing Office.

Neutze, Max. 1968. *The Suburban Apartment Boom.* Washington, D.C.: Resources for the Future.

Pollock, Richard L., and Donald C. Shoup. 1977. "The Effect of Shifting the Property Tax Base from Improvement Value to Land Value: An Empirical Estimate." *Land Economics* 52, no. 1: 67-77.

Richman, Raymond L. 1965. "The Theory and Practice of Site-Value Taxation in Pittsburgh." In *1964 Proceedings of the Fifty-Seventh Annual Conference on Taxation.* Harrisburg, Pa.: National Tax Association.

Robinson, Joan. 1933. *The Economics of Imperfect Competition,* London: Macmillan and Co.

Shoup, Donald C. 1970. "The Optimal Timing of Urban Land Development." *Papers of the Regional Science Associaton* 25: 33-44.

Turvey, Ralph. 1957. *The Economics of Real Property.* London: George Allen and Unwin.

U.S. Bureau of the Census. 1973. *Governmental Finances in 1971-72.* Series GF 72-No. 5. Washington, D.C.: U.S. Government Printing Office.

Vargha, Louis A. 1964. *An Economic View of Leasehold and Fee Simple Tenure of Residential Land in Hawaii.* Land Study Bureau Bulletin no. 4. Honolulu: University of Hawaii.

Vickrey, William S. 1970. "Defining Land Value for Taxation Purposes," In *The Assessment of Land Value,* ed. Daniel M. Holland, pp. 25-36. Madison: University of Wisconsin Press.

Winter, Sidney G. 1964. "Economic 'Natural Selection' and the Theory of the Firm." *Yale Economic Essays* 4, no. 1: 225-72.

Woodruff, A. M., and L. L. Ecker-Racz. 1969. "Property Taxes and Land Use Patterns in Australia and New Zealand." In *Land and Building Taxes, Their Effect on Economic Development,* ed. Arthur Becker, pp. 147-86. Madison: University of Wisconsin Press.

6 Gail C. A. Cook

Toronto Metropolitan Finance: Selected Objectives and Results

Introduction

Both the academic and popular literature have expressed considerable interest in topics relevant to analyzing the advantages and disadvantages of political fragmentation and various forms of consolidation in metropolitan areas. The most recent academic literature has attempted to illuminate such questions as the potential trade-off between jointness and distributional efficiency and whether redistribution is a local public good. The popular contributions, on the other hand, examine major metropolitan reorganizations in both Canada and the United States, evaluating them primarily in administrative and political terms and making superficial, if any, economic assessments on the basis of limited evidence.

These recent academic and popular approaches leave out a major potential contribution of economic analysis to the evaluation of the economic impact of alternative types of organization. This has happened, in part, because the academic literature has been normative in nature while the popular literature has tended to deify any form of rationalization of public service provision in metropolitan areas. This is to some

This essay is based on work financed by the Ministry of State for Urban Affairs, Canada, while the author was a professor in the Department of Political Economy and Research Associate, Institute for the Quantitative Analysis of Social and Economic Policy, University of Toronto.

Table 6.1. Distribution of Responsibilities between Metropolitan Toronto and Area Municipalities, 1954 (M = municipality of metropolitan Toronto, A = area municipalities)

Function	M	A
Finance and taxation		
Assessment of property	M	
Courts of revision	M	A
Taxation of property		A
Debenture borrowing	M	
Local improvement charges		A
Planning		
Official plans	M	A
Subdivision approval	M	A
Zoning		A
Recreation and community services		
Regional parks	M	
Local parks		A
Recreation programs		A
Community centers and arenas		A
Municipal golf courses	M	
Municipal zoo	M	
Public libraries		A
Grants to cultural organizations	M	A
Road construction		
Expressways	M	
Arterial roads	M	
Local roads		A
Bridges and grade separations	M	A
Snow removal	M	A
Street cleaning	M	A
Sidewalks		A
Traffic control		
Traffic regulations	M	A
Cross-walks	M	A
Traffic lights	M	
Street lighting		A
Pavement markings	M	A
Public transit		
Toronto Transit Commission	M	
Water supply		
Purification, pumping, and trunk distribution system	M	
Local distribution		A
Collection of water bills		A
Sewage disposal		
Sanitary trunk systems and disposal plants	M	
Connecting systems		A
Storm drainage	M	A
Garbage collection and disposal		
Collection		A
Disposal sites	M	A
Air pollution		
Air pollution control	M	
Public education		
Operation of public school system		A
School sites, attendance areas, and building programs	M	A
Operating costs	M	A
Capital costs	M	A
Housing		
Elderly persons housing	M	
Low-rental family housing	M	A
Moderate-rental family housing		A
Welfare		
Welfare assistance	M	A
Hospitalization of indigents	M	
Assistance to children's aid societies	M	
Homes for the aged	M	
Other services		A
Health		
Public health services		A
Chronic and convalescent hospital	M	
Hospital grants		A
Police and fire protection		
Police	M	
Fire		A
Administration of justice		
Magistrates' courts	M	
Court house and jail	M	
Juvenile and family court	M	
Coroner's office	M	
Registry and land titles offices	M	
Licensing and inspection		
Business licensing	M	
Dog licensing and pound		A
Marriage licenses		A
Building by-laws		A
Civil defense		
Emergency Measures Organization	M	
Other municipal services		
Collection of fines	M	A
Collection of vital statistics		A
Distribution of hydro-electric power		A
Harbor		A
Island airport		A
Municipal parking lots		A
Preparation of voters' lists and administration of civic elections		A
Redevelopment		A

Source: Metropolitan Toronto Council (1963, p. 47).

extent explainable by the context in which these issues are raised. With fragmentation of political units in the United States being blamed for many urban ills, it is not surprising that alternatives to fragmentation are regarded as the answers to these problems. Such an approach, however, avoids critical analysis of other alternatives.[1] The first part of this chapter, therefore, will outline briefly the history and objectives of reorganization in the Toronto metropolitan area, while the remainder will present quantitative results on the outcome of the reorganizations, with emphasis on the 1967 reorganization.

Metropolitan Reorganization in Toronto: History and Objectives

Prior to the reorganization in 1954 which formed the well-known metropolitan government in Toronto, the greater Toronto area was composed of thirteen autonomous municipalities which cooperated when necessary through intermunicipal agreements. Rapid population growth in the late 1940s and early 1950s put considerable pressure on this structure, which separated the high demand areas (the suburbs) from the major source of the tax base (the central city). The suburban municipalities required sewer facilities, education facilities, and roads to meet the requirements of their rapidly expanding population. Provision of such services required access to capital markets, yet the tax base upon which to borrow was limited. Moreover, the municipalities were in the position of competing with each other in the capital markets.

In response to this overall situation, as well as to specific requests by selected municipalities in the Toronto metropolitan area for rationalization of their positions with respect to particular public services, in 1954 the Ontario government passed Bill 80, "An Act to Provide for the Federation of the Municipalities in the Metropolitan Area." A compromise structure was embodied in this act. The thirteen local units of government were retained, while a metropolitan level of government was superimposed over them. As is evident in table 6.1, the responsibility for most services was shared between the local and metropolitan levels of government. The two-tiered federated system reflected the interest of the legislators in achieving autonomy over some aspects of service at the local level while permitting decisions potentially affecting other municipalities to be undertaken at the metropolitan level.

As the Department of Economics of the Province of Ontario set them out in *A Report on the Metropolitan Toronto System of Government* (1961) the objectives of the 1954 federation were to be that it should (1)

---

1. For an elaboration of the importance of the context and the constitution within which reorganized governments operate, see Cook (1973a).

make an effective contribution toward unifying the main services common to the whole area; (2) remove the fetters inhibiting the growth of suburban municipalities which had the geographical area but not the financial strength to provide schools and other local services; (3) provide for an effective pooling of costs which would facilitate the construction of public projects such as highways and water and sewage facilities throughout the whole area; (4) contain the power to plan on a regional scale; (5) avoid producing an upsurge in aggregate municipal costs and taxes; and (6) not impose a sudden or intolerable tax burden upon any municipality or group of people. These six objectives can be reduced to two: the new political organization was to provide a decision-making structure permitting overall planning and planning for particular services in the metropolitan area (objectives 1 and 4) and to redistribute the tax base such that basic services could be provided in the rapidly growing municipalities with the small tax bases without increasing costs and taxes in the metropolitan area as a whole (objectives 2, 3, 5, and 6).

Earlier work examined the expenditure effects of the 1954 reorganization using the largest single budgetary item—education—as an example (Cook, 1973b). The results contained there show that a significant increase in expenditures followed reorganization and that this increase was significant relative to other municipalities in the province of Ontario over the same period. Indeed, analysis of the changes involved in reorganization should not make these results surprising. To provide services where none existed and to upgrade the quality of existing services cannot be done without additional expenditures. Implicit in the objective of reorganizing without raising expenditures and tax rates in the metropolitan area as a whole seemed to be the hope that the rationalization of service provision would result in some economies of an offsetting nature. When the potential economies of scale are inherent in new and expanded services, an expenditure reduction cannot be expected.

Closely related to the objective of better enabling the greater Toronto area to respond to population growth was the implied concern about inequities across the municipalities. Identical public expenditures per capita (or per pupil in the case of education) involved quite different levels of tax effort in each municipality. Early in the history of metropolitan government in the Toronto area, however, those municipalities which were suffering on the basis of rapid population growth were also those municipalities which required a high tax effort to maintain a given level of service provision. As time went on, however, concern with variations in service levels became paramount and during discussions prior to the 1967 reorganization took on primary importance along with the problem of political representation at the metropolitan level. The 1967 consolidation of the thirteen municipalities into six municipalities reduced the variation in tax bases among the local units and permitted representation of the municipalities at the metropolitan level more in accordance with population.

Two sets of changes raise the question as to the future of the federated system of government in which there is a real sharing of important responsibilities between the metropolitan and local units of government. These include a limit placed on expenditures out of own tax sources (for education purposes) imposed in 1967 and the progressive reduction in numbers of local units within the federated structure and transfer of powers from the local level between 1954 and the present.

Prior to 1967 the local municipalities were permitted to finance from their own education levy those expenditures which exceeded the amount to be paid from the metropolitan levy. In 1967, however, major responsibility for education budgeting was placed at the metropolitan level and a stringent *limit* on taxation for elementary and secondary purposes was placed on the local municipalities.

The introduction of such a limit suggests that the objective of metropolitan government as seen by some was not to redistribute income at the local level and then allow the expression of priorities, but rather to reduce the range in expenditures per pupil, quite a different objective.

If application of the philosophy behind the limits is extended into the noneducation sector, the two-tiered structure loses all relevance. If all the real responsibility is to be placed at the metropolitan level for most services, either because more and more functions are regarded as having areawide implications or because of an interest in reducing the range of expenditures per capita or per pupil, the two-tiered system becomes irrelevant.

Given Canadian experience, one can even speculate as to whether a two-tiered system should not be regarded as merely an intermediate step between full autonomy of local units and their complete consolidation. Supporting that view is experience from both the greater Toronto and greater Winnipeg areas. The Toronto area moved from full autonomy of the thirteen municipalities, to metropolitan government with shared responsibilities between the metropolitan and local governments, and, finally, to consolidation of local units within the metropolitan structure combined with the transfer of more responsibilities to the metropolitan level. The Winnipeg experience ranged from full autonomy through metropolitan government (similar to that in Toronto) and finally to full consolidation.

From this experience it appears that the response to metropolitan problems has been continuous centralization. It is not clear that in some cases this does not merely transfer the problem to another level of government rather than assisting in solving it.

Expenditure Effects of 1967 Consolidation

As pointed out earlier, the 1967 reorganization involved the consolidation of thirteen municipalities into six within the metropolitan structure and the transfer of selected powers to the metropolitan level, the most important of which was budgetary power over education. Corresponding to these two structural changes were two means by which budgetary patterns could be affected. The 1967 reorganization could alter the environment internal to the new consolidated municipality (decision-making unit) or could alter the environment external to the consolidated unit. Hypotheses related to potential reactions (internal and external) to the newly consolidated units will be examined here.

Equalizing-up Hypothesis

One simple hypothesis suggests that public service expenditures increase significantly after consolidation when consolidation involves the reduction of numbers of decision-making units. This short-run expenditure effect results from a pressure to equalize expenditures of the consolidated unit at the level of the highest expenditure municipality (preconsolidation) within the new unit. The institution of a uniform tax rate in the consolidated units results in pressure for a reduction in former expenditure differentials. The hypothesis further implies that resistance to lowering expenditures is stronger than the resistance to tax increases required to finance the increased expenditures, the burden of which is spread throughout the consolidated unit. Three services, police protection, fire protection, and elementary and secondary education, which were affected differently by consolidation, are analyzed.

Police protection has been the responsibility of the metropolitan level of government since 1957. Since the 1967 structural change did not directly affect police protection, it provides a control for the fire and education functions. Fire protection has always been a local function in the metropolitan area. Consolidation simply reduced the number of political units providing the service, which permits a direct test of the equalizing-up hypothesis.

The case of elementary and secondary education is slightly more complicated. The year 1967 brought a change in the financing of education as well as its consolidation. Education services were to be financed almost entirely[2] from the metropolitan levy rather than about 48 percent

2. A ceiling of one-and-a-half mills for elementary schools and one mill for secondary schools was placed on taxation from local sources.

from the metropolitan levy and 52 percent from local levies as was the case in 1966.

Two different interpretations of the equalizing-up hypothesis as applied to education can be given. With complete power over financial matters being vested in the Metropolitan School Board in 1967, pressure may have existed to equalize toward the highest expenditure municipality in the metropolitan area. Alternatively, however, in accepting or altering budgets submitted by the local boards the Metropolitan School Board may have given priority to equalizing within consolidated school districts rather than to the level of the highest expenditure municipality in the metropolitan area. Both alternatives will be tested.

The effect of consolidation on police, fire, and education expenditures in the metropolitan area will also be tested, followed by a disaggregated borough analysis.

Metropolitan Area Expenditures.—Time series regression equations were estimated. Inclusion of a dummy variable of value 0 prior to 1967 and 1 for 1967 and subsequent years indicates whether expenditures altered after consolidation. Police expenditures showed no significant increase in expenditures after consolidation, a result consistent with the equalizing-up hypothesis. Since no consolidation of the police function took place in 1967, no significant increase in expenditures should be observed.

The specific formulation of the equation appears in table 6.2, line (1). The dependent variable is real police expenditures expressed per number

Table 6.2. Estimated Equations for Police and Fire in Metropolitan Toronto

Real expenditure	Constant	Real income	Population	Dummy	R^2	D.W.
(1) Police[a]	—30.15 (— 3.27)	.018[b] (3.57)	— .00002 (—1.72)	.43 (.37)	.94	2.01
(2) Fire[a]	—18.84 (— 1.46)	.015[b] (2.11)	— .000015 (—1.14)	— .97 (— .60)	.77	1.20
(3) Fire[c]	— 8.34 (— 3.57)	.0085[d] (4.29)	— .000011 (—2.55)	1.17 (2.76)	.97	1.90
(4) Fire[c]	— 4.55 (— 0.97)	.0014[e] (1.05)	.0000078 (5.13)	2.91 (3.12)	.92	1.10

[a] Dependent variable is expenditures per taxable return.

[b] Income is defined as income from taxable returns for Toronto (Department of Revenue, Taxation income tax statistics) deflated by the consumer price index for Toronto.

[c] Dependent variable is per capita expenditures.

[d] Income series obtained by applying the pattern of income growth between 1961 and 1970, and 1957 and 1961, to the 1961 Census of Canada wage and salary income.

[e] Assessed valuation of property deflated by an index for housing based on value of multiple listed sales.

of taxable returns to match the income variable, which is income per taxable return in metropolitan Toronto.

Both police expenditures and income were deflated by the consumer price index for Toronto. Population was inserted as a measure of density, and the dummy variable was included to pick up the effect of any shift in expenditures resulting from consolidation.

Comparable equations were estimated for fire protection. Three formulations of the basic equation were estimated, with two of the three equations supporting the equalizing-up hypothesis by showing significant increases in expenditures subsequent to consolidation.

The equations for fire protection were estimated with two series of income data. In table 6.2, line (2), income is defined as real income per taxable return for metropolitan Toronto, information obtained from the Department of National Revenue, Taxation income tax statistics. In line (3) an estimated income series,[3] which was required for subsequent disaggregated regressions, was utilized to permit comparison of consistency between the aggregated and disaggregated results. The coefficient on the dummy variable is not significantly different from zero in line (2), but is significantly different from zero in line (3). The results in line (2) are inconsistent with the hypothesis, while those in line (3) are consistent with the hypothesis.

Given the unreliability of the data, similar equations were estimated, replacing income by assessed valuation as an independent variable. Fire expenditures per capita were deflated by the consumer price index for Toronto and assessed valuation per capita by a housing price index for Toronto. The results of the equation are consistent with the hypothesis. In the case of fire protection, therefore, the results of two of the three formulations of the test support the hypothesis.

All equations for per pupil expenditures on education consistently show a significant increase in expenditures per pupil as indicated by the coefficient on the dummy variable being significantly different from zero in all equations following consolidation (see table 6.3).

The dependent variable in lines (5) and (6) in table 6.3 is expenditures from local sources (exclusive of provincial grants). Provincial grants were introduced as an explanatory variable primarily to assist in obtaining the most accurate coefficient on the dummy variable and not to test for the extent of substitution between local and provincial funds. Given the high correlation between income per capita and provincial grants per pupil,

3. The 1961 wage and salary income is obtained from the 1961 Census of Canada. Income figures back to 1954 and forward to 1970 are obtained by applying the time distribution indicated by the Department of National Revenue, Taxation income tax statistics series.

Table 6.3. Estimated Equations for Education Expenditures in Metropolitan Toronto

Real expenditure[a]	Constant	Real income	Provincial grants	Dummy	R^2	D.W.
(1) Local education	−136.80	.08[b]	1.15	56.62	.98	1.59
	(− .87)	(1.81)	(2.18)	(3.08)		
(2) Local education	− 10.13	.05[c]	1.36	56.10	.98	1.63
	(− .09)	(1.40)	(2.58)	(2.83)		
(3) Local education	182.54	− .02[d]	2.05	33.54	.98	1.56
	(2.54)	(− .51)	(11.44)	(1.27)		
(4) Total education	−136.87	.08[b]	2.15	56.52	.99	1.59
	(− .87)	(1.81)	(4.07)	(3.08)		
(5) Total education	− 10.18	.05[c]	2.36	56.10	.99	1.63
	(− .09)	(1.40)	(4.47)	(2.83)		
(6) Total education	182.54	− .02[d]	3.05	33.54	.99	1.56
	(2.54)	(− .51)	(17.01)	(1.27)		

[a] Total real education expenditures per pupil minus provincial grants.
[b] Income is defined as income from taxable returns for Toronto (Department of Revenue, Taxation income tax statistics) deflated by the consumer price index for Toronto.
[c] Income series obtained by applying the pattern of income growth between 1961 and 1970, and 1957 and 1961, to the 1961 census wage and salary income.
[d] Assessed valuation of property deflated by an index for housing based on value of multiple listed sales.

the effects of the two variables cannot be separated. To the extent that the coefficient on the provincial grant variable is meaningful, it suggests that the administrative arrangements for grants are such that they are regarded as matching grants. Thus, as provincial grants increase, expenditures from local sources also increase.

In summary, for the metropolitan Toronto area as a whole the expenditure regressions for the police and education functions are consistent with the equalizing-up hypothesis. No significant expenditure increase is noted for police, a function transferred entirely to the metropolitan level ten years before the 1967 consolidation. Significant expenditure increases were obtained for education, which experienced both consolidation and transfer of increased financial power to the metropolitan level. For fire expenditures the results are mixed, with two of the three formulations indicating support for the equalizing-up hypothesis.

The general consistency of the results with the equalizing-up hypothesis suggests support for more detailed analysis of education and fire expenditures by borough.

Borough Expenditures.—The more specific test of the equalizing-up hypothesis is twofold: to estimate the change in expenditures in each borough in 1967 and subsequently, holding the effect of other variables constant, and to relate the size of the expenditure changes thereby

Table 6.4. Total Real Education Operating Expenditures Per Pupil, by Borough

	Constant	Real income per capita	Dummy	R^2	D.W.
North York	—720.65	.23	110.67	.97	.88
	(— 6.81)	(10.62)	(4.50)		
Scarborough	—590.29	.21	64.99	.94	1.51
	(— 5.05)	(8.21)	(2.39)		
Etobicoke	—716.76	.22	121.95	.95	1.39
	(— 4.91)	(7.59)	(3.59)		
East York	—796.73	.28	70.36	.98	1.25
	(— 10.29)	(15.78)	(3.91)		
York	—698.32	.29	143.37	.98	1.27
	(— 9.24)	(14.28)	(8.17)		
Toronto	—981.32	.41	118.92	.98	1.89
	(— 8.94)	(13.33)	(4.66)		

Table 6.5. Real Fire Expenditures Per Capita, by Borough

	Constant	Real income	Population	Dummy	R^2	D.W.
North York	— 7.41	.003	.000002	— .005	.97	2.44
	(— 1.89)	(2.83)	(.44)	(— .02)		
	— 9.04	.003		— .02	.97	2.43
	(— 6.98)	(12.92)		(— .08)		
Scarborough	—14.10	.005	— .00001	.91	.93	2.45
	(— 1.62)	(1.91)	(— .54)	(1.34)		
	— 9.66	.004		1.12	.93	2.37
	(— 3.45)	(6.33)		(2.13)		
Etobicoke	—18.46	—.006	— .00003	.88	.97	2.65
	(— 4.91)	(6.20)	(—3.35)	(2.20)		
	— 7.66	.003		1.43	.94	1.44
	(— 2.84)	(6.13)		(2.82)		
East York	—16.67	.009	— .0002	.02	.97	1.40
	(— 3.80)	(7.39)	(—1.63)	(.05)		
	—22.86	.007		— .40	.97	1.15
	(— 9.63)	(13.41)		(— .90)		
York	—11.06	.01	— .0001	— .13	.98	2.37
	(— 1.81)	(7.82)	(—1.84)	(— .31)		
	—21.66	.008		.24	.98	2.04
	(— 9.74)	(13.32)		(.57)		
Toronto	— 3.13	.009	— .00002	2.42	.97	.73
	(— .13)	(8.53)	(— .55)	(3.51)		
	—16.05	.008		2.41	.97	.78
	(— 4.54)	(8.80)		(3.61)		

obtained to a measure of the 1966 discrepancy in expenditures for municipalities which consolidated in 1967.

Time series regression equations were estimated for each of the six boroughs and school districts over the period 1954-70.[4] Again, the inclusion of a dummy variable permitted a test of the effect of consolidation on expenditures. The coefficients on the dummy variables were then correlated with a weighted expenditure differential. A high positive correlation is consistent with the equalizing-up hypothesis, indicating the greater the preconsolidation expenditure differentials among municipalities later consolidated, the greater the increases in expenditures in that consolidated unit.

Equations estimating per pupil expenditures on education (inclusive of provincial grants) appear in table 6.4. In all equations the coefficients on the dummy variables are significantly different from zero, indicating a significant increase in expenditures beginning in 1967.

Similarly, equations with fire expenditures per capita as the dependent variable are estimated in table 6.5. The equations were estimated with and without population as an independent variable. Only in the borough of Etobicoke does the population variable enter with a coefficient significantly different from zero. Fire expenditures increased significantly following consolidation, as indicated by coefficients significantly different from zero on the dummy variable in the borough of Etobicoke and the city of Toronto.

Since two municipalities (North York and Scarborough) underwent no consolidation in 1967, an additional internal test of the equalizing-up hypothesis is available. To the extent that pressure for equalization is internal to the consolidated unit, one would expect no significant increase in expenditures arising from this source in these two municipalities. In the case of fire expenditures North York did not experience a significant increase in expenditures, while Scarborough approached significance at the 95 percent confidence level when the population variable was dropped. In addition, East York and York experienced no significant increase in expenditures, while Etobicoke and Toronto showed significant increases.

In the case of education all municipalities (including North York and Scarborough) experienced a significant increase in expenditures per pupil. Although not consistent with upward equalization within consolidated units, these results are consistent with an overall increase in expenditures in an effort to equalize at the highest expenditure munici-

4. The eleven school districts prior to 1967 were reduced to six to provide a consistent series.

pality in the metropolitan area.[5] Since both consolidation and transfer of
budgetary power to the metropolitan level occurred simultaneously, there
is no way of assessing in advance whether the budgetary system would
favor the overall upward equalization or equalization within consolidated
units.

The coefficients on the dummy variables obtained above are to be
explained by weighted expenditure differentials computed as follows:
The highest expenditure municipality in the metropolitan area or in the
1967 consolidated unit was identified from tables 6.4 (education) and 6.5
(fire protection) and the difference between its expenditure and that of
the other municipalities computed. These expenditure differentials
were then weighted by pupils in the case of education and population in
the case of fire protection to reflect the relevant population for whom this
expenditure differential must be equalized.

The weights for each school district or municipality were as follows:

$$W_{ij} = \frac{S_{ij}}{S_j},$$

where W_{ij} is the weight for school district i in consolidated unit j, where
$i = 1\text{-}11$, $j = 1\text{-}6$, and for municipality i in consolidated unit j, where
$i = 1\text{-}13$, $j = 1\text{-}6$; S_{ij} is the student population in school district i, consolidated unit j, and the population of municipality i, consolidated unit
j; and S_j is the student population in consolidated unit j, and the
population in consolidated unit j. The weights add to one within a consolidated unit in order to permit comparison with the coefficient on the
dummy variable, which is estimated using consolidated units.

In the case of education, these weights were applied to the difference
in expenditures per pupil between each low expenditure school district
and the highest expenditure school district in its consolidated group and
the highest expenditure school district in the metropolitan area to give
weighted differences in expenditures (tables 6.6 and 6.7). In the case of
fire protection the weights were applied to the difference between the

5. Another possible explanation is that changes in provincial policy affecting all school
expenditures in Ontario took place which were not included in the simple specification of
the regression equation. Extension of the analysis to control municipalities in Ontario
would suggest whether the metropolitan or provincial explanation were more likely.
Unfortunately, however, most school districts in Ontario underwent structural changes
themselves in the late 1960s as part of the provincial government's policy to reduce the
number of school districts.

high and low expenditure municipalities in the consolidated unit (tables 6.8 and 6.9).

These weighted expenditure differentials were then used as an explanatory variable in an equation wherein the dependent variable was the size of the expenditure increase subsequent to consolidation (estimated

Table 6.6. Operating Expenditures on Education by Municipality, 1966 and 1967

1966		1967	
Toronto	$710.00 ⎫		
Forest Hill	806.00 ⎬	Toronto	$873.00
Swansea	602.00 ⎭		
Etobicoke	591.00 ⎫		
Lakeshore	627.00 ⎭	Etobicoke	699.00
East York	580.00 ⎫		
Leaside	755.00 ⎭	East York	725.00
York	543.00 ⎫		
Weston	551.00 ⎭	York	704.00
North York	578.00	North York	704.00
Scarborough	520.00	Scarborough	610.00

Table 6.7. Calculation of Weighted Expenditure Differential for Education

	Expenditure differential				Weighted expenditure differential	
	Method 1[a]	Method 2[b]	Weight		Method 1[a]	Method 2[b]
Toronto	96.00	96.00	.96430 ⎫			
Forest Hill	.00	.00	.02795 ⎬ Toronto		94.15	94.15
Swansea	204.00	204.00	.00773 ⎭			
Etobicoke	36.00	215.00	.87980 ⎫ Etobicoke		31.67	210.68
Lakeshore	.00	179.00	.12020 ⎭			
East York	175.00	226.00	.76236 ⎫ East York		133.41	184.41
Leaside	.00	51.00	.23764 ⎭			
York	8.00	263.00	.88267 ⎫ York		7.06	262.06
Weston	.00	255.00	.11733 ⎭			
North York	.00	228.00	1.00000	North York	.00	228.00
Scarborough	.00	286.00	1.00000	Scarborough	.00	286.00

[a] Difference between expenditure in each municipality and expenditure of the highest expenditure municipality in the consolidated unit.

[b] Difference between expenditure in each municipality and expenditure of the highest expenditure municipality in the metropolitan area.

Table 6.8. Operating Expenditures on Fire by Municipality, 1966 and 1967

1966			1967	
Toronto	$18.95	⎫		
Forest Hill	14.23	⎬	Toronto	$22.77
Swansea	6.79	⎭		
Etobicoke	11.30	⎫		
Mimico	7.67	⎪		
New Toronto	18.28	⎬	Etobicoke	12.44
Long Branch	9.34	⎭		
East York	10.27	⎫		
Leaside	18.89	⎭	East York	13.31
York	10.87	⎫		
Weston	16.21	⎭	York	11.70
North York	9.85		North York	11.06
Scarborough	10.98		Scarborough	12.01

Table 6.9. Calculation of Weighted Expenditure Differential for Fire

	Expenditure differential[a]	Weight		Weighted expenditure differential
Toronto	.00	.95230 ⎫		
Forest Hill	4.72	.3384 ⎬	Toronto	.33
Swansea	12.16	.1386 ⎭		
Etobicoke	6.98	.83254 ⎫		
Mimico	10.61	.7242 ⎪		
New Toronto	.00	.4686 ⎬	Etobicoke	7.01
Long Branch	8.94	.4818 ⎭		
East York	8.62	.77680 ⎫		
Leaside	.00	.22320 ⎭	East York	6.70
York	5.34	.92113 ⎫		
Weston	.00	.7887 ⎭	York	4.92
North York	.00	1.00000	North York	.00
Scarborough	.00	1.00000	Scarborough	.00

[a] Difference between expenditure in each municipality and expenditure of the highest expenditure municipality in the consolidated unit.

by the coefficient on the dummy variable). Both expenditure differentials between each municipality and that of the highest expenditure municipality (school district) in the consolidated unit and expenditure differentials from the highest expenditure municipality (school district) in the metropolitan area were used.

Table 6.10. Selected Expenditure Increases Related to Preconsolidation Expenditure Differentials

Coefficient on dummy variable	Constant	Weighted expenditure differential	R^2	D.W.
(1) Education	112.09	—.155	.079	1.68
	(6.25)	(—.59)		
(2) Education	121.55	—.077	.029	2.61
	(2.45)	(—.34)		
(3) Fire[a]	1.03	—.099	.13	.64
	(1.80)	(—.77)		

[a] The dummy variable is taken from the equation which included population as an explanatory variable.

The results presented in table 6.10 indicate that the coefficient on the weighted expenditure differential is not significantly different from zero for either education or fire protection. We must, therefore, conclude that the results of this test do not support the hypothesis that the greater the differences in preconsolidation level of expenditures among school district or municipalities later to consolidate, the greater the post-consolidation increase in expenditures.

Conclusion.—This cross-section formulation provides a severe test of the hypothesis and is not inconsistent with equalizing-up within each unit. The expenditure analysis shows a significant increase in expenditures in Toronto. Our test of equalizing-up requires that the expenditure increases relate positively *on a cross-section basis* to the observed expenditure differentials. Thus, although the evidence does not support equalizing-up according to this strong test we cannot reject the possibility that some equalizing-up occurred. The evidence does, however, indicate that expenditures on fire and education, functions affected by consolidation, increased, while expenditures on police, a function unaffected by consolidation, did not increase subsequent to reorganization.

External Determinants

We now examine the effect of the external change involving transfer of the budgetary responsibility and revenue raising almost entirely to the metropolitan level. Consolidation and transfer of increased budgetary power to the metropolitan level has the potential to alter the burden and benefits of metropolitan government in such a way as to redistribute income in the metropolitan area and/or alter the tax price of public services to the boroughs.

The existence of a tax-price effect would require that the behavior of the municipality at the margin could affect its receipts from the metropolitan government. The formula for distributing metropolitan-level expenditures were based on parameters which could not readily be altered by the municipalities. In addition, since metropolitan decisions are made by officials elected at the local level, one must establish that decisions at the metropolitan level are not influenced by previous decisions at the local level in such a way that a tax-price effect is implicit in the formula chosen for disbursing metropolitan funds. For example, if by raising expenditures and its borough tax rate for education a municipality could affect the favor with which it was regarded at the metropolitan level and thereby affect its funds, a tax-price effect is possible. In fact, however, the only flexibility exercised at the metropolitan level over the period being analyzed was to alter the formula, leaving little flexibility for an indirect tax-price effect.

Throughout the period the metropolitan expenditures in a borough may have been greater, less than, or equal to the revenue raised by the borough for metropolitan purposes. More precisely, this net subsidy resulting from the operation of metropolitan government is the expenditures accruing to the municipality from the metropolitan level minus the revenues raised from the borough.

Analysis here attempts to explain total expenditures on education by borough in terms of a number of variables, one of which is net subsidy from metropolitan government for educational purposes. Ideally, of course, the explanatory variable should be net subsidy from the operation of metropolitan government with respect to all services. That is, the net overall subsidy, positive or negative, should be included as an explanatory variable in the equation for each public service expenditure. Since that net figure requires the attribution of all metropolitan public service expenditures by borough where the margin of error may be very high, the procedure was not followed.

Partial support for the use of the net subsidy from metropolitan government through education can be given on two grounds. First, there are separate education and general levies at the metropolitan level. Furthermore, the Metropolitan Council in this period was effectively a rubber stamp, accepting but not altering the budget of the Metropolitan School Board. This independence between the decision-making unit responsible for education and for other public services would provide partial support for the use of the net redistributive effect of metropolitan government in education as an explanatory variable in an equation explaining education expenditures.

An alternative assumption, which is difficult to evaluate, is that the total net redistributive effect of metropolitan government by borough is proportional to the net redistributive effect through education alone.

The purpose of the analysis is to examine whether the income redistribution caused by the 1967 consolidation affected total expenditures on education. Analysis was done using boroughs as units of observation. The municipalities combined to form boroughs in 1967 were aggregated prior to 1967 to form comparable units. The dependent variable was total expenditures on education per pupil. Regression equations were estimated for each borough, using data from 1954 to 1968. The basic equation estimated real expenditures on education per pupil as a function of real income, per pupil (per capita); the price of education relative to all other services; and the price of reorganization, represented by a dummy variable (value 0 prior to 1967 and value 1 for 1967 and subsequently).

The coefficient on the dummy variable is significantly different from zero in the income per capita formulations in five of the six boroughs. The second set of equations dropped the dummy variable and replaced it with the net subsidy. The net subsidy variable enters with a coefficient significantly different from zero in four of the six municipalities. In three of the four cases the subsidy has a positive sign. Expenditures respond positively to this easing of the budget constraint.

More specifically, the internal redistribution, exclusive of the effect of provincial grants, resulted in municipalities receiving positive subsidies increasing their expenditures in response and those receiving negative subsidies not altering their expenditures. The net effect was consequently to increase expenditures on the part of all municipalities combined. The same analysis, including the effect of provincial grants, provided an offsetting effect in the case of Toronto, which responded negatively to its negative subsidy. Thus as the negative subsidy increased, Toronto expenditures declined. This effect of the increase of expenditures in the other municipalities outweighed the expenditure reduction in the case of Toronto, giving rise to confirmation of the prediction that internal redistribution results in expenditure increases.

In the third set of equations the dummy variable and the net subsidy variable were both included. The purpose was to see if the specific variable (net subsidy) which could have been altered by reorganization would replace the dummy variable as an explanation of expenditures. In all five municipalities with a coefficient significantly different from zero on the dummy variable the significance of the dummy variable was reduced when the net subsidy variable was added. In three of the five

Table 6.11. Changes in Residential Property Value Attributable to 1967 Consolidation

East York		Toronto	
East York	$3,068	Toronto	$10,370
	(6.39)		(1.95)
Leaside	$ 460	Forest Hill	$13,430
	(.21)		(1.63)

cases the coefficient on the dummy variable was no longer significantly different from zero.

Redistributive Effects of 1967 Consolidation

The existence of a redistributive effect resulting from the consolidation of units within the metropolitan structure was established in the previous section. This section presents estimates of the extent to which capitalization of these fiscal transfers took place.[6]

To determine the degree of capitalization of fiscal transfer, a sample of real estate transactions was taken from four jurisdictions (prior to 1967) which formed two jurisdictions following 1967 (see Cook and Hamilton, 1974). The change in property values resulting from the 1967 consolidation was estimated after excluding the effect of other major determinants of real estate values through use of a hedonic price index.

Mixed results were obtained from the two samples used. The East York-Leaside results were both predictable and understandable, while the Toronto-Forest Hill results exhibited extreme property value increases. Since it is assumed that these results are due to the very small sample size, they should be reestimated when a larger sample is collected. Table 6.11 shows the changes in residential property values attributable to 1967 consolidation. These are the coefficients obtained on a dummy variable having value 0 prior to 1967 and 1 in 1967 and afterwards. Relative property values changed by $3,528 in the East York-Leaside case and $3,060 in the Toronto-Forest Hill case.

To interpret these results estimates of the fiscal transfer which occurred in 1967 are required. It is assumed here that the fiscal transfer results from the consolidation of tax bases of two formerly autonomous political units. Estimates of the resulting tax base changes are the actual

6. It should be noted that estimates of fiscal transfers used in this section do not correspond precisely to those used in the previous section. Estimates here are based on transfers through the tax side alone while in the previous section both the expenditure and revenue sides were included.

tax base per capita in 1966 minus the tax base per capita of consolidation having taken place in 1966. The net result on a per household basis is that East York gained $78.50, while Leaside lost $286.00; Toronto gained $4, and Forest Hill lost $33.56.

These figures, along with assumptions concerning discount rates, provide us with some indication of the extent of short-run capitalization. In this case the observed increase in East York property values relative to Leaside is consistent with full capitalization of the transfer at a discount rate of 10 percent. The results in the city of Toronto and Forest Hill are unreasonable, resulting from the particular nature of a very small sample. Although unsatisfactory at this stage, the most that can be said is that there is presumptive evidence that short-run capitalization of the transfers took place. This evidence suggests that the property owners at the time of the consolidation (or more correctly at the time the effect of consolidation was discounted) bore the effects of redistribution. The extent to which the effects were passed on to residents thereafter depends on the nature of long-run supply responses.

Conclusions

Conclusions from the research undertaken on metropolitan reorganization in Toronto are of both a methodological and substantive nature. The preceding discussion has illustrated that generalizations cannot be made about the performance of metropolitan government or the changes that can be expected from political reorganization. The institutional context within which reorganization takes place, including such considerations as the nature of intermunicipal agreements and the role of senior levels of government, will determine the effectiveness of the old and new structures and the changes to be expected after transition. The particular constitution will determine those considerations given priority, which in turn will affect budgetary patterns.

Substantively, research based on both the 1954 federation and the 1967 consolidation indicates that significant increases occurred in the expenditures of functions affected by reorganization, resulting in a redistribution of income in the metropolitan area. Those services not affected by reorganization did not experience this expenditure increase. For one of two samples, estimates of fiscal transfers arising from the 1967 consolidation are consistent with full capitalization of the transfers at a discount rate of 10 percent. The time period over which these capitalized effects are sustained because of lack of supply responses awaits the data from subsequent years.

References

Cook, Gail C. A. 1973a. "Metropolitan Government: The Significance of Context and Form." In *Proceedings of the Conference on Urban Economics,* ed. John M. Mattila and Wilbur R. Thompson. Detroit: Wayne State University.

Cook, Gail C. A. 1973b. "The Effect of Metropolitan Government on Resource Allocation: The Case of Education in Toronto." *National Tax Journal* 26, no. 4.

Cook, Gail C. A., and Bruce W. Hamilton. 1974. "Distributional Effect of the Reorganization of Local Governments." Paper presented at the Eastern Economic Association Convention, State University of New York, Albany, N.Y.

Metropolitan Toronto Council. 1963. *Metropolitan Toronto 1953-1963: 10 Years of Progress.* Toronto: The council.

Ontario Department of Economics. 1961. *A Report on the Metropolitan Toronto System of Government.* Prepared for the Special Committee of the Metropolitan Council on Metropolitan Affairs. Toronto: The department.

7 *Roy W. Bahl*

Urban Property Taxation
in Less Developed Countries:
Fiscal and Growth Management Dimensions

Introduction

Taxes on property are the single most important source of locally raised revenue for urban governments in less developed countries and play a major role in guiding and financing urban expansion. Moreover, since central governments have generally preempted the sales and income tax bases, and since urban government expenditure needs and urban expansion requirements continue to press, it seems likely that the role of urban property taxes will become even more important. This increased use of property taxation will result mostly from discretionary actions by local governments, and therefore will lead to further modifications in the property tax structure, which will in turn affect the elasticity, equity, and allocative features of the tax. The presumption of this essay is that such modifications are, at best, made on a basis of a priori reasoning and with little knowledge of the experience other cities have had with such changes. I hope to take a step toward filling this gap by descriptively comparing the property tax structure and performance of a selected group of large city governments in less developed countries.

Generally, the focus here is on the compatability of the revenue-growth, distributional, and urban development-management features of taxes on urban property in less developed countries. The specific concerns in this essay are a comparison of alternative systems of general urban property taxation, a description of the use of taxes on property to guide urban expansion and to affect urban renewal, and a general statement of the considerations necessary to evaluate the equity, elasticity, and allocative effects of alternative systems.

The first of these issues is descriptive, its object being to provide a cross-section of the property tax structures presently in use. Existing surveys of urban property taxation in less developed countries tend to focus on country practices (for good examples of country surveys, see Yoingco, 1971; and Lent, 1974), thereby ignoring wide variations among cities within a country in the specifics of the tax. For example, the systems in Bogotá and Cartagena, Colombia, are markedly different, and each possesses unique and possibly transferable features. A general description of property tax practices in Colombia would miss these features. Particularly for policy purposes, it is important to identify the full range of possibilities so as to suggest what alternative structural reforms in present systems are feasible.

Yet another reason for detailed description is the need to develop a set of norms against which to evaluate the performance of any given system, that is, to develop a basis for estimating "average" effective rates, levels of assessed value, property tax revenue growth rates, tax burdens, and so on. Country surveys, while providing useful general description, do not enable the development of such norms. The usefulness of comparative norms for tax policy purposes has been debated in the literature, but the comparative experience continues to be used in tax reform analyses.[1] In theory, desired levels of assessed value, for example, should be determined normatively for any given city in the context of what the property tax is intended to accomplish, but in practice comparative "norms" are more likely to be persuasive evidence. This is a result of the absence of a useful model (and/or data) to estimate the equity and allocative effects of the property tax and of the fact that policy makers tend to view the feasibility of any particular discretionary action in terms of what is done elsewhere. In short, comparative description will fill an important gap in knowledge about the structure and performance of urban property taxation in less developed countries.

The second aim of this essay is to explore the implications of these various property tax structures for urban renewal—particularly for the maintenance/reinvestment decision of homeowners and for the holding of vacant land from the market. The hypothesis here is that cities have adopted a wide variety of approaches to using taxes on property to induce renewal but have contradictory, offsetting features elsewhere in

1. One such area is the comparison of tax effort to establish "average" levels of taxation. See, for example, Bahl (1971), Chelliah (1971), and Manvel (1971).

the tax structure. The third concern of this analysis is with the manner in which property taxes have been used to guide and finance urban expansion. The focus here is on innovative uses of the property tax and on the compatibility of the revenue-raising goals of the tax with its intended allocative and distributional effects. The fourth goal of this study is to make some rough evaluation of the elasticity, equity, and allocative effects of various property tax forms.

Comparative analysis, such as that proposed here, requires detailed description and annotated data which can only be assembled by means of detailed case study. The case study cities were chosen on a basis of geographic and cultural diversity and population size. Detailed studies have been carried out for Cartagena and Bogotá, Colombia; Manila City, Philippines; Lusaka, Zambia; Jakarta, Indonesia; Bombay and Ahmedabad, India; Seoul, Korea; and Tunis. Additional data have been gathered for Calcutta, Singapore, and Hong Kong, and these are presented on a selected basis at certain points in the analysis.[2]

To give some perspective to the claim of the importance of urban property taxes in less developed countries, it would seem to be worth examining the relative dependence of these local governments on property tax financing. From national statistics, the property tax would appear to be of little revenue importance in less developed countries. Chelliah (1971) reported the average ratio of property tax revenues to income among fifty-two developing countries to be less than one percent.

This implied unimportance is misleading for at least two reasons. First, most property taxes are collected by local governments and may not be fully included and/or classified as property taxes in the national accounts. For example, various forms of land development taxes are not typically classified by the central government—or even by the local government—as taxes on property. Second, and perhaps even more important, while the property tax may not be a major source of revenue for central governments, it is clearly a major source of revenue for local governments. Even when land development taxes are excluded, annual taxes on the assessed value of property account for a significant proportion of total local government financing (see table 7.1). The proportion of total expenditures (current plus capital) financed with the property tax is between 10 and 20 percent for most of the cities studied here, implying that major variations in the property tax could have measurable distribution and service level effects.

2. These case study results are drawn from a larger research project on Urban Public Finances in developing countries for the Urban and Regional Economics division of the World Bank. The studies are listed in the sources to table 7.1 and are not repeated below.

Table 7.1. The Importance of Property Tax Revenues in Local Government Finances

Cities		Property tax revenues as a percentage of total expenditures	Population[a]	Per capita income (in $)
Cartagena	(1972)	12%	357,668 (5.0)	$ 254
Bogotá	(1971)	6	2,849,400 (5.3)	518
Manila	(1972)	41	1,330,000 (N.A.)	422
Lusaka	(1972)	17	347,900 (13.7)	148
Jakarta	(1973)	12	4,200,000 (6.7)	160
Bombay	(1971)	19	5,971,000 (3.7)	256
Ahmedabad	(1972)	18	1,588,379 (2.8)	80
Seoul	(1971)	6	5,850,925 (9.1)	434
Singapore	(1968)	12	1,990,000 (2.2)	697
Hong Kong	(1973)	N.A.	4,266,000 (2.0)	1,177
Tunis	(1971)	58	538,000 (4.0)	222
New York City	(1972)	29	11,575,740[c]	5,900
Chicago[b]	(1972)	55	6,978,733[c]	5,191

Sources: *Cartagena:* Johannes Linn, "Urban Public Finances in Cartagena," Urban Public Finance Project, mimeographed (Washington, D.C.: Urban and Regional Economics Division, IBRD, 1974); *Bogotá:* Johannes Linn, "Urban Public Finances in Bogotá, Colombia," Urban Public Finance Project; *Manila:* Roy W. Bahl, "Metropolitan Financial Administration and Structure," Manila Urban Survey Mission Report, mimeographed (Washington, D.C.: Urban and Regional Economics Division, IBRD, 1974); Pamela Brigg, "Local Government Structure and Finance," Manila Urban Survey Mission Report, mimeographed (Washington, D.C.: Urban and Regional Economics Division, IBRD, 1973); *Lusaka:* Robert J. Saunders, "A Survey of the Public Finances of Lusaka, Zambia with Special Reference to a Proposed Sites and Services and Squatter Upgrading Projects," mimeographed (Washington, D.C.: IBRD, 1973); *Jakarta:* Johannes Linn, "Urban Public Finances in Jakarta," Urban Public Finance Project; Dietrich Lerche, "The Revenue Potential of the Land Tax for Urban Finance in Indonesia" (paper presented at a conference on land use and land taxation in Asia, Singapore, 1974); *Bombay:* Francine Bougeoun, "Urban Public Finances in Bombay, India," Urban Public Finance Project; Roy W. Bahl, "Urban Public Finance and the Efficiency of Urban Development in Bombay," Bombay Urban Survey, mimeographed (Washington, D.C.: Urban Projects Department, IBRD, 1971); *Ahmedabad:* Roy W. Bahl, "Urban Public Finances in Ahmedabad," Urban Public Finance Project; *Seoul:* Roy W. Bahl and Michael J. Wasylenko, "Urban Public Finances in Seoul, Korea," Urban Public Finance Project; *Hong Kong: Annual Departmental Report by the Commissioner of Rating and Valuation for 1972-1973* (Hong Kong, 1973); *Tunis:* Remy Prudhomme, "Urban Public Service in Tunis," Urban Public Finance Project; *New York and Chicago:* U.S. Bureau of the Census, *City Government Finances in 1972,* series GF75, no. 4 (Washington, D.C.: U.S. Government Printing Office, 1976).

[a] Figures in parentheses are average annual growth rates of population, over a period which varies from five to eight years.

[b] Composed of overlapping local governments in the metropolitan area.

[c] 1970 statistics.

Pressures on urban governments will probably lead to an increasing reliance on property taxation in large cities in developing countries.[3] Moreover, the United States example would suggest an increasing local government reliance on the property tax as development and urbanization proceed. Compare, for example, the level of reliance on property taxation in the urban areas of less developed counties with that in New York and Chicago (see table 7.1). Many of the same factors which drove American urban governments to increased use of property taxation are present in the less developed country case: higher levels of government preempting the sales and income tax bases and leaving local governments with major expenditure responsibilities; a heavy population migration to urban areas, leading to increased public service financing requirements; and increasing concentrations of the poor, who typically have less taxpaying ability than public expenditure needs.

Comparison of Property Tax Systems

In theory the property tax base may be seen as either annual rental value or capital value, with the latter including land or improvements or both. In practice, however, the number of different tax structure possibilities is considerably greater because of wide variations in assessment practices. These variations are illustrated in the following discussion of assessment practices and rate structures. Attention is then turned to the development of comparative norms for property tax systems.

Tax Base and Assessment Practices

The property tax base for residential property in the case of countries using an annual value system is "expected" or notional rents. The English courts have described the narrowness of this rent concept (see Paddington, 1965, p. 993; and Copes, 1970, p. 65):

The rent prescribed by the statute is a hypothetical rent, as hypothetical as the tenant. It is the rent which an imaginary tenant might be reasonably expected to pay to an imaginary landlord for the tenancy of this dwelling in this locality, on the hypothesis that both are reasonable people, the landlord not being extortionate, the tenant not being under pressure, the dwelling being vacant and to let, not subject to any control, the landlord agreeing to do the repairs, and pay the insurance, the tenant agreeing to pay the rates, the period not too short nor yet too long, simply from year to year. I do not suppose that throughout the length and breadth of Paddington you could find a rent corresponding to this imaginary rent.

3. For a discussion of urban fiscal problems in developing countries, see Smith (1974) and Smith and Smith (1971).

Among countries using the annual value basis, there are wide differences in assessment techniques. In Singapore an average rent is estimated for an area—block or neighborhood—and a given type of structure, and this average is taken as the assessment of annual value for all similar properties in the area. If actual rents paid vary about this mean, the residuals are ignored on the grounds that the proper assessment is on reasonably expected annual rent and that an arithmetic average best approximates the norm. A similar approach to valuing residential property is taken in the Indian cities of Bombay and Ahmedabad. In Ahmedabad, however, owner-occupied residential properties are assessed on yet a different basis—a formula basis which determines rental value per square meter and, it is argued, results in a preferential assessment of owner-occupied properties. Among the important considerations in the formula assessment of owner-occupied dwellings are the location of the property within the city, the specific amenities of the property, construction material, ventilation, and carpet area. While there are graduated assessment rates depending on these considerations, the judgment of the assessor plays a major role. In Bombay, while there is no differentiation between owner-occupied and rented properties, properties included under a 1948 rent control ordinance are assessed at the controlled rent amount (Mohan, 1974). Finally, it should be noted that only Bombay among these three cities permits a reduction (10 percent) in assessed value to compensate for the cost of repairs and insurance.

There are similar variations in residential property assessment practices among the cities in this sample which use a capital value basis for assessment. The extremes are Jakarta and Cartagena, which use a formula basis for assessment, and Seoul, which uses a great deal of judgmental valuation evidence. In Jakarta, properties are classified according to land use (actual and zoned), zone location, and condition of adjacent roads and streets. An assessed value per square meter of land for each of these cross-classifications is read from a table which serves as a kind of tabular assessment manual. The land values included in this table are not derived from any current land value information nor is the assessment table updated. Hence, the growth in assessed value is almost exclusively from additions of new properties to the tax rolls.

A formula assessment method is also used in Cartagena, but differs from the Jakarta system in that it employs current property value data and in that both land and improvements are assessed. In this approach a "key" value is identified via comparative sales analysis (by examination of sales records *and* realtor opinions) in each of some six hundred "neighborhood" areas. These key values are then linked with a set of isovalue lines and assessed values for all remaining properties are interpolated. This assessment method is centrally administered through the Augustin Codazzi Institute in Bogotá.

In the cases of Seoul and Manila, land and improvements are assessed separately. In Seoul, land values are assessed by using realtor estimates for each of seventy land "classes" in some three hundred neighborhood areas. Improvements are valued by formula: first, properties are grouped into eight classes according to roof and wall materials and second, a current construction cost is estimated for each. In Manila, land values are assessed as a residual. Property values are first estimated on a basis of comparative sales, and improvement value on the basis of a construction cost formula.

These approaches to valuation are sufficiently different that one would not expect them to result in comparable levels of assessed value even if applied to the same tax base. Hence, one might argue that there are as many property tax systems as there are cities and that explanation of intercity variations in the equity, elasticity, and allocative performance of

Table 7.2. Statutory Rate Structures in Selected Cities Using Annual Value Systems

Annual value ($)	Rate	Comments
Ahmedabad		
0–67	.175	
68–133	.235	
134–400	.325	
401–667	.395	
over 667	.425	
Bangkok	.1259–.13	Improvements are taxed only if structure is rented or used for commercial purposes.
Bombay		
0–75	.352	Includes both the city rate and the state education
75–299	.402	cess; this rate is for central area, lower rates are in
over 299	.415	effect in outer suburbs.
Calcutta		
0–133	.155	Rate reduced to 0.083 percent in unserviced areas
134–400	.185	and 0.065 percent if water supply not provided.
401–1,600	.225	
1,601–2,000	.275	
over 2,000	.335	
Karachi (1971)		
0–385	.125	Includes municipal and provincial rates.
386–3,850	.150	
over 3,850	.200	
Singapore	.36	General rate in the central area; rates vary by location and are as low as 0.12 percent in some areas.

Sources: See Table 7.1.

Table 7.3. Statutory Rate Structures for Selected Capital Value Systems

City	Assessed value class ($)	Land	Improve-ments	Total tax rate	Comments
Bogotá				.1520	Includes general rate, CAR rate, and refuse collection rate.
Cartagena	25			.0084	Selected levels of assessed value.
	152			.0175	
	381			.0140	
	1,776			.0135	
	4,568			.0127	
	8,121			.0130	
	25,380			.0125	
	45,685			.0126	
	76,142			.0124	
	91,370			.0121	
Jakarta		.003			Improvements taxed only for industrial and commercial properties.
Kingston	0–167			.045	
	168–333			.049	Kingston Parish only.
	334–500			.053	
	501–833			.053	
	834–1,667			.060	
	1,668–4,167			.084	
	4,168–8,333			.103	
	8,334–16,667			.107	
	over 16,668			.113	
Lusaka		.03	.0085		
Manila City				.03	
Nairobi		.0375	0		By 1975 the rate had been increased to 5.75 percent.
Seoul		.02	.04		There is also a surcharge on the property tax on improvements which varies from 20 to 80 percent depending on value class.

Sources: See table 7.1.

various systems may have to rest, at least partially, on variations in assessment practices.

Tax Rates

Urban governments in LDCs have chosen broad differences in rate structure and therefore have effected differences in the level of revenues, the elasticity of the system, the distribution of tax burdens, and the incentives to own, maintain, and locate housing. There are five basic patterns for statutory rate schedules: a single proportional rate applied to all properties, a rate which is graduated by assessed value class of the base, a rate which is different for land versus improvements, a rate which differs by location in the city, and a rate which differentiates between renters and owner-occupiers. Most cities have developed tax structures which combine two or more of these features.

As may be seen from the data in tables 7.2 and 7.3 there are wide variations in the type of rate structure applied. Bombay, Singapore, and

Hong Kong follow a practice of differentiating among areas within the city by charging a lower property tax rate in the areas where public services are thought to be the poorest, for example, the outermost suburbs or rural areas. It would appear that such a practice results in double counting in that lower service levels should already be reflected in lower rental values and hence lower assessments. To the extent the property tax is large enough to have a measurable effect on location decisions, such a practice will induce a decentralization of the pattern of urban residential settlements.

In the subcontinent cities and in Cartagena and Kingston, the rate structures are graduated by assessed value class in order to build a greater degree of tax burden equity (in an ability-to-pay sense) into the property tax system. But these piecemeal practices may do less to improve system equity than it would appear. For example, in the case of Ahmedabad higher income owner-occupiers are given a preferential assessment which effectively increases the overall regressivity of the system and then are subjected to a differentially higher property tax rate which reduces the overall regressivity of the system. Overall, it is not clear how the goal of equity is served under such a system. There is evidence in the other cities as well of assessment bias which favors higher income homeowners.

Lusaka, Seoul, and Manila tax land and improvements at different rates, but Seoul and Manila tax some improvements more heavily, while Lusaka taxes land more heavily. This, in theory, suggests that the pattern in Seoul and Manila is one of discouraging the optimal allocation of land use.

It would appear that local governments attempt to make rate structure adjustments for both equity and allocative effects, but it does not appear that these adjustments are made so as to conform with assessment practices. Because of this, the total distributional effects of the property tax cannot be properly evaluated by separate reference to rate or assessment adjustments. The kinds of partial analysis inferences drawn here must be viewed in terms of this limitation.

Property Tax Norms

It would be difficult to identify an "average" or "normal" level of performance of the property tax for urban governments in LDCs—there is no single comparable compilation of these data. On a basis of the data gathered in these case studies, however, some very crude comparisons might be made. The level of the property tax base, assessed value adjusted for income level, varies substantially among the cities which use a capital value basis of assessment. From these limited data a normal assessed value would appear to be roughly an amount equivalent to two times the level of per capita income (see table 7.4). On this basis the Colombian cities show a relatively low level of assessed value, while Manila and Lusaka have relatively high levels of assessed property values. These differences in the assessed value—income ratio (V/Y)—are translated into a rough measure of property tax effort, that is, the product of property taxes as a percentage of income (T/Y) and the effective tax rate (T/V). Since the pattern of effective tax rates are similar—Manila and Lusaka are highest—the differences in tax effort

Table 7.4. Comparative Levels of Property Tax Effort

City		Per capita total property taxes	Per capita assessed value	Assessed value as a percentage of income	Taxes as a percentage of assessed value	Property taxes as a percentage of income
Cartagena	(1972)	$ 2.76	$ 518	204.0%	0.5%	1.0%
Manila City	(1972)	14.20	1,276	246.3	1.1	3.4
Lusaka	(1972)	9.60	845	570.9	1.1	6.4
Bogotá	(1971)	3.49	653	126.0	.5	.7
Seoul	(1971)	2.20	840	193.5	.3	.5
Bombay	(1971)	4.80	18	6.8	27.4	1.9
Singapore	(1968)	14.30	32	4.6	44.4	2.1
Hong Kong	(1973)	15.20	131	11.1	11.6	1.3
Tunis	(1971)	10.00	143	64.4	6.9	4.5
Calcutta	(1971)	5.73	14	8.0	40.9	3.3
Ahmedabad	(1972)	3.75	15	18.7	24.9	4.7

Sources: See Table 7.1.

Table 7.5. Comparisons of Assessed Value–Income Ratios among Annual Value and Capital Value Systems

	If the percentage of rental value to capital value was 5.0, the percentage of capital assessed value to income would be	If the percentage of rental value to capital value was 2.0, the percentage of capital assessed value to income would be	Rental to capital value percentage necessary for percentage of capital assessed value to income to be 200
Bombay	136%	340%	3.4%
Singapore	92	230	2.3
Hong Kong	222	555	5.5
Tunis	1288	3220	32.2
Calcutta	159	398	3.9
Ahmedabad	374	935	9.3
Cartagena	204		
Manila	246		
Lusaka	571		
Bogotá	126		
Seoul	194		

Sources: See Table 7.1.

are proportionately greater than that in the assessment income ratio. This particular result suggests a negative relationship between city personal income levels and city property tax effort.

As among the cities using a comparable rental value system the assessment level in Ahmedabad appears relatively high, though with the variation observed a norm is difficult to identify. A similar pattern of variation is observed for the distribution of effective rates; hence it is difficult to develop any notion of "normal" tax effort.

From the data in table 7.4 it is not possible to compare the relative assessment levels between cities using capital and annual value systems. In order to make such a comparison we have assumed, alternatively, annual value/capital value ratios of 5 and 2 percent. The result from using this assumption (see table 7.5) shows that the annual value system assessment levels are roughly comparable to the capital value systems at a rate of 5 percent. A comparison of the eleven cities observed here on this basis does not show any systematic relationship between assessed value and income. An alternative comparison involves solving for that annual/capital value percentage which just equates any city's annual value/income percentage with two hundred, the approximate average of the capital value cities. These results suggest relatively low levels of assessment in Bombay, Calcutta, and Singapore.

The growth in the property tax base and in property tax revenues has varied markedly among these cities, and a "normal" rate is difficult to identify (see table 7.6). These data indicate, however, that both total property tax revenues and assessed values grew at a higher rate in

Table 7.6. Growth in Property Tax Revenues and Property Tax Base

	Annual rates of increase[a]			Population Elasticity[b]			
				Property tax revenues		Assessed value	
	Property tax revenues	Assessed value	Prices	Actual	Real	Actual	Real
Cartagena	16.5	22.5	9.0	3.3	1.4	4.4	2.5
Lusaka	16.3	14.8	6.8	1.2	.6	1.1	.5
Bogotá	13.2	19.4	9.0	2.5	.7	3.7	1.8
Seoul	38.0	31.0	12.0[c]	4.2	2.5	3.4	1.9
Bombay	8.0	7.2	7.1	2.2	.2	1.9	.02
Singapore	10.8	9.1	1.0	4.9	4.4	4.1	3.6
Hong Kong	6.9	18.7	1.8	3.4	2.5	9.4	8.3
Tunis	4.8	6.8	3.6	1.2	.3	1.7	.8
Calcutta	4.5	4.0	7.1	6.4	−3.4	5.7	−4.1
Ahmedabad	5.6	6.7	5.5[c]	2.0	.04	2.4	.4

[a] The number is the annual increase in prices for the country in which the city is located from 1964 to 1970. See *International Financial Statistics* 24, no. 6 (June 1971).

[b] Percentage increase in property tax revenues per one percent increase in population.

[c] Actual rate of inflation in the city.

countries using the capital value system than in countries using the annual value system. Only in about half the cities was there an increase in the intensity of property taxation, that is, in the effective rate. When these data are adjusted for population and price levels changes, the pattern of increase becomes less clear. The population elasticity of real property tax revenue growth exceeds unity only in Cartagena, Seoul, Singapore, and Hong Kong. Since there were increases in real per capita income in all of these countries, and since the revenue increases presented here include discretionary changes, it would appear that the income elasticity of the property tax in these cities is generally below unity.

Urban Renewal and Urban Sprawl

Features have been built into the system of property taxation in these cities which affect the renewal and maintenance decisions of private owners and developers. With scarce public sector resources to be devoted to the renewal problem, there is a premium on using tax policy to induce private sector housing investment. Urban governments in less developed countries have approached this issue of how to encourage (or at least not discourage) investment in housing with property taxation in two ways: (1) by employing marginal adjustments in the property tax rate structure and/or assessment practices, and (2) by the institution of specific property tax coercive measures.

Marginal Rate or Base Changes

Several cities have instituted rate or base adjustments either to stimulate private investment in construction/maintenance/repair of buildings or to improve the overall use of land by penalizing the speculation in idle land. Various forms of preferential tax rates or preferential assessments for lower valued homes (Ahmedabad), or for owner-occupiers (Singapore), are used, and Bombay permits a 10 percent reduction in gross rateable value for repairs and insurance. Such forms of property tax relief, while they may encourage homeownership and thus, housing investment, do not provide any direct incentives for housing renovation but rather have only an income effect on the property tax payee. On the other hand, Singapore assesses certain vacated plots and plots containing vacated structures at 5 percent of capital value—over twice the rate ordinarily applied. This higher rate is in some cases applied to occupied properties of unusually low land intensities; if a factory, for example, occupies more land than seems warranted (by the assessor), the "excess" land may be considered vacant and assessed at 5 percent of capital value.

Finally, there are the perverse systems wherein improvements are assessed at a higher rate than land, and therefore optimal uses of land are discouraged. Examples of this are Seoul's property tax rate structure and the assessment of certain vacant properties at lower rates in Bombay. In such cases, housing investment—if accompanied by reassessment—is discouraged.

Effective methods of managing and controlling urban expansion with tax policy require an effect on relative prices, that is, they require a reduction in the relative cost of housing versus other investments or an increase in the relative cost of land speculation. Most property tax adjustments designed to affect urban renewal or land speculation have not generally recognized this need.

Bombay Repairs Board

A novel and potentially successful approach to stimulating investment in housing renovation is a special authority for housing repair which has been set up by the state of Maharashtra for the city of Bombay. State government involvement in urban redevelopment had in the past been limited to the slum clearance program of the Housing Board and a relatively small grant to the Bombay Municipal Corporation for slum clearance. This was expanded in 1969 to encompass rehabilitation of selected core city housing. The State Building Repairs and Reconstruction Board was created to provide for the repair or reconstruction of dangerous buildings and to provide for the rehousing of their occupiers. The board, which operates only in the city area of greater Bombay, has the responsibility and authority to carry out structural repairs and receive no compensation, to move the state government to acquire properties beyond repair for purposes of reconstruction, and to take action for the demolition of dangerous or delapidated buildings.

For these purposes the board is authorized to levy a property tax, with the Bombay Municipal Corporation acting as collecting agent. All residential properties in the city area are subject to the cess, with the exception of those owned by government, those rented on a leave and

Table 7.7. Repairs and Reconstruction Board Property Tax Rates

Class of property	Date constructed	Normal rate	Rate if structurally repaired	Rateable value (in millions of dollars)	Property tax assessed (in millions of dollars)
A	Before 1940	25	40	1.74	.33
B	1940–50	20	30	.34	.05
C	After 1950	15	20	2.92	.48

Source: Data are for 1970 and were supplied by Maharashtra state government officials.

license basis, and certain newer properties. For purposes of assessing the tax liability, buildings are classified according to date of construction, with rates higher for older buildings and for buildings which have undergone repair under the act (see table 7.7). In each case the owners' share of the tax is 10 percent of rateable value, with the remainder being paid by the tenant in the form of a higher controlled rent. It may also be seen in table 7.7 that the greatest portion of the cess is collected from the oldest class of property and that total collections are equivalent in amount to approximately 10 percent of total property tax collections of the Bombay Municipal Corporation.

Urban Fringe Development Schemes

The problem of urban growth management in developing countries is qualitatively different from that in developed countries. First, population growth rates are considerably greater than those in developed countries, hence there is greater pressure for physical expansion of the urban area. This pressure is heightened by the already overcrowded situation which typically exists in the core city and the always large housing deficit. Second, since urban infrastructure is already grossly inadequate in urban areas of LDCs, there are substantial claims on public resources, and physical extensions of the urban area may be a relatively low priority use of general tax resources. Third, central governments have generally preempted the major tax bases and therefore have limited the revenue-raising ability of local governments. Moreover, local government tax administrations are not yet well developed and tend to be grossly understaffed. Finally, the private sector has little interest in financing and developing physical extensions of the city, particularly if the aim of such extension is settlement of low income families. Consequently, while in the United States taxation designed to manage urban growth is generally restrictive, the problem in LDCs is to use the public sector to guide urban expansion but at the same time to generate resources adequate to finance the expansion.

In fact, urban governments in some developed countries have responded to this problem by implementing innovative approaches to expanding and financing expansions of the urbanized area. Where these approaches have been successful (as in Seoul), there has been a markedly favorable effect on the fiscal position of the local government. In cases where land development schemes have not been effectively used (Jakarta, Manila), both the fiscal position of the city government and the expansion schemes for the physical urban area have lagged. To illustrate the response of urban governments to the need for self-financing land development schemes two prominent examples are reviewed in the following sections: Seoul's land adjustment scheme and Bogotá and Cartagena's valorization program.[4]

Seoul: Land Adjustment

Seoul Special City (SSC) has a land adjustment scheme under which certain areas of the city are designated for improvement. The improvement consists of rearranging the shape of plots, land grading, laying out and constructing roads, and provision of other basic infrastructure. The objectives of the program are to facilitate the development of areas, usually on the city's urban fringe and usually difficult to develop because of their physical characteristics (plot shape, size, or topography), and to recover public sector costs from such development. Fiscal transactions under this scheme are made through a land adjustment special account and administered by the Land Adjustment Bureau of the SSC government. The Land Adjustment Bureau has no maintenance responsibilities after the development takes place.

The city administration has a five-year plan with respect to areas designated for land adjustment. The decisions on which lands are to be adjusted are made by the mayor and the city administration. Technically, it is required that a majority of landowners agree to the program.

The finances of the land adjustment program are entirely in the special account, with the fiscal resources for the program derived primarily from borrowing, with repayment made from proceeds from the resale of land. The landholders must surrender some of their land to the government as payment in lieu of the improvements they receive on their land. More specifically, the landowner whose land will be improved donates to the government an amount of the land adequate to meet the costs of the improvement plus an amount for general uses such as parks, roads, and open spaces. The government then resells the land to recoup the improvement cost. As of October 1972 thirty-eight land adjustment schemes had been undertaken, twenty-seven of which were complete, and the expenditure for the adjustment of land amounted to about 40 billion won ($100 million) in Seoul city. This amount is equivalent to 49.8 percent of the SSC budget.

Land adjustments can be initiated either by decree of the minister of construction or by those who are connected with the lands which are being adjusted, for example the city government, the housing corporation, or any land-owner association which is formed for that purpose. In the latter case the land adjuster must submit an application

4. Other programs are described in Grimes (1974).

to and obtain formal permission from the Ministry of Construction. The land adjuster first designates a certain area as the area for land adjustment. Next, the land adjustment scheme is announced to the public and remains open to those concerned for public reference for a period of fourteen days. The proposed scheme, the method of covering costs, and other matters must be approved by at least two-thirds of the landowners. If the landowners approve, the land adjuster then submits the land adjustment scheme to the Ministry of Construction and procures a permit.

Technically all the costs of land adjustment are borne by the landowners in the adjusted area, but the land adjuster, usually the Seoul city government, undertakes the planning and execution of the scheme. These costs are allocated among landowners by formula, generally based on the difficulty of improving the land and on the location of the adjusted plot.

In addition to the "cost equivalent" amount of land some common rate of land is surrendered by all landowners to allow land for public parks, public squares, open spaces, and other public uses such as markets and schools. A proportion of 25-35 percent was mentioned by Seoul authorities as being commonly required for institutional use. Finally, there is an additional amount of land which must be surrendered for roads, with the amount surrendered differing according to whether the road is in the front or beside the property.

If there is a discrepancy between the actual cost of the adjustment project and the revenue from sales of cost equivalent land then the difference will either be returned to the landowners or invested in further improvement of the area. It is rare, however, that the price of the land after improvement is overestimated.

Bogotá and Cartagena: Valorization[5]

The Colombian valorization scheme is similar to Korean land adjustment in that the intent is to cover project costs through special assessments on benefiting landowners. Projects executed under the system of valorization up to now have included primarily construction of roads, streets, public squares, and sewage works. In the case of road construction the valorization department has been responsible almost exclusively for all the construction in the city of Bogotá, while the district secretary of public works is in charge of only marginal investment programs in areas where the valorization system cannot be used to recoup project

---

5. A more complete description of this program may be found in Linn (1974). The summary here is drawn from these case studies.

costs. To date, the valorization approach has not been taken in the opening and complete development of new land on the urban fringe.

If the cost of the project is taken as the total burden to be distributed among landowners, the following factors must be considered in computing total project cost: (1) land purchases; (2) all construction costs, including those of complementary works (for example, sidewalks, drainage canals, and so on); (3) all compensation paid on account of the project; and (4) up to 20 percent of the sum of 1-3 for administrative overhead. The statutes also provide for a benefit measurement of the total value of the project, which is the increase in overall land values which results because of the investment. In fact, only in a few cases has a serious effort been made to determine expected land value increments, and the general practice has been to rely on estimated project costs as the amount to be redistributed.

During the process of determining the total benefit/cost of the project the geographic area which is likely to benefit from the project is limited. The "zone of influence" is defined as the area over which the benefits of the project are presumed to affect land values, and this area may be separated into two subzones: the zone of direct influence and that of indirect influence. The former would typically consist of all the properties directly bordering on the project works; the latter would be the properties not directly bordering on the project. In practice, in Bogotá a pragmatic approach appears to have been followed in the determination of the boundaries of the zone of influence. In the case of small projects in homogeneous neighborhoods, a parallel zone of influence method is frequently employed, while in the case of larger, more complex projects affecting nonhomogeneous neighborhoods (nonhomogeneous in terms of topography, socioeconomic characteristics, and capacity to pay) boundaries of varying width on either side of the project are defined.

Once the zone of influence is determined and the survey of properties in the zone is concluded, the distribution of the valorization payment proceeds by one of two alternative methods: Under the first, a series of equidistant parallel lines are drawn parallel to the project. Each zone which is thus formed between the parallel lines is assigned a coefficient which declines continuously from the zone that is closest to the project to the zone that is farthest away. Then the area and the frontage of each property are multiplied separately by the factor of the zone in which it is situated, thus determining what is called "adjusted area" and "adjusted frontage." Then a choice is made as to how much of the total tax burden is to be distributed according to area and what part according to frontage; the former amount is divided by the sum of the adjusted areas, the latter by the sum of the adjusted frontages, which results in a "conversion coefficient" for area and a "conversion coefficient" for frontage, which in turn are multiplied respectively by the adjusted area and the adjusted frontage of each property; finally, by summing the resulting amounts for each property (the taxes on area and frontage, respectively), the total tax burden placed on the property is obtained.

Alternatively, a detailed study is made for each property of the circumstances which may determine the degree to which it benefits from the project that is undertaken. In this the following factors are to be given special attention: the area of the property; the relationship between frontage and area; the distance of the property from the project, as a measurement of the degree of accessibility; the economic aspects of the street to be constructed or improved, taking into consideration such factors as transport demand, accessibility, and so on; the form of the property; the topography of the land; the natural conditions of the property, such as streams and flood land; the proximity of the property to poor neighborhoods; the voluntary contributions which the property owner has made to facilitate the execution of the project; and the change which the project occasions in the potential for economic utilization of the property. Each of these factors is expressed in the form of a coefficient or weight, each ranging between two limits chosen to reflect the relative maximum and minimum benefit that may be derived from the work. These coefficients are determined by local officials and reviewed after having obtained the opinions of the owners' representatives. Each of the coefficients is then multiplied by the area of the respective property to obtain the adjusted area. As in the previous method the total amount to be distributed is divided by the sum of adjusted areas of all properties, and the resulting quotient is multiplied with each adjusted area to obtain the final value of the valorization tax per property.[6]

Conclusion

Little is known about the structure and performance of urban property taxes in developing countries. Since comparative quantitative analysis of property tax yield and the property tax base do not exist, it is not possible to identify "average" performance levels. It follows that there

6. Linn (1974) formulates this operation algebraically as follows:

$$A_i \pi_j K_i^j = A_i^a, \quad \frac{C}{\Sigma A_i^a} = f, \quad \text{and} \quad A_i^a f = C_i,$$

where A_i is the area of property i; A_i^a, the adjusted area of property i; C, the total cost of the project; C_i, the valorization tax burden as property i; K_i^j, the coefficient concerning factor j for property i; π_j, the product operator; and f, the conversion coefficient.

are no accepted standards against which the performance of any particular system might be measured. The analysis here, based on a number of intensive case studies and some supplementary data, demonstrates the feasibility of such empirical comparison and is suggestive of the level of variation in property tax effective rate and base levels.

These data suggest, indirectly, a relatively low income elasticity of property tax revenues. In some cities, property taxes have grown at a rate which is considerably less than the increase in the price level. This relatively low growth in property tax revenues is due in large part to the inability to reassess property so that actual property value growth is matched by growth in the assessed value base. Among the cities in the sample here, there would appear to be little relationship between the growth in the tax base and either income level or the form of the property tax. This low elasticity, coupled with increasing fiscal pressures on city governments and the general absence of other major tax bases, implies an increasing long-term reliance on the property tax.

No attempt is made here to estimate empirically the distributional effects of the property tax. Even if the problem of the incidence of the tax were solved, there is a paucity of data on housing consumption expenditures and/or the distribution of property incomes by income class. Moreover, in terms of vertical equity, there are no studies of biases in assessment practices among properties of different values. There are features of the property tax systems studied here which, if viewed partially, would seem to suggest discretionary attempts to effect a more equitable distribution of tax burden. Other features of the tax system, however, preferential treatment of owner-occupiers, for example, may tend to offset intended progressivity adjustments.

The property tax practices observed in these case study cities suggest a host of allocative effects. Simply in terms of the partial effects of certain features of property tax systems, it would appear that discretionary policy has been designed to encourage homeownership and decentralization of population within the urban area and to discourage speculation in idle land. Moreover, the generally differentially higher rate on land than on improvements is designed to bring about an improved allocation of land use.

A basic difference between developed and developing countries in urban property taxation is the aggressive use in LDCs of taxes on property to guide and finance development as well as to renew the already built-up areas of the city. Whereas urban property tax policy in the United States is restrictive and probably of secondary importance in managing urban growth, in developing countries it is designed to induce particular forms of development and to finance this development.

References

Bahl, Roy W. 1971. "A Regression Approach to Tax Ratio and Tax Effort Analysis in Developing Countries." *International Monetary Fund Staff Papers* 18, no. 3: 570-612.

Chelliah, Raja. 1971. "Trends in Taxation in Developing Countries." *International Monetary Fund Staff Papers* 18, no. 2: 254-331.

Copes, John M. 1970. "Reckoning with Imperfections in the Land Market." In *The Assessment of Land Value,* ed. Daniel M. Holland, pp. 55-82. Madison: University of Wisconsin Press.

Grimes, Orville. 1974. "Urban Land and Public Policy: Social Appropriation of Betterment." IBRD, Bank Staff Working Paper no. 179. Mimeographed. Washington, D.C.

Lent, George E. 1974. *The Urban Property Tax in Developing Countries.* *Finanzarchiv,* N.F., 33, no. 1: 45-72.

Linn, Johannes. 1974a. "Urban Public Finances in Bogotá." Urban Public Finance Project, Urban and Regional Economics Division, IBRD. Mimeographed. Washington, D.C.

Linn, Johannes. 1974b. "Urban Public Finances in Cartagena." Urban Public Finance Project, Urban and Regional Economics Division, IBRD. Mimeographed. Washington, D.C.

Manvel, Allen D. 1971. "Differences in Fiscal Capacity and Effort: Their Significance for a Federal Revenue-Sharing System." *National Tax Journal* 24, no. 2: 193-204.

Mohan, Rakesh. 1974. "Indian Thinking and Practice Concerning Property Taxation and Land Policies." Discussion Paper 47. Mimeographed. Princeton, N.J.: Woodrow Wilson School, Princeton University.

Paddington, R. V. 1965. *Ex Parte Peachey Property Corporation Ltd.* Reported in *The State Gazette* 19: 993.

Smith, Roger S. 1974. "Financing Cities in Developing Countries." *International Monetary Fund Staff Papers* 21, no. 2: 329-88.

Smith, T. M., and R. S. Smith. 1971. "Municipal Finance." *Bulletin of Indonesian Economic Studies* 7, no. 1: 80-102.

Yoingco, Angel. 1971. *Property Taxation in Asian Countries.* Manila: Republic of the Philippines Joint Legislative-Executive Tax Commission.

III. PROPERTY TAX REFORM

8 *Larry D. Schroeder and David L. Sjoquist*

Property Tax Exporting and Differential Incidence of the Homestead Exemption

Among the institutional devices intended to ease the burden of the local property tax is the homestead exemption. In 1971 eleven states granted partial exemption from the property tax through its use, the relative size of the exemptions ranging from 0.3 percent (North Dakota) to 23.5 percent (Mississippi) of the state's gross assessed property tax base. Of more interest, however, is that according to the *Census of Governments* (1967 and 1972) there was an increase during 1966-71 in the use of the homestead exemption as a device for lessening the property tax load. Thus, in the 1967 *Census of Governments* only six states, primarily southern, were reported utilizing outright homestead exemptions (many others exempted some property of veterans or other property), while in the 1972 *Census* eleven states reported use of this device as of 1971. Among the additional states were California, Nebraska, Nevada, North Dakota, and Oregon, all nonsouthern states. Furthermore, on a local level a major legislative issue within the state of Georgia was whether or not to increase homestead exemptions, and, in fact, the Georgia constitution was recently amended to provide this type of property tax relief to the homeowners of Atlanta.

While it appears that the homestead exemption is a rather important policy tool, there appears to be little economic analysis of its effects in the literature. Our objective in this essay is to determine the incidence effect of increasing the local homestead exemption while maintaining constant property tax yields through an increase in the tax rate. Analysis was carried out in a modified general equilibrium model similar to those used by Arnold Harberger, Peter Mieszkowski, and Charles McLure. We used Atlanta as a case study, first determining the exporting of the property tax and then the incidence across income classes of the non-exported proportion of the tax.

The Model

As with most tax incidence studies we employed a theoretical model to draw implications concerning the incidence of the taxes and then applied these implications to obtain empirical estimates of tax incidence. The model we used is a general-equilibrium model similar to those described by Harberger (1962), Mieszkowski (1967), and McLure (1970, 1971).[1] Since the basic model has been presented elsewhere, in the interest of space we will present the model with little elaboration.

Consider three geographic sectors, x, y, and z, which are meant to represent the city of Atlanta, the rest of the Atlanta SMSA, and the rest of the United States, respectively. Assume that sectors y and z each produce one aggregate product, denoted Y and Z, respectively, while sector x produces two products, H, or residential housing, and X, which includes rental housing. Note that H does not refer to the construction of housing but rather to the production of housing services. These four products are produced using capital, K, and labor, L, according to production functions that are homogeneous of degree one and in industries that are perfectly competitive.

We assumed that goods are perfectly mobile throughout the economy and adopted McLure's (1970) assumption regarding the mobility of factors, that capital is perfectly mobile throughout the entire economy while labor is perfectly mobile within the region (the SMSA), but perfectly immobile between the SMSA and the rest of the United States. We assumed that labor is in fixed supply within the SMSA and is fully employed at all times.

All quantities were defined such that all prices are initially equal to unity. Further, we assumed that the price of z is the numeraire and that the prices of the factors of production are equal to the value of their marginal product.

As is normal, we assumed that the distribution of income has no effect on product demand for any of the products; hence demand is solely a function of price ratios.

1. The use of the general-equilibrium model in the analysis of tax incidence has been ably reviewed by Mieszkowski (1969) and Break (1974).

Since sectors x and y are small relative to sector z, we assumed that any action by the firms in the SMSA will have no effect upon the price of capital throughout the United States. In other words the market for capital was assumed to be perfectly competitive, with the firms in the SMSA being one buyer in that market and therefore unable to affect the price of capital.

Within the framework of this model we considered a tax on capital used in the production of residential housing services and a tax on all capital employed in sector x. We considered each tax separately, noting the differential burden of each and assuming that each tax is replacing a neutral tax yielding the same revenue.

These assumptions enabled us to express the model in terms of the following set of fourteen equations with fourteen unknowns:

$$(1) \qquad \frac{dH}{H} = E_{HH}dP_H + E_{HX}dP_X + E_{HY}dP_Y + E_{HZ}dP_Z,$$

$$(2) \qquad \frac{dX}{X} = E_{XX}dP_X + E_{XH}dP_H + E_{XY}dP_Y + E_{XZ}dP_Z,$$

$$(3) \qquad \frac{dY}{Y} = E_{YY}dP_Y + E_{YX}dP_X + E_{YH}dP_H + E_{YZ}dP_Z,$$

$$(4) \qquad \frac{dH}{H} = f_K dK_H + f_L dL_H,$$

$$(5) \qquad \frac{dX}{X} = g_K dK_X + g_L dL_X,$$

$$(6) \qquad \frac{dY}{Y} = h_K dK_Y + h_L dL_Y,$$

$$(7) \qquad dP_H = f_L dP_L + f_K(t_{KH} + t_{Kx}),$$

$$(8) \qquad dP_X = g_L dP_L + g_K(t_{Kx}),$$

$$(9) \qquad dP_Y = h_L dP_L,$$

$$(10) \qquad \frac{dK_H}{K_H} - \frac{dL_H}{L_H} = -S_H(t_{KH} + t_{Kx} - dP_L),$$

$$(11) \qquad \frac{dK_X}{K_X} - \frac{dL_X}{L_X} = -S_X(t_{Kx} - dP_L),$$

$$(12) \qquad \frac{dK_Y}{K_Y} - \frac{dL_Y}{L_Y} = -S_Y(-dP_L),$$

$$(13) \qquad dL_H + dL_X + dL_Y = 0,$$

$$(14) \qquad dP_Z = 0,$$

where d is the derivative operator; E_{ij} is the elasticity of the ith product with respect to the jth price; f_K, g_K, and h_K represent the capital-output ratios in the production of H, X, and Y, respectively; f_L, g_L, and h_L represent the labor-output ratios in the production of H, X, and Y, respectively; S_H, S_X, and S_Y represent the elasticity of substitution in production for H, X, and Y, respectively; t_{KH} represents a tax on the use of capital in the production of H; t_{Kx} represents a tax on the use of capital in sector x, that is, on the production of H and X; and the subscripts on L, K, and P represent the particular product. Equations 1–3 are the demand equations; equations 4–6 the production relations; equations 7–9 the factor share equations; equations 10–12 the factor substitution equations; equation 13 the labor supply equation; and equation 14 the numeraire.

A few comments are in order regarding the demand equations since they differ from those used in the usual two-sector model. Since there is no income effect, demand is a function of price ratios and will be homogeneous of degree zero in prices. We expressed the percentage change in amount demanded as a function of the percentage changes in prices and the own and cross-elasticities which are elasticities of the compensated demand since there is no income effect. If all prices, including P_Z, increase by the same percentage, then the change in the amount demanded will be zero due to homogeneity property. Thus, the sum of the elasticities for any product will be zero.

The definition of tax burden we used is the loss of income resulting from reduced factor prices plus the loss of spending power resulting from the changes in product prices.[2] Given the assumptions in the model, it follows that the burden, B, of a tax is given by

$$(15) \qquad B = -(dP_L L) + (dP_X X) + (dP_Y Y) + (dP_H H),$$

where $L = L_X + L_H + L_Y$. The tax burden on Atlanta residents, B_A, is given by

$$(16) \qquad B_A = -(dP_L L^A) + (dP_X X^A) + (dP_Y Y^A) + (dP_H H^A),$$

where L^A is the labor force made up of Atlanta residents and X^A, Y^A, and H^A are the amounts of X, Y, and H, respectively, consumed by Atlanta residents.

To determine the burden it is necessary to solve the model for the changes in the prices of the products and labor. To simplify the model we assumed that $E_{HZ} = E_{HY} = E_{YH} = E_{XY} = E_{YX} = 0$. Thus, the only cross effect is between H and X. Based on these assumptions it follows that for t_{KH}

2. This definition is the same as that used in Musgrave (1959) and McLure (1971).

(17) $$dP_L = -\frac{f_K t_{KH}(S_H L_H + E_{XH}L_X + E_{HH}L_H)}{\phi},$$

where

(18) $$\phi = E_{XX}g_L L_X - S_X g_K L_X + E_{YY}h_L L_Y - S_Y h_K L_Y + E_{HX}g_L L_H$$
$$+ E_{XH}L_X f_L - S_H f_K L_H + E_{HH}f_L L_H.$$

The expression for dP_H can be obtained directly from equation 7, given equation 17.

Depending upon the value of the various parameters, the tax on K_H may or may not be borne by homeowners, that is, $dP_H \geq 0$. If $dP_H = f_K t_{KH}$, then homeowners bear the entire burden of the tax on K_H. If not, then part of the burden on t_{KH} will be borne by workers in the form of lower wage rates. The lower wage rate will result, in turn, in lower product prices for H net of tax and for X and Y.

Turning to the tax on K_x and K_H and again solving for dP_L we obtain

(19) $$dP_L = -\frac{f_K t_{KX}(\alpha)}{\phi} - \frac{g_K t_{KX}(\beta)}{\phi},$$

where

(20) $$\alpha = E_{HH}L_H + S_H L_H + E_{XH}L_H,$$
(21) $$\beta = E_{XX}L_X + S_X L_X + E_{HX}L_H,$$

and ϕ is as defined above.

The first term on the right side is the same as the expression for the change in P_L when only the capital in housing is being taxed. The second term is due, then, to the expansion of the tax base to include the capital used in the production of X. Again the sign of dP_L cannot be determined.

dP_L can be either positive, zero, or negative, depending upon the values of the cross-elasticities. If the cross-elasticities in equation 17 were zero, then the denominator would be clearly negative, since the sign of the own elasticities are presumed negative. The sign of dP_L would then depend upon the relative values of S_H and E_{HH}. Thus, nothing a priori can be said concerning the sign of dP_L. Suppose however, that H and X are substitutes, so that E_{XH} is positive. Since L_X is much larger than L_H, the numerator of equation 17 would likely be positive, while the denominator would likely be negative. In this case dP_L is positive for a tax on K_H. Such a result is reasonable because, since H and X are substitutes, an increase in P_H causes the amount of X produced to increase. f_L, however, is likely to be much smaller than g_L so that the demand for labor increases as a result of the tax and therefore its price increases.

Suppose that a tax is imposed on capital used to produce both H and X and that all of the revenues are then rebated to K_H. Such a case would be, for example, an increase in the homestead exemption, with a corresponding increase in property tax rates for all classes of property so that total revenue to the government did not change. The resulting change in P_L would be given by

$$(22) \qquad dP_L = -\frac{r_H K_H}{K_H + K_X}\left(\frac{f_K \alpha + g_K \beta}{\phi}\right) + \frac{r_H f_K \alpha}{\phi},$$

where

$$(23) \qquad r_H K_H = t_{KX}(K_H + K_X),$$

where r_H is the rebate rate to K_H; α, β, ϕ, and t_{KX} are as defined above.

Estimation of Tax Exporting

To estimate the extent to which Atlanta is able to export the tax burden it is necessary to determine the value of the parameters of equations 16, 17, and 19. For certain of these parameters we either estimated their value directly or used previously estimated values. In other cases it was necessary to assume particular values.

Consider first the values of the demand and production elasticities. We have previously assumed that $E_{HY} = 0$. In addition, we now assume that $E_{HZ} = 0$ and $E_Y = E_X = -1$. It follows from the homogeneity property of our demand function that $-E_H = E_{HX}$. Given that E_H is the elasticity of the compensated demand we selected a value for E_H of -0.6 based on the following: Estimates of the price elasticity of the ordinary demand for housing are in the neighborhood of -0.8, while estimates of the income elasticity for housing are in the neighborhood of 0.7 (see Carliner, 1973). Employing the theoretical relationship between these elasticities and the assumption that housing expenditures constitute about 25 percent of a homeowner's total expenditures, we arrived at our estimate for E_H. It then follows that $E_{HX} = +.6$. Since only Atlanta residents are affected by a change in the price of H, while there are many non-Atlantans who consume X, the value of E_{XH} will be small, particularly given that E_{HX} is small. We thus assumed that $E_{XH} = 0.1$.

Estimates of the elasticity of substitution in production for manufacturing have been in the neighborhood of one (see Lucas, 1969). Based on this we assumed that S_Y and S_X are both equal to one. The value of S_H, the elasticity of substitution in the production of housing services, is probably low but we had no estimate on which to base our selection. We therefore selected a value for S_H of 0.3. (We repeated the calculations using $S_H = 0.7$. The results were not significantly different.)

Based upon these values of the elasticities, equations 17 and 19 reduce to the following:

$$(17') \; dP_L = -\frac{f_K t_{KH}(S_H L_H + .1 L_X + .6 L_H)}{-L_X - L_Y + .6 g_L L_H + .1 f_L L_X - S_H f_K L_H - .6 f_L L_H}, \; \text{and}$$

$$(19') \qquad dP_L = -\frac{f_K t_{KX}(A)}{D} - \frac{g_K t_{KX}(.6 L_H)}{D}.$$

We will refer to equation 17′ as model A and equation 19′ as model B. In addition to these two models we generated incidence estimates under the more classical assumption that the property tax is borne entirely by consumers in the form of higher prices. In these additional models, denoted A′ and B′, we thus assumed that the price of labor does not change, that is, $dP_L = 0$.

We now turn to selection of values for the input-output ratios and the amount of labor in each of the sectors. In all cases we employed data for 1970. To measure the labor-output ratio we calculated the ratio of labor income to net national product using national data (by industry sector) as listed in the *Survey of Current Business*. Starting with the value of employee compensation for the SMSA from the *Survey of Current Business* and using a number of data sources we estimated the value added (output) by industrial sector for Atlanta and for the rest of the SMSA. Capital-output ratios are one minus the labor-output ratios. The value of the capital stock was then determined using the capital-output ratios and the value added. The implied value of capital net of the real estate sector was considered the nonresidential portion of the tax base.

To measure the value of capital in sector H we assumed that the ratio of K_H to total capital in Atlanta is the same as the ratio of owner-occupied housing to the total property tax base for the city of Atlanta. We assumed that the labor-output ratio in sector H was the same as in the real estate sector net of the imputed rental value of owner-occupied housing.

The values of L, L_H, L_X, and L_Y followed directly from the labor-output ratios and the value of output in each sector. The values of the parameters in equations 17 and 20 are thus specified, and we are left with determining the percentage of the output from each of the sectors that is consumed by Atlanta residents and the value of L^A. We first estimated the percentage of output of each of the industrial sectors, as reported in the *Survey of Current Business*, that are consumed by Atlanta residents. Atlanta residents consume 100 percent of the owner-occupied and rental housing. Since the property tax is an allowable deduction on the federal income tax, part of the tax on owner-occupied housing is offset. (The calculation of this offset is explained below.) For the other industrial sectors there were no direct estimates of the percentage of the output that is consumed by Atlanta

residents. Based on a number of assumptions and many different calculations we arrived at estimates of the percentage of the various outputs consumed by Atlanta residents.[3] To estimate the value of L^4 we used information on place of work as presented in the *Census of Population*.

Based upon the above we calculated the percentage of the two different
taxes (a tax on K_H and a tax on $K_H + K_X$) exported under the different
models. The results are as follows: (1) for model A, 27.2 percent of the tax
change is exported; (2) for model B, 52.7 percent of the tax change is exported; (3) for model A′, 21.3 percent of the tax change is exported; and
(4) for model B′, 50.9 percent of the tax change is exported. We will postpone a discussion of these values until we have presented our estimates
of the incidence of the taxes across income classes, to which we now proceed.

Incidence

Before estimating the incidence of the policy change it is necessary to
indicate the form of income distribution used in analyzing the incidence
of the tax. Although we relied primarily upon 1970 *Census of Population*

Table 8.1. Final Income Distribution

Income class[a]	Families		Unrelated individuals		Class mean income
	Number	Percentage of total income	Number	Percentage of total income	
0–1	3,297	2.76%	14,982	21.74%	$ 127
1–2	1,066	.89	3,941	5.72	1,669
2–3	2,441	2.04	8,944	12.98	2,552
3–4	4,294	3.60	4,941	7.17	3,541
4–5	4,649	3.90	6,016	8.73	4,469
5–6	6,191	5.19	5,467	7.93	5,452
6–7	7,549	6.33	5,140	7.46	6,448
7–8	8,354	7.00	4,667	6.77	7,446
8–9	7,607	6.38	3,195	4.64	8,470
9–10	6,713	5.63	2,395	3.48	9,528
10–12	13,649	11.44	3,228	4.68	10,953
12–15	15,406	12.91	2,474	3.59	13,394
15–25	25,827	21.65	2,154	3.12	18,692
>25	13,624	10.27	1,376	2.00	42,601
Total	120,667	99.99	68,920	100.01	

[a] In this and the following tables we denote the income classes $0–999, $1,000–1,999,
$2,000–2,999, . . . as 0–1, 1–2, 2–3 . . . .

3. For a discussion of the procedure for arriving at these estimates, see Schroeder and
Sjoquist (1975).

data to determine the local distribution of income, there are certain weaknesses in this distribution which are sufficiently important to be corrected before estimating the tax burdens by income class. A relatively simple method was devised to adjust for the underreporting of incomes to the census and the exclusion of nonwage labor incomes, imputed rental incomes, and realized capital gains incomes from the census definition of income. The exact procedures used are contained in Sjoquist and Schroeder (1974), in which a distribution of incomes by income type, income class, and family sizes is generated for 1969 incomes in Atlanta. Table 8.1 contains a summary of this broad-based income distribution.

The conclusions of the model presented above require that when the local incidence of the policy change is estimated, one must consider the impact on five different "bases": tax effect on owner-occupied housing, input price effect on owner-occupied housing, price effect on rental housing, effect on prices for goods produced either in or outside the taxing jurisdiction but purchased by residents of the jurisdiction, and the effect on the price of labor. We will briefly describe the estimation method for each of these effects in turn.

For the tax effect on owner-occupied housing the crucial assumption in the estimation process centers on the relationship between housing value and income. At least two alternative methods of approaching this question are possible. First, one can use the published income/housing value tabulations as published in the 1970 *Census of Housing* (1972) and directly allocate the owner-occupied portion of the local tax base according to the distribution implied in that cross-tabulation. Second, one can simply assume a particular stable relationship between income and housing (a constant income elasticity of demand for housing) and, on the basis of the income distribution, estimate a distribution of gross housing values. While these two approaches can lead to divergent results (see Schroeder and Sjoquist, 1975), we have chosen the latter approach for our estimates here.

To accomplish this estimation we assumed that the income elasticity of demand for owner-occupied housing is 0.75 and constant over all income classes. This estimate is near the mid-range of the more recent estimates of housing elasticities.[4] Further, the estimation process explicitly accounts for the conclusion from a large sample of sale/assessed value ratios that the assessment ratio in Atlanta was 33.1 percent. Basically,

4. For example, de Leeuw (1971) found estimates in the range 0.7-1.5, while Carliner (1973) estimated the elasticity to be in the range 0.5-0.75. Other studies of interest include those by Lee (1968) and Maisel, Burnham, and Austin (1971).

the method uses these assumptions together with the assumed level of homestead exemption to derive housing value estimates for each income class such that the resulting total net residential property tax base on owner-occupied housing is equal to that holding in Atlanta in 1970.

The input price effect on owner-occupied housing is allocated over income classes in the same proportion as is the value of owner-occupied housing as derived from the 1970 *Census of Housing,* with the income concept adjusted to conform to the income definition used here.

The price effect on rental housing is allocated over income classes using a method analogous to that used for owner-occupied housing. That is, the method is based on an assumed level of income elasticity of demand for rental housing which we here assume to be 0.50.[5] In addition the method explicitly accounts for the income levels of occupants of rented public housing on whom we assume there is no property tax burden.

To estimate the incidence of the price effect on items produced in sectors x or y (but not z) and that are consumed in sector x, we relied on an income/consumption matrix estimated from the results of the 1960-61 *Survey of Consumer Expenditures* (1965). This matrix includes all expenditures other than those on housing-related items and accounts for differential spending levels within income classes by family size.

The price effect on labor incomes is estimated directly from the distribution of estimated wage and salary incomes underlying the final income distribution. It was assumed that the proportion of the total burden falling on the price of labor within any one income class is equal to the proportion of total wage and salary income earned by that class.

With this brief background concerning the methods used to estimate each of the tax and price effects stemming from a change in property taxes, we can now turn to a discussion of the estimates of each of these effects for income groups in Atlanta in 1970. We are interested in the differential incidence of the policy of increasing homestead exemptions for the local property tax from $2,000 to $5,000. Since one of the measures of incidence used below is sensitive to the absolute sizes of tax burdens by income class, we assumed for our analysis a desired total yield of the property tax to be $21.6 million, approximately equal to the amount of property tax collected by the city of Atlanta in 1970 for general fund uses.

From the model above it is apparent that the total effect of the policy change can be considered in consecutive steps. First, the increase in the homestead exemption can be considered equivalent to a decrease in the

---

5. This estimate is near the lower bound of most estimates of income elasticities. Compare de Leeuw (1971) or Carliner (1973).

effective rate of the property tax on owner-occupied housing only. Such a decrease in effective rates means, of course, a fall in tax yields. Since we are interested in differential incidence, as the second step in the analysis we will consider the additional burdens of an across-the-board increase in the property tax rates on all properties, including housing.

The homestead exemption obviously treats homeowners differently from renters. It is, therefore, of interest to consider the relative effects on owners and renters within the same income classes. We utilized the 1970 census data together with the results of our income construction method to determine for each income class the proportion of homeowners and renters. Assuming the mean incomes for each of these groups within an income class are the same, we then determined a distribution of total income by income class for each of the two residential types. This assumption does create a difficulty, however, since imputed rental incomes are earned only by owner-occupants. We therefore adjusted the relative weights of incomes earned by renters and owners for types of incomes other than imputed rental incomes to reflect this difference while still maintaining the assumption that overall means of incomes for the two groups of residences are equal. The adjustment has the effect of making mean incomes for renters for income types such as wages and salaries, transfers, and so on, somewhat greater than the means for owners within the same income class. Finally for this distribution we assumed that the family size distribution by income class as determined for the entire population holds for both renters and owners. The resulting distribution for renters and owners is shown in table 8.2.

Table 8.2. Income Distribution of Owner-Occupiers and Renters

Income class	Owners' percentage of total number[a]	Renters' percentage of total number[b]
0–1	6.29%	11.95%
1–2	1.72	3.27
2–3	3.92	7.44
3–4	3.41	5.88
4–5	3.87	6.84
5–6	4.20	7.50
6–7	4.75	8.06
7–8	5.17	8.07
8–9	4.80	6.35
9–10	4.36	5.15
10–12	8.99	8.95
12–15	11.73	8.04
15–25	23.06	9.51
>25	13.74	2.98

[a] Total number of owners is 74,436.
[b] Total number of renters is 113,775.

In order to make direct comparisons of the income distribution effects of $2,000 and $5,000 homestead exemptions, we first estimated changes in tax burdens by income class due to the decreased owner-occupier taxes, then turned our attention to the increased burdens necessary to offset the revenue loss. Further, as in the previous section, two cases concerning the wage response to a change in the property tax will be considered: $dP_L = 0$ and $dP_L \neq 0$. The latter case involves estimation of all possible effects of the property tax; we will consider its effects in detail since a decomposition of the total effects provides interesting insight to the overall incidence of the tax. In the remaining cases we will only present the results and comment briefly on the findings.

Case A: Decrease in the Tax on Housing with $dP_L \neq 0$

With a $2,000 homestead exemption allowed, the existing net property tax base in 1970 was approximately $1.9 billion in Atlanta. This base would have been decreased an additional $300 million if the homestead exemption were increased to $5,000. At the original tax rate this decrease in the tax base would mean a decrease in tax revenue of $3.5 million. Thus, one can consider the increase in the homestead exemption as equivalent to a decrease in the rate of a property tax on housing such that the yield of the tax would fall by $3.5 million. The tax base, together with the desired decrease in yield, determines the necessary base-altered tax rate, which, in turn, when applied to the total price effects as estimated from the model in the previous section, determines the sizes of the various price effects generated by the policy change. The three most important of these price effects are, of course, $dP_X X^A$, $dP_R R^A$, and $dP_H H^A$. Although case A involves a decrease in tax liabilities, we will discuss the case in terms of positive burdens, realizing that for the net effect the negative case A will be offset by positive case B.

The price effects $dP_R R^A$ and $dP_H H^A$ are the effects on renters and owners, respectively (excluding the tax offset provisions and the input price effect on housing consumption). The methods outlined above were then used to estimate burdens by income class on renters and owners. The log linear estimation equations used to estimate housing values by income class while at the same time satisfying the restriction that the computed tax base equaled the actual tax base were $lnHV = 2.881 + 0.75I$ and $lnHV = 4.255 + 0.50I$ for owners and renters, respectively, where HV is the estimated housing value of the class and I is the estimated income class mean.

With these assumptions the estimated relative burdens by income class resulting from price increases on housing are shown in the first two columns of table 8.2, where the entries show the burden as a proportion of class income (allocated to owners and renters as explained above). The

Table 8.3. Relative Tax Burdens Due to Separate Price Effects (burden/class income)

Income class	Owners' tax effect	Renters' price effect	Consumption price effect[a]
0–1	0	.00023	.00339
1–2	0	.00006	.00032
2–3	.00026	.00005	.00024
3–4	.00132	.00003	.00026
4–5	.00180	.00003	.00026
5–6	.00211	.00003	.00026
6–7	.00230	.00003	.00026
7–8	.00242	.00003	.00025
8–9	.00250	.00003	.00024
9–10	.00255	.00003	.00023
10–12	.00260	.00003	.00023
12–15	.00263	.00002	.00022
15–25	.00262	.00002	.00020
>25	.00239	.00001	.00019

[a] Includes both renters and owners.

$2,000 homestead exemption means that the lowest income class home-owners pay no property taxes and that the relative burdens increase with income levels. Conversely, this means that an across-the-board cut in taxes on housing will not benefit the lowest income homeowners at all and will provide relatively larger savings for higher income persons. The change in the tax on housing also affects renters but in a very minor way.

While $dP_x X^A$ is quantitatively much more important than $dP_x Y^A$ (the price effect of goods produced outside the city but consumed within the city), since the method of allocating these price increase burdens does not differ we present the overall burden estimates in the third column of table 8.3. These estimates are combined for renters and owner-occupiers and are later disaggregated according to the proportions shown in table 8.2. From the entries in table 8.3, it is obvious that the burden of these price effects of a change in the tax on housing weigh more heavily upon those in the lower income classes than on those in the upper income classes.

The third price effect considered acts as a partial offset to the burdens thus far considered. This is the wage change due to the tax change. The model of the previous section concludes that wages move in the same direction as the tax change; thus a decrease in the tax on housing is predicted to have a depressing effect on wages, thus partially offsetting the decreased tax burdens. An increase in the tax on housing thus increases wages, with the negative "burdens" allocated over income classes proportionately to the distribution of wages and salaries earned in the various income classes.

The final price effect, the input price effect on homeowners, is extremely small, but is an additional positive burden imposed by the change in the housing tax. It has the effect of altering the burden only on the homeowners.

The remaining effect of a change in the housing tax is not a direct tax effect but instead is due to the deductibility of local taxes in determining the federal income tax. (Note that this applies only to the statutory portion of the property tax and not to the secondary effects which may have additional federal tax-related consequences.) To estimate the federal tax offset we utilized information from the Internal Revenue Service. From its data for 1969 we determined the proportion of returns with itemized deductions and the average marginal tax rate, each by adjusted gross income class. We then determined the adjusted gross income of each of our income classes and determined from the estimates of the direct property liability on homeowners the amount of federal tax offset obtainable in each income class. The offset, of course, also acts as a negative burden in the sense that it lightens the burden of increased taxes and decreases the benefit of lowered taxes.

When all of these effects of a change in the tax on housing are accounted for, the distribution of burdens by income class for renters and owners are as shown in table 8.4. In the first and third columns of that table are shown the relative burdens of a change in the tax on housing as measured by the proportion of before-tax income such a change in tax would represent. To provide some perspective of the absolute amounts being considered the second and fourth columns have been

Table 8.4. Incidence results—Case A

Income class	Renters		Owners after offset	
	Burden/ income	Burden/ unit	Burden/ income	Burden/ unit
0–1	.00266	.34	.00119	.15
1–2	.00014	.24	.00015	.26
2–3	.00009	.22	.00023	.58
3–4	.00008	.27	.00135	4.77
4–5	.00004	.17	.00167	7.46
5–6	—.00000	— .00	.00186	10.13
6–7	—.00005	— .34	.00191	12.29
7–8	—.00010	— .77	.00191	14.21
8–9	—.00017	— 1.44	.00192	16.28
9–10	—.00020	— 1.94	.00194	18.45
10–12	—.00022	— 2.46	.00194	21.24
12–15	—.00028	— 3.70	.00189	25.32
15–25	—.00031	— 5.73	.00190	35.46
>25	—.00024	—10.11	.00149	63.42

added to indicate the absolute dollar change in tax burden of a change in the tax on housing. While more will be said below concerning the implications of these results, note that the negative amounts shown in the rental columns indicate that the wage effect on renters more than offsets the price effects, thus leading to the conclusion that a decrease in the tax on housing via the increase in the homestead exemption would decrease burdens for all owners and on low income renters but would increase burdens on higher income renters even before the revenue-loss offsetting increase in other property taxes is accounted for (case **B** below).

Case A': Decrease in the Tax on Housing with $dP_L = 0$

Under the more common assumption that $dP_L = 0$ the estimation method regarding the incidence of the policy change on taxation of housing is much simpler; in fact, it is only the direct effect on owner-occupiers that must be considered. The distribution of these burdens after accounting for federal tax offsets is shown in table 8.5. The results shown in that table indicate that an increase in homestead exemptions would benefit higher income groups slightly more although this decrease in tax burden is weakened by diminished tax offsets available to owner-occupiers.

Case B: Increase in the Tax on Capital with $dP_L \neq 0$

While cases A and A' were concerned only with the diminished tax burdens stemming from the increased homestead exemptions, it is

Table 8.5. Incidence Results—Case A'

Income class	Owners after offset	
	Burden/ income	Burden/ unit
0–1	0	0
1–2	0	0
2–3	.00026	.65
3–4	.00130	4.62
4–5	.00170	7.59
5–6	.00193	10.52
6–7	.00202	13.06
7–8	.00207	15.44
8–9	.00211	17.88
9–10	.00213	20.31
10–12	.00215	23.57
12–15	.00211	28.22
15–25	.00212	39.61
>25	.00161	68.59

Table 8.6. Incidence Results—Case B

Income class	Renters		Owners after offset	
	Burden/ income	Burden/ unit	Burden/ income	Burden/ unit
0–1	.01136	1.44	.00172	.22
1–2	.00220	3.67	.00018	.30
2–3	.00163	4.11	.00010	.24
3–4	.00121	4.29	.00013	.47
4–5	.00126	5.64	.00010	.46
5–6	.00117	6.39	.00011	.60
6–7	.00111	7.15	.00026	1.67
7–8	.00114	8.46	.00033	2.48
8–9	.00108	9.12	.00042	3.54
9–10	.00100	9.54	.00047	4.48
10–12	.00093	10.15	.00053	5.79
12–15	.00079	10.61	.00059	7.94
15–25	.00063	11.83	.00070	13.08
>25	.00040	17.18	.00070	29.74

reasonable to suspect that given the demands for public services in urban areas there would necessarily be an offsetting increase in overall tax rates such that final tax yields are equal. In this instance we consider the incidence of such an increase in rates on all capital, including owner-occupied housing, but under the assumption that $5,000 homestead exemptions hold. As in case A there are five separate price effects to consider as well as the federal tax offset effect.

Using the methods outlined above we derived the estimates shown in table 8.6 for renters and owners after federal tax offsets. From the entries in that table we observe the general regressive nature of the tax on renters, with the effects on owners being almost proportional. Further, by comparing renters and owners within an income class, we see that except for the highest two income classes the relative burden on renters is greater than that on owners.

Case B′: Increase in the Tax on Capital with $dP_L = 0$

With the assumption that there are no wage effects of the tax change we need consider only three price effects in addition to the federal tax offset effect: the effects on the price of housing, on the price of rental housing, and on the prices of goods produced and consumed in sector x. There are no offsetting price effects on wages nor on the prices of goods produced in sector y nor on the prices of goods consumed in housing.

We have not presented the results of these three estimates since they are very similar to the results in table 8.6. This follows from the fact that the aggregate effect of the three price changes omitted under the assumption that $dP_L = 0$ are all quite small.

Summary and Conclusions

In this chapter we have presented a model of the local property tax from which it is possible to estimate the incidence of a policy designed to exempt certain portions of the tax base. More specifically we have considered the incidence of a change in the level of homestead exemption allowed to homeowner-occupiers since this appears to be one policy which states have attempted to use to decrease the burdens of the local property tax. Furthermore, this particular policy has recently been put into effect in the city of Atlanta; therefore it is most appropriate that we have used Atlanta data to estimate the incidence of this policy change.

The model presented in the first section of the chapter is a general equilibrium model not unlike those employed by Harberger, Mieszkowski, and McLure. This model was constructed with two factor inputs, three geographical areas, and four products considered. Given certain assumptions regarding the mobility of factors and other common assumptions regarding the competitiveness of markets and further assumptions regarding elasticities of demand, the model was solved.

From the solved model, and under certain other assumptions regarding elasticities of demand and substitution in housing, we estimated the extent to which a tax falling only on owner-occupied housing as well as a tax on all capital including housing would be exported from the taxing jurisdiction. Further, these estimates were made both under the assumption that the effect of a local tax on local wage rates is zero and nonzero. For a change in the tax on housing only (with $dP_L \neq 0$) the extent of exporting was estimated to be 27.2 percent when exporting includes the effect of decreased total tax liabilities due to federal tax deductibility of local taxes.

With a change in taxes on all capital a substantially greater proportion of the local tax would be exported to nonresidents. Under the assumption that $dP_L \neq 0$, over half (52.7 percent) of the tax is exported via increased prices on goods consumed outside the taxing jurisdiction and in the form of federal tax offsets. The net change, therefore, of an equal yield decrease in housing tax rates via increased homestead exemptions and increased tax rates on all capital would be to increase the overall portion of the local tax that is exported.[6]

6. Similar exporting coefficients hold for the case of $dP_L = 0$, with the estimates being 21.3 percent and 50.9 percent for taxes on housing and all capital, respectively.

Table 8.7. Final Incidence of Policy Change (case B minus Case A)[a]

Income class	Renters		Owners	
	Burden/income	Burden/unit	Burden/income	Burden/unit
0–1	.00870	1.10	.00053	.07
1–2	.00206	3.43	.00003	.04
2–3	.00154	3.89	—.00013	— .34
3–4	.00113	4.02	—.00122	— 4.30
4–5	.00122	5.47	—.00157	— 7.00
5–6	.00117	6.39	—.00175	— 9.53
6–7	.00116	7.49	—.00165	—10.62
7–8	.00124	9.23	—.00158	—11.73
8–9	.00125	10.56	—.00150	—12.74
9–10	.00120	11.48	—.00147	—13.97
10–12	.00115	12.61	—.00141	—15.45
12–15	.00107	14.31	—.00130	—17.38
15–25	.00094	17.56	—.00120	—22.38
>25	.00064	27.29	—.00079	—33.68

[a] Negative entries indicate decreased burden; positive entries indicate increased burden.

Turning to the incidence of the tax policy change we first constructed a broad-based income distribution for the city of Atlanta for 1969. Then, using several estimating techniques we analyzed the effects of the local income distribution of a change in the tax on housing as well as on all capital. Under the assumption that there is a wage effect from the tax change, we found that the decreased tax on housing would benefit all owners of housing, with this benefit increasing very slightly as income increases. On the other hand, for renters there is a slight benefit to low income groups but an increase in tax burdens placed on higher income renters due to the decreased wages induced by the tax reduction.

For the equal-yield increase in tax on all capital with a $5,000 homestead exemption we found that owners' burdens are very slightly progressive, with rental burdens decreasing as income increases. Furthermore, except for the highest income classes, relative burdens by income class are greater for renters than for owners.

The overall net effect of these two policies by income class are shown in table 8.7, from which it is apparent that the bulk of the lower income homeowners (except for those in the very lowest income classes who, under the assumption regarding the demand for housing used here, would not be currently paying any property tax) would gain from the change in policy. This gain by owners decreases relative to total class income of owners as incomes increase; therefore, the policy is definitely progressive with respect to the homeowning group. On the other hand, all renters would experience increased burdens of taxation as estimated here. In addition, the increase in burdens is relatively greater for those in lower income classes than for those in higher income classes; thus, the policy change would be regressive for home renters. Of course, since a greater proportion of the tax would be exported, the relative change in the incomes of any group would be quite small—in all cases less than one percent of total class income.

In conclusion, it is of interest to consider in another way the distributional impacts of the policy change being considered here. A summary measure of distributional impact is observed in changes in the Gini coefficient of income concentration. This coefficient is directly related to the level of income inequality within a population. For the distribution of broad-based definition of income shown in table 8.1 and disaggregated for renters and owners as in table 8.2 the Gini coefficients are .4312 and .4527 for owners and renters, respectively. We can then compare the Gini coefficients for these two groups after imposition of a $21.6 million property tax both under the assumption of a $2,000 and a $5,000 homestead exemption. Under the assumption that $dP_L \neq 0$, the Gini coefficients are as follows:

	Owners	Renters
$2,000 H.E.	.4312	.4527
$5,000 H.E.	.4309	.4529

Thus, according to the model and estimates made here, the policy of increasing homestead exemptions to provide property tax relief has the effect of increasing income inequality for renters (as measured by the Gini coefficient) while decreasing this inequality for owners.

References

Break, George. 1974. "The Incidence and Economic Effects of Taxation." In *The Economics of Public Finance,* ed. Alan Blinder et al., pp. 119-237. Washington, D.C.: Brookings Institute.

Carliner, Geoffrey. 1973. "Income Elasticity of Housing Demand." *Review of Economics and Statistics* 55: 528-32.

deLeeuw, Frank. 1971. "The Demand for Housing: A Review of Cross-Section Evidence." *Review of Economics and Statistics* 53: 1-10.

Harberger, Arnold. 1962. "The Incidence of the Corporation Income Tax." *Journal of Political Economy* 70: 214-40.

Internal Revenue Service. 1971. *Statistics of Income—1969, Individual Income Tax Returns.* Washington, D.C.: Government Printing Office.

Lee, Tong Hun. 1968. "Demand for Housing: A Cross Section Analysis." *Review of Economics and Statistics* 50: 480-90.

Lucas, Robert. 1969. "Labor-Capital Substitution in U.S. Manufacturing." In *The Taxation of Income From Capital,* ed. Arnold Harberger and Martin Bailey. Washington, D.C.: The Brookings Institute.

Maisel, S. J., J. B. Burnham, and J. S. Austin. 1971. "The Demand for Housing: A Comment." *Review of Economics and Statistics* 53: 410-13.

McLure, Charles. 1970. "Taxation, Substitution and Industrial Location." *Journal of Political Economy* 78: 112-32.

McLure, Charles. 1971. "The Theory of Tax Incidence with Imperfect Factor Mobility." *Finanzarchiv* 30: 27-48.

Mieszkowski, Peter. 1967. "On the Theory of Tax Incidence." *Journal of Political Economy* 75: 250-62.

Mieszkowski, Peter. 1969. "Tax Incidence Theory: The Effects of Taxes on the Distribution of Income." *Journal of Economic Literature* 7: 1103-24.

Musgrave, Richard. 1959. *The Theory of Public Finance.* New York: McGraw-Hill.

Schroeder, L. D., and D. L. Sjoquist. 1975. *The Property Tax and Alternative Local Taxes: An Economic Analysis.* New York: Praeger.

Sjoquist, D. L., and L. D. Schroeder. 1974. "A Method for Construction of Distributions of Broad-Based Income for Metropolitan Areas and Central Cities." Unprocessed. Working Paper 7374-04. Atlanta: Georgia State University.

U.S. Bureau of the Census, Census of Housing. 1972. *1970 Metropolitan Housing Characteristics.* HC(2)-15. Washington, D.C.: Government Printing Office.

U.S. Bureau of Labor Statistics. 1965. *Consumer Expenditures and Income, Survey of Consumer Expenditures, 1960-61.* BLS Report no. 237-38. Washington, D.C.: Government Printing Office.

9 *Daniel M. Holland and Oliver Oldman*

Estimating the Impact of Full Value Assessment on Taxes and Value of Real Estate in Boston

Introduction

While Massachusetts law requires the property tax base to be the full market value of taxable property, in fact current assessments in Boston depart considerably from this valuation.[1] Moreover, current assessments depart differentially or unequally rather than uniformly from market values, so that replacing these assessments by market values would lead to higher property taxes for some classes of properties and lower taxes for others.

In this report we will measure and evaluate the pattern of real property tax redistribution which would occur if Boston were to base its property tax on full market value rather than on current assessments. We undertook this study in the expectation that the findings might be timely since pressures were building up in the direction of full-value assessment. In fact, soon after we completed the estimates, the Massachusetts Supreme Judicial Court, in a decision handed down on December 24, 1974, mandated the full-value base for all property tax jurisdictions in the commonwealth, directing the commissioner of corporations and taxation "to take such action as will produce uniformity throughout the Common-

---

1. For legal references and other information, see Oldman and Aaron (1965), Black (1960), and Woodbury (1970).

wealth in valuation and assessments."[2] And it is worth noting that uniformity is an issue in other states as well.

Given the judicial order to implement the full-value basis and the imminence of a shift thereto, the time is ripe for speculation on the impact of the change. Our data are rather courageous estimates that fall far short of being definitive. In our judgment, however, they are good enough to help define the broad outlines of the major areas of impacts. And we are encouraged in this assessment by the fact that two other studies, while differing importantly from each other and from our study in the proportions each major class of property constitutes of the total, do give substantially the same indications as to the major impacts.[3]

To help evaluate the impact of full-value assessment we have developed as of 1972 estimates of market and current assessed value of taxable properties by broad categories: residential, commercial (further subdivided into "new"—built since 1960—and "old"—built prior to 1960), and "other" (primarily vacant land). These estimates are based on fragmentary data and numerous assumptions, many of them questionable. Yet we believe that they are sufficiently accurate to suggest the orders of magnitude of the redistribution of tax liabilities attendant on changing the basis of property valuation for tax purposes.

We must emphasize that our work is far from definitive. Before the full implications of full-value assessment (or one of the alternatives discussed in the body of our report) can be understood, much more study of Boston market values is in order. Our data are good enough only for a first pass at some of the main effects that appear so broad and persuasive as to rise above the deficiencies of our estimates. Our approach,

2. *Town of Sudbury* v. *Commissioner of Taxation,* 321 N.E.2d 641 (Mass. 1974). The court therein declared "that (1) the commissioner [of corporations and taxation] has the power and the duty to direct local assessors to take such action as will tend to produce uniformity throughout the Commonwealth in valuation and assessments; (2) the [state tax] commission has the power and the duty to direct city and town officers to furnish such returns and statements relative to the amount and value of taxable property in the city or town as it deems necessary to enable it to determine and establish for each city and town an equalized valuation which shall be the fair cash value of all property in such city or town subject to local taxation as of January 1 in each even-numbered year; and (3) the functions of the commissioner and the commission in these respects are to command and not merely to advise or educate, and it is the legal duty of the assessors to obey their lawful commands."

3. The other two sources for comparable estimates are: (1) estimates by the Bureau of Land Assessing of the Department of Corporations and Taxation of the Commonwealth of Massachusetts of assessed and market value of taxable property by broad categories in Boston as of the end of 1973; and (2) the 1974 Equalization Study of the Department of Corporations and Taxation of the Commonwealth of Massachusetts (unpublished) which has estimates, as of the end of 1973 of assessed and market value, by major classes of taxable property in Boston. A comparison of all three bodies of data (the two cited above and ours) appears in appendix A.

we should note, fails to come to grips with the many "practical" problems full-valuation assessment would face. For example, we have not allowed for the special case of rent-controlled property, or the possibility that Boston might, as a result of full-value assessment throughout the commonwealth experience a reduction in state aid, and so on. We stress these caveats, but we also feel that the major impacts we identify—call them tendencies if you will—are supportable despite data deficiencies. We believe, that is, that the direction and general order of the magnitudes of change are correct, but that the specific value of our estimates of any one of them could be off substantially.

Redistribution of tax and changes in property values are the foci of our study. Total revenue from the property tax in Boston is taken as given (at its 1972 level) and the changes in the shares of this total that fall on different types of property are explored. These changes are the essence of the conflict of interests whose uneasy resolution is the prime objective of tax policy. In fact the estimates in our study can be viewed as more useful for political discussion than for refined economic analysis. Estimates of the sort we have made are the raw materials from which political debate is fashioned. They belong in the political arena because they constitute the balance sheet of who would lose and who would gain on the first round. The taxpayer is keenly interested in what his new tax bill will be and what will happen to the value of his property. Answers will be sought, and, in any event, answers will be forthcoming. It is in this spirit that we offer our estimates.

Most discussions of tax redistributions portended by changes in the basis of assessment focus on the magnitudes of what we call the "initial impact." These are derived simply by an arithmetic exercise that allocates the current total tax among categories of property on the basis of their respective shares of total assessed value and then allocates the same total tax on the basis of the proportions these categories compose of total market value. A comparison of the two amounts of tax liability indicates by how much property tax would increase or decrease for each category.

Some behavioral support can be given for proceeding this way, at least as a first approximation, by arguing that assessors concerned with justifying their assessments to irate citizens or producing validating evidence in a suit in court would, under full-value assessment, set a value on the property equal to its current market value. But the estimates of tax redistributions obtained by this method necessarily would have a limited duration of relevance. For with change in property tax liabilities would come changes in market values, and with the change in market values would come still another change in tax liabilities, and so on. It is possible to treat this as a process: the "initial impact" tax change setting up a "first iteration" value change, which sets up a second tax change, which sets up new market value, etc. An exercise along these lines appears in appendix B.

But it is quite unlikely that this infinite series of successive iterations converging on a central set of values in the limit would in fact eventuate. Assessors and investors are always searching for the determinants of value and in the process are constantly attempting to get to the heart of the matter by adjusting and capitalizing the new net income stream (net of all expenses but property tax) to arrive at an estimate of the equilibrium value. In the absence of change this estimate of the "equilibrium" value will tend to persist over time; therefore, we refer to estimates derived in this way as "steady state" estimates.[4] In our judgment the "steady state" estimates are more relevant than the "initial impact" estimates since we think they capture the more likely result. But we remind the reader that both the "initial impact" and the "steady state" estimates embody extreme assumptions which necessarily render the estimates closer to illustrative of what *might* eventuate than predictive of what *will* happen. Our emphasis at this point is on developing techniques rather than numbers per se. At a later date when more information is available and a better basis for estimation exists, we hope to get a better handle on the numbers.

In an earlier discussion of our findings we were not properly perceptive of this point and emphasized the "initial impact" results at the expense of the "steady state" estimates (Holland and Oldman, 1974). This is unfortunate; the "initial impact" estimate is always more severe (like the first swing of a pendulum which is always more extreme than the succeeding swings), either by way of tax increase (and attendant decline in the value of property) or tax decrease (and associated rise in property value), than is the "steady state" estimate.

Now to back up a bit and explain one more designation, found in table 9.1. Column 5 in that table is labeled "first iteration." This is the value counterpart of the "initial impact" tax change estimates. In deriving it we capitalized the property's income[5] as modified by the "initial impact" tax change.

Our primary interest at this point is to display our results and discuss their significance, to which we now proceed. The reader, however, who feels the need for a deeper understanding of our methodology should turn to appendix B and then come back to the next section.

---

4. It can be shown that under reasonable assumptions the "steady state" value is the same as the limiting value in the convergent series generated by the successive iterations described above.

5. More accurately, we should refer to capitalizing the income of a class of properties.

Table 9.1. Estimated Effect of Full-Value Assessment on Market Value of Taxable Property, Boston, 1972 (in millions of dollars)

Property category	Current assessed value (1)	Proportion of total (2)	Current market value (3)	Proportion of total (4)	Market value—"first iteration" (15% capitalization rate) (5)	Proportion of total (6)	Change in value (7)	Percentage change in value (8)	Market value—"steady state" (15% capitalization rate) (9)	Proportion of total (10)	Change in value (11)	Percentage change in value (12)
"New" commercial	$ 127	.0841	$ 696	.1496	$ 562	.1208	−$134	−19%	$ 603	.1296	−$ 93	−13%
"Old" commercial	669	.4430	1,279	.2749	1,622	.3486	+ 343	+27	1,518	.3262	+ 239	+19
"All" commercial	796	.5271	1,975	.4245	2,184	.4694	+ 209	+11	2,121	.4558	+ 146	+ 7
Residential	663	.4391	2,456	.5278	2,275	.4889	− 181	− 7	2,330	.5008	− 126	− 5
Other	51	.0338	222	.0477	194	.0417	− 28	−13	202	.0434	− 20	− 9
Total	1,510	—	4,653	—	4,653	—	—	—	4,653	—	—	—

Table 9.2. Estimated Effect of Full-Value Assessment on Tax Liability of Taxable Property, Boston, 1972 (dollar amounts in millions)

Property category	Current property tax (1)	Current effective rate of tax (on market value) (2)	Property tax—"initial impact" (3)	Change in tax (4)	Percentage change in tax (5)	Effective rate of tax—"initial impact" (6)	Property tax—"steady state" (7)	Change in tax (8)	Percentage change in tax (9)	Effective rate of tax—"steady state" (10)
"New" commercial	$ 25.77	3.7%	$ 45.84	+$20.07	+78%	6.6%	$ 39.70	+$13.93	+54%	6.6%
"Old" commercial	135.74	10.6	84.23	− 51.51	−38	6.6	99.96	− 35.78	−26	6.6
All commercial	161.51	8.2	130.07	− 31.44	−19	6.6	139.66	− 21.85	−14	6.6
Residential	134.54	5.5	161.72	+ 27.18	+20	6.6	153.43	+ 18.89	+14	6.6
Other	10.36	4.7	14.61	+ 4.25	+41	6.6	13.30	+ 2.94	+28	6.6
Total	306.40	6.6	306.40	—	—	6.6	306.40	—	—	6.6

Major Findings and Their Policy Implications

The major findings and policy implications of full-value assessment on taxes and value of real estate in Boston were as follows (estimates are drawn from tables 9.1 and 9.2):

1. As of the end of 1972 the market value of taxable real property in the city of Boston was $4,653 million (column 3 in table 9.1). Slightly more than half (53 percent) was accounted for by residential property— $2,456 million in all. Commercial property made up most of the rest— $1,975 million (42 percent of the total)—with other property (primarily vacant land) accounting for the remaining 5 percent (column 4).

2. While ostensibly required to assess for property tax at market value, the city of Boston (and most other local governments in the United States as well), whether by default or design, does not achieve this objective. Assessed value is lower than market value and, more important, is distributed in different proportions among categories of property than is market value. We estimate the aggregate assessed value of taxable real property at $1,510 million (column 1 in table 9.1) and note by way of comforting comparison that our independently estimated total is close to the official figure of $1,532 million tabulated by the city assessor's office from the tax rolls. Our concern is primarily with the proportions of this total accounted for by the various categories of property since this, in turn, determines each category's share of the property tax. As with market value, residential and commercial properties together account for all but a small percentage (3.4) of the total assessed value. But their relative importance is reversed. Residential makes up 44 percent of the tax base; commercial accounts for 53 percent.

3. Therefore, were the city of Boston to assess all taxable properties at their current full market value and raise an amount of property tax revenue equal to what was collected in 1972 ($306.4 million), a significant redistribution of tax liabilities could be expected. Business in the aggregate would pay less, and residences would pay more. Total property tax collected from residential property would increase from $135 to $162 million (columns 1 and 3 in table 9.2) or by 20 percent (column 5); commercial property, on the other hand, would enjoy a decline of 19 percent (column 5) in the property tax it was responsible for, that is, a fall from $162 million to $130 million (columns 1 and 3). Under full market value assessment, of course, the effective rate of real property tax would be the same for all properties—6.6 percent. For residential property this would be a substantial rise over the present effective rate of 5.5 percent, while for commercial property 6.6 percent would mean a rate considerably less than the 8.2 percent currently levied on it (column 2).

4. The market values and new distribution of tax liabilities set forth in paragraphs 1, 2, and 3 above are "initial impact" results which do not take into account the effects of increases and decreases of taxes on the market values of the properties affected. To the extent that commercial property enjoys a decline in tax liability its value will rise, while to the extent that residential property suffers an increase in property tax it would command less in the market. Property values (and, along with them, of course, tax liabilities) would adjust to the initial redistribution of tax liabilities and might, in fact, adjust in anticipation thereof. Therefore, a major consequence, if not *the* major consequence, of adoption of full market value assessment can be expected to be a substantial change in the current market value of taxable properties, involving significant windfall gains and losses to present holders. Current owners of properties would enjoy or suffer these gains and losses. Through "tax capitalization" later holders would buy "free" of these tax changes.

5. The tax liabilities that would apply to different classes of property in the "steady state" are, of course, different from those that they bear now. Similar to the "initial impact" results, new commercial properties as a group, the residential property sector, and other property would all be liable for more tax than they are at present and old commercial properties for less. But the steady state tax changes would be less severe (compare columns 5 and 9 in table 9.2). Between them these two columns encompass the range of real possibilities. We may conclude, then, that as a result of assessment at full market value the residential property sector would have a tax increase on the order of 14 to 20 percent, "new" construction an even sharper rise of between 54 and 78 percent, while "old" commercial would enjoy a tax decline of 26 to 38 percent. These numbers are no more valid than the assumptions used in their derivation, so it is worth noting that had we used a capitalization rate of 10 percent rather than 15 percent (which is the more valid assumption in our opinion), the tax liability changes in the "steady state" would have been slightly less pronounced: a rise of 12 percent for residential, 47 percent for "new" commercial, and a decline of 23 percent for "old" commercial. We repeat our judgment that the "steady state" results are the more likely to obtain, not simply in the long run, but in a relatively short time. The reader is reminded, however, that the basic estimates of their fair market value of commercial properties used in this study are based on a very small sample which does not enable us to say with confidence that a more careful or thorough study might not have produced a set of fair market value estimates that would differ significantly from those that served as the basis for this entire study. The need for a careful additional original study of Boston property characteriza-

tics and their fair market value is the essential underpinning for estimates sufficiently good to be a basis for policy decisions.

6. As property tax liabilities change, the net returns available from
those properties that enjoy a tax decrease would go up, and they would
fetch a higher price in the market. Conversely properties subject to
higher taxes would be worth less than they are now. Tax changes then
will lead to changes in value. This statement borders on tautology since
the value change is simply the present value of the stream of increased
(or decreased) tax payments for which holders of the property are liable.

We cannot give a precise estimate of how severe the changes in value
would be, but we can suggest a range that would encompass reasonable
expectations as to order of magnitude. As with the possible tax change
we have two "models" of the valuation process—"first iteration" and
"steady state"—hence two estimates of changes in property values. The
"first iteration"—the logical complement of the "initial impact" measure
of tax change—takes tax change as measured by the latter and capital-
izes it to arrive at a new market value. Thus this method estimates the
first change in value, if the valuation process proceeded in such steps. As
we have two "models" of the valuation process—"first iteration" and
of an infinite series of tax-cum-market value changes that converge on
the same value as the "steady state."

This latter value, however, is not to be viewed as something reached
only after elapse of a considerable period of time. Rather, as already
suggested, it is likely to eventuate in short order because it reflects the
way assessors and investors generally would value a piece of property.

Turning to the estimates in table 9.1, we note first that the change in
the value of properties would be *proportionately* less severe than the
change in tax liability that caused them. Compare, for example, column
5 of table 9.2 and column 8 of table 9.1 or column 9 of table 9.2 and
column 12 of table 9.1. For residential property in the aggregate, the two
estimates of declines are 7 percent or 5 percent. "Old" commercial
property would increase substantially in value—somewhere between 19
and 27 percent. And the decline in the value of "new" commercial property would be on the order of 13 to 19 percent.

7. These results point up two sensitive areas. Politically, the residential sector is of prime importance, for voters are renters or homeowners. Tax increases in the range of 14-20 percent are not popular with
voters. Phased in over a five-year period, however, they could perhaps be
tolerated. Moreover, residential property would change only moderately
in value, say on the order of 5 to 7 percent. Once again, not a cause of
elation in the electorate, but still moderate enough, it is hoped, to be
absorbed. "New" commercial property, however, would be more severely

hit. Benefiting now from lower effective rates of tax than other major categories of property, it would suffer a tax increase of between one-half and three-quarters. And its market value would fall by 13 to 19 percent. Changes of this magnitude could make further development in Boston unattractive. Indeed, it was the presumption that this was already the case that led to the special arrangements that have moderated the property tax on "new" commercial development.

8. The findings cited to this point are based on averages for very broad classifications of property. These are the basic data of our report, but it would be unduly remiss on our part to fail to note that a wide diversity of experience for individual properties is subsumed under these averages. Thus it is trite but true that about half of the individual properties in each category would experience smaller proportionate tax increases than average, and half would have larger than average increases. In fact, the dispersions could conceivably be so large as to show a sizable number of properties having a tax increase when the average result was a decrease, and vice versa. A great many of the tax redistributions *within* categories will be larger than the redistributions, on the average, *between* categories. We have not studied this matter in any depth, but we can cite data that illustrate its importance.

9. For commercial properties we can give a sense of the within-a-category dispersion in two ways: one on the basis of averages for subgroups of commercial properties and the other on the basis of inferences about the dispersion of tax burden redistribution variation drawn from the standard deviations of the assessment-sales ratios developed in the course of our study.

10. A different burden of real property tax presently falls on "new" and "old" commercial property, as summarized in tables 9.1 and 9.2. Commercial properties built since 1960 have generally been assessed under agreement with the city at values low enough to permit earning a rate of return sufficient to induce the developers to undertake the project. As a consequence such properties—primarily office and retail—are currently bearing a tax of between 3 and 4 percent of market values. We estimate that "old" property, however, pays a tax equal to 10 to 11 percent of its market value. With full value as the tax base and all property uniformly levied on at 6.6 percent of market value, "new" commercial will have a tax increase on the order of 54 percent to 78 percent, while "old" commercial properties would enjoy a tax cut in the range of 26-38 percent (columns 5 and 9 of table 9.2).

11. But again we note that the figures show the average experience for properties in these respective categories. Within each category, a good number of individual properties would have even more startling changes in tax burden. Suggestive of this result is the high standard deviation of

Table 9.3. Frequency Array of Assessment-Sales Ratios of Properties in "Old" Commercial Sample

Value of ASR	Number of properties	Percentage of total properties
0–.10	2	1.1%
.10–.20	17	9.0
.20–.30	38	20.1
.30–.40	34	18.0
.40–.50	29	15.3
.50–.60	19	10.1
.60–.70	18	9.5
.70–.80	10	5.3
.80–.90	11	5.8
.90–1.00	1	.5
Over 1.00	10	5.3
Total	189	100.0

the assessment-sales ratios (ASRs) for "old" commercial properties. For the sample we used in developing our estimates the unweighted ASR was .47 and its standard deviation .26. What this means more particularly is brought out by the frequency array of individual ASRs for the 189 properties in the "old" commercial sample in table 9.3. Citing the "initial impact" estimates first and the "steady state" estimates in parentheses, an average "old" commercial property, that is, one currently assessed at about 52 percent of market value, would enjoy a decline in property tax of 38 (26) percent if full market value replaced current assessments as the basis of the tax. With reference to the frequency distribution, about 15 percent of properties (those in ASR class .40–.50) would, in fact, experience a decline of this order of magnitude. Thirty-seven percent (those in ASR classes .50 and above) would have a decline in tax liability proportionately greater than 38 (26) percent; some 15 percent of "old" commercial properties could well have their liability cut by 50 (33) percent or more. Similarly, about 48 percent of "old" commercial properties (those with ASRs under .40) would find their tax liability under market value assessment declining less than 38 (26) percent. In fact, those in the lowest three ASR classes (with ratios of .30 or less) would find that their property tax had gone up.

12. As for taxable residential property it is also important to recognize the wide dispersion of individual outcomes around our estimated "average" experience: an increase of 20 percent ("initial impact" estimate) or 14 percent ("steady state" estimate). While the variability around the average has not been a major concern of our study (but should be in future extensions of it) we can suggest some of the relevant orders of magnitude by drawing on some recent (as yet unpublished) work of Robert Engle.

Table 9.4. Estimated Percentage Change in Property Tax Liability under Full-Value Assessment for Residential Property in Each Boston Redevelopment Authority (BRA) Planning District, Boston, 1972 (dollar amounts in millions)

BRA planning district (1)	Percentage of total residential assessed value (2)	Estimated current tax liability[a] (3)	Percentage of total residential market value (4)	Estimated tax liability under full-value assessment ("initial impact" method)[b] (5)	Percentage change in tax liability under full-value assessment ("initial impact" method)[c] (6)	Estimated tax liability under full-value assessment ("steady state" method)[d] (7)	Percentage change in tax liability under full-value assessment ("steady state")[e] (8)
East Boston	4.10%	$ 5.5	4.16%	$ 6.7	+ 22%	$ 6.4	+ 16%
Charlestown	.86	1.2	1.62	2.6	+126	2.2	+83
South Boston	2.96	4.0	3.72	6.0	+ 51	5.4	+35
Central/North	4.61	6.2	5.67	9.2	+ 48	8.3	+34
Back Bay/Beacon Hill	13.54	18.2	10.58	17.1	− 6	17.4	− 4
South End	2.19	3.0	3.09	5.0	+ 70	4.4	+47
Fenway/Kenmore	9.35	12.6	8.41	13.6	+ 8	13.3	+ 6
Allston/Brighton	11.12	15.0	13.30	21.5	+ 44	19.5	+30
Jamaica Plain/Parker Hill	6.69	9.0	5.58	9.0	0	9.0	0
Washington Park/Model City	9.61	12.9	5.83	9.4	− 27	10.5	−19
North and South Dorchester	10.83	14.6	10.12	16.4	+ 12	15.8	+ 8
Roslindale	5.72	7.7	6.58	10.6	+ 38	9.7	+26
West Roxbury	7.63	10.3	9.61	15.5	+ 51	13.9	+35
Hyde Park	5.24	7.1	6.60	10.7	+ 51	9.6	+35
Mattapan/Franklin	5.55	7.5	5.13	8.3	+ 11	8.1	+18
Total	100.00	134.5	100.00	161.7	+ 20	153.4	+14

Source: Unpublished estimates prepared by Robert Engle for Boston Redevelopment Authority, 1972. In the calculations we assumed that the value of tax-exempt residential property, excluded from our estimates, was distributed among BRA planning districts proportionately to the value of all residential property.

[a] Column 3 = column 2 × $134.5 million.
[b] Column 5 = column 4 × $161.7 million.
[c] Column 6 = [(column 5 − column 3)/column 3] × 100.
[d] Column 7 = column 4 × $153.4 million.
[e] Column 8 = [(column 7 − column 3)/column 3] × 100.

Table 9.5. Frequency Array of Estimated Percentage Changes in Residential Property Values in the Fifteen Boston Redevelopment Planning Districts

Tax change on full-value assessment	Number of planning districts ("initial impact")	Number of planning districts ("steady state")
Decline	2	2
Increase of under 10%	2	3
Increase of 10–20%	2	2
Increase of 20–30%	1	1
Increase of 30–50%	3	6
Increase of 50–100%	4	1
Increase of over 100%	1	0

Source: See Table 9.4.

He has estimated assessed values and market values of residential property for each of the fifteen planning districts by which the Boston Redevelopment Authority (BRA) divides up the city. We allocated the $134,540,000 of property tax now levied on taxable residential properties (column 1 of table 9.2) in proportion to their share of total assessed value, then did the same but on the basis of market value for their tax burden of $161,720,000 "initial impact" estimate (column 3) and the $153,430,000 that would be forthcoming from taxable residential property under the "steady state" assumption (column 7). The difference between the two—current assessment tax liability and full value tax liability—is calculated as a percentage in table 9.4.

The data, procedures, and results appear in table 9.4. Among the fifteen planning districts the change in tax liability (and tax rate) would vary tremendously in importance. Under the aggregate average increase of 20 (14) percent for taxable residential properties in the city lie such disparate results as a 27 (19) percent average decrease for homes in Washington Park/Model City and a 126 (83) percent average increase for Charlestown. The changes are summarized in table 9.5.

The "steady state" estimates point to smaller changes in tax liability. Under this method, which we think the more appropriate one, five planning districts would have moderate tax increases of under 10 percent or would enjoy tax decreases; the "initial impact" method has four districts in this category. Under this latter method five districts would have property tax increases on their residential property of 50 percent or more; the "steady state" estimate is that only one district would experience a tax increase this sharp.

While property tax changes would generally be the more immediately perceived impact, residential property values, too, would change differentially among the planning districts as the existing disparities in assessment-sales ratios were removed under full-value assessment. As noted in table 9.1 (column 12), residential property, in the aggregate, would decrease in value by 5 percent ("steady state" method, 15 percent capitalization rate) because of the higher property tax due from it.

But encompassed by this average is a wide diversity of results for subdivisions thereof. In table 9.6 we illustrate this for residential property arrayed by BRA planning districts, with value changes as estimated by the "steady state" assumptions with a capitalization rate of 15 percent. To cite some extremes, residential property in the Charlestown planning district would, we estimate, fall in value by 17 percent, which is more than three times the average decline, and there are five other

Table 9.6. Estimated Percentage Change in Value of Residential Property under Full-Value Assessment for Residential Property in Each BRA Planning District, Boston, 1972 ("steady state" assumption, 15 percent capitalization rate)

BRA planning district	Estimated percentage change in value
East Boston	− 6%
Charlestown	−17
South Boston	−10
Central/North	−10
Back Bay/Beacon Hill	+ 2
South End	−12
Fenway/Kenmore	− 2
Allston/Brighton	− 9
Jamaica Plain/Parker Hill	0
Washington Park/Model City	+11
North and South Dorchester	− 3
Roslindale	− 9
West Roxbury	−10
Hyde Park	−10
Mattapan/Franklin	− 3
Total residential property	− 5

Source: See table 9.4.

Table 9.7. The Diversity of Assessment-Sales Ratios for Residential Property in Boston

Type of residential property	ASR (1962)[a]
Single family, one structure	.341
Two family or apartments	.412
Three to five families or apartments	.520
Six or more families or apartments	.579
Multifamily, more than one structure	.650

Source: Oldman and Aaron (1965, p. 40).

[a] All of Boston for each type of property, excluding questionable sales.

planning districts in which the values would fall by 10 percent or more, that is, at least twice the average. On the other hand in the Washington Park/Model City district residential properties would increase in value by 11 percent.

Finally, we remind the reader that this by no means exhausts the catalog of diversity. For every one of the entries in table 9.6 is itself an average—in this case for a planning district—around which the experience of individual properties will exhibit a wide degree of dispersion.

We do not have any additional value estimates to carry the story further, but we can cite data that are strongly suggestive in this connection and tend to confirm the view that dispersions of ASRs (and hence redistributions of property tax and value changes) are greater within each category (as illustrated in tables 9.4 and 9.6) than they are between major categories (as indicated in tables 9.1 and 9.2).

13. In addition to regional variation within the city, ASRs also vary systematically by category of residential property, tending to rise with size (the number of families housed in the property) and, within a given category, tending to fall with value. If we assume in both these connections that the relative ranking of ASRs was the same in 1972 (the year we are interested in) as in 1962 (the year for which we have relevant data) we can cite evidence suggestive of the extent of dispersions in tax liability changes that would accompany full-value assessments with respect to type of residence and value.

As summarized in table 9.7 ASRs vary systematically with class of residence. Typically the smaller the residence (that is, the fewer the number of families housed in it), the lower the ASR and, therefore, the greater the expected property tax increase under full-value assessment.

Table 9.8. The Diversity of Assessment-Sales Ratios, Arrayed by Selling Price, Boston (1962)

Price range	Single family, one structure	Two families or apartments	Three to five families or apartments	Six or more families or apartments
Under $5,000	.603	.887	.880	—
5,000–10,000	.437	.523	.606	.928
10,000–20,000	.312	.380	.478	.709
20.000–35,000	.320	.343	.387	.562
35,000–50,000	.345	.361	.419	.565
50,000–100,000	.371	.327	.369	.476
100,000–250,000	—	—	—	.548
250,000–1,000,000	—	—	—	.476

Source: Oldman and Aaron (1965, p. 44).

The average tax increase for single- and two-family houses would be the most pronounced, the tax change for apartments the most modest relatively. We lack the underlying control total necessary for estimating more precise percentage changes, so we cannot say whether the average apartment house will experience a modest tax increase or an actual decline. Since there is dispersion within any category, however, we can conjecture with some certainty that a good number of apartment houses would enjoy a decline in tax and many others a modest increase at worst, while very few single- or two-family residences could expect such an outcome.

In table 9.8 we carry the dispersion story one step further, this time with respect to price ranges within given types of residential property. The ASRs have a characteristic behavior for each category of residential property. They are highest for the least expensive properties, which suggests that these modest properties would experience a smaller average proportionate property tax increase or, in some cases, recognizing dispersion for individual properties within each price range, a more pronounced average decline in property tax, if Boston went over to market value assessments. The selling prices are as of 1962; ten years later, 1972, house prices were much higher. The classes in table 9.8, then, should be interpreted as "low," "medium," and "high" rather than as absolute numbers. Compared to the overall average, "low" price houses, as we have said, would experience a less vigorous increase than the average in tax liability under full-value assessment. "Medium" and "high" price houses, however, now relatively underassessed, would experience a higher than average tax increase. Again we note that these results are averages for each price class. With considerable additional dispersion to be expected within each class around its average, a number of "low" price homes might well enjoy a cut in taxes. For "medium" and "high" price houses this would be a less frequent result.

14. The estimates of the last several paragraphs suggest that multi-family residences, particularly apartment houses, would experience a relatively modest tax increase under full-value assessment (a not inconsiderable number of them in all likelihood might receive reductions in tax) while single-family houses in, say, the West Roxbury-Hyde Park area would be subject to sharply increased burdens. The existing dispersion of effective rates may reflect quite closely, by broad classes of property and regions of the city, the political effectiveness of taxpayers and their attitude toward the property tax. If tenants as a whole do not think they bear much of the property tax and have no particular sympathy for relieving the tax burden on landlords and if some of the recent speculation about the incidence of the property tax is correct in stating

that the tenants are at least in part right in their intuition, then the case for a substantial reduction in the burdens on apartment houses may be difficult to make.[6] Conversely, the owners of single-family homes in the West Roxbury-Hyde Park area constitute an important group of voters who would be reluctant to lose the benefit from the city's practice of only rarely raising assessments even in areas of rising property values and who are not particularly concerned that other taxpayers not so favorably situated bear the burdens not borne by West Roxbury-Hyde Park.

15. If one looks at the city public as a whole, from the point of view of who gains and who loses, an important advantage of going to 100 percent valuation is public awareness of the policy and the possible assistance of the public in policing it. At present the lack of public awareness of assessment policy or of changes in it makes it easy for the city to engage in one or another kind of tax deal. The situation is ripe for abuse and the entrenchment of existing differentials and distortions. One device that may be found useful to the city to assist in the policing of the 100 percent valuation policy (or any other publicly announced, legal policy) is the one used in Wisconsin, perhaps in some other states, and in New Zealand. Under this device a statute would enable two or three taxpayers to petition the local administration (and if no action is taken there, the State Tax Commission) to revalue a property which the petitioners think is underassessed. Since assessment records are public already, the comparisons of assessments by taxpayers would provide a useful general check which would identify flagrant underassessment.

16. While group averages, then, by no means tell the whole of the story, they are sufficient data for suggesting that there may well be political obstacles in the way of complete and immediate implementation of the legally required full-value assessment. The discussion of the next several paragraphs is based, for convenience, on the "initial impact" estimates of tax liability change. While they tend to overstate the amount of tax change, we are interested here primarily in the relative picture for the different major property categories and the direction of change in relative burden attendant upon one or another modification of uniform full-value assessment. And these general points are not affected by the upward bias of the "initial impact" estimates vis-a-vis those based on the "steady state" assumption.

An average increase in property tax on residences of 20 percent, an average decline of property tax of 38 percent for "old" commercial properties, and an average rise of 78 percent for "new" commercial

6. For surveys of references to literature on recent property tax incidence studies, see Ladd (1973) and Netzer (1973).

Table 9.9. Percentage Difference in Property Tax Burden of Specified Categories of Real Property under Six Alternative Bases Compared with Current Tax, Boston, 1972 ("initial impact" estimates)

Category	Market value	New commercial freeze	50% adjustment new commercial	50% adjustment all property	50% adjustment residential	Residential freeze
All commercial						
New	+78	0	+39	+59	+95	+111
Old	—38	—33	—36	—29	—32	— 26
Total	—19	—28	—24	—15	—12	— 4
Residential	+20	+29	+25	+15	+10	0
Other	+41	+52	+47	+31	+54	+ 68
All taxable property	0	0	0	0	0	0

properties may simply be too severe a change to be implemented in full. Moreover, it could be that even if the political will to effectuate such a change existed, the moral force behind agreements made by the city with property owners may preclude instantaneous and complete application of full valuation to "new" commercial properties, even though the agreements may be without legal force. In recognition of these considerations, we have analyzed the redistributive consequences of five alternative courses of action between doing nothing and going to 100 percent valuation for all. The estimates on which our discussion is based appear in table 9.9.

17. If it should turn out that the city of Boston is, in effect, committed by its contractual arrangements to a "freeze" on "new" commercial property, the portion of the total property tax load borne by other categories of property would, perforce, be higher than if the "new" commercial were also to be assessed at full value. Residential property would, on the average, bear a tax 29 percent higher than at present rather than 20 percent higher, while "old" commercial properties would experience a more modest decline, albeit of about one-third, compared to the 38 percent decline under full-value assessment for all properties. Obviously, a mayor caught between a judicial directive to tax uniformly at full market value and a "new" commercial "freeze" would be in the unenviable position of having to adjust property tax liabilities so homeowners and renters (all voters) experienced an average rise of 29 percent in their property tax, while the property tax of "new" commercial properties was unchanged, and the load on "old" commercial properties fell by a third.

18. Under such pressure the mayor might well decide (if the law gave him some scope) that while he would have to show special solicitude for

those properties with tax compacts, he could not afford not to raise somewhat the tax due from them. He might, for example, as regards "new" commercial property make half of the adjustment called for by the principle of full-value assessment. Our estimates suggest, however, that there is not much political nourishment in such a policy. It is true that homeowners would have a smaller tax increase than under the "new" commercial "freeze," but an average increase of 25 percent over present levels could still be considered "crushing." Moreover, if it is true that the compacts were necessary at the margin of choice to get new development to locate in Boston and not elsewhere, a 39 percent average increase in the tax that would otherwise be due from a newly constructed commercial project might significantly curtail new construction. "Old" commercial properties would, of course, enjoy a 36 percent average decline in property tax, but it is doubtful that the gratitude from this sector would go far toward placating irate homeowners or relieving those concerned with the possible decline in new commercial construction.

19. The mayor then might consider a compromise that affected all categories of taxable property "equally." One possibility would be to move halfway toward full value from present assessments and tax accordingly. Residential property currently relatively more underassessed (compared with the market value benchmark) would, of course, have to pay more than at present under this alternative too. But the average experience would be less of a jolt than in the various policies discussed in the several preceding paragraphs. The average property tax of residential properties would increase by 15 percent and "old" commercial properties would enjoy a 29 percent decline in property tax, while "new" commercial properties would find their property tax up by more than 50 percent. Homeowners would be less upset than under the other alternatives reviewed up to this point, but commercial developers could well find a 59 percent increase in taxes definitely discouraging.

20. Even more concern could be shown for the homeowner. Illustrative of these possibilities is a policy of adjusting residential properties in part to the new basis—the example we chose involved making half the adjustment called for—and making up the rest of the required tax revenue from the commercial sector. The average tax increase experienced by residential properties under this arrangement would be quite modest, about 10 percent. "Old" commercial properties would, nonetheless, enjoy a 32 percent cut in property tax payments, but "new" commercial properties would find their tax increased by an average of 95 percent. With this policy the mayor would be keeping the unhappiness of homeowners to a relatively modest level, but at the expense of severe discouragement to new commercial development.

21. Of course freezing the tax due from residences would be even more popular with homeowners. And it would also permit a slight fall in the tax on commercial properties (at the expense of "other" property) as compared with liabilities under current assessments. But within the commercial sector "new" properties would experience, on the average, more than a doubling of tax due, while "old" properties would find the property tax about 26 percent lighter.

22. All these policies reflect the conflicting pressures operating on the mayor in going from the current assessments to full-value assessment. That step would raise taxes on residences by more than a fifth and on "new" commercial properties by nearly 80 percent. Thus he would feel the wrath of voters (homeowners and renters) and face the prospect of a sharp curtailment of property development in the city. To the extent that he attempted to mollify the former he would accentuate the latter, and vice versa. Of course this is no new discovery. It is simply the specific property tax version of the iron law of politics. To the extent that the size of the pie is fixed you can only give more of it to A at the expense of less to B.

23. While these reflections are based primarily on the average results, they would be substantially modified if we were to take account of the diversity around the average. Some modest efforts in this connection are reported above; the results whet our appetites for more extensive work in this connection. Certainly that task is high on our list of further work to be done. Nonetheless, the inferences possible now without further extensive study suggest that taking account of the diversity of experience will illuminate still more difficult areas of trade-off. Thus in moving to full-value assessment we think it likely that a number of residential properties in Roxbury would enjoy a tax cut, since the divergence (in an upward direction) of their assessment from the residential average is greater than that sector's divergence (downward) from the average for all properties. But at the same time, political benefits from this prospect might be nullified by the large increase in tax liability on the homeowners in the other sections of the city.

What Can the Mayor Do?

While no elected official is likely voluntarily to undertake a tax policy irritating to sensitive sectors—the voting public (in their guise as homeowners and renters) and property developers—the mayor of Boston (and his counterparts in other cities and towns in the commonwealth) will not be able to avoid doing so, since the Massachusetts Supreme Judicial Court has mandated putting the property tax on a market value base.

In carrying out that mandate the mayor could avoid the large re-distribution of tax liability, described earlier as likely, by finding more revenue. This can come from extending the property tax to real estate that the city does not now reach, or by getting more revenue from an additional tax not now levied by the city, or by stepped up grants-in-aid from the commonwealth or the federal government. With the additional revenues in prospect Boston could lower the effective rate of property tax on properties presently taxable and thus moderate the tax increases that most homeowners and others would otherwise experience on the adoption of market value assessment. For example, if $55 million could be obtained from some other source and the property tax take were reduced by this amount, it would become an effective levy of 5.4 percent on market value, so that, generally, residential property, which is paying at just about that rate now, would find its property tax liability un-changed. And if even more were forthcoming, say $75 million, then most residential properties would pay a lower property tax even under market value assessment.[7] The $55 to $75 million required is between 20 and 25 percent of the present level of property tax collections. Where could such a sum come from? The answer obviously is a major study in itself. The several conjectures that make up the rest of this section are not the major contribution of our study. We bring them up here in the hope that they will induce others to join the discussion of alternatives or additional measures that might be employed. Our remarks are quite selective; the failure to cover a number of well-thought-out proposals already put forth should not be taken to imply criticism of them.

1. For a start, it is not unlikely that more could be wrung out of the property tax by identifying and placing on the rolls taxable property that is not now there and by getting new property on the rolls more rapidly. The Jacobs Company report (1971) pointed to a substantial shortfall between what the construction data suggested additions to the taxable rolls should be and what they in fact were. Whether this property is really "missing" or whether the explanation lies in a long lag in administration is not really important. Whether "found" or more speedily put on the rolls, some property not now taxed could be. Property tax revenues could be increased, or for an unchanged amount of property tax collections mill rates could be lowered. The amount of

7. Of course "old" commercial properties presently taxed would enjoy even more sub-stantial declines than those suggested in our tables. But the envy that this would cause among owners of residential property is not likely to be as distressing politically as their anger in the face of full-value assessment with no cut in the mill rate.

Table 9.10. Volume of New Construction Compared with Annual Increase in Assessed Values, Boston, 1967 and 1968 (in millions of dollars)

	New construction reported by building department			Value increases reported by assessing department
	Total	Nontaxable	Net taxable	Total
1967	$231	$66	$165	$36
1968	211	32	179	22
Total	442	98	344	58

Source: Jacobs Company (1971, p. 83).

property involved here is not enough to solve the problem, but it might help substantially.

The report by the Jacobs Company provides the data found in table 9.10 that permit a comparison of new construction and increases in the valuation roll over several years.

While building department records indicated $344 million of net taxable construction over the two years 1967 and 1968, taxable valuations rose by only $58 million. Discrepancies of this magnitude are probably not due to a single factor. By way of explaining the shortfall we can suggest these possibilities: (1) assessed values are below market value; (2) some properties get "lost"; or (3) there is a lag in getting properties on to the tax rolls. To the extent that the two latter reasons explain the gap (the Jacobs report, 1971, page 84, implies they are important in this connection) then by improving the administration of the property tax Boston could raise the same amount of revenue it currently does with a lower mill rate.

This is only one instance of the rate reduction potential of administrative improvements in the property tax. For a careful documentation of the opportunities (or needs, if one prefers) in this connection, see the Jacobs report noted above.

In summary, then, one answer to the question "What can the mayor do?" is simply to improve property tax administration. This is something he should do in any case in order to make the most of the new property record system now in the process of installation, but it could be that a mandated shift to full-value assessment would sharpen the perception of the need and energize the will to undertake the task.

2. A tempting area to search for additions to the property tax base would appear to be property presently exempt from tax. In Boston the assessed value of tax-exempt property at $1,725 million (in 1970) exceeds taxable property of $1,617 million. Even more to the point, whereas taxable real property increased by $280 million between 1960 and 1970, the value of tax-exempt property rose by $850 million. If relative rates of

Table 9.11. Distribution of Exempt Property in Boston, 1969

Category	Percentage of total
United States of America	4.0%
Commonwealth of Massachusetts	42.3
City of Boston	33.3
Literary and scientific	6.1
Charitable and benevolent	3.9
Religious	2.7
Cemeteries	6.1
Other	1.4

Source: Jacobs Company (1971).

growth of this order of magnitude were to continue for the next decade, merely slowing down the additions to the tax-exempt sector by a more rigorous interpretation of the exemption privilege could add importantly to the tax base.

The present stock of tax-exempt real property, appears a tempting target, but the allure dissipates quickly when one examines its composition (see table 9.11). Boston is a capital city; consequently the vast mass of tax-exempt property, 80 percent, is owned by government. But this concentration, in fact, suggests an opportunity. While government property cannot now be taxed, the city could well seek payments from the commonwealth and the federal government in lieu of taxation. Mayor Kevin White has recently made a proposal in this connection to the effect that the commonwealth pay in lieu of property tax a sum equal to 20 percent of the property tax that would have been due if their properties had been subject to tax. If accepted this proposal alone would permit a 4-5 percent cut in the mill rate. A further cut of the same magnitude could be supported by getting half the nongovernment properties presently exempt from tax on the tax rolls.[8] This is probably unlikely to be accomplished, but, needless to say, the mayor should push as hard as he can in this area. Also, of course, he need not remain content with in-lieu payments equal to one-fifth of the tax that might have been due, but could press for a higher percentage.

Given his present fiscal powers these two attempts—improving property tax administration and curbing and reversing tax exemption and obtaining in-lieu payments with respect to it—exhaust the opportunities available to the mayor of Boston, who basically is limited to the real

8. New York City has recently successfully added to the tax rolls the property of bar associations and scientific organizations as a result of legislative and judicial decisions. See *Association of the Bar of the City of New York* v. *Lewisohn,* 34 N.Y.2d 143 (1974).

property tax in his search for revenue. Of course the mayor can also levy charges and fees, and undoubtedly there is some revenue potential in this source, but as a quick judgment (and necessarily, therefore, provisional) there does not seem to be enough new revenue here to offset substantially the need for property tax revenue. Moreover, the mayor would be well advised to pay appropriate attention to allocation effects, as well as maximum revenue, in designing the structure of fees and charges.

3. Right now the mayor would probably like the power to tap a new major revenue source. Were he required to tax property at full market value, he would feel the need more intensely. Were he able to add some points to the sales tax for city use or to institute a city income or payroll tax, the city could raise enough to support a sizable cut in the property tax rate. So another course of action for the mayor is to seek the power to levy one or several new major taxes.

Of course to relieve the rate of property tax it is not necessary that the city do the job. It could be effectuated (and, perhaps in a superior fashion) by actions at the state level. Increased state income and sales tax revenues could be used by the state to finance or assume the operation of selected municipal programs such as mass transportation, parks, refuse disposal, courts, and libraries or to finance all or part of the cost of state-mandated property tax exemptions based on personal characteristics (age, widow, veteran) of the owner-occupant. A particularly promising approach, we think, is embodied in the Master Tax Plan Commission proposal which would, in essence, (1) abate the effective rate of property tax for local governments in the commonwealth by converting the tax substantially to an almost uniform, statewide levy for local governments' use; (2) keep the property tax to a specified (and lower than at present) fraction of total commonwealth and local revenues; and (3) have the state increase sales and income taxes to raise the additional funds needed by local government. The mayor of Boston could only applaud any recasting of revenue structure to give the state and the broad revenue raisers it has exclusive use of—income and sales taxes—a greater role and the property tax a lesser one, provided Boston received its proper share of the revenues so raised.[9] One more thing the mayor can do, then, is to support and encourage greater use of the income tax (and possibly the sales tax as well) and a smaller role for the property tax. Given the present distribution of fiscal powers between the

9. Changes of the sort envisioned by the Master Tax Plan Commission carry with them a complete overhaul of the formulas and arrangements for state aid to local government. Moreover, the *Sudbury* decision may well precipitate state legislative action on state aid distribution. It may therefore be only of temporary importance to note that full valuation under current state aid arrangements may be costly to Boston.

commonwealth and its cities and towns, this means exhorting and encouraging the commonwealth to undertake the initiative and responsibility. A strong effort to get the Master Tax Plan Commission to issue its final report would be an important first step.

4. Another interesting proposal is the subject of a recent report by the Boston Urban Observatory (1973). In this study a case is made for state assumption of responsibility for a range of municipal services including public transit and safety, solid waste and sewage, health and hospitals, regional parks and recreation, and some others. The tax saving involved for Boston would, it is estimated, "be equivalent to about 26 percent of the 1973 property tax levy."

In brief summary, it appears that there are real possibilities of raising additional revenues from other sources and/or shifting the fiscal responsibility for some expenditures currently financed by Boston to permit a shift to full-value property taxation without unduly increasing the taxes due from the "average" homeowner.[10] But the mayor of Boston cannot pull the necessary levers on his own. Cooperation and involvement at the state level will be required.

5. Finally, more for serious consideration than immediate implementation, we suggest the possibility of a levy, separate and distinct from the property tax, on land value per se. It would be applicable to all properties, including, therefore, those exempt from the property tax. The levy on land value could be considered a charge to be paid by all properties in the city because they all make some demand on city facilities and require city services. Structured as a charge, it should, in principle, be applicable also to real estate exempt from the property tax. To view such a charge as a modest rental fee for occupying space at the Hub of the World might be one of the more appealing ways of presenting the idea.

With land estimated at one-fourth to one-third of the total value of property, and with the value of tax-exempt property at least as great as taxable property, the land value charge at a rate equivalent to 1 percent would raise on the order of $24-32 million and might have a healthy impact on the allocation of land uses. (If the levy were limited to taxable property, revenue would be between $12 and $16 million.) Either sum could replace an equivalent amount of property tax, lowering the latter's effective rate and moderating the impact of full-value assessment. Moreover, it is likely that the land value charge would further work to moderate the strength of the redistributions to be expected from full-value assessment, because it would fall differently from the property tax.

10. Attendant upon the new assessment, however, residential properties now grossly relatively under-assessed or over-assessed would have major changes in their tax bill.

Presently in Boston for each property separate assessments are made for the land and improvement components. While no pretense is made at accuracy for each component (the primary interest attaching to the accuracy of the assessment of the property per se, that is, the land plus improvements), the ratio of land to total value if different enough among different categories of property is probably truly different. The ratio appears to differ significantly for "old" and "new" commercial properties. From the sample of commercial properties we used in estimating assessment-sales ratios, we separated "old" (181 properties) and "new" (35 properties) and calculated the ratio of land to total property value. For "old" it came to 0.4, while for "new" it was 0.2. (Too much weight should not be given to these two numbers, however. We were unable to obtain sufficient information to be confident about the magnitude of the difference.) These results generally conform to what might be expected since "old" properties built in periods of lower land prices would be less intensively developed than "new" properties. Thus the land value charge at the same rate (percentage) for all properties would bear more heavily on "old" than on "new" commercial properties, which would have an impact that would tend to soften somewhat the tax blow on "new" commercial properties to be expected from assessment at 100 percent of market value and also to tone down the tax decrease that "old" commercial properties would experience.

APPENDIX A: Methods Used in Deriving Estimates of Market Value and Assessed Value for Taxable Real Property, as of 1972, in Boston

In this appendix we will summarize briefly the methods by which we estimated market and assessed value by class of taxable property. And we will also compare our estimates with those of other studies. A detailed description of the procedures employed can be found in Holland and Oldman (1974, section 3).

First, in table 9.12 we will take up the estimates of market value for most categories of taxable commercial real property, for which a common methodology was used. Then we will briefly explain the remainder of the market value estimates. Finally, we will indicate in table 9.13 assessment-sales ratios which, together with the estimated market values, furnished the estimates of assessed value.

Since 1960, we take it, most of the commercial real property built in the city of Boston has been covered by agreements between the developers and the city which set the property tax liability at a specified fraction of gross income from the property, with the result that assessed values and effective rates of tax run lower than those that apply to commercial

Table 9.12. Estimation of Market Value of Various Categories of Commercial Real Property, Boston, 1972

Category of property (1)	Estimated physical amount (millions of square feet) (2)	Estimated replacement cost per square foot (3)	Land as percentage of total value (4)	Estimated land value per square foot[a] (5)	Depreciation factor (6)	Estimated improvement value per square foot[b] (7)	Total value per square foot[c] (8)	Total market value in category[d] (millions of dollars) (9)
Office								
New	6.7	$ 43.18	25%	$ 14.39	4.2%	$ 41.37	$ 55.76	$374
Old								
Class B	5.3	24.54	25	7.88	25.9	18.41	26.29	139
Class C	11.9	18.02	25	6.00	25.0	13.52	19.52	232
Total	23.9							745
Retailing								
New	3.7	34.56	27	12.78	4.2	33.11	45.89	170
Old	18.3	16.43	25	6.08	25.0	12.32	18.40	337
Total	22.0							507
Hotels								
New[e]	1,563[f]	30,000[g]	25	7,500[g]	4.2	21,555[g]	29,055[g]	45
Old[e]	4,643		25		25.0		13,011	60
Total	6,206							105
Manufacturing								
New	1.0	25.16	20	6.04	6.8	22.52	28.56	29
Old	29.0	11.34	20	2.84	25.0	8.51	11.35	329
Total	30.0							358
Warehousing								
New	2.0	17.04	25	5.63	5.5	16.10	21.73	43
Old	10.0	9.43	25	3.14	25.0	7.07	10.21	102
Total	12.0							145

[a] Column 5 = [column 3 ÷ (100.0 − column 4)] −column 3.
[b] Column 7 = column 3 × (100.0 − column 6).
[c] Column 8 = column 5 + column 7.
[d] Column 9 = column 2 + column 8.

[e] Since in our hotel estimates column 2's costs include land, the estimation of market values is different for this category than for the others in the table.
[f] Number of rooms.
[g] Per room.

properties of earlier vintage. Therefore, we developed separate estimates for these two categories of taxable commercial real property. In what follows, properties constructed before 1960 will be referred to as "old," while those built from 1960 on will be designated as "new."

While market values were developed separately for "old" and "new" commercial property, similar methods were employed in making the estimates. Market value is derived as the product of a physical amount of property[11] and the per unit cost (construction and land) of reproducing the property.[12]

By way of summary, then, our basic assumptions in deriving market values of most classes of taxable commercial real property were that the current value of that property is equal to the sum of the construction costs of replacing the structure (depreciated back to the time of construction, on the average)[13] and the value of the land on which the structure stands.

Table 9.12 summarizes the estimates for most categories of commercial property.

Property Categories Not Explained in Table 9.12

Commercial Personal Services Not Included in Office Space (SNIOS)

For one major category of commercial property there is not sufficient information for estimating market values in the manner just described. This category is made up of a vast variety of personal services, including laundries, barber shops, beauty parlors, repairs of all kinds, auto and equipment rentals, motion pictures, amusements and recreation, edu-

---

11. Square feet for all categories but hotels, for which the physical unit was number of rooms.

12. For estimates of the physical amount of property by category (office, retail, hotels, manufacturing, and warehousing) we are indebted to the Boston Redevelopment Authority (BRA) and wish to thank Alex Ganz and Susan Houston particularly. Replacement costs (exclusive of land) for the most part came from the *Stevens Valuation Quarterly*. Land costs (values) were estimated on the basis of typical ratios of land to other costs suggested by Theodore R. Smith of the Harvard Law School International Tax Program. Smith has cautioned that these ratios are approximations subject to wide margins of error. We thank him for his help and absolve him from blame in our specific use of the information he provided.

13. The cost approach to valuation is well recognized in this state and elsewhere, especially with respect to properties which are not obsolete in use or are relatively new. See, for example, Commonwealth of Massachusetts, Department of Corporations and Taxation (1973); Bonbright (1937, chap. 8, pp. 144-45); *Seagram* v. *Tax Com'n*, 18 App. Div. 2d 109, 238 N.Y.S. 2d 228 (1963), affirmed 14 N.Y. 2d 314, 251 N.Y.S. 2d 460, 200 N.E. 2d 447; and *Matter of 860 Fifth Ave. Corp.* v. *Tax Com'n*, 8 N.Y. 2d 29, 32, 167 N.E. 2d 445, 456 (1960).

cation, museums, and so on. To arrive at a figure for the market value of commercial property in this category, we utilized payroll data relying on the assumption that in the main the ratio of payrolls to market value of premises is substantially similar across industries, so that this sector's share of payrolls in Boston would be a reasonable proxy for its share of commercial property.

Utilities and Transportation

Utilities (electricity, gas, and telephone) hold extensive amounts of property in Boston, but very little of it shows up in the tax rolls in a way that is germane to our study. Most of what utilities own is, apparently, classified as personal property, while two very important transportation facilities are not on the taxable rolls, one being owned by the Boston Redevelopment Authority and the other by the Massachusetts Bay Transit Authority.

Thus, the five utility companies—American Telephone and Telegraph, New England Telephone, Western Union, Boston Edison, and Boston Gas—were assessed on the taxable rolls in 1972 for $7.1 million of real property (this is the figure relevant for our study) and $154 million of personal property. With respect to transportation, the Greyhound Terminal was assessed at $1 million, Trailways Terminal at $175 thousand, North Station (difficult to identify in the records) at something like this or less, while South Station, owned by the BRA, and Back Bay Station, owned by the MBTA, were, of course, exempt from the property tax.

With identified taxable utility real property assessed at around $7 million and taxable transportation real property assessments on the order of $1.5 million, a total of $10 million for this category seemed reasonable. On the assumption that these properties are assessed by the state at 100 percent of market value, we estimated both the assessed value and market value of taxable properties in this category as $10 million. In the tabulations, we put all of this category of real property under "old."

Residential

An estimate by the Boston Redevelopment Authority (BRA) which appeared in a memorandum of April 30, 1973, explains its derivation of the value of all residential property as follows:

The total residential figure was developed primarily from a BRA report entitled "The Housing Stock of the City of Boston by Neighborhood." This source, based on 1970 census material, presented the aggregate 1970 market value of all housing for each neighborhood in Boston. Briefly, the market value figures were, for single-family housing, based on captalization of rents. Capitalization rates were developed for each neighborhood on the basis of information on vacancies, trends of residential sales prices, and family income. To update the 1970 values to 1972, price indices were used. These indices were developed for the same neighborhoods as were presented in "The Housing Stock" and reflected the change in sales prices for all residential property that had been sold at least twice. These indices were applied to each of the neighborhood market value figures for 1970, and, with some modifications for actual changes in the housing stock, the resulting 1972 values were summed to the total figure of $2.602 billion.

But this figure, based on approximately 232,000 dwelling units, includes all taxable and tax exempt residential properties. Taxable properties alone number about 214,000.

Adjusting simply on the proportion of the number of exempt residential units to the total number of dwelling units (that is, taking $\frac{214,000}{232,000}$ of the total value of $2.6 billion) would be inappropriate, since tax-exempt housing (primarily public housing) generally has a lower average value than taxable housing. From a study on subsidized housing by the Boston Urban Observatory (1972) an estimate of $21,000 per subsidized dwelling unit ("new" construction) was obtained, and Mark Gilman and Robert Earsy of the BRA estimated an order of magnitude cost of $30,000 per dwelling unit for "new" private construction. Assuming these two figures to indicate the *relative* values of exempt and taxable dwelling units, respectively, we lowered $2.6 billion by (1— $\frac{214,000}{232,000} \times \frac{\$21}{\$30}$) to get $2,456 million as our estimate of the market value of taxable residential property.[14]

Other

This category is derived by working backwards from the assessed value estimates of table 9.13 and an ASR of .23—the same as that reported in U.S. Bureau of the Census (1973, p. 127) for vacant platted land, since vacant lots represented virtually the whole of locally assessed taxable real property not accounted for by commercial and residential in 1966, the most recent year for which such estimates are available.

Specifically, in Boston in 1966 residential and commercial and industrial (which combined category we have been referring to as commercial) made up 96.6 percent of the total; vacant lots accounted for 3.1 percent;

14. The data on number of housing units used in this estimate are available due to the generosity of Susan Houston of the BRA.

and what the Census of Governments designated as "other and un-allocable" represented 0.3 percent. Our "other," amounting to 3.4 percent, is the sum of these two latter categories (for the data see U.S. Bureau of the Census, 1968, p. 132). Having estimated the assessed values for commercial and residential as described in the notes for table 9.13, we were able to derive a figure for "other" on the assumption that

Table 9.13. Derivation of Current Assessed Value of Real Property from Estimated Market Value, Boston, 1972

Property category	Estimated market value (millions of dollars)	Assessment-sales ratio	Estimated assessed value (millions of dollars)
Commercial			
Office			
New	$ 374	.18	$ 67
Old	371	.52	193
Total	745		260
Retail			
New	170	.18	31
Old	337	.52	175
Total	507		206
Hotel			
New	45	.18	8
Old	60	.52	31
Total	105		39
Manufacturing			
New	29	.32	9
Old	329	.52	171
Total	358		180
Warehousing			
New	43	.14	6
Old	102	.52	53
Total	145		59
Personal services (SNIOS)			
New	35	.18	6
Old	70	.52	36
Total	105		42
Utilities and transportation (tabulated with old)	10	1.00	10
All commercial			
New	696		127
Old	1,279		669
Total	1,975		796
Residential	2,456	.27	663
Other	222	.23	51
All taxable property	4,653		1,510

this category represented the same percentage of total assessed value in Boston in 1972 as it did in 1966.

Then, as explained above, we estimated the market value of other property on the assumption that the assessed value was 23 percent of market value, ending up with $222 million.

Assessed Values

Introduction

From the market values whose derivation has been explained above, we obtained estimates of assessed value for each category of taxable real property by application of assessment-sales ratios, that is, ratios assembled from the data of real property sales whose numeratory is the assessed value of the property sold and whose denominator is the selling price. In table 9.13, we list the assessment-sales ratios used for each category of property, and in the discussion that follows the table we explain very succinctly the source of each.

Derivation of Assessment-Sales Ratio for "Old" Commercial Properties

For "old" commercial properties we developed an assessment-sales ratio based on sales of commercial properties in 1972. For this purpose commercial was taken to mean all taxable real properties other than residences.

The sample used in deriving the ratio was drawn from a data base consisting of all reported sales of commercial properties in 1972. From the 240 seemingly separate transactions that made up the basic data, 51 were excluded as invalid or inappropriate. The final sample, therefore, contained 189 sales.

"New" Commercial Properties

To obtain the equivalent of ASRs for "new" commercial properties, we calculated weighted averages of the ratios of assessed value to development costs for particular properties in each of four categories. For fifteen commercial office space buildings the ratio (weighted by development cost which was assumed equal to market value) was .18, in our sample of thirteen retail properties it was .18, a sample of six manufacturing properties had a ratio of .32, while for nine warehousing facilities it was .14. For "new" hotels we made no survey but used the .18 for an ASR, since this appeared to be the typical value for "new" commercial properties. And we did the same for SNIOS.

The ASR of 1.00 for utilities and transportation, as has been explained above, reflects our understanding that the state values such properties at 100 percent of market. In any event the value of taxable property in this category is very small, so an error in the ASR is inconsequential.

"Old" and "New" Residential Property

The ASR of .27 for all residential property—"old" and "new"—is the figure given for all residential (nonfarm) property for Boston in U.S. Bureau of the Census (1973, p. 127).

Other Property

As noted earlier the ASR of .23 is that reported for vacant platted land (the predominant component of "other") in U.S. Bureau of the Census (1973, p. 127).

Evaluating Our Estimates

We noted above that while at every juncture we chose those assumptions and data that seemed most "appropriate," the wide variety of plausible alternatives not chosen suggests that our estimates cannot be validated on a priori grounds, but, like the pudding of the proverb, can only be evaluated in the eating.

Therefore it is quite comforting to find that the assessed value estimates conform very closely to two control totals:

1. The Boston Assessors Office tabulation of taxable assessed value in 1972 was $1,532 million. Our estimate of taxable assessed value, independently derived from our market value estimates, is $1,510 million, which differs from the tabulated total by less than 2 percent.

2. For 1966 (the most recent year for which such a breakdown was available), the *Census of Governments, 1967* puts commercial property at 55.4 percent of total assessed value of taxable real property, residential at 41.1 percent, and other property at 3.4 percent. Our estimates for 1972 for these three classifications are 52.7, 43.9, and 3.4 percent, respectively. The similarity in the proportion accounted for by other property in the two totals simply reflects our methodology. But the close correspondence for the other two categories suggests to us that some measure of confidence can be placed in our estimate of market values and the assessed values derived from them.

Of course, the results just reported could be consistent with major errors in the specific categories making up the commercial total or in the division between "old" and "new." This suggests that we can place more confidence in the broad redistribution of property tax liability between commercial and residential that is indicated by our estimates than we can in the redistributions within the commercial total. But, after all, it is the former redistribution, not the latter, that is our prime concern. The judgment that the direction of the redistributions we have identified and their general orders of magnitude are rather "robust" results is reinforced by a comparison of our estimates of market value with those made by others.

We have found two other sets of estimates of the assessed value and the market value of taxable property in Boston as of substantially the same date as ours. As we have already explained, while it is our judgment that our estimates are the "best" we could make, they are far from definitive. Therefore it is useful to compare them with the other available estimates to judge how our results would be modified were we to use these other sources as the basis for estimating the tax redistribution among classes of property.

The other two studies (see footnote 3) and ours all employ somewhat different classifications of taxable property; comparability among them is possible only on the broadest bases. Specifically we compare the tax burden redistribution with respect to just two broad sectors: between residential property and "all others" (which makes up the rest of taxable property).

One of the studies, hereinafter designated "Bureau," was the annual equalization study undertaken by the Bureau of Land Assessing of the Department of Corporations and Taxation of the Commonwealth of Massachusetts, and consists of estimates of assessed value and market value as of the end of 1973. (We are indebted to William C. Wheaton for bringing this source to our attention.) The study groups taxable property in four classes: residential, industrial, commercial, and personal. We excluded personal property from our study and subtracted it from the bureau's totals in the comparisons we will make. In deriving the entries of table 9.14, their commercial and industrial were summed to get "all other," which with residential adds up to a total taxable property figure comparable with our aggregate.

The other independent source, hereinafter designated "Equalization," as yet unpublished, is the 1974 equalization study of the Department of Corporations and Taxation of the Commonwealth of Massachusetts. Again as of the end of 1973, assessed values and market values are estimated for commercial, industrial, land, and residential properties. For comparison we lumped the first three under the category of "all other."

Finally, our own estimates (Holland and Oldman, 1974) are arrayed

Table 9.14. Comparison of Three Estimates of Assessed and Market Value of Taxable Property in Boston and Tax Burden Redistributions[a]

Source	Assessed value (millions of dollars)	Market value (millions of dollars)	Residential				All other			
			Proportion of total		Percentage of total tax redistributed	Relative change in tax	Proportion of total		Percentage of total tax redistributed	Relative change in tax
			Current assessed value	Market value			Current assessed value	Market value		
"Bureau"	$1,529	$4,353	.5186	.6552	+13.66	+26%	.4814	.3448	−13.66	−28%
"Equaliza-tion"	1,535	4,880	.3211	.4207	+ 9.96	+31	.6789	.5793	− 9.96	−15
Holland and Oldman (1974)	1,510	4,653	.4391	.5278	+ 8.87	+20	.5609	.4722	− 8.87	−16

[a] See text for sources and explanations of method.

into a comparable classification, by summing up "new" commercial, "old" commercial, and "other" to obtain an "all other" category which together with residential accounts for aggregate taxable property as of the end of 1972.

For purposes of table 9.14 tax burden change is calculated by the "initial impact" method.[15]

Turning to that table we note that the three estimates show remarkable agreement with respect to the aggregates. This is not as noteworthy for assessed value as for market value, since two of the three sources had available to them a *tabulated* breakdown of assessed value among categories of property.[16] But the close correspondence of the three estimates of market value is truly surprising.

Other things equal, the similarity among these three independent estimates would be encouraging. But other things are not equal. The sharp disparity in the proportions that residential and all other property constitute of total current assessed value and total market value in the three studies removes much of the encouragement. It is clear there is a great variation in the estimates of the components of the total, most likely due to differences in the basis of classifying larger residential properties which at least one of the other sources probably tabulates under commercial.

There is no way to determine which estimate is most correct.

We have Pygmalion's preference for our own creation, but have no strong basis other than parental pride to credit it above the others. There is a lesson, however, in table 9.14. Our method provides both the smallest amount of tax redistribution (see the percentage total tax redistributed figures) and the smallest relative change in taxes. We may conclude, therefore, that to the extent that either of the others or both are truly more correct than Holland and Oldman (1974), we have understated the amount of tax burden redistribution to be expected from 100 percent of market value assessment and the relative change in sector tax burdens caused thereby. And therefore we have understated the change in value of properties caused by the redistribution of tax liabilities among classes of property.

15. Specifically, to allocate the property tax burden on the basis of current assessed values, we use pro rata shares of the assessed value total; to allocate it on the basis of market values, we use each class's proportion of the total market value. The relative (percentage) tax change is the ratio of the difference between the shares on these respective bases and the share that the classification currently bears.

16. We remind the reader that Holland and Oldman (1974) did not. We, in effect, estimated assessed value from market value.

Table 9.15. Explanation of the Derivation of "Initial Impact" Tax Change Estimate, Boston, 1972 (dollar amounts in millions)

Property category	Assessed value (1)	Proportion of assessed value (2)	Current property tax (3)	Current market value (4)	Proportion of current market value (5)	Property tax based on market value (6)	Effective rate of property tax on current market value (8)	Change in property tax (8)	Percentage change in property tax (9)	Effective rate of tax "initial impact" (10)
"New" commercial	$ 127	.0841	$ 25.77	$ 696	.1496	$ 45.84	3.7%	+ $20.07	+ 78%	6.6%
"Old" commercial	669	.4430	135.74	1,279	.2749	84.23	10.6	− 51.51	−38	6.6
All commercial	796	.5271	161.51	1,975	.4245	130.07	8.2	− 31.44	−19	6.6
Residential	663	.4391	134.54	2,456	.5278	161.72	5.5	+ 27.18	+20	6.6
Other	51	.0338	10.36	222	.0477	14.61	4.7	+ 4.25	+41	6.6
Total	1,510	1.0000	306.40	4,653	1.0000	306.40	6.6	—	—	6.6

In short, as compared with our study the other available estimates suggest larger property tax liability redistributions than ours, relatively heavier changes in tax burdens by class of taxable property, and more pronounced changes in property values.

APPENDIX B: Explanation of Methods of Estimating Property Tax and Property Value Changes

In this appendix we will explain the methods of estimating tax and value changes that were used in our study.

"Initial Impact" and "First Iteration"

A straightforward way to estimate property tax redistributions to be expected from full value assessment is to (1) allocate a given amount of property tax among specified categories of assessed value on the basis of their proportionate share of total assessed value; (2) do the same on the basis of market value proportions; and (3) take the difference between the two tax liabilities in each category of property to be the tax change to be expected from a shift to market value on the basis of assessment for property tax purposes. Tax changes estimated this way, we call "initial impact" estimates. The magnitudes associated with their derivation appear in table 9.15.

By way of specific example, "old" commercial property had an assessed value of $669,000,000 (column 1), which came to .4430 of total assessed value of taxable property (column 2). Currently (as of 1972), then, this category is subject to .4430 of total property tax collections or $135,740,000 (column 3). But "old" commercial property, relatively over-assessed, constitutes a lower fraction of market value, .2749 (column 5). Applying this proportion to the total tax of $306,400,000 indicates the tax due from "old" commercial property on a market value basis would be $84,230,000 (column 6). Thus, under full value assessment the property tax on "old" commercial property would decline by $51,510,000 (column 8) or by 38 percent (column 9). Finally, a summary measure, with reference to market value, the current property tax on "old" commercial property is at an effective rate of 10.6 percent (column 7). Under 100 percent of market assessment, this category, and all others, would be subject to an effective rate of 6.6 percent.

This simple arithmetic exercise is one way of estimating the distributive impact of full-value assessment. While we call it the "initial impact" method, in fact redistributions as severe as this might not occur even initially. In any event the "initial impact" magnitudes would be

Table 9.16. Explanation of the Derivation of "First Iteration" Value Change Estimate, Boston, 1972 (dollar amounts in millions)

Property category	Change in value due to change in tax[a] (1)	"First iteration" market value[a] (2)	Change in value due to change in property tax[b] (3)	"First iteration" market value[b] (4)
"New" commercial	−$134	$ 562	−$201	$ 495
"Old" commercial	+ 343	1,622	+ 515	1,794
All commercial	+ 209	2,184	+ 314	2,289
Residential	− 181	2,275	− 272	2,184
Other	− 28	194	− 43	179
Total	—	4,653	—	4,653

[a] Assumes capitalization rate of 15 percent.
[b] Assumes capitalization rate of 10 percent.

quite ephemeral. We use this measure because of its simplicity and directness, and because this is the measure that has been most commonly employed in discussions of property tax redistribution.

The "initial impact" method might also be justified by the argument that with shift to a new basis for tax purposes, assessors, facing the possibility that their valuations will be challenged and, perhaps, brought to litigation, will base their assessments on the evidence a court would accept, that is, what the property could sell for in the market at the time of valuation. This is not a very supportive argument for anything more than a very brief life, if any, for the "initial impact" estimates.

For as soon as a new distribution of a given total tax liability is struck, every property can be expected to have a new market value that reflects the change in its tax. In the aggregate the market value of property in Boston will remain the same (since the total tax levied on it would not change), but all properties whose taxes are now higher will fall in value, while those enjoying lower tax liabilities will be worth more than before. So a second set of market values would be established by going to full-value assessment, aggregate tax collections remaining unchanged. But this set of market values, too, will prove evanescent, as a new distribution of tax liabilities based on them will, once again, induce a change in the underlying structure of values, and so on.

Specifically, were "old" commercial property to enjoy a tax decrease of $51,510,000 it would become more valuable than at present. Assuming first that current market values do not reflect expectations of a shift to full value for tax purposes in any way and second that the capitalization rate for real estate in Boston in 15 percent, "old" commercial property would be worth $343,000,000 more (column 1 of table 9.16). This is the change in value as estimated by the "first iteration" method which is the logical counterpart of the "initial impact" tax change. In our judgment a rate of 15 percent is appropriate for capitalizing properties in Boston, but we have also provided in table 9.16 estimates based on a 10 percent rate (columns 3 and 4).

But the "first iteration," too, may, in fact, never occur; and if it did, it could have a very limited time span of relevance. For, if the value of "old" commercial properties increases by $343,000,000, they would be subject to higher property tax payments, which, in turn, would cause a change in value, and so on. Even within their rigid framework, then, the "initial impact" and "first iteration" estimates are not likely to be relevant for more than a brief period, and if investors expect the shift to full-value assessment to take place, these values will never transpire. Thus the "initial impact" and "first iteration" estimates are more appropriately considered the upper bound on a range of possible values.

The Iterative Process

We have been sketching out a process of tax change leading to a value change that could be spun out interminably, since there would be an infinite number of changes in market value determined by the process. This is not a realistic description of how the market would operate, but it is useful to analyze the process, since our "steady state" estimates are equivalent to the limiting values of the iterative process.

Our understanding of this process and the analysis that follows draws very heavily on the work of Dickstein (1974). Following Dickstein, we define V_i as the value of property at time i, T_i as the tax on property at time i, C as the capitalization rate, and E as the effective rate of tax on market value.

Start the process of tax change, value change, tax change, etc., after the first set of new tax liabilities which determine the tax change, ΔT_1, under full value assessment have been determined. Then for any given property or class of property, Dickstein derives the following:

(1) $\qquad \Delta V_1 = \Delta T_1/C$;

(2) $\qquad \Delta T_2 = \Delta V_1 \cdot E, \qquad$ and $\quad \Delta T_2 = \Delta T_1(E/C)$;

(3) $\qquad \Delta V_2 = \Delta T_2/C, \qquad$ and $\quad \Delta V_2 = \Delta T_2/C$;

$\qquad\qquad\quad = \Delta V_1 \cdot E/C \qquad\qquad\qquad\; = \Delta T_1(E/C^2)$

(4) $\qquad \Delta T_3 = \Delta V_2 \cdot E, \qquad$ and $\quad \Delta T_3 = \Delta V_2 \cdot E$;

$\qquad\qquad\quad = \Delta V_1 \cdot E^2/C \qquad\qquad\qquad = \Delta T_1(E^2/C^2)$

(5) $\qquad \Delta V_3 = \Delta T_3/C, \qquad$ and $\quad \Delta V_3 = \Delta T_3/C$;

$\qquad\qquad\quad = \Delta V_1 \cdot E^2/C^2 \qquad\qquad\qquad = \Delta T_1(E^2/C^3)$.

Or, in the general case,

(6) $\qquad\qquad\qquad \Delta V_n = \Delta V_1 \cdot E^{n-1}/C^{n-1}$, and

(7) $\qquad\qquad\qquad \Delta T_n = \Delta T_1(E^{n-1}/C^{n-1})$.

If $E > C$, then the changes in tax and value get larger with successive iterations in the process since the value of $(E/C)^{n-1}$ increases with n. If $E = C$, the value of $(E/C)^{n-1}$ is constant. The process would not converge. The same tax and value changes would occur period after period. If $E < C$, $(E/C)^{n-1}$ approaches zero as n gets larger, hence the tax and property value change would be smaller with successive periods. The process tends to converge toward a limiting value. This limiting value is the same as our "steady state" estimates to which we now turn.

Table 9.17. Explanation of the Derivation of "Steady State" Estimates of Tax and Property Value Changes, Boston, 1972 (15% capitilization rate) (dollar amounts in million)

Property category	Current market value (V_0)	Capitalization rate (r)	Capitalization rate times current market value (rV_0)	Current property tax (T_0)	Estimated revenues gross of tax (R)	New property tax rate (t_1)	Capitalization rate plus new property tax rate ($r+t_1$)	"Steady state" market value (V_1)	Change in market value (ΔV)	Percentage change in market value	"Steady state" property tax (T_1)	Change in property tax (ΔT)	Percentage change in tax
"New commercial	$ 696	.15	$104.40	$ 25.77	$ 130.17	.06585	.21585	$ 603	−$ 93	−13%	$ 39.70	+ 13.93	+ 54
"Old commercial	1,279	.15	191.85	135.74	327.59	.06585	.21585	1,518	+ 239	+ 19	99.96	−35.78	−26
All commercial	1,975	.15	296.25	161.51	457.76	.06585	.21585	2,121	+ 146	+ 7	139.67	−21.85	−14
Residential	2,456	.15	368.40	134.54	502.94	.06585	.21585	2,330	− 126	− 5	153.43	+18.89	+14
Other	222	.15	33.30	10.36	43.66	.06585	.21585	202	− 20	− 9	13.30	+ 2.94	+28
Total	4,653	.15	697.95	306.40	1,004.36	.06585	.21585	4,653	—	—	306.40	—	—

"Steady State"

Were assessors and investors to expect a shift to full valuation for tax purposes, and act with perfect knowledge, values would be set which short-circuited the "iterative" process, and which, in principle, reached the limiting value at once. Our judgment is that the "steady state" is the more realistic of the two sets of estimates and the values toward which value and tax adjustments would tend. The "steady state" estimates of tax and value changes are always smaller than the "initial impact" and "first iteration." Thus the "steady state" is a lower bound on our "predictions" and the "initial impact" and "first iteration" an upper bound. Our judgment is that tax and value changes toward the "steady state" end are more likely to eventuate.

If a property yields a return of R, net of all costs but property tax, T_o, the present value of the returns to the owner of the property, V_o, is $R - T_o$ discounted at the rate appropriate for investments of that class, r.

$$V_o = \frac{R - T_o}{r}, \quad \text{and} \quad rV_o + T_o = R.$$

R is derived in table 9.17.

To illustrate with the data for "old" commercial property: V_o = \$1,279,000,000; T_o = \$135,740,000; and r = .15. Therefore

$$R = rV_o + T_o,$$
$$= .15(\$1,279,000,000) + \$135,740,000,$$
$$= \$191,850,000 + \$135,740,000,$$
$$= \$327,590,000.$$

Having R, we can estimate what the market value would be *given the tax rate* that would apply under full-value assessments by noting that the new market value, V_1, would equal the return gross of tax capitalized by the sum of the capitalization rate and the effective rate of property tax, t_1. The latter, of course, under full-value assessments would be the same for all properties.

$$V_1 = \frac{R - t_1V_1}{r}, \quad rV_1 + t_1V_1 = R, \quad \text{and} \quad V_1 = \frac{R}{r + t_1}.$$

Under a full-value assessment scheme t_1 is the same for all properties. Specifically, in our study t_1 is .06585 (that is, 6.585 percent) the rate which if applied to all taxable property would yield the sum actually raised by property tax in Boston in 1972: \$306,400,000.

Table 9.18. Explanation of the Derivation of "Steady State" Estimates of Tax and Property Value Changes, Boston, 1972 (10% capitalization rate) (dollar amounts in millions)

Property category	Capitalization rate (r)	Capitalization rate times current market value (rV_0)	Estimated revenues gross of tax (R)	Capitalization rate plus new property tax rate ($r + t_1$)	"Steady state" market value (V_1)	Change in market value (ΔV)	Percentage change in market value	"Steady state" property tax (T_1)	Change in property tax (ΔT)	Percentage change in tax
"New" commercial	.10	$ 69.60	$ 95.37	.16585	$ 575	−$121	−17%	$ 37.86	+ $12.09	+47
"Old" commercial	.10	127.90	263.64	.16585	1,590	+ 311	+24	104.70	− 31.40	−23
All commercial	.10	197.50	359.01	.16585	2,165	+ 190	+10	142.56	− 18.95	−12
Residential	.10	245.60	380.14	.16585	2,292	− 164	− 7	150.93	+ 16.39	+12
Other	.10	22.20	32.56	.16585	196	− 26	−12	12.91	+ 2.55	+25
Total	.10	465.30	771.70	.16585	4,653	—	—	306.40	—	—

Once again using the data for "old" commercial property to illustrate:

$$R = \$327,590,000,$$

$$r = .15,$$

$$t_1 = .06585,$$

$$V_1 = \frac{R}{r + t_1},$$

$$= \frac{\$327,590,000}{.15000 + .06585} = \$1,517,674,000.$$

V_1 is greater than V_o because, under full valuation assessment, "old" commercial property would be subject to a lower property tax rate. Currently, the effective rate of tax on property in this category is

$$\frac{T_o}{V_o} = \frac{\$135,740,000}{1,279,000,000} = .10613.$$

And under full-value assessment it would be .06585.

The behavior implicit in our "steady state" method estimates is that assessors and investors capitalize the income from the property employing for this purpose the appropriate discount rate plus the property tax rate derived from the ratio of required revenues (the current property tax levied) to the aggregate value of taxable property.

Finally, "steady state" tax liabilities, T_1, are calculated by applying the overall effective rate, .06585 in our case, to the "steady state" market values V_1. For "old" commercial properties

$$T_1 = V_1 t_1,$$

$$= \$1,518,000,000 \,(.06585),$$

$$= \$99,960,000.$$

While it is our judgment that 15 percent is the appropriate capitalization rate for commercial and residential property (see table 9.17), table 9.18 has estimates based on a capitalization rate of 10 percent.

The "steady state" estimates are not very sensitive to the capitalization rate assumed. With the higher rate (15 percent) value changes are somewhat more moderate and tax changes a little sharper than with the lower (1 0 percent) one.

Acknowledgments

In preparing this essay we have drawn heavily on the estimates prepared for our earlier study, "Estimating the Impact of 100% of Market

Value Property Tax Assessments of Boston Real Estate," prepared for the Boston Urban Observatory in August 1974. With the observatory's generous permission we have included in this essay, substantially unchanged, some parts of the earlier study.

In carrying out that study we were helped by many people. Alexander Ganz and Joseph S. Slavet were twin sources of encouragement, counsel, guidance, and critical insight from start to completion. We are grateful to Dennis Jones and Arthur Perry, who assembled the basic data in the early stages of the project, and to Larry Green, who succeeded to this task and, in addition, assisted in the preparation of the final estimates. Without the generous help of members of the research staff of the Boston Redevelopment Authority, The Boston Urban Observatory study would not have been possible. In addition to Alexander Ganz, we wish to thank Susan Houston, Dennis Dickstein, Peter Menconeri, Stewart Forbes, and Mark Gilman.

We benefited from the expert judgment of Jack Hall, Theodore R. Smith, and Stuart Traver and from the analytical insights of Dennis Dickstein, incorporated in his undergraduate thesis for MIT. And we thank Robert Engle for permission to use his unpublished estimates of assessment-sales ratios.

In the preparation of the present essay we are indebted additionally to Sudeep Anand, Ronald Grieson, Daniel Rubinfeld, and Eli Schwartz for helpful criticism and advice.

References

Black, D. E. 1969. "Inequalities in Effective Property Tax: A Statistical Study of the City of Boston." Ph.D. diss., Department of Economics, MIT.

Bonbright, J. C. 1937. *Valuation of Property.* New York: McGraw-Hill.

Boston Urban Observatory. 1972. "Reconnaissance Report of the Subsidized Housing Study." Multilithed. Boston, Mass.

Boston Urban Observatory. 1973. *Reallocation of Responsibilities and/or Financing for Selected Municipal Services to the State: A Municipal Finance Alternative.* Boston: The Observatory.

Commonwealth of Massachusetts, Department of Corporations and Taxation. 1973. *Massachusetts Property Tax Law Handbook.* Paragraphs 16-19. Boston: The department.

Dickstein, Dennis. 1974. "The Effect Property Taxes Have on Property Values: A Study of a Specific Situation." Undergraduate thesis, Department of Urban Studies and Planning, MIT.

Holland, Daniel M., and Oliver Oldman. 1974. *Estimating the Impact of 100% of Market Value Property Tax Assessments of Boston Real Estate.* Boston: Boston Urban Observatory.

Jacobs Company, Inc. 1971. "The Assessing Function in Boston: A Study of the Property Assessment Process in the City of Boston and the Impact of Existing Tax Laws." Multilithed. Prepared for the Boston Finance Commission.

Ladd, Helen. 1973. "The Role of the Property Tax: A Reassessment." In *Broad-Based Taxes,* ed. R. A. Musgrave. Baltimore, Md.: The Johns Hopkins University Press.

Netzer, Dick. 1973. "The Incidence of the Property Tax Revisited." *National Tax Journal* 26: 515-35.

Oldman, Oliver, and Henry Aaron. 1965. "Assessment-Sales Ratios Under the Boston Property Tax." *National Tax Journal* 18: 36-49. Reprinted, with data through 1966, in *Assessors Journal* 4 (1969): 13-29.

U.S. Bureau of the Census. 1968. *Census of Governments, 1967.* Vol. 2, *Taxable Property Values.* Washington, D.C.: U.S. Government Printing Office.

U.S. Bureau of the Census. 1973. *Census of Governments, 1972.* Vol. 2, *Taxable Property Values and Assessment-Sales Price Ratios, Part 2: Assessment-Sales Price Ratios and Tax Rates, U.S.* Washington, D.C.: U.S. Government Printing Office.

Woodbury, M. G. 1970. "Experiments in Restructuring the Property Tax." Master of Science thesis, Sloan School of Management, MIT.

10 *Arthur P. Becker and Hans R. Isakson*

The Burden on the City of Milwaukee and Its Residents of the Real Property Tax Compared with the Individual Income Tax

Introduction

The financial burden of large central cities in the United States has been of critical proportions since the 1960s and continues so into the 1970s. The concentration of the poor, aged, and minorities in our central cities and the flight of middle and upper income whites to the suburbs have been both cause and effect of these financial burdens. This trend has not yet stabilized, although its pace may have slowed down somewhat.

The two most notable programs that were adopted in the early 1970s to alleviate these financial burdens were federal revenue sharing and increased federal assumptions of financial responsibility for welfare. The revenue sharing program poured federal funds into our ailing, and not so ailing, cities. It gave a new lease on life to those in serious financial conditions . . . temporarily. Financial pressures were diverted for several years, but this has not removed the cause of rising financial pressures, which continue to build up. It is clear that further measures are necessary: both those that will deal in a satisfactory way with the causes

The research and studies forming the basis for this chapter were conducted pursuant to a contract between the Department of Housing and Urban Development and the National League of Cities. The substance of such research and studies is dedicated to the public. The authors are solely responsible for the accuracy of statements or interpretations contained herein.

of these financial burdens as well as those that can ease the financial burdens of central cities "permanently."

A great many proposals have been advanced for alleviating the financial burdens of large central cities in the United States. They include the use of new revenue sources, an increased reliance upon existing non-property tax revenue sources, a reallocation of existing financial resources by changing priorities for local public services, and a shifting of responsibility for the financing of selected services from local to state governments. Of all of these fiscal alternatives, the one with the greatest intuitive appeal, that is, the method which appears to be the most feasible for providing significant tax relief, is the shifting of financial responsibility for public services from local and state governments and from the local property tax to a state progressive individual income tax, such as that utilized by the State of Wisconsin.

This study will analyze the effects of changes like these in the Milwaukee area. Its first task was to prepare an inventory of services provided to City of Milwaukee residents by local governments, namely, the City of Milwaukee, the County of Milwaukee, the School Board (District) of the City of Milwaukee, the Milwaukee Vocational, Technical, and Adult Education District no. 9, and the Metropolitan Milwaukee Sewerage District. This involved the identification of both services and jurisdictions responsible for financing and performing the services, of revenue sources used in 1970 to finance the services, and of 1970 expenditures on the services as well.

The next task was to select a limited number of services (from the inventory) for careful analysis of the proposition that would shift their financial responsibility from local governments to the state by increasing individual income tax burdens and reducing property tax burdens. The public services selected for intensive investigation were those which seem to have considerable popular and political support. For example, it appears that the idea of transferring financial responsibility for public welfare to the state and federal government is widely approved by state citizens and also has considerable political support.

The desirability of transferring the financial responsibility of a public service to the state, however, should depend upon a defensible rationale rather than popular or political caprice. Transferring financial responsibility by governmental jurisdiction and revenue source should be based upon economic, political, and social criteria. While presumptive conformity to these relevant criteria is essential, it is not sufficient. The complexities involved in local government and fiscal responsibilities for providing various services are so considerable that the change in financial responsibility of a particular public service may not support that shift, even though the logic or rationale is very strong. For example, such a divergence of rationale and fiscal fact would occur if the financial responsibility for public education were shifted, as is frequently proposed.

Because a strong rationale for alternative fiscal measures must be supported by fiscal facts, this study is designed to measure the impact or effect (in dollars) of several alternative fiscal measures. More specifically, this study will examine the impact on the property taxes and individual income taxes paid by residents in the City of Milwaukee if the financial responsibility of a selected group of public services were to be transferred to the state government from the local jurisdictions to which city residents pay property taxes. The dollar impact of such a shift in financial responsibility on the various governmental jurisdictions involved will be ascertained initially.

The next part of the study is an analysis of the impact of the shift in the financial responsibility of certain public services (to state government from local jurisdictions) on the tax burden of families by income class and size. The method of arriving at a quantitative measure of the impact of these shifts required the making of a number of assumptions. The making of assumptions (where it was unavoidable) was guided by judgments as to what was reasonable and conservative so that the results would reflect maximum probability or reliability.

An Inventory of Local Public Services

The first task of this study was to take an inventory of the various public services performed by local governments for residents of the City of Milwaukee and nonresidents who take advantage of these services in the city. An inventory of such services can serve a variety of useful purposes. The basic knowledge that it provides is essential for analysis to determine the efficiency and equity both within and between local governmental units as well as between local and state levels of government. If efficiency and equity can be related to particular forms of governmental organization and financial responsibility in the provision of specific local services, such information may be of considerable value in suggesting improved forms of government organization and financial responsibilities.

Similar inventories and studies of efficiency and equity were carried on in other cities with federal financial support (Atlanta, Boston, Denver, Baltimore, San Diego, Nashville, and both Kansas Citys). It is hoped that these will eventually provide valuable information as to why and how some cities achieve greater efficiency or equity than others. The ultimate purpose of such comparative analyses is to uncover approaches utilized by some central cities which either reduce tax burdens or increase the quantity and quality of services, or both.

The primary purpose for taking an inventory of public services in this study, however, is to bring these services into perspective so that several can be selected for an intensive kind of financial analysis. Moreover, in this study it is assumed that greater equity will be achieved if the financial responsibility for certain local services is transferred to the state government. Furthermore, it is hypothesized that such shifts will indeed reduce tax burdens of residents in the City of Milwaukee. The study should either verify or disprove this hypothesis.

The sources of the inventory were many and varied. Published and unpublished financial reports and operating statements of local governments, their departments, and agencies were tapped to assemble the inventory and related expenditures in 1970. A great deal of time was spent with local government personnel knowledgeable with expenditures and administration in order to determine the need for making adjust-

Table 10.1. List of Local Public Services to City of Milwaukee Residents

Census category	Number of subcategories	Number of services
Police protection	6	19
Parks and recreation	10	65
General control	16	51
Natural resources	1	4
Parking facilities	2	3
Protective inspection and regulation	2	2
Water transportation and terminals	2	9
Other and unallocable	16	35
Financial administration	15	41
General public buildings	6	10
Airports	5	10
Public welfare	9	18
Education	18	45
Libraries	2	7
Correction	4	10
Sewerage and sanitation	13	45
Highways	10	33
Fire department	2	8
Housing and urban renewal	4	18
Health and hospitals	14	35
Total	157	468

Source: Becker and Isakson (1975, app. A).

ments in local data so that services might be listed in conformity with
United States Bureau of the Census categories.

Local public services provided for City of Milwaukee residents and
other users were identified and classified according to the categories of
services established by the Census Bureau. No less than 468 local public
services[1] were identified under 157 subcategories. These, in turn, were
grouped under twenty Census Bureau categories of expenditures (see
table 10.1).

Normally only one local government exercises the responsibility for
providing services in a given subcategory. In some cases, however, both
the City and County of Milwaukee have assumed spending responsibilities for services in the same subcategories, indicating rivalry in interests,
although not necessarily duplication in effort. A considerable overlap
occurs also for the Sewerage Commission of the City of Milwaukee and
the Metropolitan Sewerage Commission of the County of Milwaukee. A
smaller coincidence occurs for some service subcategories of the City of
Milwaukee School Board and the Vocational, Technical, and Adult
School District no. 9.

Listing total expenditures by local governments in various categories
and subcategories of services marks only the starting point in this
investigation of present tax burdens on city residents and the possibility
of reducing them. Since the local tax burdens arising out of expenditures
by local governments is reduced to the extent that these are financed via
federal and state financial assistance as well as by possible service
charges, it is essential to know the magnitude of these sums. These data
were ascertained but because they are so voluminous cannot be presented
here for lack of space.

Federal and state government payments to local governments in the
Milwaukee area to help finance services could not be applied to many
subcategories of service because of the impossibility of disentangling
the fiscal threads. The problem of allocating funds from the federal and
state governments becomes even more difficult if one attempts to trace
such allocations to a specific service. As one can readily see from table
10.2, the effect of federal and state financial assistance and the levying of
local service charges has a substantial effect in reducing the amounts of
money that local governments must raise through taxation. This is
especially evident in the financing of health and hospitals, housing and
urban renewal, highways (and streets), sewerage and sanitation, edu-

1. The exact number of services found by an investigator will depend in part upon the
concept of service that is utilized, that is, whether the service is broadly or narrowly viewed.
"Subcategories" of public services as utilized in this study correspond to customary usage
by the various local governments.

Table 10.2. Total Expenditures by Unit of Government in 1970 (in thousands of dollars)

Function	Federal government	State government			Special districts	County government	City government	Charges			Total expenditures
		To county	To city	To special districts				To county	To city	To special districts	
Police services						$ 2,065	$27,692	$ 977	$ 3,318		$ 29,757
Parks and recreation						13,506	8,134				25,935
General control		$10,146	$ 1,162			8,346	3,630				11,976
Health and hospital	$ 19					(782)^a	4,010	436	38,198		53,189
Housing and urban renewal	5,141						15,994	3,365			24,500
Highways		15,024	4,929		$ 630^b	(1,826)	15,583	538			34,878
Fire services							11,433				11,433
Sewerage and sanitation	2,913^b			$ 2,696^c	23,464	265	12,796	226		$3,418	45,778
Correction						5,290	146				5,436
Libraries							5,905				5,905
Education	1,554^d	132	105,077	30,076^e	86,728					4,665^f	123,155
Public welfare		40,901			234^b	41,996	3				83,134
Airports						1,788			2,443		4,231
General public buildings						1,403	1,193				2,596
Financial administration						1,837	3,645				5,482
Natural resources						111					111
Parking facilities							(200)	1,743			1,543
Protective inspection and regulation							2,264				2,264
Water transportation and terminals							(542)	1,217			675
Other and unallocable	2,299^g	14,109			1,517^h	(6,769)	(92,468)	1,495	4,860		30,120
Total	11,926	80,312	105,077	32,772	112,573	67,230	19,218	9,997	48,819	8,083	502,098

Source: Becker and Isakson (1974, vol. 1, app. B).

^a Figures in parentheses represent surpluses of revenue over expenditures for 1970.

^b Received from other local governments (unspecified).

^c To Sewerage Commission of the City of Milwaukee.

^d To Milwaukee School Board.

^e Of this figure, $27,147 was received by the Milwaukee School Board and $2,929 was received by the Vocational, Technical, and Adult School District no. 9.

^f Of this figure, $2,832 were charges of the Milwaukee School Board and $1,833 were charges of the Vocational, Technical, and Adult School District no. 9.

^g Of this figure, $201.00 was received by the County of Milwaukee and $1,492 was received by the City of Milwaukee.

^h Of this figure, $750.00 was received by the County of Milwaukee from other local governments (unspecified) and $767.00 was received by the City of Milwaukee from other local governments (unspecified).

cation, public welfare, airports, parking facilities, water transportation and terminals, as well as other services.

The Rationale for Shifting the Financial Responsibility of Selected Local Public Services to the State

The intent of this study is to analyze the change in tax burdens on Milwaukee residents as a group as well as individually if the local financial responsibility for providing certain services were transferred to the state government. Services that were selected for analysis are those for which the strongest justification might be made for advocating such a transfer. Thus the selection is based largely upon what is believed to be rational and most consistent with recognized and relevant guidelines. These guidelines were set forth in an earlier study which anticipated the importance of justifying any major change in public policy (see Becker, 1974, chap. 2).

In this earlier study sixteen broad categories of local public services were analyzed. These constitute the most costly services that are provided in nearly all local jurisdictions. They were analyzed in terms of their characteristics and what would seem to be an ideal model of administrative responsibility, financial responsibility, and method of financing.

As to "characteristics," each service was examined to see if it constituted a natural monopoly, whether the service was exchangeable or exclusive (or only of general benefit), whether the service provided spillover benefits to others than the recipients (or if the absence of the service would result in spillover costs of general disadvantage), and lastly whether the service was primarily "people-related," "land-related," or both. Next, guidelines for allocating public services and raising public revenue were reviewed, and these guidelines were applied to each of the sixteen services, keeping in mind their essential characteristics. By this method it is possible to determine more or less objectively which level of government should ideally assume the administrative and/or financial responsibility for each service as well as how the latter might best be financed.

The results of this analysis show that six of the local public services so studied are prime candidates for a fiscal transfer from the local to the state level of government, namely, welfare, health, hospitals, education, courts, and correction. That is to say, according to the guidelines used for providing for and paying for services, it seems logical for the state to finance these services out of its individual income tax to the point where the property taxpayers of local jurisdictions might be relieved of these burdens completely.

Welfare, Health, and Hospitals

These three services have similar characteristics in that they are clearly people-related. Poverty and ill health, as well as the public costs that they cause, cannot be localized. Instead, they affect much of remaining society either directly or indirectly. Moreover, the poor and sick tend to gravitate toward and concentrate in or near our large central cities. Thus, high spillover effects arise both in the concentration of the poor and sick in large urban areas as well as in the outwardly expanding influence (cost) of poverty and sickness. The concentrating effect places a moral obligation on persons living in all areas, those from whence the poor and sick originated as well as those areas which are excluded. It is also in the self-interest of these areas to protect themselves from any possible adverse influence of these miseries by providing assistance to minimize poverty and ill health. According to this rationale the financial responsibility for providing these services rests properly with the state and the federal governments.

Since welfare, health, and hospital services are rendered to the needy, their financing by means of user charges or taxes based on the benefits-received principle are automatically eliminated. It is perfectly clear, then, that the services must be financed on the basis of ability to pay. Many of those persons with the greatest ability to pay live outside of the central city or county where the bulk of these social services is demanded. Tax contributions from these affluent persons can be accomplished only if financing is managed by the state and federal governments which have the requisite wide taxing jurisdiction. Furthermore, Wisconsin and federal individual income taxes most clearly embody the ability-to-pay principle, which cannot be achieved with a local income tax because of its limited jurisdiction and administrative inefficiencies.

Education

There is a little dispute with the view that public education (primary and secondary) is essentially a people-related service with high spillover effects. The general level of education affects the quality of life in many ways for a large and perhaps major portion of all persons living in a community. Educational spillover costs arise also in the absence of educational opportunities as people move into other local jurisdictions to acquire their education at those jurisdictions' expense. Should a person move after receiving his education from a local jurisdiction, he deprives it of expected benefits which he confers as a windfall gain on the local jurisdiction in which he settles.

In recent years it has become apparent that central cities are losing the benefits of their educational services via the out-migration of those who benefited most from their education. Thus, the central city must bear the rising costs of educating a larger proportion of hard-to-educate students, while at the same time it loses the benefits of those graduates who were the best learners and then moved away. In this fashion the disparity between costs and benefits in public education has been growing for large central cities.

Most of the spillover effects and their accompanying injustices can be eliminated by placing primary responsibility with the states and secondary responsibility with the federal government for financing all compulsory education of an agreed-upon standard of quality. The individual income taxes utilized by these levels of government are generally regarded as the best ability-to-pay taxes that are available today. This study attempts to determine whether this view is valid for the City of Milwaukee.

Education, however, is also land-related. It is well known that the demand for land and its value are influenced by the quality of education available in a school district and neighborhood. It seems to be appropriate, therefore, for landowners to bear a part of the cost of education in each school district. Funding from this source, too, would give support to local administrative control of schools, a method widely and intensely preferred over state or federal control. Furthermore, it would allow school districts to institute variations in educational opportunities that reflect values that are held high in local esteem.

Vocational, technical, and adult education is regarded by many as a service that benefits the recipient to a greater extent with increased employment and income opportunities than does primary or secondary education. For that reason it can be argued that it is entirely appropriate to levy fees (or user charges) similar to university fees. The size of fees for both types of these postsecondary educational services would have to depend upon the tax-paying ability of the state.

Courts and Correction

Although some of these services pertain to and benefit land (by increasing their value), their costs and benefits are largely people-related. All of society is presumed to benefit from its judicial and correctional activities. Because of these high spillover effects and people-related characteristics, it is appropriate to center financial responsibility in the hands of the state rather than local government.

Indeed, because of the high mobility of people, a strong case can be made for federal financial assistance to local and state correctional functions and facilities.

Assumptions and Modifications in the Present Study

Even though our functional finance model sees a logical place for user charges and a land value tax to finance a portion of the expenses of education, courts, and corrections, the following analysis of property tax burden versus individual income tax burden (if the shift had occurred in 1970) is based on the assumption that all user charges, where used, would continue but that all real property tax burdens would be removed. Furthermore, because of local differences in classifying services (as compared with the Census Bureau) our analysis identifies the services discussed above as follows: the education category of the Census Bureau is divided into two categories; thus "education" refers to public schools and vocational, technical, and adult education; the two census categories of health and hospitals are combined since these services are not divisible on the local level; courts are included under both legal and judicial services; and corrections stands as a single category.

Methodology of Analyzing Changes in Tax Burdens

If financial responsibility for this study's selected public services were transferred from the local property tax to the state individual income tax, the effects of that transfer would be felt in two ways. It would change the tax burden of (1) the units of government involved in the transfer, and (2) the individual taxpayers who are obligated to the units of government. This study emphasizes the effects of the transfers on individuals and pays somewhat less attention to the change in tax burdens on the units of government involved.

In examining the changes in the impact of tax burdens on individual residents in the City of Milwaukee, it is desirable to do so in terms of family income and size, as well as in the aggregate. The concept of real income is used in the study in order that tax burdens and any changes in them will be more meaningful. "Real income" is far more than merely "taxable income" in that it includes wages and salaries, proprietorship income, social security and public assistance income, property income (including imputed rents), and capital gains.[2] Because of the difficulties of coming up with "hard" estimates, real income as used in the study

2. This concept of real income is the same as that used by Bahl (1972).

does not include assistance in kind (housing, food) or do-it-yourself income such as home and auto repairs and maintenance and gardening. Family size, as utilized in the study, is defined as the number of related individuals living in the household.

The analysis of the impact of the shift in the financial responsibility of certain public services from local jurisdictions to the state of Wisconsin was carried out in three major steps: (1) property tax burdens, in the aggregate as well as by family income and size, and related to each public service selected, were estimated for residents in the jurisdiction being studied (the City of Milwaukee); (2) the share of increased income tax payments of residents in the aggregate, as well as by family income and size in the jurisdiction being studied (the City of Milwaukee), if the financial responsibility of the public service were transferred to the State of Wisconsin, was estimated; and (3) the difference between burdens before and after the shift from local property tax to state income tax was calculated for City of Milwaukee residents, in the aggregate as well as by family income and size. This analysis of the change in tax burdens was conducted for each of the public service functions selected for trans-ference of local property tax financing to state income tax financing. This change in tax burden was determined for each representative class of taxpayer. Lastly, the change in tax burden on local residents was calculated if the local property tax were replaced with a local income tax.

Estimating Aggregate Property Tax Burdens

As stated above, it is necessary to determine current property tax payments of city residents in order to finance certain public services at their present levels of quality. This determination is simple in the case of special purpose governments (such as education) where the property tax levy on residents is earmarked.

The problem is only slightly complicated if the special purpose government provides its services to more than one municipality, as is the case of the Metropolitan Milwaukee Sewerage District and the Milwaukee Vocational, Technical, and Adult Education District no. 9. But the total levy for all jurisdictions is divided among those municipalities that are included. Thus, a municipality's share of such a (larger) special purpose government's levy can be found in the records as a specific amount and portion of the municipality's total levy.

If the public service whose burden is being studied is provided by a general purpose government, such as a municipality or county which levies one tax in order to finance many services, however, it is necessary to estimate that share of the levy that can be attributed to the particular service that is being analyzed. Throughout this study it is assumed that the property tax levy for a given service is proportional to the expenditures for the service.[3] Furthermore, if more than one unit of government supplies a particular service, the property tax levies necessary to support that service by each unit must be added together in order to find the total property tax levy for that service.

The above procedures are necessary for determining the property tax levies for related services. But these levies measure only the impact rather than the incidence or burden of those property tax levies. Discrepancies between the impact and incidence of the property tax may arise out of the fact that all local property taxpayers are not city residents and that part of the property tax may be shifted forward to renters or buyers or backwards to landowners, labor, or lenders.

An unknown, but probably substantial, portion of the taxes paid on property located within the City of Milwaukee is paid by nonresident owners of the property. This might apply to any property except owner-occupied residences within the city. On the other hand, city residents may own property located in other jurisdictions to which they would pay property tax. Inasmuch as it is difficult to formulate a reasonable judgment with respect to the relative outflow or inflow of property taxes, it is assumed in this study that the two effects cancel each other out.

Further, it is assumed in this study that taxes on improvements are shifted forward. Accordingly any owner of income-producing property (mercantile, manufacturing, or residential) whose costs rise due to increased taxes on improvements will "tend" to reduce the supply of such property in time and allow for an increase in rentals sufficient to cover the tax increases. In turn, the tenants, if mercantile or industrial, would be able to increase the prices of goods and services that they provide to the public.

The property tax levies on improvements can be transferred outside Milwaukee to the extent that goods and services produced in Milwaukee are sold to customers outside Milwaukee. The reverse situation holds to the extent that Milwaukee residents who purchase goods and services outside pay part of the taxes on improvements of outside municipalities. The net effect of this geographic transfer of shifted property taxes on improvements depends upon the size and composition of the city's "imports" and "exports" with the "outside" economy.

It was beyond the scope of this study to determine anew the net effect

---

3. In algebraic terms, the tax levy for a given public service can be expressed as $\frac{e}{E} T$, where e = the expenditures for the given public service, E = total expenditures, and T = total property tax levy.

Table 10.3. Adjustments in Real Estate Assessments for the City of Milwaukee (1970) to Allow for the Partial Shifting of the Incidence of the Property Tax (dollar amounts in thousands)

Class of property	Land assessment (1)	Improvement assessment (2)	Total assessment[a] (3)	Adjustment factor for shifting of tax burden[b] (4)	Improvement assessment (adjusted)[c] (5)	Total assessment (adjusted)[d] (6)
Residential	$342,219	$ 790,734	$1,132,953	1.00	$ 790,734	$1,132,953
Commercial	187,613	400,962	588,575	.95	380,914	568,527
Manufacturing	50,559	299,713	350,272	.20	59,943	110,502
Agriculture	5,378	183	5,561	1.00	183	5,561
Total	585,769	1,491,592	2,077,361	.87492[e]	1,305,024	1,890,793

Source: City of Milwaukee, Tax Commissioner (1971).

[a] Column 1 plus column 2.
[b] See University of Wisconsin Tax Study Committee (1959, pp. 44–45).
[c] Column 2 times column 4.
[d] Column 1 plus column 5.
[e] Ratio of column 6 to column 3.

of exporting the property tax. Instead, the estimates of another study were utilized. That study concluded that approximately 80 percent of Wisconsin's manufacturing output is sold to nonresident buyers but that only 5 percent of all retail sales are made to out-of-state buyers (University of Wisconsin Tax Study Committee, 1959, pp. 44-45). These same proportions were utilized in determining the allocation between residents and nonresidents of the City of Milwaukee of property tax burdens shifted by city manufacturing and commercial property.

The technique used to reflect these shifts is to reduce the assessed value of each class of taxable property (and thus the burden borne by taxpayers) by the net exports (in percentage terms) of the property tax from the City of Milwaukee for various classes of property. This adjustment is made only in the assessed value of improvements. Inasmuch as the tax on land is assumed to be borne by the owners land assessments are not adjusted. (Residential assessments are also left unchanged since the property tax burden on this class of property is not transferred outside the City of Milwaukee.) The results of these adjustments are shown in column 6 of table 10.3. The table shows that about 12.5 percent of the property tax levies on property within the city limits of

Table 10.4. 1970 Net Property Tax Payments on City of Milwaukee Property (dollar amounts in thousands)

Local taxing unit	Gross amount of property tax levied	Less percentage share of state property tax relief ($16,841)	Property tax payment net of state relief
City of Milwaukee School Board	$ 89,239	36.884%	$ 83,028
City of Milwaukee	85,754	35.443	79,785
Milwaukee County	54,670	22.596	50,864
Vocational, Technical, and Adult Education District no. 9	6,771	2.798	6,300
Milwaukee Metro Sewerage District and Commission	5,511	2.277	5,127
Total	241,945		225,104

Sources: City of Milwaukee, Tax Commissioner (1971), Wisconsin Department of Revenue, Bureau of Local Fiscal Information (1971), and City of Milwaukee, Comptroller (1971).

Milwaukee are shifted outside the city. Therefore, the property tax burden on *residents* (because of property tax financing) for a given public service would have to be regarded as about 87.5 percent of the property tax levy for that service. If this property tax levy were replaced dollar for dollar by an individual income tax, the tax burden of the city would increase by the amount of the property tax shifted outside the city. According to our estimates, the loss in property tax revenues to the city, or the increase in tax burdens with an income tax, would be about 12.5 percent of the tax levy on real property situated within the city limits.

In determining the burden of property taxes in Wisconsin it is necessary to make a further adjustment to allow for state property tax relief. Although the sums of money provided for property tax relief are paid to units of local government in Wisconsin, such relief is accounted for as a property tax reduction to all owners of taxable real estate. Thus, gross property tax levies must be reduced by an amount equal to the property tax relief paid by the state to the locality. Table 10.4 summarizes this adjustment for the five units of local government to which owners of property in Milwaukee pay property taxes.

Estimating Aggregate Income Tax Burdens

As shown above, if the revenue generated by the local real property tax in Milwaukee were raised, instead, by increasing the Wisconsin state individual income tax, tax burdens would increase on city residents. Since a portion of the real property tax levied in the city is shifted outside of the state, Wisconsin would have to increase its individual income tax revenues by more than the sum of all of the property tax burdens on state residents.

In order to determine how much the state individual income tax must be increased to transfer the financial responsibility of selected services to the state, we must calculate the extent to which those services are currently financed by the local property tax. Property tax levies for special purpose governments require only the adjustment for property tax relief payments. The aggregate property tax levies for selected services provided by general purpose local governments, however, are allocated to each service according to its share of total expenditures. No adjustments are made for altering service levels since this would introduce an extraneous determinant and render the study in comparative financing less meaningful.

In 1970 City of Milwaukee residents paid about 16.9 percent of the

Table 10.5. City of Milwaukee Real Property Tax Payments and Burdens (1970) If Several Expenditure Categories Were Financed by Increasing the State Individual Income Tax and the Real Property Tax Were Reduced Accordingly (dollar amounts in thousands)

Expenditure category (1)	Total expenditures by local governments (2)	Real property tax payments (levies) in Wisconsin for each expenditure category (3)	Real property tax payments (levies) in the City of Milwaukee for each expenditure category in column 2 (4)	Real property tax payments in the City of Milwaukee as a percentage of total real property tax payments in Wisconsin[a] (5)	Real property tax burden in the City of Milwaukee after adjustments for shifting of tax incidence[b] (6)	Real property tax burden in the City of Milwaukee as a percentage of total real property tax payments in Wisconsin[c] (7)	Alternative Wisconsin individual income tax payments by residents of the City of Milwaukee for each expenditure category (8)	Change in tax payments for city taxpayers with alternative financing for each expenditure category[d] (9)	Change in tax burden for city taxpayers with alternative financing for each expenditure category[e] (10)
Public education	$123,155	$664,218	$83,028	12.50%	$72,643[f]	10.94%[g]	$112,253	$29,225	+$39,610
Vocational, technical, and adult education	14,138	35,995	6,300	17.50	5,512	15.31	6,083	− 217	+ 571
Public welfare	76,326	31,469	13,205	41.96	11,553	36.71	5,318	− 7,887	− 6,235
Health and hospitals	58,797	35,216	9,651	27.40	8,444	23.98	5,951	− 3,700	− 2,493
Legal and judicial	7,828	5,014	1,259	25.10	1,101	21.96	847	− 412	− 254
Correction	4,357	1,356	753	55.53	659	48.60	229	− 524	− 430
Total	284,601	773,268	114,196	14.76	99,912	12.92	130,681	+ 16,485	

Source: Data in columns 2, 3, and 4 taken from Becker and Isakson (1974, vol. 1, app. B).

[a] Column 4 divided by column 3.
[b] Column 4 times .87492.
[c] Column 6 divided by column 3.
[d] Column 8 minus column 4.
[e] Column 8 minus column 6.
[f] The difference between columns 4 and 6 is the amount of the real property tax that we assume to be exported (shifted) to persons outside of the State of Wisconsin. This amount would be lost to the state as well as to the City of Milwaukee if the real property tax were reduced by increasing the individual income tax. The City of Milwaukee would actually lose even more because a part of its real property tax is also exported to other Wisconsin residents as well as out-of-state residents.
[g] City of Milwaukee residents pay 16.9 percent of the total Wisconsin individual income tax yield. Thus, city residents will benefit by financing an expenditure function with the income tax only if the property tax burden of that function is greater than 16.9 percent.

state's total individual income tax payments (Wisconsin Department of Revenue, 1973). It is assumed in this study that this local share of total income tax revenues will remain constant. Accordingly, the burden of financing a given service (previously financed by the property tax) with the individual income tax will be equal to 16.9 percent of the increase in the total revenues of the state's individual income tax which is required to accomplish the change in method of financing. Thus if the property tax burden of city residents for financing a given service is less than 16.9 percent of total statewide property tax levies, city residents will have to pay more with individual income tax financing of that service. Similarly, if the city residents' share of total statewide property tax levies for that particular service is greater than 16.9 percent, city residents will be better off with the transfer in financing to the individual income tax.

After having determined present property tax burdens for selected public services and the probable increases in individual income tax burdens, the difference in the two will indicate the changes in tax burdens if the method of financing were shifted to the individual income tax. Aggregate figures are shown in table 10.5 for each of the services that are examined in the study.

Tax Burdens by Family Income and Size

Although the total effect of a particular transfer may make Milwaukee residents, taken all together, worse off, as shown above, it is still possible for some income classes to be better off than before. In order to determine this effect it is necessary to distribute the increase in income tax payments among city families by income and family size. Then, a simple comparison of the "before" and "after" burdens provides for a meaningful analysis of the proposed transfer in the method of financing the service.

Thus, once the overall magnitude of the property tax burden on Milwaukee residents is determined, an attempt can be made to distribute the total burden among families by income class and family size. The property taxes paid by residents is reflected by the assessed value of property on which residents pay taxes. Therefore, the method for accomplishing this tax distribution is to allocate the assessed value of property taxes paid by residents as follows: The assessed value of residential (including agricultural) property is allocated among income classes in proportion to the distribution of property income (including imputed rents). The assessed value of commercial and manufacturing property on which residents pay taxes is distributed among the various income classes in proportion to the distribution of money income among those classes.

Table 10.6. The Distribution of 1970 Real Estate Assessments in Milwaukee by Family Income Class (in thousands of dollars)

Family income	Money income[a]	Property income[a]	Residential and agricultural amounts[b]	Commercial and manufacturing amounts[b]	Total amounts[b]
$ 0– 1,000	$ 679,109	$ 427,302	$ 824	$ 226	$ 1,050
1,001– 2,000	3,641,906	1,394,698	2,689	1,212	3,901
2,001– 3,000	22,755,318	9,237,521	17,811	7,575	25,386
3,001– 4,000	39,146,363	16,620,903	32,046	13,028	45,074
4,001– 5,000	40,001,011	15,774,149	30,413	13,312	43,725
5,001– 6,000	55,527,465	15,727,048	30,323	18,479	48,802
6,001– 7,000	77,539,281	20,311,071	39,162	25,805	64,967
7,001– 8,000	118,306,777	24,883,689	47,977	39,372	87,349
8,001– 9,000	131,170,508	26,009,819	50,148	43,653	93,801
9,001–10,000	145,724,066	21,996,315	42,410	48,496	90,906
10,001–12,000	396,100,067	47,207,726	91,019	131,819	222,838
12,001–15,000	454,726,320	61,496,591	118,569	151,330	269,899
15,001–25,000	699,679,503	107,473,427	207,214	232,848	440,062
Over 25,000	636,122,544	221,937,888	427,907	211,697	639,604
Total	2,821,120,238	590,500,148	1,138,512	938,852	2,077,364

[a] Bahl (1973).
[b] City of Milwaukee, Tax Commissioner (1971).

Table 10.7. 1970 Distribution of City of Milwaukee Families by Income and Size

Family income	Number of persons in family						Total
	1	2	3	4	5	6 and up	
$ 0– 1,000	12,870	1,440	656	598	281	403	16,248
1,001– 2,000	1,774	354	118	89	50	45	2,430
2,001– 3,000	8,290	1,498	342	234	139	149	10,652
3,001– 4,000	9,071	2,548	580	252	196	294	12,941
4,001– 5,000	5,936	2,783	582	310	213	291	10,115
5,001– 6,000	6,188	2,854	835	441	316	419	11,053
6,001– 7,000	6,347	3,440	1,309	824	433	711	13,064
7,001– 8,000	7,793	4,018	1,959	1,543	818	979	17,110
8,001– 9,000	6,733	3,360	2,059	1,986	1,256	1,311	16,705
9,001–10,000	5,274	3,777	2,315	2,233	1,412	1,474	16,485
10,001–12,000	7,218	8,647	6,254	6,765	4,573	4,965	38,422
12,001–15,000	3,926	9,073	6,560	7,098	4,798	5,210	36,665
15,001–25,000	2,105	8,823	8,270	8,323	5,987	7,194	40,702
Over 25,000	1,058	4,534	3,468	3,686	2,767	3,496	19,009

Source: Bahl (1972).

Table 10.8. Wisconsin State Income Tax Yields by Family Income for Milwaukee Residents (1970)

Family income class	Money income as a percentage of real income (1)	Wisconsin taxable income as a percentage of money income (2)	State income tax yields by taxable income class (3)	Adjustment A[a] (4)	Adjustment B[b] (5)	Adjustment C[c] (6)	State tax yields by real income class (Adjustment D)[d] (7)
$ 0– 1,000	70.14%	63.68%	$ 45,292	$ 31,768	$ 34,186	$ 21,770	$ 23,462
1,001– 2,000	82.62	38.86	499,834	412,963	444,389	172,690	186,108
2,001– 3,000	84.37	42.02	921,446	777,424	836,586	351,533	378,847
3,001– 4,000	87.05	58.53	1,293,801	1,226,254	1,319,572	772,345	832,356
4,001– 5,000	87.95	70.63	1,946,007	1,711,513	1,841,759	1,300,834	1,401,909
5,001– 6,000	92.01	79.77	2,553,818	2,349,768	2,528,585	2,017,053	2,173,778
6,001– 7,000	90.81	86.88	3,190,309	2,897,120	3,117,591	2,708,563	2,919,024
7,001– 8,000	92.79	89.96	4,008,120	3,719,135	4,002,161	3,600,344	3,880,091
8,001– 9,000	92.76	93.17	4,869,508	4,516,956	4,860,696	4,528,717	4,880,592
9,001–10,000	93.30	93.78	5,552,335	5,180,329	5,574,552	5,227,815	5,634,016
10,001–12,000	93.63	95.23	12,063,212	11,294,785	12,154,318	11,574,557	12,473,900
12,001–15,000	93.24	95.80	15,933,307	14,856,215	15,986,773	15,315,328	16,505,329
15,001–25,000	93.28	96.61	18,118,451	16,900,891	18,187,049	17,570,508	18,937,736
Over 25,000	93.84	98.57	10,557,153	9,906,832	10,660,742	10,508,293	11,324,788
Total			81,552,593	75,781,953	81,552,592	75,670,344	81,552,593

Sources: Wisconsin Department of Revenue (1973) and Bahl (1972).

[a] Column 1 times column 3.

[b] Column 4 times (total of column 3 divided by total of column 4, i.e., 1.0761). Because of rounding in making adjustments, the actual total does not conform to the total of the entries in this column.

[c] Column 5 times column 2.

[d] Column 6 times (total of column 3 divided by total of column 6, i.e., 1.077). Because of rounding in making adjustments, the actual total does not conform to the total of the entries in this column.

Table 10.6 shows the distribution of real property assessments among
income classes which can serve as a proxy for the property tax burden of
residents. While the property tax burden varies according to income size
in our methodology, it is assumed, however, that the property tax burden
is constant in terms of family size. The number of families in each
income class and the number of families in each size category in
Milwaukee is contained in table 10.7. Since the total property tax burden
on resident families is distributed in proportion to the distribution of the
assessed values of property found in the last column of table 10.6, the
tax burden for each income class can be distributed, then, by family size,
holding the property tax burden constant for each family regardless of
size within a given income class. The resulting 14 × 6 matrix of real
property tax burdens arising out of financing selected public services is
disaggregated by income class and family size in the following sections of
this chapter.

The disaggregation according to family income and size of the increase
in income tax payments by city residents is accomplished with reasonable, yet simplifying, assumptions. State individual income tax collections by family adjusted gross income class were corrected to be more
closely aligned to real income classes. Using money income as a percentage of real income and adjusted gross income as a percentage of
money income, various adjustments are made to obtain a better estimate
of state individual income tax yields by real income classes for Milwaukee residents. Money income includes transfer payments whereas
adjusted gross income does not. Moreover, imputed rents of homeowners
must be added to money income to arrive at real income.

Furthermore, Wisconsin taxes capital gains at the same rate as other
income. The distribution of state income tax yields by taxable income
will generally overstate the tax payments by the lower real income groups
while understating the tax payments of higher real income groups. The
procedure used to adjust the data reallocates tax yields from the lower
income classes to the higher income classes in accordance with the
known distributions of money income and taxable income.

Table 10.8 summarizes the method used to estimate Wisconsin state
individual income tax yields for 1970 by family real income classes of
City of Milwaukee residents. Basic data used include money income as a
percentage of real income (column 1), Wisconsin taxable income as a
percentage of money income (column 2), and state income tax yields by
taxable income class (column 3). The adjustments in the remainder of
the table (columns 4-7) must be made because the tax yields reported by
the Wisconsin Department of Revenue are by taxable income classes,

whereas it is necessary to distribute these taxes across classes of real income.

Adjustment A in column 4 (the percentage figure in column 1 times the corresponding tax yield in column 3) brings the tax yields closer to the pattern of real income. The total of column 4, however, does not equal the total tax yield, which necessitates adjustment B in column 5. This adjustment is undertaken to correct the total to equal the known tax yield total. Adjustment C in column 6 is made to provide the final link between the real income classes and the Wisconsin state taxable income classes. Since Wisconsin state taxable income is far less than money income, adjustment C must be made and corrected for (columns 6 and 7). The increase in the state individual income tax due to the transfer of property tax financing of a given service to individual income tax financing is distributed among Milwaukee families by income class directly proportional to the figures in column 7 of table 10.8.

In order to distribute the change in income by family size it is assumed that the increase (or decrease) per family in a given income class remains constant. Even though Wisconsin families are given tax credits according to their size, inasmuch as we are dealing with a change in the income tax burden and not the *entire* burden, each family will have already claimed whatever tax credits it is entitled to because of its size, that is, number of dependents. Since there is no change in these tax credits the assumption of a constant per-family change for each income class is reasonable.

A Municipal Individual Income Tax

The comparative burden of financing selected local government services with an individual income tax or the real property tax is placed in sharper focus when it is assumed that a municipal income tax can be levied that is proportional to the present state individual income tax. This would be the case if a municipal income tax were enacted to ride "piggyback" on the state individual income tax.

Since this study is concerned with an income tax alternative to the real property tax, each dollar of property tax revenue lost by local governments which levy property taxes on city residents is always less than a corresponding levy on individual income because of the shifting of a part of the tax levies on nonresidential (commercial and manufacturing) property to nonresidents of the city. For this reason the burdens of a municipal individual income tax levied upon city residents will increase tax burdens on residents even if the property tax levy were decreased by an equal number of dollars. The burden of the tax change upon families of different incomes and sizes, however, may not always increase.

According to this analysis of the comparative burdens of the real property tax and individual income tax, the incidence of the burden will be the same regardless of which municipal service is being financed.

Public Education

This section focuses on the financing of local public education, including kindergarten through high school (K-12). An analysis is made of the probable change in tax burdens for city residents if all public school districts in Wisconsin had been financed in 1970 by the state individual income tax rather than the local property tax.

In 1970 there were 369 public school districts in Wisconsin, enrolling 993,735 students and levying $664,218,000 in property taxes (Wisconsin Department of Public Instruction, 1971). The School Board of the City of Milwaukee alone levied $83,028,000 in property taxes in its district (City of Milwaukee, Comptroller, 1971). This amounted to about 12.5 percent of all statewide property taxes for public education. In contrast, it was noted earlier that city residents paid about 16.9 percent of the state's individual income tax revenues. Accordingly, if spending levels for public education were unchanged in 1970 throughout the state, city residents would experience an increase in tax burdens if the state were to take over the responsibility of financing public education by raising individual income taxes with proportionally higher rates for all income brackets. But this differential burden of the property tax and individual income tax is only one reason for an increased tax burden on city residents with income tax financing.

Another reason, as stated earlier, lies in the generally held view that a portion of the property tax burden levied in the City of Milwaukee, about 12.5 percent, is shifted outside the city. Thus, the total increase in the tax burdens of city residents would have amounted to $39,610,000 in 1970 had the state taken financial responsibility for all local public education tax burdens by increasing income tax rates sufficiently. Table 10.5 contains a detailed summary of the pertinent data.

The above analysis does not take into consideration the "power-equalization" formula for school aids that was recently adopted in Wisconsin. For the school district with higher than average property taxes, the new state aid program would reduce still further the burden of school financing by means of the property tax compared with the individual income tax. For the school district with lower than average property tax rates the power-equalization formula for school aids would tend to offset the tax export "bonus" if that school district has commercial and/or manufacturing property. If such a school district is entirely residential, the new formula will place an extra burden upon the

Table 10.9. Public Education (K–12): Changes in Tax Burdens on City of Milwaukee Residents If Real Property Tax Financing Were Replaced by Individual Income Tax Financing, by Family Income Class and Size, 1970 (in thousands of dollars)

Family income	Number of persons in family						Total	Average per household (in dollars)
	1	2	3	4	5	6 and up		
$ 0– 1,000	— 3.524	.394	.180	.136	.074	.110	4.418	.274
1,001– 2,000	87.450	17.451	5.817	4.387	2.465	2.218	119.788	49.296
2,001– 3,000	— 284.934	51.487	11.755	8.043	4.778	5.121	— 366.118	— 34.371
3,001– 4,000	— 311.297	87.442	19.904	8.648	6.726	10.089	— 444.106	— 34.318
4,001– 5,000	235.266	110.301	23.067	12.286	8.442	11.533	400.895	39.634
5,001– 6,000	719.928	332.042	97.146	51.307	36.764	48.748	1285.935	116.343
6,001– 7,000	848.562	459.911	175.007	110.165	57.890	95.057	1746.592	133.695
7,001– 8,000	1041.625	537.052	261.843	206.240	109.335	130.855	2286.950	133.662
8,001– 9,000	1385.958	691.641	423.836	408.809	258.542	269.864	3438.650	205.846
9,001–10,000	1464.329	1048.686	642.761	619.994	392.043	409.257	4577.070	277.651
10,001–12,000	1762.051	2110.897	1526.720	1651.465	1116.356	1212.051	9379.540	244.119
12,001–15,000	1422.382	3287.129	2376.674	2571.591	1738.305	1887.572	13283.653	362.298
15,001–25,000	552.433	2315.494	2170.365	2184.275	1571.219	1887.982	10681.768	262.438
Over 25,000	— 377.148	—1616.249	—1236.249	—1313.960	— 986.361	—1246.230	— 6776.197	—356.473
Total	8543.081	9155.032	6435.148	6489.732	4293.422	4693.587	39610.002	

property taxpayer. It is uncertain whether this would be sufficient, however, to offset the income tax burden if residents enjoy higher than average taxable incomes. For the City of Milwaukee the additional school aid under the power-equalization formula would have been far less than the amount of property taxes that were exported.

We have seen that the property tax burden may be less than that of an alternative income tax because a portion of the taxes on property located in the city may be (1) borne by owners living in other tax jurisdictions, or (2) exported since some of the goods and services produced on that property are sold outside of the city, whereas the individual income tax is borne by the resident of the city. But a determination of the change in the aggregate tax burden with a change in revenue source is an incomplete analysis. While the aggregate tax burden for residents of the city may rise, the tax burden of individual households may fall.

The methodology for distributing tax burdens among households of different incomes and family size, as presented in the preceding section of this chapter, was applied to those public educational outlays that were financed with the real property tax in 1970. Next, the distribution of tax burdens among households of different incomes and family size was determined on the assumption that the state would take over the financial responsibility of public education and increase individual income taxes as a replacement of real property tax financing of public education.

The change in tax burdens that probably would have occurred in 1970 had real property tax financing of public education been replaced with the individual income tax are shown by income class and family size in table 10.9. Although the total tax burden would rise by $39,610,000, some income classes would experience a decrease in their tax burdens. The average decrease in the tax burdens per household for four of the fourteen income classes, namely, the 0-$1,000, $2,001-$3,000, $3,001-$4,000, and the over $25,000 income classes were $.27, $34.37, $34.32, and $356.47, respectively.

The tax burden increase for the $1,001-$2,000 income class seems out of place at first glance. This group, however, is very small in absolute size and consists of a large percentage of households with only one person and thus eligible to take only the minimum personal tax credit in the state income tax. Persons in this class also own very little taxable property. Thus, the $1,001-$2,000 income class of households loses rather than gains if the income tax replaces the property tax for public school financing.

The three lowest income classes (0-$1,000, $2,001-$3,000, and $3,001-$4,000) that would gain with a change in financing to the income tax would gain only moderately. The gains are due primarily to personal tax credits available to the larger families in these income classes. Furthermore, the large number of families in these classes make the average income tax burden even smaller (see average per household change in table 10.9.)

An interesting disclosure in table 10.9 is the inconsistency in the magnitude of the change in burden among income classes. This is especially noticeable in the average change in tax burden per household among income classes. Households in the $12,001-$15,000 income class experience a total increase in tax burdens of $13,283,653 as well as the largest dollar increase in tax burden per household, namely $362.30. Households with an income over $25,000 would pay $6,776,197 less and receive the largest dollar decrease in tax burden per household, namely $356.47.

These changes in tax burdens are probably more meaningful when expressed as percentages of individual income and property tax burdens for various income classes (see table 10.10). But the same inconsistencies that were observed above show up again. In terms of present property tax burdens, those households in the $1,001-$2,000 and $5,001-$15,000 income ranges would bear the greatest increase in tax burdens. The present tax burdens of households in these income brackets (except for households with $7,001-$8,000 income) would more than double and reduce their disposable real income between 2 and 3 percent. The income class over $25,000 would enjoy an average reduction in tax

Table 10.10. Public Education: Changes in Tax Burdens on City of Milwaukee Residents

| Family income | Change in tax burdens as a percentage of | |
	Property taxes paid for public education	Median income
$ 0- 1,000	—12.035%	— .456%
1,001- 2,000	87.812	2.718
2,001- 3,000	—41.246	—1.357
3,001- 4,000	—28.176	— .988
4,001- 5,000	26.219	.882
5,001- 6,000	75.353	2.131
6,001- 7,000	76.881	2.045
7,001- 8,000	74.872	1.786
8,001- 9,000	104.833	2.433
9,001-10,000	143.984	2.932
10,001-12,000	120.368	2.217
12,001-15,000	140.746	2.724
15,001-25,000	69.414	1.421
Over 25,000	—30.297	—1.000

Table 10.11. Vocational, Technical, and Adult Education: Changes in Tax Burdens on City of Milwaukee Residents If Real Property Tax Financing Were Replaced by Individual Income Tax Financing, by Family Income Class and Size, 1970 (in thousands of dollars)

Family income	Number of persons in family						Total	Average per household (in dollars)
	1	2	3	4	5	6 and up		
$ 0– 1,000	— .826	.092	.042	.032	.017	.026	— 1.035	— .064
1,001– 2,000	— 2.579	.515	.172	.129	.073	.065	— 3.533	— 1.454
2,001– 3,000	— 30.423	5.497	1.255	.859	.510	.547	— 39.091	— 3.670
3,001– 4,000	— 40.831	11.469	2.611	1.134	.882	1.323	— 58.250	— 4.501
4,001– 5,000	— 6.712	3.147	.658	.350	.241	.329	— 11.437	— 1.131
5,001– 6,000	18.292	8.437	2.468	1.304	.934	1.239	32.674	2.956
6,001– 7,000	22.046	11.949	4.547	2.862	1.504	2.470	45.378	3.473
7,001– 8,000	26.273	13.546	6.605	5.202	2.758	3.301	57.685	3.371
8,001– 9,000	46.433	23.171	14.199	13.696	8.662	9.041	115.202	6.896
9,001–10,000	57.295	41.032	25.150	24.259	15.340	16.013	179.089	10.864
10,001–12,000	63.737	76.356	55.225	59.737	40.381	43.842	339.278	8.830
12,001–15,000	55.161	127.478	92.169	99.728	67.413	73.202	515.151	14.050
15,001–25,000	12.676	53.131	49.801	50.120	36.053	43.322	245.103	6.022
Over 25,000	— 47.436	— 203.284	— 155.489	— 165.264	— 124.060	— 156.745	— 852.278	— 44.835
Total	178.264	132.126	90.281	89.398	47.408	33.525	571.002	

burden equal to 30 percent of their present property tax burdens arising out of local financing of public education and on that account a 1.0 percent increase in disposable income.

In summary, a change in the financing of public education from the local real property tax to the state income tax appears to lower the tax burden of households in only a few low income categories. It lowers it for taxpayers in the highest income class, too, but all other income classes, and thus most of the households in the City of Milwaukee, are faced with moderate to substantial increases in tax burdens.

Vocational, Technical, and Adult Education

Public vocational, technical, and adult education in Wisconsin is provided by eighteen special districts embracing the entire state. The City of Milwaukee is part of Vocational, Technical, and Adult Education District no. 9. Altogether, the eighteen districts levied $35,995,000 in property taxes in 1970, whereas district no. 9 alone levied $6,771,049. After subtracting its share of general property tax relief, the net property tax levied by district no. 9 was $6,300,000. But after subtracting the taxes shifted out of the city, the actual property tax burden on city residents was only $5,512,000.

If Wisconsin were to assume full responsibility for financing all of the vocational, technical, and adult education districts throughout the state, it would have to raise an additional $35,995,000. If the state's individual income tax were raised so that it would yield this additional amount city residents would pay $6,083,000 more in income taxes. Thus, the net effect on city residents would be an overall increase in tax burdens by $571,000 (see tables 10.5 and 10.11).

Although total tax burdens on city residents would increase with income tax financing, some residents would gain while others would lose. Table 10.11 shows the net change in tax burdens by family income and size. The last column in the table shows the dollar change for the average household in each income category. It is interesting to note that the changes in tax burden by family income categories are similar to the changes with respect to income tax financing of public education. In this case, however, the $4,001-$5,000 income class also experiences a fall in tax burdens. Furthermore, the average gain for the highest income household is substantial ($44.84) while the gain for the average household with the lowest income is insignificant ($0.064).

Families within the $8,001-$15,000 range will bear the greatest increase in tax burdens due to the change in financing. In absolute dollar amounts, however, the increases for these households can be described as moderate, whereas the increase for households in the $1,001-$2,000 and $5,001-$8,000 categories are very modest.

Families with the highest income, over $25,000, would benefit by an aggregate tax reduction of $852,278, or an average of $44.84 per household. Families with incomes of $12,001-$15,000 would have to pay $515,151 more in total taxes, or an average of $14.05 per household.

The change in financing would increase tax burdens in the aggregate for families of all sizes. Single persons, however, would have to bear the greatest increase in tax burden ($178,264) compared with families of any other size. As family size increases, the impact of the change in financing falls—the smallest increase would be borne by families of six ($33,525). As a group, two-member households with incomes over $25,000 would receive the largest decrease in tax burdens ($203,284), whereas two-member households with incomes from $12,001-$15,000 would experience the largest increase in tax burdens as a group ($127,478).

The impact of changing the financing of vocational, technical, and adult education from the property tax to the state individual income tax can also be summarized in terms of the relative (percentage) change of the tax burden in terms of present property tax burdens and by size of income. This is shown in table 10.12.

According to this type of analysis, those families with incomes from $0-$1,000, $2,001-$5,000, and over $25,000 receive the greatest benefits

Table 10.12. Vocational, Technical, and Adult Education: Changes in Tax Burdens on City of Milwaukee Residents

| | Change in tax burdens as a percentage of | |
Family income	Property taxes paid for vocational, technical, and adult education	Median income
$ 0– 1,000	—37.177%	—.107%
1,001– 2,000	34.131	.080
2,001– 3,000	—58.039	—.145
3,001– 4,000	—48.705	—.130
4,001– 5,000	— 9.857	—.025
5,001– 6,000	25.233	.054
6,001– 7,000	26.324	.053
7,001– 8,000	24.889	.045
8,001– 9,000	46.287	.081
9,001–10,000	74.247	.115
10,001–12,000	57.381	.080
12,001–15,000	71.934	.106
15,001–25,000	20.991	.033
Over 25,000	—50.220	—.126

in terms of their incomes as well as their present property taxes. The pattern of change in tax burdens in terms of income is crudely progressive for income classes between $4,001 and $10,000, after which the pattern wobbles for incomes up to $15,000, and thereafter collapses and becomes strongly regressive.

Public Welfare

Public welfare services in Wisconsin may be provided either by municipalities or counties. In Milwaukee County it is the county itself that administers a considerable list of public welfare programs. In 1970 the county levied $50,864,000 in property taxes net of state property tax relief on property located in the city (see table 10.4). It is assumed that 25.96 percent of the county property tax on property located in the city is levied to finance public welfare programs inasmuch as the county allocated the same percentage of its total budget to public welfare programs. [4] Thus, the net real property tax levy by the county upon real property in the city for public welfare purposes is $13,205,000. Moreover, considering that approximately 12.5 percent of the property tax burden on property located in the city is "shifted" outside of the city, about $11,553,000, or 87.5 percent of the $13,205,000 of the public welfare portion of the real property tax, bears on city residents.

Now any plan that would transfer the local financial burden of public welfare from Milwaukee County to the State of Wisconsin would have to do the same for all local governments throughout the state to the extent that public welfare is supported by the property tax. Table 10.13 summarizes total property taxes levied throughout Wisconsin in 1970 for the purpose of public welfare. The method of arriving at the total is to determine first the property taxes levied for public welfare for each class of municipality and county. Again, it is assumed that the percentage of total property tax levies in each category that is utilized for public welfare is the same as the percentage which public welfare disbursements are of total disbursements for all programs for each class of municipality and county. In this way it is estimated that the public welfare programs placed a total tax burden on real property in the amount of $31,469,000 in 1970. Thus, if the state were to have lifted from taxpayers the property tax burden caused by public welfare, it would have had to increase the

4. From Wisconsin Department of Administration, State Bureau of Municipal Audit (1971a). The percentage is 62.47 percent if public welfare expenditures ($41,996,000) financed by means of the real property tax is compared with total county expenditures financed by funds raised from the real property tax ($67,230,000).

Table 10.13. Property Tax Levies by All Local Governments in Wisconsin in 1970 for Public Welfare Purposes (in thousands of dollars)

Unit of government	Total disbursements for all purposes (A)	Total disbursements for public welfare (W)	Total property taxes levied (P_t)	Property taxes levied for public welfare (P_w^a)
Counties	$1,236,622	$152,229	$251,130	$30,914
Cities	3,238,154	1,515	736,668	368
Villages	245,484	54	110,243	23
Towns	425,566	265	265,146	164
Total				31,469

Source: Wisconsin Department of Administration, State Bureau of Municipal Audit (1971b).

$^a P_w = P_t(\frac{W}{A})$.

yield of the Wisconsin individual income tax by this amount. We are assuming no change in welfare benefits, not only because the nature of such changes is debatable, but also because it would introduce a variable that would obscure the effect of the "take-over," and the major objective of this study is to demonstrate this effect with maximum clarity.

Since residents of the City of Milwaukee paid 16.9 percent of the state's total income tax payments in 1970, they would have had to pay that percentage of $31,469,000, which amounts to $5,318,000 (see table 10.5). Simultaneously the aggregate property tax burdens of city residents would have been reduced by $11,553,000, a net savings of some $6,235,000 for city residents.

Whereas the transfer of financial responsibility for public education (including vocational, technical, and adult education) to the state resulted in higher tax burdens for city residents in the aggregate, our findings show that the same pattern does not apply when the financial burden for public welfare is transferred from local government units to the state. This seems to be the case because Milwaukee County accounts for such a large share of all state expenditures for public welfare services. Because of this the residents of the city bore 36.71 percent of all real property tax payments to the state. Thus, any program designed to finance a greater portion of public welfare services out of the state income tax rather than the property tax will greatly benefit city residents. According to the plan analyzed here, in which the burden of welfare services on the property tax is completely replaced by increasing the income tax, residents of the City of Milwaukee would have gained by $6,235,000 in 1970.

Table 10.14. Public Welfare: Changes in Tax Burdens on City of Milwaukee Residents If Real Property Tax Financing Were Replaced by Individual Income Tax Financing, by Family Income Class and Size, 1970 (in thousands of dollars)

Family income	Number of persons in family						Total	Average per household (in dollars)
	1	2	3	4	5	6 and up		
$ 0- 1,000	— 3.437	— .385	— .175	— .133	— .072	— .108	— 4.310	— .267
1,001- 2,000	— 6.977	— 1.392	— .464	— .350	— .197	— .177	— 9.557	— 3.933
2,001- 3,000	— 90.638	— 16.378	— 3.739	— 2.558	— 1.520	— 1.629	— 116.462	— 10.933
3,001- 4,000	— 138.116	— 38.796	— 8.831	— 3.837	— 2.984	— 4.476	— 197.040	— 15.226
4,001- 5,000	— 89.050	— 41.750	— 8.731	— 4.651	— 3.195	— 4.365	— 151.742	— 15.002
5,001- 6,000	— 72.577	— 33.474	— 9.793	— 5.172	— 3.706	— 4.914	— 129.636	— 11.729
6,001- 7,000	— 83.046	— 45.010	— 17.127	— 10.781	— 5.666	— 9.303	— 170.933	— 13.084
7,001- 8,000	— 106.000	— 54.653	— 26.646	— 20.988	— 11.126	— 13.316	— 232.729	— 13.602
8,001- 9,000	— 81.965	— 40.903	— 25.066	— 24.177	— 15.290	— 15.960	— 203.361	— 12.174
9,001-10,000	— 44.190	— 31.647	— 19.397	— 18.710	— 11.831	— 12.350	— 138.125	— 8.379
10,001-12,000	— 79.985	— 95.820	— 69.302	— 74.965	— 50.675	— 55.018	— 425.765	— 11.081
12,001-15,000	— 45.462	— 105.062	— 75.962	— 82.192	— 55.559	— 60.330	— 424.567	— 11.580
15,001-25,000	— 62.695	— 262.785	— 246.314	— 247.893	— 178.317	— 214.267	— 1212.271	— 29.784
Over 25,000	— 156.872	— 672.265	— 514.207	— 546.530	— 410.268	— 518.359	— 2818.501	— 148.272
Total	— 1061.010	— 1440.320	— 1025.754	— 1042.937	— 750.406	— 914.572	— 6234.999	

The distribution of this reduction in tax burdens among households of various incomes and sizes is shown in table 10.14. The data are the difference between the distribution of property tax burdens arising out of financing public welfare and the income tax burdens, following the state assumption of financial responsibility. The outstanding feature of the data in table 10.14 is the universal benefit that would be enjoyed by each and every household group regardless of income and family size.

A closer examination of the findings reported in table 10.14 reveals a familiar pattern.[5] The average dollar gain per household resulting from the alternative plan, state assumption of local financial responsibility for public welfare (the last column in table 10.14), shows that the largest tax reductions would be received by households with incomes over $15,000, whereas the least benefits would go to the lowest ($0-$2,000) income households. Households between $2,001 and $15,000 would receive relatively stable tax reductions in terms of dollars. Variations in tax reduction for households in this range ($2,001 and $15,000) bear no regular or predictable relationship to income.

An analysis of the tax burden effects of the fiscal alternative for financing public welfare according to family size shows that the greatest reduction in tax burden would go to two-person households. In this

Table 10.15. Public Welfare: Changes in Tax Burdens on City of Milwaukee Residents

Family income	Change in tax burdens as a percentage of	
	Property taxes paid for public welfare	Median income
$ 0- 1,000	—73.796%	—.445%
1,001- 2,000	—44.053	—.217
2,001- 3,000	—82.498	—.432
3,001- 4,000	—78.605	—.438
4,001- 5,000	—62.401	—.334
5,001- 6,000	—47.765	—.215
6,001- 7,000	—47.310	—.200
7,001- 8,000	—47.908	—.182
8,001- 9,000	—38.983	—.144
9,001-10,000	—27.321	—.088
10,001-12,000	—34.356	—.101
12,001-15,000	—28.285	—.087
15,001-25,000	—49.534	—.161
Over 25,000	—79.236	—.416

5. The basic explanation for this pattern may be found in an often expressed view that the ownership of total taxable property is more highly concentrated in the hands of higher income households than total taxable income.

analysis, all households of a given size are lumped together regardless of income. Households of one, three, four, and more than five all receive about the same tax reductions, on the average. Households of two receive the largest reduction, whereas households of five receive the smallest dollar reductions. Yet the overall range of tax reductions for families of all sizes is small, $750,410 to $1,440,320.

If we consider both income and family size simultaneously, the largest benefits ($672,265) would go to two-person family households, as a group, in the highest (over $25,000) bracket and the smallest benefit ($72,000) to households of five persons with the lowest income, $0-$1,000. Moreover, it is clear that the ownership of taxable property is concentrated in households with two or more persons with higher incomes. It appears that most high income persons are married.

The above changes in tax burdens of City of Milwaukee residents can be expressed as a percentage of property taxes paid and the median income in each income class, as shown in table 10.15. Had the fiscal alternative been in effect in 1970, the property taxes paid by the highest (over $25,000) income group would have been reduced by an average of 79.24 percent. Several of the lowest income groups of households, that is, $0-$1,000, $2,001-$3,000, and $3,001-$4,000, would have enjoyed an equally substantial percentage reduction. Households with incomes ranging between $8,001 and $15,000 would have received the smallest reduction in their tax burdens expressed as a percentage of the respective property taxes that they paid.

The same pattern of effects shows up if the median of each group of households is utilized as the basis of analysis. The percentage increase in real income due to the fiscal change is large for households below $5,000 (except for the $1,001-$2,000 group) and those over $25,000. Households in the $8,001-$15,000 brackets would enjoy the smallest increases in real income. But for all groups of households the change in tax burden would increase real income by less than one-half of one percent.

Health and Hospitals

All forms of multifunctional local governments in Wisconsin may provide health and hospital services. These general local governments include counties, cities, villages, and towns. Residents of the City of Milwaukee receive health and hospital services from both the county and city governments, at differential rates, however. In 1970 the county allocated 18.41 percent of its total expenditures for health and hospital purposes. In the same year, the city spent only .36 percent of its total budget on these services.

In dollars, the county levied property taxes (net of property tax relief)

Table 10.16. Real Property Tax Levies by All Local Governments in Wisconsin in 1970 for Health and Hospital Services (in thousands of dollars)

Unit of government	Total disbursements for all purposes (A)	Total disbursements for health and hospitals (W)	Total property taxes levied (P_t)	Property taxes levied for health and hospitals ($P_w{}^a$)
Counties	$1,236,622	$154,382	$251,130	$31,341
Cities	3,238,154	19,133	736,668	3,683
Villages	245,484	371	110,293	110
Towns	425,566	132	265,146	82
Total				35,216

Source: Wisconsin Department of Administration, State Bureau of Municipal Audit (1971b).

$^a P_w = P_t(\dfrac{W}{A})$.

in the amount of $9,364,000 in 1970 on city residents, and the city itself levied some $287,000 for health and hospital purposes, for a total of $9,651,000. After we subtract that portion believed to be borne by noncity residents, the residents of the city are left with an aggregate tax burden of $8,444,000 for health and hospital services for 1970.

Property taxes levied throughout the state in 1970 for health and hospital services are shown in table 10.16. Calculated as a fraction of total disbursements the property taxes levied for these services are estimated (for 1970) to be $31,341,000 for counties, $3,683,000 for cities, $110,000 for villages, and $82,000 for towns—a total of $35,216,000 for all of these local jurisdictions throughout the state. If the state were to take over the financing of this amount from the local units of government, it would have to raise the yield of the individual income tax by this $35,216,000. Of this amount, City of Milwaukee residents would pay $5,951,000 more in the aggregate in their state income taxes. At the same time, city residents would receive a reduction of $8,444,000 in their property tax burdens. Thus, the net aggregate effect on tax burdens to all city residents would be a decrease of $2,493,000 (see table 10.5).

We can now examine the effects of this transfer of financial responsibility on the tax burdens of individual Milwaukee households of various incomes and family size. The distribution of real property tax burdens for public health and hospital services in 1970 (in terms of the average amount of dollars per household) indicates clearly that higher income households pay more than lower income households. Moreover, the larger families in the lower income classes appear to pay less property taxes than smaller families. Family size appears to have little effect on property taxes paid among the higher income classes.

Table 10.17. Health and Hospitals: Changes in Tax Burdens on City of Milwaukee Residents If Real Property Tax Financing Were Replaced by Individual Income Tax Financing, by Family Income Class and Size, 1970 (in thousands of dollars)

Family income	Number of persons in family						Total	Average per household (in dollars)
	1	2	3	4	5	6 and up		
$ 0– 1,000	— 2.038	— .228	— .104	— .079	— .043	— .064	— 2.556	— .158
1,001– 2,000	— 1.660	— .331	— .110	— .083	— .047	— .042	— 2.273	— .936
2,001– 3,000	— 58.783	— 10.622	— 2.425	— 1.659	— .986	— 1.057	— 75.532	— 7.091
3,001– 4,000	— 86.357	— 24.257	— 5.522	— 2.399	— 1.866	— 2.799	— 123.200	— 9.520
4,001– 5,000	— 44.260	— 20.751	— 4.340	— 2.311	— 1.588	— 2.170	— 75.420	— 7.456
5,001– 6,000	— 22.240	— 10.257	— 3.001	— 1.585	— 1.136	— 1.506	— 39.725	— 3.594
6,001– 7,000	— 24.799	— 13.441	— 5.114	— 3.219	— 1.692	— 2.778	— 51.043	— 3.907
7,001– 8,000	— 32.739	— 16.880	— 8.230	— 6.482	— 3.437	— 4.113	— 71.881	— 4.201
8,001– 9,000	— 10.113	— 5.046	— 3.092	— 2.983	— 1.886	— 1.969	— 25.089	— 1.502
9,001–10,000	13.329	9.546	5.851	5.644	3.569	3.725	41.664	2.527
10,001–12,000	.859	1.029	.744	.805	.544	.591	4.572	.119
12,001–15,000	11.510	26.600	19.233	20.810	14.067	15.275	107.495	2.932
15,001–25,000	— 21.031	— 88.152	— 82.627	— 83.156	— 59.817	— 71.876	— 406.659	— 9.991
Over 25,000	— 98.701	— 422.977	— 323.530	— 343.867	— 258.134	— 326.142	— 1773.351	— 93.290
Total	— 377.023	— 575.767	— 412.267	— 420.564	— 312.452	— 394.925	— 2492.998	

The increase in state individual income taxes that would have been necessary in 1970 had local property tax financing been eliminated for health and hospital services by income class and family size was then calculated. The pattern of correlation between increased income tax liability and size of family income is less stable than is the case with property tax financing. The relationship, however, is positive, with higher income households being liable usually for a greater increase in individual income taxes. The pattern of tax liability by family size is similar to that found with the property tax.

The changes in tax burdens by family income and size are shown in table 10.17. The most striking feature of these results is a significant increase in tax burdens of only those families with incomes from $9,001-$10,000 and $12,001-$15,000. At the same time, the highest income class, over $25,000, receives enormous tax cuts, while the lowest income categories, that is, all those receiving less than $9,001, receive far smaller tax reductions. The pattern of change in tax burden according to family size is not much different than that found previously. The lower income classes appear to pay less if their family size increases. No general or clear pattern emerges for higher income classes that correlates tax burdens with family size.

The change in tax burdens by income class can be expressed as a percentage of total (in each class) property taxes paid in 1970 and as a percentage of the median income of each income class (see table 10.18).

Table 10.18. Health and Hospitals: Changes in Tax Burdens on City of Milwaukee Residents

| | Change in tax burdens as a percentage of | |
Family income	Property taxes paid for health and hospitals	Median income
$ 0– 1,000	−59.881%	—.264%
1,001– 2,000	−14.343	—.052
2,001– 3,000	−73.204	—.280
3,001– 4,000	−67.243	—.274
4,001– 5,000	−42.434	—.166
5,001– 6,000	−20.026	—.066
6,001– 7,000	−19.329	—.060
7,001– 8,000	−20.245	—.056
8,001– 9,000	− 6.580	—.018
9,001–10,000	11.275	.027
10,001–12,000	.505	.001
12,001–15,000	9.798	.022
15,001–25,000	−22.734	—.054
Over 25,000	−68.210	—.262

The percentage change in property tax burdens reveals a pattern in which the highest and lowest income classes receive the largest reductions in tax burdens. The pattern among the middle income classes is inconsistent. When we use income as the basis for measuring change in tax burdens, the pattern is similar.

In summary, our analysis reveals that most city residents would receive a sizable reduction in their aggregate tax burdens with a transfer of the local financial responsibility for public health and hospital services from the real property tax to the state individual income tax. But all households would not share the benefits of this tax reduction equally. In fact, some households ($9,001-$15,000) would actually experience an increase in tax burdens. The households which would benefit the most are classes with the low incomes ($0-$1,000 and $2,001-$4,000) and all of the classes with income over $25,000.

Legal and Judicial

All forms of multifunctional local governments in Wisconsin provide legal and judicial services. These general local governments include counties, cities, villages, and towns. Residents of the City of Milwaukee receive legal and judicial services from their county and city governments.

Property taxes levied throughout Wisconsin in 1970 for legal and judicial services are shown in table 10.19. These figures are estimates arrived at by taking that fraction of total property taxes levied which total disbursements for legal and judicial purposes bear to total disburse-

Table 10.19. Property Tax Levies by All Local Governments in Wisconsin in 1970 for Legal and Judicial Purposes (in thousands of dollars)

Unit of government	Total disbursements for all purposes (A)	Total disbursements for legal and judicial purposes (W)	Total property taxes levied (P_t)	Property taxes levied for legal and judicial purposes $(P_w{}^a)$
Counties	$1,236,622	$ 19,253	$251,130	$ 3,908
Cities	3,238,154	2,670	736,668	604
Villages	245,484	512	110,243	229
Towns	425,566	440	265,146	273
Total				5,014

Source: Wisconsin Department of Administration, State Bureau of Municipal Audit (1971b).

$^a P_w = P_t(\frac{W}{A})$.

Table 10.20. Legal and Judicial: Changes in Tax Burdens on City of Milwaukee Residents If Real Property Tax Financing Were Replaced by Individual Income Tax Financing, by Family Income Class and Size, 1970 (in thousands of dollars)

Family income	Number of persons in family						Total	Average per household (in dollars)
	1	2	3	4	5	6 and up		
$ 0– 1,000	— .249	— .028	— .013	— .010	— .005	— .008	— .313	.019
1,001– 2,000	— .098	— .020	— .007	— .005	— .003	— .002	— .135	.055
2,001– 3,000	— 7.408	— 1.339	— .306	— .209	— .124	— .133	— 9.519	.894
3,001– 4,000	—10.758	— 3.002	— .688	— .299	— .232	— .349	—15.348	1.186
4,001– 5,000	— 5.054	— 2.370	— .496	— .264	— .181	— .248	— 8.613	.851
5,001– 6,000	— 1.839	— .848	— .248	— .131	— .094	— .125	— 3.285	.297
6,001– 7,000	— 1.998	— 1.083	— .412	— .259	— .136	— .224	— 4.112	.315
7,001– 8,000	— 2.729	— 1.407	— .686	— .540	— .286	— .343	— 5.991	.350
8,001– 9,000	.396	.197	.121	.117	.074	.077	.982	.059
9,001–10,000	3.309	2.370	1.452	1.401	.886	.925	10.343	.627
10,001–12,000	2.154	2.580	1.866	2.019	1.365	1.482	11.466	.298
12,001–15,000	3.041	7.028	5.081	5.498	3.716	4.035	28.399	.775
15,001–25,000	— 1.889	— 7.917	— 7.420	— 7.468	— 5.372	— 6.455	—36.521	.897
Over 25,000	—12.320	—52.797	—40.384	—42.923	—32.221	—40.710	—221.355	—11.645
Total	—35.442	—58.656	—42.140	—43.073	—32.613	—42.078	—254.002	

ments for all purposes. Of all local governments the counties spend by far the most on legal and judicial services and levy the most property taxes for this purpose. Altogether, counties levied a total of $3,908,000 in property taxes to support legal and judicial services out of a total of $5,014,000 spent by all local governments for these purposes.

In 1970 the County of Milwaukee spent $6,998,000 (2.38 percent of its total disbursements), while the City of Milwaukee spent $830,000 (.06 percent of its total disbursements) for legal and judicial services. Given the total property tax levies of both governmental units, it was estimated that $1,211,000 was levied on real property in the city by the county and $48,000 by the city for a total levy of $1,259,000. After making adjustments in this figure for the shifting of some of this burden to non-residents, however, it was concluded that the real property tax burden on city residents for legal and judicial services amounted to $1,101,000.

Had Wisconsin taken over in 1970 the complete financial responsibility for legal and judicial services from local governments by increasing the yield of the individual income tax, the aggregate tax burden of City of Milwaukee residents would have decreased by $254,000, or 23 percent. But the effect on individual households is not at all what this would suggest.

The distribution by family income and size of the $1,101,000 in real property tax burdens on city residents for legal and judicial purposes shows that the average dollar burden per household is relatively constant for families with income between $4,001 and $12,000. For families with incomes of $12,000 and less, the tax burden varies inversely with the size of the family. On the other hand, for families with incomes of over $12,000 the tax burden varies directly with family size.

The increase in state individual income taxes that would have been necessary in 1970 had local property tax financing been eliminated for legal and judicial services shows a positive correlation between increased income tax liability and size of family income. The burden generally declines for families of more than one person with an income of $10,000 and less and for two-person families if the income is above $10,000.

The changes in tax burdens by family income and size are shown in table 10.20. While residents of the City of Milwaukee would receive a tax cut of $254,000, more than that amount, namely, $257,876, would go to families with incomes of over $15,000. Families with incomes between $8,000 and $15,000 would have their tax burdens increased by $51,190. Families with incomes below $8,000 would enjoy a reduction in tax burdens of $47,316. Tax burdens seem to diminish with increasing family size for households with incomes less than $12,000. There seems to be no general pattern to the changes in tax burdens according to family size for households with incomes of more than $12,000.

The change in tax burdens by income class can be expressed as a percentage of total property taxes (in each class) paid in 1970, and as a percentage of the median income of each income class (see table 10.21). The percentage reduction in property tax burdens is the greatest for families with incomes below $1,000, from $2,001 to $5,000, and over $25,000. The pattern of change in tax burden based on income is similar.

Table 10.21. Legal and Judicial: Changes in Tax Burdens on City of Milwaukee Residents

	Change in tax burdens as a percentage of	
Family income	Property taxes paid for legal and judicial services	Median income
$ 0– 1,000	−56.207%	−.032%
1,001– 2,000	− 6.499	−.003
2,001– 3,000	−70.750	−.035
3,001– 4,000	−64.243	−.034
4,001– 5,000	−37.163	−.019
5,001– 6,000	−12.702	−.005
6,001– 7,000	−11.941	−.005
7,001– 8,000	−12.941	−.005
8,001– 9,000	1.975	.001
9,001–10,000	21.465	.007
10,001–12,000	9.708	.003
12,001–15,000	19.853	.006
15,001–25,000	−15.658	−.005
Over 25,000	−65.299	−.033

Table 10.22. Property Tax Levies by All Local Governments in Wisconsin in 1970 for Correctional Purposes (in thousands of dollars)

Unit of government	Total disbursements for all purposes (A)	Total disbursements for correctional purposes (W)	Total property taxes levied for all purposes (P_t)	Property taxes levied for correctional purposes ($P_w{}^a$)
Counties	$1,236,622	$ 6,680	$251,130	$ 1,356
Cities	3,238,154	—	736,668	—
Villages	245,484	—	110,243	—
Towns	425,566	—	265,146	—
Total				1,356

Source: Wisconsin Department of Administration, State Bureau of Municipal Audit (1971b).

$^a P_w = P_t(\dfrac{W}{A})$.

In summary, our analysis reveals that if the State of Wisconsin were to assume the financial responsibility of locally financed legal and judicial services and accomplish this shift with an increase in the individual income tax, the net effect on tax burdens would be mixed for various income classes. The bulk of the tax savings—over 100 percent of the total $254,000—would be received by families with income over $15,000 per year. Tax savings for families below $8,000 would be very small, ranging between $1.19 to $.02 per family. Families with income between $8,001 and $15,000 would have their tax burdens increased by enough to pay not only for the reductions enjoyed by lower income families but also for part of the tax reductions of higher income families.

Correctional Services

All local correctional services in Wisconsin are provided by county governments (see table 10.22). In fact, most of the correctional facilities in Wisconsin are owned, operated, and financed by the state government. But county governments in Wisconsin spent an aggregate of $6,680,000 or .5 percent of their total expenditures for correctional purposes. Of this amount, about $1,356,000 was financed by property tax levies in 1970.

The County of Milwaukee spent 1.48 percent of its total disbursements for correctional purposes. In order to finance part of this amount the county levied $753,000 in taxes on real property located in the City of Milwaukee. After taking into account that portion shifted out of the city, the net tax burden remaining on city residents was $659,000.

If the state had assumed complete responsibility for all local (county) correctional facilities and services in 1970, the state individual income tax yield would have had to be increased by $1,356,000 to replace the local property tax for that purpose. Since residents of the city pay 16.9 percent of each dollar of the state's individual income tax yield, they would have had to increase their individual income tax payments by only $229,000. Thus the tax burdens on city residents would have decreased by $430,000 in the aggregate. While all city residents would not share equally, the pattern of tax savings is surprisingly stable, as we shall see.

The distribution of the average amount of real property tax burdens in 1970 in Milwaukee per household of various income and size for correctional services is positively related to family income. Tax burdens increase arithmetically and unfailingly from the lowest to highest income classes and are generally progressive. Real property tax burdens are generally smaller for larger families (up to five) with incomes less than $12,001.

The increase in state individual income taxes that would have been

Table 10.23. Correction: Changes in Tax Burdens on City of Milwaukee Residents If Real Property Tax Financing Were Replaced by Individual Income Tax Financing, by Family Income Class and Size, 1970 (in thousands of dollars)

Family income	Number of persons in family						Total	Average per household (in dollars)
	1	2	3	4	5	6 and up		
$ 0– 1,000	− .213	− .024	− .011	− .008	− .004	− .007	− .267	.017
1,001– 2,000	− .522	− .104	− .035	− .026	− .015	− .013	− .715	.294
2,001– 3,000	− 5.439	− .983	− .224	− .154	− .091	− .098	− 6.989	.656
3,001– 4,000	− 8.404	− 2.361	− .537	− .233	− .182	− .272	− 11.989	.926
4,001– 5,000	− 5.830	− 2.733	− .572	− .304	− .209	− .286	− 9.934	.982
5,001– 6,000	− 5.249	− 2.421	− .708	− .374	− .268	− .355	− 9.375	.848
6,001– 7,000	− 6.030	− 3.268	− 1.244	− .783	− .411	− .676	− 12.412	.950
7,001– 8,000	− 7.658	− 3.948	− 1.925	− 1.516	− .804	− .962	− 16.813	.983
8,001– 9,000	− 6.469	− 3.228	− 1.978	− 1.908	− 1.207	− 1.260	− 16.050	.961
9,001–10,000	− 4.164	− 2.982	− 1.828	− 1.763	− 1.115	− 1.164	− 13.016	.790
10,001–12,000	− 6.699	− 8.025	− 5.804	− 6.279	− 4.244	− 4.608	− 35.659	.928
12,001–15,000	− 4.205	− 9.717	− 7.026	− 7.602	− 5.138	− 5.580	− 39.268	−1.071
15,001–25,000	− 4.469	−18.733	−17.558	−17.671	−12.711	−15.274	− 86.416	−2.123
Over 25,000	− 9.523	−40.810	−31.215	−33.177	−24.905	−31.467	−171.097	−9.001
Total	−74.874	−99.337	−70.665	−71.798	−51.304	−62.022	−430.000	

necessary in 1970 had local property tax financing been eliminated for correctional services shows that tax burdens increase with income, as with the property tax, but the pattern is less progressive. Similarly, as with the property tax, income tax burdens generally decrease for larger families (up to five members) with incomes of $10,000 or less. At higher incomes, income tax burdens generally decrease for families of more than two members but less than six.

The distribution of the change in tax burdens by family income and size had local financial responsibility for correctional services been transferred in 1970 is shown in table 10.23. Tax burdens would fall for all family income classes. The reduction in burdens would have been almost uniform for all income classes from $3,001 to $15,000, while families with lower incomes would have lesser tax cuts and families with incomes above $15,000 would enjoy substantially larger tax reductions. The change in tax burdens by family size is similar to the tax burdens of an increased income tax noted above.

The change in tax burdens by income class is expressed in table 10.24 as a percentage of total (in each class) property taxes paid for correction services in 1970, and as a percentage of the median income of each income class. Families with incomes from $8,001 to $15,000 would receive property tax reductions ranging from 45.13 percent to 53.9 percent, whereas all other income groups would have received larger percentage reductions in their property taxes. A similar pattern of

Table 10.24. Correctional Services: Changes in Tax Burdens on City of Milwaukee Residents

| | Change in tax burdens as a percentage of | |
Family income	Property taxes paid for correctional services	Median income
$ 0- 1,000	—80.219%	—.028%
1,001- 2,000	—57.765	—.016
2,001- 3,000	—86.787	—.026
3,001- 4,000	—83.848	—.027
4,001- 5,000	—71.616	—.022
5,001- 6,000	—60.567	—.016
6,001- 7,000	—60.224	—.015
7,001- 8,000	—60.675	—.013
8,001- 9,000	—53.938	—.011
9,001-10,000	—45.134	—.008
10,001-12,000	—50.444	—.008
12,001-15,000	—45.862	—.008
15,001-25,000	—61.903	—.011
Over 25,000	—84.325	—.025

change in tax burden obtains when expressed in terms of the median income of each family income class.

In summary, our analysis finds that City of Milwaukee residents would be able to transfer successfully the bulk of the burden of correctional services if the state assumed financial responsibility by means of an increase in the state individual income tax. Based on 1970 figures city residents would have saved $430,000 in taxes in the aggregate, which is 65 percent of the property taxes paid for correctional services. Families of all sizes and income classes would have had a reduction in tax burdens, with the greatest benefit going to the heavy property tax payers in the over $25,000 income class.

The Differential Tax Incidence of the Real Property Tax Compared with a City Income Tax

The six preceding sections of this chapter focused on the changes in tax burdens that would have resulted from the transfer of the local financial responsibility for six selected public services to the state level of government in Wisconsin. Our findings demonstrate clearly that effects would vary from service to service. While the overall effects are not the same for each of the services studied, some general patterns emerge. In this section we will attempt to isolate and quantify these basic patterns. We will highlight the changes in tax burdens for families of various incomes and sizes that would occur if part of the real property tax were replaced with a municipal income tax in the City of Milwaukee.

In our differential tax incidence study we assume that one million dollars of real property tax payments to the city are to be replaced with an equal amount of revenues from a city income tax designed as a supplement (or "piggyback" as it is sometimes called) to the Wisconsin state individual income tax by increasing the rates of all income brackets by such amounts that the same percentage of income taxes for each class of real income would be maintained. A city income tax of this design accepts the same progressive rate structure inherent in the Wisconsin individual income tax, with its rates ranging from 3.1 percent on the first $1,000 of taxable income up to 11.4 percent on income over $14,000. By replacing part of the real property tax with an income tax modeled along the foregoing lines, we should be able to determine clearly the basic effect on tax burdens of residents of the City of Milwaukee if the state assumption of local financial responsibility were to be managed by increasing the state's individual income tax. It should be understood that this exercise is unrelated to the financing of any particular local service. Actual tax burdens will be affected also by the degree of concentration of

Table 10.25. Distribution of Real Property Tax Relief to City of Milwaukee Residents If Levy Were Reduced by $1,000,000, 1970 (in dollars)

Family income	Number of persons in family						Total	Average per household
	1	2	3	4	5	6 and up		
$ 0- 1,000	352.675	39.460	17.976	13.647	7.426	11.043	442.227	.027
1,001- 2,000	1199.443	239.348	79.783	60.175	33.806	30.426	1642.981	.676
2,001- 3,000	8320.312	1503.477	343.250	234.856	139.508	149.545	10690.948	1.004
3,001- 4,000	13306.676	3737.781	850.829	369.671	287.522	431.282	18983.761	1.467
4,001- 5,000	10807.220	5066.794	1059.603	564.393	387.793	529.801	18415.604	1.821
5,001- 6,000	11507.048	5307.226	1552.745	820.072	587.626	779.162	20553.879	1.860
6,001- 7,000	13293.560	7204.954	2741.653	1725.838	906.903	1489.164	27362.072	2.094
7,001- 8,000	16755.938	8639.210	4212.099	3317.646	1758.804	2104.974	36788.671	2.150
8,001- 9,000	15923.032	7946.144	4869.378	4696.739	2970.344	3100.415	39506.052	2.365
9,001-10,000	12248.979	8772.164	5376.637	5186.191	3279.400	3423.397	38286.768	2.323
10,001-12,000	17631.218	21121.799	15276.481	16524.687	11170.346	12127.874	93852.405	2.443
12,001-15,000	12171.834	28129.153	20339.062	22006.032	14875.309	16152.638	113673.028	3.100
15,001-25,000	9585.315	40176.357	37658.220	37899.560	27262.365	32758.553	185340.370	4.554
Over 25,000	14993.179	64252.432	49145.882	52235.214	39211.838	49542.678	269381.223	14.171
Total	158096.429	202136.299	143522.598	145654.721	102878.990	122630.952	874919.989	

Table 10.26. Distribution of Individual Income Tax Burdens on City of Milwaukee Residents If a Municipal Individual Income Tax Were Enacted to Yield an Additional $1,000,000 from City of Milwaukee Residents, by Family Income Class and Size, 1970 (in dollars)

Family income	Number of persons in family						Total	Average per household
	1	2	3	4	5	6 and up		
$ 0– 1,000	229.463	25.674	11.696	8.879	4.832	7.185	287.729	.018
1,001– 2,000	1666.216	332.492	110.831	83.593	46.962	42.266	2282.360	.939
2,001– 3,000	3615.815	653.376	149.169	102.063	60.627	64.989	4646.039	.436
3,001– 4,000	7069.133	1985.685	452.001	196.386	152.745	229.118	10085.068	.779
4,001– 5,000	10089.434	4730.272	989.227	526.908	362.037	494.613	17192.491	1.700
5,001– 6,000	14924.655	6883.479	2013.912	1063.635	762.151	1010.574	26658.406	2.412
6,001– 7,000	17391.978	9426.249	3586.907	2257.915	1186.502	1948.274	35797.825	2.740
7,001– 8,000	21672.826	11174.312	5448.103	4291.181	2274.910	2722.661	47583.993	2.781
8,001– 9,000	24124.238	12038.830	7377.366	7115.808	4500.229	4697.293	59853.764	3.583
9,001–10,000	22104.883	15830.516	9702.845	9359.159	5918.107	6177.967	69093.477	4.191
10,001–12,000	28738.106	34427.598	24899.988	26934.509	18207.171	19767.899	152975.271	3.981
12,001–15,000	21674.135	50089.002	36215.568	39185.687	26448.155	28762.669	202415.216	5.521
15,001–25,000	12011.116	50343.981	47188.567	47490.985	34161.784	41048.918	232245.351	5.706
Over 25,000	7729.928	33126.176	25337.798	26930.543	20216.173	25542.371	138882.989	7.306
Total	193041.926	231067.642	163483.978	165547.251	114342.385	132516.797	999999.979	

Table 10.27. Change in Tax Burdens on City of Milwaukee Residents If Real Property Tax Financing of $1,000,000 Were Replaced by Individual Income Tax Financing, by Family Income Class and Size, 1970 (in dollars)

Family income	Number of persons in family						Total	Average per household
	1	2	3	4	5	6 and up		
$ 0– 1,000	− 123.212	− 13.786	− 6.280	− 4.768	− 2.594	− 3.858	− 154.498	− .010
1,001– 2,000	466.774	93.144	31.048	23.418	13.156	11.840	639.380	.263
2,001– 3,000	− 4704.497	− 850.101	− 194.082	− 132.793	− 78.881	− 84.556	− 6044.910	− .567
3,001– 4,000	− 6237.543	− 1752.096	− 398.829	− 173.284	− 134.777	− 202.165	− 8898.694	− .688
4,001– 5,000	− 717.786	− 336.523	− 70.376	− 37.485	− 25.756	− 35.188	− 1223.114	− .121
5,001– 6,000	3417.607	1576.253	461.167	243.563	174.526	231.412	6104.528	.552
6,001– 7,000	4098.418	2221.295	845.254	532.078	279.599	459.111	8435.755	.646
7,001– 8,000	4916.888	2535.103	1236.005	973.535	516.106	617.687	10795.324	.631
8,001– 9,000	8201.207	4092.686	2507.988	2419.070	1529.885	1596.878	20347.714	1.218
9,001–10,000	9855.905	7058.353	4326.208	4172.968	2638.706	2754.570	30806.710	1.869
10,001–12,000	11106.888	13305.799	9623.507	10409.822	7036.824	7640.025	59122.865	1.539
12,001–15,000	9502.300	21959.849	15877.506	17179.655	11612.846	12610.031	88742.187	2.420
15,001–25,000	2425.802	10167.625	9530.348	9591.425	6899.418	8290.365	46904.983	1.152
Over 25,000	− 7263.251	− 31126.256	− 23808.084	− 25304.671	− 18995.666	− 24000.307	− 130498.235	− 6.865
Total	34945.500	28931.345	19961.380	19892.533	11463.392	9885.845	125079.995	

total expenditures for that local service in Milwaukee as well as the city's percentage of total property taxes levied throughout the state for financing that local service. Nevertheless, in this chapter we are focusing our attention solely on the relative burdens produced by these two taxes on city residents.

If the real property tax levy in the City of Milwaukee were reduced by one million dollars, the aggregate tax burden removed from the residents of the city would be about $874,920 because of the exporting of about 12.5 percent of the property tax burden (as explained above).

Since the individual income tax cannot be shifted, however, the full one-million-dollar income tax levy would be borne by city residents. The difference of $125,000 represents the increase in total tax burdens on city residents in the aggregate.

If the real property tax levy were reduced by $1,000,000 the aggregate reduction in property tax burdens of $874,920 would be distributed by family income and size, as shown in table 10.25. The average reduction in property tax burden is greater per household (see the last column in the table) as income increases. Reductions in real property tax burdens range from an average $.027 for families in the 0-$1,000 bracket up to over $14.17 for families with incomes over $25,000. The distribution of the benefits of this simulated plan for real property tax relief is similar to that encountered in the previous sections, that is, while the amount of tax relief generally decreases for larger families, the relative amount of relief according to family size (of more than two and up to five members) is greater for households with incomes of less than $10,000.

The distribution according to family income and size of the individual income tax burden of $1,000,000 on residents of Milwaukee is shown in table 10.26. The average burden per household for each income class is positively correlated in general, although not regularly so, with all income class (that is, income tax burdens ordinarily rise according to income). Increases in individual income tax burdens range from an average of $.02 for families in the 0-$1,000 bracket up to over $7.31 for families with incomes over $25,000. The pattern of distribution according to family size is similar to that of the real property tax.

The differential tax incidence, or the net change in tax burden, for City of Milwaukee residents if the city had to choose between raising $1,000,000 in revenues with a real property tax and an individual income tax with the same degree of progressivity found in Wisconsin's individual income tax was calculated next. The distribution of net benefits or losses according to family income and size of our simulated study are found in table 10.27. The distributional pattern of net change per household for the various income classes is inconsistent and of doubtful equity. Tax

burdens will increase for households in the $1,001-$2,000 and $5,001-
$25,000 income brackets. On the other hand, the tax burden would drop
an average of $.01 per household for the 0 to $1,000 income class and
between $.12 and $.69 on the average for households with incomes
between $2,001-$5,000. By far the largest benefit—in the amount of
$6.87 per household on the average—flows to households with incomes
over $25,000. The increase in net tax burden for households ranging
from $12,001-$25,000 would be more than enough to provide the
reduction (of $130,498) in tax burdens for those households with incomes
of over $25,000. The increase in tax burdens on households with incomes
from $7,001-$12,000 would fall short of the lost portion of the real
property tax that is exported, $125,000.

When the distribution of net changes in tax burdens are expressed in
terms of percentages of property taxes paid by each income class to help
raise its share of the $874,919.99 levy on city residents and median
income of each class (see table 10.28) the same pattern emerges. The
greatest benefits (46.9 percent to 56.5 percent of real property taxes)
would be reaped by those households with incomes from $2,001-$4,000
and over $25,000. In striking contrast, households in the $8,001-$15,000
income ranges would be required to increase their tax payments from

Table 10.28. General Property Tax Relief Changes in Tax Burdens on City of Milwaukee
Residents If Financed by Enacting a City Individual Income Tax[a]

| | Change in tax burdens as a percentage of | |
Family income	Real property taxes paid to raise a levy of $874,919.96	Median income
$ 0– 1,000	—34.936%	—.016%
1,001– 2,000	38.916	.015
2,001– 3,000	—56.542	—.022
3,001– 4,000	—46.875	—.020
4,001– 5,000	— 6.642	—.003
5,001– 6,000	29.700	.010
6,001– 7,000	30.830	.010
7,001– 8,000	29.344	.008
8,001– 9,000	51.505	.014
9,001–10,000	80.463	.020
10,001–12,000	62.996	.014
12,001–15,000	78.068	.018
15,001–25,000	25.307	.006
Over 25,000	—48.444	—.019

[a] The income tax compared in this simulation study has the same degree of progressivity
as the Wisconsin state individual income tax in 1970.

Table 10.29. Percentage Change in Tax Burdens on City of Milwaukee Residents Using Property Taxes For Each Function (Before Change) as the Base, 1970 (average per household in each income class)

Family income	Public education	Vocational, technical, and adult education	Public welfare	Health and hospitals	Legal and judicial	Correction	Per $1,000,000
$ 0– 1,000	– 12.035%	–37.177%	–73.796%	–59.881%	–56.207%	–80.219%	–34.936%
1,001– 2,000	87.812	34.131	–44.053	–14.343	– 6.499	–57.765	38.916
2,001– 3,000	– 41.246	–58.039	–82.498	–73.204	–70.750	–86.787	–56.542
3,001– 4,000	– 28.176	–48.705	–78.605	–67.243	–64.243	–83.848	–46.875
4,001– 5,000	26.219	– 9.857	–62.401	–42.434	–37.163	–71.616	– 6.642
5,001– 6,000	75.353	25.233	–47.765	–20.026	–12.702	–60.567	29.700
6,001– 7,000	76.881	26.324	–47.310	–19.329	–11.941	–60.224	30.830
7,001– 8,000	74.872	24.889	–47.908	–20.245	–12.941	–60.675	29.344
8,001– 9,000	104.833	46.287	–38.983	– 6.580	1.975	–53.938	51.505
9,001–10,000	143.984	74.247	–27.321	11.275	21.465	–45.134	80.463
10,001–12,000	120.368	57.381	–34.356	.505	9.708	–50.444	62.996
12,001–15,000	140.746	71.934	–28.285	9.798	19.853	–45.862	78.068
15,001–25,000	69.414	20.991	–49.534	–22.734	–15.658	–61.903	25.307
Over 25,000	– 30.297	–50.220	–79.236	–68.210	–65.299	–84.325	–48.444

Table 10.30. Percentage Change in Tax Burdens on City of Milwaukee Residents Using Median Income of Each Class as the Base, 1970

Family income	Public education	Vocational, technical, and adult education	Public welfare	Health and hospitals	Legal and judicial	Correction	Per $1,000,000
$ 0– 1,000	–.456%	–.107%	–.445%	–.264%	–.032%	–.028%	–.016%
1,001– 2,000	2.718	.080	–.217	–.052	–.003	–.016	.015
2,001– 3,000	–1.357	–.145	–.432	–.280	–.035	–.026	–.022
3,001– 4,000	–.988	–.130	–.438	–.274	–.034	–.027	–.020
4,001– 5,000	.882	–.025	–.334	–.166	–.019	–.022	–.003
5,001– 6,000	2.131	.054	–.215	–.066	–.005	–.016	.010
6,001– 7,000	2.045	.053	–.200	–.060	–.005	–.015	.010
7,001– 8,000	1.786	.045	–.182	–.056	–.005	–.013	.008
8,001– 9,000	2.433	.081	–.144	–.018	.001	–.011	.014
9,001–10,000	2.932	.115	–.088	.027	.007	–.008	.020
10,001–12,000	2.217	.080	–.101	.001	.003	–.008	.014
12,001–15,000	2.724	.106	–.087	.022	.006	–.008	.018
15,001–25,000	1.421	.033	–.161	–.054	–.005	–.011	.006
Over 25,000	–1.000	–.126	–.416	–.262	–.033	–.025	–.019

51.51 percent to 80.46 percent of what they had previously paid in real property taxes. It is clear that many households would gain or lose substantial amounts that would not be according to any regular or defensible pattern of equity.

In summary, our study shows that the replacement of $1,000,000 in city property taxes by a city income tax as progressive as the state individual income tax would produce $125,080 in benefits to persons outside the city, $130,498 in benefits to households with incomes over $25,000, $16,167 in benefits for households with incomes from $2,001-$5,000, and $154 in benefits for all families with incomes from 0-$1,000. Of a total of $271,899 in benefits, $255,578 or 94 percent would go to outsiders or residents with income of more than $25,000. Households with incomes of $1,001-$2,000 and $5,001-$25,000 would have to provide these benefits (about 74 percent of all households in the City of Milwaukee, according to estimates for 1970).

Summary and Conclusions

We can now summarize the effects of shifting completely the local financial responsibility for certain public services from the real property tax to the state government with the necessary increase in its individual income tax (see tables 10.29 and 10.30).

In our analysis of the six public services of our study we have found two general factors at work which will determine whether the shift in the financing of any service will produce a net increase or decrease in the aggregate burdens on residents in the City of Milwaukee. The first of these factors is the fact that a portion of the property taxes paid in the city is exported. This portion is conservatively estimated at about 12.5 percent (see above and table 10.5). Furthermore, since the individual income tax cannot be shifted, any transfer of financing from the real property tax to t'se state individual income tax means that only 87.5 percent of real property tax relief can be realized for every dollar increase in income tax burdens for city residents. This factor would apply to the transfer of all of the services studied as well as to any others for which such a transference of financial responsibility may be contemplated.

The second basic determinant of whether city taxpayers will gain or lose in a transference of any local-property-financed services to state income tax financing is the relative proportion of real property and individual income taxes paid by city residents compared with total real property and individual income taxes paid in the entire state (see above and table 10.5). Thus, in view of the fact that city residents pay 16.9 percent of the total Wisconsin individual income tax yield, it would be disadvantageous for the city to transfer financial responsibility of any local public service for which residents pay a lesser percentage of the total amount of real property taxes spent for that service throughout the state.

In summary, of the six services analyzed, the city would suffer an amount of $39,610,000 in greater tax burdens in 1970 if the city transferred local financial responsibility for public education from the real property tax to the state's individual income tax. The city pays 16.9 percent of the latter tax while it pays only 10.94 percent of the total real property tax levied in the entire state for that service (see columns 7 and 10 in table 10.5). Aggregate tax burdens would also rise if real property tax financing for vocational, technical, and adult education were replaced by increasing state individual income taxes for city residents. Inasmuch as city residents pay 15.31 percent of total state property taxes for that service compared with 16.9 percent of the state income tax yield the extra tax burden in the aggregate would be $571,000.

While the city's "responsibility ratio" for the real property tax (10.94 percent and 15.31 percent) is lower than for the individual income tax (16.9 percent) our analysis found the city's "responsibility ratio" for the real property tax to be higher for the other four services. Consequently residents of the city would realize lower aggregate tax burdens if local financial responsibility for these public services were shifted to the state and its individual income tax. The city's "responsibility ratio" is highest for the real property tax which is used to provide financial support to correctional and public welfare services (48.60 percent and 36.71 percent, respectively). The significance of these high ratios is apparent in that it enables each and every family income class to enjoy a reduction in tax burdens.

Since the city's real property tax "responsibility ratio" is 23.98 percent for health and hospitals and 21.96 percent for legal and judicial services, it is not surprising that fewer income classes would benefit from a shift from local financial responsibility for these compared with correction and public welfare.

Our analysis of the distribution of changes in tax burdens according to classes of income discovered several noteworthy and dominant patterns. Thus, despite the exporting of part of the real property tax and regardless of whether the "responsibility ratio" of the city's real property tax is more or less than that of the city's portion (16.9 percent) of the state's individual income tax yield, shifting local financial responsibility of all six public services to individual income tax financing would lower tax burdens for families with incomes from 0-$1,000, $2,001-$5,000, and $25,000 and over.

The reasons for lower tax burdens among these income classes are not hard to find. In the 0-$1,000 income class, fewer families have taxable incomes and those that do pay something pay very little because of tax credits for personal exemptions. The tax credit for personal allowances plus the standard deductions seem to account for the lower income tax burdens compared with the real property tax burdens for families with $2,001-$5,000 in annual incomes. The reduction of tax burdens for families with incomes over $25,000 is due to the concentrated ownership of taxable real property in this income class. Moreover, for families with incomes of $15,001-$25,000 the net tax burden increases less than (or decreases more than) families with incomes of $8,001-$15,000. In other words, the concentration of the ownership of taxable property makes the property tax more progressive than do the effective rates of the state individual income tax.

Thus, since our findings show a reduction in both the aggregate tax burden on residents of the City of Milwaukee as well as in the average change per household for all income classes where public welfare and correction services are concerned, it can be recommended without reservation that the local financial responsibility for these two services be shifted to the state and that they be financed by an increase in the individual income tax.

Furthermore, it is true that aggregate tax burdens for city residents would drop if local financial responsibility for health and hospitals and legal and judiciary services were transferred to the state. It is also true, however, that a shift in the financing of health and hospitals would cause an increase in burdens for households with incomes of $9,001-$15,000 and a shift in the financing of legal and judiciary services would increase tax burdens for households with incomes of $8,001-$15,000. Despite this drawback, the shifting of these services from the real property tax to the state income tax can be recommended. The benefit of tax reductions in the aggregate as well as for a large group of families—those income classes up to $8,000 and over $15,000—makes this recommendation generally feasible. It is made with some reservations, however, because these changes project increased burdens on middle income families with incomes between $8,001 and $15,000.

Finally, and most important, our findings show it would be of doubtful wisdom to shift the local financing of public education from the real property tax to the state and its income tax. The increase in tax burdens on city residents in 1970 would have been very substantial ($39,610,000) if this shift had been made. Moreover, most of the family income classes (ten out of fourteen) would have had to pay more in taxes. The bulk of the tax reductions would have gone to real property owners with incomes of over $25,000 and persons living outside of the City of Milwaukee. While less money is involved, the rationale against shifting local financing responsibility for public education can be applied equally well to the vocational, technical, and adult educational services.

The accuracy of the findings of this study suffers slightly since residential property values and taxes throughout the city and state exclude (by state law) multifamily properties with more than eight dwelling units and all properties with mixed commercial and residential users. If we assume that a higher percentage of such residential property is located in the city than elsewhere in the state, it means that our calculations of property tax burdens on city residents are slightly understated.

If our residential property taxes within the city and the remainder of the state were adjusted for this understatement, the probable effect would be marginal and our recommendations would very likely remain unchanged except for vocational, technical, and adult education.

References

Bahl, Roy W. 1972. "An Estimated Income Distribution for Metropolitan Areas: Methodology." Mimeographed. Syracuse, N.Y.: Metropolitan and Regional Research Center of The Maxwell School of Citizenship and Public Affairs, Syracuse University Research Corporation.

Bahl, Roy W. 1973. "Special Report to The National League of Cities." Mimeographed. Syracuse, N.Y.: Metropolitan and Regional Research Center of The Maxwell School of Citizenship and Public Affairs, Syracuse University Research Corporation.

Becker, Arthur P. 1974. *Local Government Finance in the Milwaukee Standard Metropolitan Statistical Area,* vol. 2, *Special Studies in Municipal Finance.* Milwaukee, Wis.: The Milwaukee Urban Observatory.

Becker, Arthur P., and Hans Isakson. 1974. *Local Government Finance in the Milwaukee Standard Metropolitan Statistical Area,* vol. 1, *Past Trends and Projections of Expenditures and Revenues.* Milwaukee, Wis.: The Milwaukee Urban Observatory.

Becker, Arthur P., and Hans Isakson. 1975. *Local Government Fiscal Alternatives in Milwaukee.* Milwaukee, Wis.: The Milwaukee Urban Observatory.

City of Milwaukee, Comptroller. 1971. *Annual Financial Report of the City of Milwaukee, Wisconsin for the Year Ended December 31, 1970.* Milwaukee, Wis.: Office of the Comptroller.

City of Milwaukee, Tax Commissioner. 1971. "1970 Assessment and Taxes for the City of Milwaukee." Intra-office typewritten report. Milwaukee, Wis.: Office of the Tax Commissioner.

University of Wisconsin Tax Study Committee (Harold M. Groves and W. Donald Knight, co-chairmen). 1959. *Wisconsin's State And Local Tax Burden.* Madison, Wis.: The committee.

Wisconsin Department of Administration. State Bureau of Municipal Audit. 1971a. *County Schedule for the Year Ending December 31, 1970. Report of Clerk (Auditor) of Milwaukee County.* Madison, Wis.: The department.

Wisconsin Department of Administration. State Bureau of Municipal Audit. 1971b. *Receipts and Disbursements of Wisconsin Counties, Cities, Villages, and Towns for Fiscal Years Ending in 1969 and 1970.* Madison, Wis.: The department.

Wisconsin Department of Public Instruction. 1971. *The Condition of the Schools: Report for the 1968-70 Biennium.* Madison, Wis.: The department.

Wisconsin Department of Revenue, 1973. Special report to the author by the tax analysis staff. Madison, Wis.: The department.

Wisconsin Department of Revenue, Bureau of Local Fiscal Information. 1971. *Town, City, and Village Taxes Levied 1970—Collected 1971.* Madison, Wis.: The department.

Henry O. Pollakowski, Provocateur and Editor

Summary Discussion and Evaluation

The final session of the conference was devoted to a summary discussion and evalution, over which Henry O. Pollakowski presided. The following is an edited transcript of that discussion.

Land Taxation: Transitional Issues

Henry O. Pollakowski: I think that it would be very useful and appropriate to discuss some of the important policy implications for urban public finance of the papers that have been presented at the conference and of the issues that have arisen in our discussions of these papers.

Concerning the issue of shifting to a system of land taxation in urban areas, either partially or fully, Donald Shoup has presented an analysis in terms of comparative statics. I'd like to complement that presentation and our ensuing discussion by discussing the dynamics of switching from a property tax system to a land tax system. In presenting a static Ricardian model, Mr. Shoup has provided us with a look at the long-run effects of a change of this type. Of course, given the fact that structures in central cities are long-lived, the short-run effects of such change are certainly of paramount concern to policy makers along with the long-run effects. Would anyone like to comment on some of these short-run transitional effects?

William H. Oakland: As far as I know, we have no evidence at all on the distribution of land ownership by income class. Until we obtain appropriate ownership data, we will have a very difficult time saying anything about the short-run distributional consequences of a change to land taxation.

William S. Vickrey: I think you have to distinguish a short, medium, and a long run. In a very short run, you could say, in effect, that nothing really changes with respect to the physical aspects of the city. Market rents remain unchanged, and thus property owners who are assessed differently than was previously the case will bear the tax differential. If you then go to a medium run in which some, but not all, of the changes in property use have occurred, you will observe some effects that may be rather the opposite of what you observed in the short run.

Let me illustrate this with an example. Suppose that you have three more or less identical downtown city lots. Lot A is used for parking; lot B has on it a six-story structure which is quite old but still in good physical shape; and lot C has a five-year-old, twenty-story office building on it. Each lot has a land assessment of $100,000, and the structure on lot B is valued at $100,000 while the structure on lot C is valued at $300,000. The total property tax base is thus $700,000. Now suppose that we levy a tax of 7 total value units. Owner A pays a tax of 1; B a tax of 2; and C a tax of 4. If we now switch to a land value tax, holding total tax revenue constant, each owner will now pay a tax of 2⅓ value units.

Now you may wish to conclude, at this point, that the owner of the vacant lot (A) loses out; that the owner of the lot with the small building (B) comes out about even; and that the owner of the lot with the large building (C) gets away tax free. But suppose that as a result of the freeing of the tax on improvements, it now becomes profitable to erect a forty-story building on one of these lots, which the owner of the vacant lot (A) proceeds to do with alacrity. His property revenue then becomes such that he can pay his 2⅓ value units of tax with very great ease. Meanwhile, competition with the forty-story building has driven down rents in the twenty-story structure on lot B. Thus, even though owner B's tax bill has changed little, his total rent revenues have decreased, and he is thus the one who suffers. The owner of lot B, however, will subsequently, perhaps immediately, be in a position to construct a forty-story structure, and he may therefore come out about even. Thus, in the medium long run the pattern of gains and losses may be exactly the opposite of the pattern that you observe by just looking at the immediate impact of the tax. Now, what occurs in the long long run is quite another matter, and I thus feel that to talk about a shift from a property tax to a land tax one needs to analyze the problem on a much more thorough basis than simply to talk of a once-and-for-all shift. In effect, the reason for changing tax bases is to increase economic efficiency, and if we increase efficiency we create a surplus to be shared. If we are improving matters, there ought to be a system of compensation payments which we can arrange that will leave nearly everybody better off. There are numerous parameters upon which we can base these compensation payments: what were the land and building assessments prior to the change; what will happen after the change; and so forth. Thus you could quite conceivably make arrangements that would lead to a tax that would balance off the short-term and long-term gains in such a way as to make nearly everybody better off, at least in the medium long run. This would consist of a combination of a shift from the property tax to a land tax, plus various kinds of tax freezes, plus some other adjustments. Of course, given a rather rigid capital structure, the gains are going to be realized quite slowly over a period of years. Nevertheless, this is an area in which a good deal of research could conceivably be done which would have important policy implications. I suggest modeling the dynamics of the situation in a manner that would incorporate all of these various elements to see if we can't find some pattern of tax transition that will overcome the opposition of the owners of land who believe that a shift to a land value tax will be to their disadvantage.

Oakland: I want to raise a question as to whether or not it is meaningful to talk about the problem in terms of a short run, an intermediate run, and a long run. Presumably, what's going to happen to land prices will happen almost immediately. The possibilities of erecting forty-story buildings will be taken into account in land prices. It seems to me that we should try to understand what the magnitude of these changes will be. I don't believe that we should have a rolling policy over time—one year, five years, ten years. I don't think it's necessary.

Vickrey: It's important to consider the liquidity problems facing taxpayers. A taxpayer facing an increased tax bill may not be in a position to redevelop immediately. Granted, the value of this property is rising. Perhaps he can mortgage it and pay the tax, and perhaps he can't. The real estate market is certainly not a perfect one.

Aubrey W. Birkelbach, Jr.: What about using a transfer of development rights?

Vickrey: That's another kind of policy that could be examined. Numerous methods could be employed to minimize the set of gains and losses involved. For example, one policy would be to freeze the assessment on old properties for a period of time while placing no new taxes on new buildings. This would be followed by a gradual reassessment based on land value. That's what I meant. I didn't mean to imply that actual compensating payments should be employed, but instead that an equivalent effect could be obtained by arranging the tax. Now, an important problem arises at this point. Not only must you determine an appropriate program and convince the legislature to adopt it, but you must make arrangements that insure that future legislators won't reverse the policy. Then, of course, you must persuade investors that the policy indeed will not be changed in the future, and that's not easy.

Bill Cook: Bill, I have some administrative reservations in terms of freezing the assessment. I achieved a similar transition by working through the rate system and not altering the assessment procedure. In this system, local government bodies are given the authority to employ two tax rates, one on land and one on improvements; we recently obtained this authority in Washington, D.C. Thus you can gradually reduce the tax rate on improvements and avoid the shock of the shift. It would be hoped that this method would lead eventually to a tax rate on improvements that would, through some ad hoc basis, be approximately equal to the cost of public services such as fire and police protection that are rendered to the improvement.

Vickrey: I disagree. Consider fire protection, for example. It should be paid for by land taxes, not improvement taxes. In most areas the cost of furnishing a given grade of fire protection for a given area is virtually independent of the amount of the improvements that are made within that area. And, although in a sense it is the improvements that are protected, the marginal cost of providing protection for an improvement in any given area is nil. Therefore, if a person insists upon having a tennis court next door to the fire department, for example, he is nevertheless using land that is provided with fire protection, and if he wants thus to displace somebody who might construct a building on the land, he certainly ought to pay for exercising that option. It's quite appropriate to pay for fire protection by land taxes and not by improvement taxes, as odd as this may seem on the basis of the usual kind of benefit taxation approach.

Oakland: But if you consider a metropolitan area containing numerous jurisdictions, I don't think your argument is quite right. Consider the case where we have a sufficient array of communities offering varied packages of public services, where migration is unrestricted, and where the system is in long-run equilibrium. In this case the amount of fire service demanded will vary with the value of the structure, and the property tax on improvements would amount to a user charge. In this system of net benefit taxation there would be no dead-weight loss. I agree with your proposition for the case of a single city, but if you consider the case in which there are many communities the situation is quite different.

Vickrey: If you build a fire station in an outlying area that is just being developed, it then becomes more attractive to build in that area and property values go up, benefiting the landowners.

Oakland: But the landowners only benefit because you have a scarcity of communities offering a given quality level of the public service in question.

Vickrey: All right.

B. Cook: I don't disagree with your theoretical thesis. I question, however, whether we want to talk about theoretical concepts that we never reach in that form of purity or whether we want to dilute the situation a little with pragmatism and get some results.

Vickrey: But first the theory, and then the pragmatic concessions, please!

B. Cook: We have to relax our assumptions.

Vickrey: But consider your example of a gradual reduction in the tax rate on improvements. A prospective builder will take into consideration the period of ten years or so of gradually declining assessments on his building and will construct less than the optimum level of improvements. I think that the way around that problem is to institute some form of freeze. While I haven't worked out the details, I think you can find a formula which makes the effect of the tax the same whether he builds a tall building or a short one. This would really accomplish what you are setting out to do and, at the same time, leave a good deal of room for maneuvering. An effort should be made to explore all the various possibilities for achieving our neutrality criterion.

Gregory H. Wassall: Suppose we apply your example to the country rather than to the city. Aren't you simply changing the location of these forty-story buildings that would be built in any case?

Vickrey: Well, not entirely. There are trade-offs. Suppose, for the moment, that you are just talking about one city. Under the property tax it becomes too expensive for some builders to build tall buildings in the center of the city relative to the country. Use of the land tax will change this. Land rents will rise in the city center and fall at the periphery. The cities will become more concentrated and transportation distances will be reduced.

Wassall: Other than the incentive effect of the removal of the tax on capital, will all this shifting of structures be efficient in any way?

Vickrey: Obviously a prospective builder is not going to construct a new building until he can effectively compete with older buildings. That is, the existence of the old structures will affect the market and the market will affect which new structures are profitable. I thus think that the optimum result indeed gets achieved.

Hans R. Isakson: Thus as a result of shifting to a land value tax the center of a city will become a stronger center of economic activity.

Vickrey: To some extent—although I wouldn't exaggerate it—the attracting power of the cities vis-a-vis the suburbs would be strengthened.

Donald C. Shoup: Some economists think of the property tax as depressing the yield on capital. Insofar as that is true, it would lessen the effect on the optimal height of buildings. I still think it would have the effect of changing the structure of the city, though perhaps not the total amount of construction.

Vickrey: Shifting to a land tax would cause a shift of investments from nonreal estate to real estate. Note that there is a countervailing force at work here in that the corporate income tax depresses the yield on equity investment, which is primarily not in real estate. Thus in my ideal world we would simultaneously abolish both the property tax and the corporate income tax!

C. Lowell Harriss: I think several points are worth making concerning the issue of transition of a property tax to a land tax. First, the total amount of savings available for investment will obviously limit the amount of investment that is possible. Thus, in emphasizing the prospective increase in capital that would occur as a result of reduction in the tax on capital—that is, on new structures—it is important to emphasize that this would be true for particular cities but not for the economy as a whole. This limit would apply unless larger sums were somehow being made available; an example today would be attracting funds from the Middle East. But each city or each state is free to act on its own; the ones that move in this direction first would have much better prospects of improving their relative positions with respect to new investment in structures.

My second point concerns the belief that land value taxation would be very hard on farmers. Excluding the urban/rural fringe problem, this point seems to me, in essence, not worthy of consideration, unless rural government expenditures are going to go up. While there may be quite large differences in the amount of structures and even machinery on farms, I doubt that the differences within neighboring areas will be large. Thus, even though farmers are large landowners, they would not be particularly affected.

Another point that has to be made and is brought home all the time is the necessity of educating the public as to what is actually involved. There exists a considerable amount of misinformation concerning the property tax. For the great majority of homeowners, the difference would probably not be very large in the short run. But fears of the difference might be quite great. While this job of educating the public in general, and politicians in particular, would seem to me to be not really difficult, there are numerous causes for pessimism. An example which comes to mind concerns recent (1974) questioning of Governor Nelson Rockefeller by a Senate committee. In response to a senator from a southern state where property taxes hardly exist by northern standards, Governor Rockefeller said, "Yes, property taxes are too high." Now, he should know better. Also, the discussions of the property tax in recent years that are growing out of the *Serrano* case and related decisions (about reliance upon property taxes for school finance) have added confusion to public attitudes about property taxation. Inequality in resources for schools and use of the property tax as an economic and revenue instrument are two quite separate matters.

In addition, one of the crosses that some of us may feel we bear results from a tendency in the past of some followers of Henry George to claim that the single tax would accomplish more good of various types than could reasonably be expected. An idea of great basic merit was somewhat discredited, I think, by overenthusiasm. Finally, there is the practical matter of educating judges and getting legal precedents in line with any other change. My guess is that these need not be difficult; but they would have to be done to make any reasonably effective transition.

Arthur P. Becker: Before we leave the issue of transition, I'd like to mention some results that I have obtained concerning the prospective short-run distributive impact of instituting a land value tax in the city of Milwaukee (Becker, 1974). Working with 1972 assessed values, I found that if we were to shift to a land value tax which yielded the same amount of revenue as we currently obtained from the real estate tax, improved property would benefit in the aggregate by a reduction in tax liability of 4 percent and that the effect would differ according to classes of use. Tax liabilities would increase almost 7 percent for residential property and about 10.5 percent for commercial property, while tax liabilities would decrease 55.5 percent in the case of industrial property. The tax liability on vacant land would increase 250 percent since the ratio of value of improvements to land value is about 2½ to 1. Examining the distribution of changes in tax liabilities, I found that about 41 percent of residential and commercial property would have lowered tax liabilities, even though in the aggregate the tax liability increased for these classes. Practically all residential property would be subject to tax decreases or increases of no more than 30 percent. In the case of commercial property about one-half of the parcels would have tax changes no greater than 30 percent. With respect to value of property, I found, almost uniformly, that properties with low-value assessments would have their taxes increased, while properties with high assessments would have their taxes decreased.

David L. Sjoquist: Thus the ratios of improvement value to land value increase as property value increases.

Eli Schwartz: That makes sense. In the case of residential property that's highly developed, land use is intensive and the land component is relatively small, though not necessarily absolutely small.

Becker: That holds generally for all kinds of property.

Sjoquist: Thus a land value tax on residential property would tend to be less progressive and more regressive.

Becker: I don't know. I wouldn't want to use the terms *regressive* and *progressive* with respect to the value of property since I don't know the income distribution of the owners of this property.

Sjoquist: This is before any capitalization that would occur?

Becker: Yes, it is the immediate impact.

Wassall: What seems to me most important is the changing land use pattern.

Vickrey: This is almost precisely what I was trying to get at in my example.

Becker: Bear in mind that the purpose of my study is to see precisely what the pragmatic problem is. Having gained some understanding of the problem by employing this approach, it is then perhaps appropriate to move on to intermediate and long-term explanations. Also, my approach thus provides a useful complement to our theoretical conclusions. It's very important to recognize that this kind of study has very little to do with equity, even though it would be interpreted as an equity study by many people. It isn't that at all. It simply gives us a measure of the initial impact of the change.

B. Cook: We did a study in Washington, D.C., of the impact of switching to an equiyield land tax (Cook, 1972). We examined the impact on each use-class and compared fifty-six neighborhoods within the city. The results supported Professor Becker's conclusion that the variation in impact response was not as great among general classes of property as one might believe.

Becker: I've also examined the spatial variation in the impact of a land tax. We identified the location of each of 153,000 parcels in the city of Milwaukee and aggregated the parcels according to which of 500 small zones called "quarter-sections" each parcel was located in. We were thus able to obtain an average change in tax liability of parcels in each quarter-section according to the type of land use: commercial, residential, and industrial. We found that taxes would decrease on property in the older parts of the city—especially the core area. This is an interesting finding and is consistent with our observation of a low demand for land in the core area and the beginnings of property abandonment.

I should also mention an important qualification to the above results. The city of Milwaukee adopted a 100 percent assessment program in 1974, and the city's Tax Department has just released some information indicating that this new 100 percent assessment system will impose a greater property tax "burden" on residential property, while lessening the "burden" on industrial and commercial property. This means that the findings in our impact study are not solely the result of switching to land value taxation, but could very well be partially reflecting the fact that tax assessments were incorrect. If we were to conduct another study of the impact of switching to a land value tax today, we might very well find that the tax liability on residential property in the aggregate will not go up at all under the new assessment system. It would be a very encouraging finding. Our frequency distributions might also be affected: we might find that more than half of residential property owners would have decreased tax bills. Great care must be taken in interpreting our results. I'm very concerned that they can be used very inappropriately as justification for not adopting land value taxation. But if the other considerations that I have just mentioned are understood, then it becomes clear that our results cannot be used as an argument against the adoption of land value taxation.

Schwartz: I made a study quite a while ago for Bethlehem, Pennsylvania (Schwartz, 1958). I found an impact pattern very similar to the one you have discovered. Regardless of whether I employed market values or assessed values, there was very little change in tax liability for most of the residential housing. There was an impact of increased taxes on the commercial property; apparently, given the value of land, they didn't use the land as intensively as they might have in the absence of the high tax on business improvements. The impact on industrial land was to reduce taxes substantially since it was essentially low value land. Given that industry tends to cluster together spatially, the demand for primarily industrial land by nonindustrial users is low.

I have a suggestion for Danny (Holland) concerning issues raised by the essay he has presented here. One possibility for reducing the initial impact of going to assessments at 100 percent of market value in Boston would be to tax improvements initially at 50 percent. Shift the differential to land and you then may find that your old commercial properties would obtain tremendous relief if you went to full market value. Now if you don't want to give them all that relief all at once, the differential could be reduced. After all, old commercial properties are probably, in terms of value at least, making rather extensive use of land.

Daniel M. Holland: That's an interesting suggestion. The land component cost estimate that was employed in estimating market value for new commercial property was based on the implicit assumption of very intensive land use.

Fiscal Responses to Metropolitan Consolidation

Pollakowski: I think it would be useful to discuss some of the issues involved in metropolitan consolidation. One topic that interests me is the question of the upward equalization of expenditures which Gail Cook has discussed in her Toronto case study. The basic idea involved here is that going to a metropolitan level of financing for one or more public services with a uniform tax rate would create a pressure to reduce expenditure differentials and that this would occur at the high end of the spectrum rather than at the low end. In other words, there would be less resistance to tax increases which, of course, are spread over the entire metropolitan area than there would be to expenditure decreases. This notion, of course, has application to not only metropolitan consolidation, but also to other types of consolidation where we are shifting financing to higher levels of government. There are thus a number of issues which we might want to pursue. For example, if this equalizing-up does indeed take place with respect to a given public service, will we observe higher taxes in general, or will we observe a change in the expenditure mix? In other words, what are the implications for the expenditures on other public services? We might also ask under what circumstances jurisdictions facing a lower tax price for a given public service actually perceive themselves as doing so. I am also interested in discussing possible alternative methods that can be employed if we wish to achieve some of the goals of metropolitan consolidation without running into these difficulties. In addition, we might think in terms of what other evidence in addition to that presented by Gail Cook could be brought to bear on the general question of fiscal responses to consolidation.

Gail C. A. Cook: First of all, I'd like to comment on the question of tax prices. The Toronto reorganizations did not involve any arrangements between the metropolitan level of government and the local municipalities which would give rise to a tax price effect. The parameters of the formulae for distributing funds were such that in the short run municipalities could not alter the amounts of funds they received. Thus under that sort of system there was no tax price effect. Economic theory tells us, however, that if the observed expenditure change by a municipality just represents an income effect, one would not expect the significant increase in expenditure that was indeed observed. I really did not expect the income effect to be quite so strong in my empirical analysis.

A second concern of mine is that there really is no theoretical justification for the equalizing-up hypothesis. While the conventional wisdom leads us to expect that there would be equalizing upward, why should there not be some sort of averaging instead? It would be very useful to come up with a sound theoretical foundation for this equalizing-up hypothesis.

Vickrey: It may be due to the differences in attitudes toward government services among different groups of the population at different income levels. Suppose there are a number of relatively low tax base areas which have well-lighted streets, pavement, and so forth which they have been enjoying at their own expense. Now suppose incorporated with them is another area which has unpaved streets and not much lighting. Given the fact of consolidation, the areawide demand for the provision of public services must be considered, and the equalization gets made at the level of services that is insisted upon by those who are more attached to a particular level of service. This effect can possibly be reinforced by the fact that those who have formerly enjoyed an inferior level of service can now enjoy the higher level of service without paying additional taxes. While people who have formerly enjoyed a high level of service now find that level more expensive, they essentially exhibit a ratchet effect response.

Only in the case of a quite wealthy community can I imagine change in the opposite direction. In this case some publicly provided services, such as swimming pools in the school, may become privately provided after consolidation because the people in the wealthy community consider extending their high level of public services to everyone too expensive.

G. Cook: Thus one would want to examine the mix of "public" services to determine whether or not the ratio of public to private provision had changed. In your first case, it is possible that the public-to-private ratio has gone up. In the second you would expect the public-to-private ratio to remain unchanged due to the substitution effect.

Becker: If you have a metropolitan government, the revenue potential of the community will be strengthened; doesn't theory predict that expenditures would then increase?

G. Cook: But revenue potential does not increase in the aggregate. You still have the same metropolitan area with the same tax base.

Becker: Correct. But it does give poorer communities an opportunity to extract more revenue from less poor communities.

Sjoquist: Bill, I would like to return to your comments about the effects of consolidation on levels of public service provision. As I perceive the situation, prior to consolidation you have, say, thirteen independent groups making decisions concerning, say, teacher-pupil ratios. After consolidation you have one agency making a decision on teacher-pupil ratios. It seems to me that the tendency would be to move toward the mean. In a situation where voting is employed as the public choice mechanism, you have people wanting low level expenditures versus people wanting high expenditures. It would seem to tend toward a mean.

Vickrey: But the people who had the higher standards are going to say very strongly that "we've been accustomed to this higher standard and you are not going to take this away from us."

Schwartz: Consider this example. What happens when, within a given school district, you construct a new high school with many excellent facilities: a new swimming pool, new tennis courts, playing fields, and so forth. What happens to the demand for improvements in the old high school, which was previously perceived as adequate? I only have a few observations, but my observation is that the people paying the same tax, who use the old high school, put tremendous pressure on the school board to do a complete remodeling job on the old high school.

Isakson: I have studied a consolidation situation in the Milwaukee area in which the opposite results occurred; there was no equalizing-up of public service provision. This was a situation in which an area had been resisting being annexed by the city of Milwaukee because the water wells in the area were sufficiently deep that they were not being contaminated by the growing pollution in adjacent areas. The people living in this area did not need to join the city government in order to obtain an adequate water supply. Thus a large unincorporated area developed in which housing was very similar to that in Milwaukee, but in which the streets were not paved, there was less street lighting, there were no sidewalks, and so forth. In about 1962 the larger township which contained this area was consolidated into Milwaukee. Due to their relatively small size compared to the size of the township, they had little influence on the decision. The result of this consolidation has been that today, over ten years later, the roads in that area are still unpaved, there are still no sidewalks, and there is still poor lighting. There has not been an equalizing-up of services.

Becker: I think that's an exception.

Isakson: I am pointing it out as an exception. I think it supports what David (Sjoquist) was observing earlier: that whether or not equalizing-up occurs is going to depend on the individual situation.

Vickrey: Is that a wealthy area or a poor area?

Isakson: It's slightly more wealthy than average.

Vickrey: That's interesting because in some areas in the Bronx where the streets are privately owned, they are more or less deliberately kept full of potholes to keep the through traffic out.

Political and Economic Motivation for Metropolitan Consolidation

Schwartz: How was it possible to effect this consolidation of the metropolitan area of Toronto? What were the perceived benefits to the richer suburbs of joining a metropolitan area?

G. Cook: It was simply imposed.

Schwartz: It was imposed from above? It was not a case of voter consensus?

G. Cook: That is correct.

Schwartz: I don't think we'll see too many such consolidations in the United States unless federal laws are changed.

Sjoquist: That same question bothers me—why in fact do municipalities consolidate?

Schwartz: In Pennsylvania we had a consolidation of school districts. The districts agreed to this consolidation because the state aid formula provided quite strong incentives for them to do so. Districts which agreed to consolidate received larger grants, while those that refused had their state aid terminated.

Isakson: The laws of consolidation vary quite a bit from state to state. For example, in Texas a large city could very easily annex an outlying area despite opposition from that area. While the situation has subsequently changed, this is indeed what occurred. Houston, for example, could easily annex an industrial park, thereby including it in the city's tax base.

B. Cook: In Wisconsin there are so many legal constraints that it is nearly impossible to annex anything.

Isakson: The case of the state of Virginia is quite interesting. In that state a payment is made to the area being consolidated, in exchange for whatever physical improvements existed there. This payment must be negotiated and settled on through a court procedure.

Vickrey: Who receives this payment?

Isakson: This is an exchange between the jurisdictions involved.

Vickrey: But does not the recipient's jurisdiction cease to exist upon consummation of the act?

Schwartz: If one jurisdiction only wants to annex a portion of another

—say, an industrial park—perhaps it would simply pay compensation for that annexation.

Isakson: I think that the central economic issue with respect to consolidation has to do with the question of the size at which economies of scale result in reduction of costs.

G. Cook: I think that the rationale of economies of scale has been quite overstressed.

Isakson: I agree, but it still remains an important issue.

G. Cook: But consider the hard services, such as sewerage and water, where the main economies of scale potentially exist. Certainly it's not very difficult to get municipal cooperation with respect to them. At least that was the case for Toronto prior to the reorganization. The reorganization wasn't necessary to meet the objective of taking advantage of economies of scale with respect to these services. I'm raising the same question again that David has raised. If metropolitan consolidation is going to give rise to fiscal transfers, why would people voluntarily enter into such an arrangement? One possible answer is that we're employing the wrong sort of model here. We may not be identifying the appropriate decision makers and beneficiaries. It's been said that in the case of Toronto those who benefited were the big landowners and development companies since they realized cost savings on infrastructure.

Vickrey: But the reorganization was effected by the Ontario government.

G. Cook: We still must consider where the real pressure was coming from.

Schwartz: I think that there were two sources of pressure in the Toronto case. The first was that the province of Ontario would have to engage in less income redistribution to the poorer areas of Toronto after reorganization; that is, Ontario could partially shift this function to the metropolitan level. The second pressure, I think, came from members of the government bureaucracy who could see the opportunity of running a consolidated system.

G. Cook: But bear in mind an important counter pressure. The Ontario government must consider the political power that a city of Toronto's size would have in a metropolitan area that would now be speaking with one voice in a province of the size of Ontario.

Becker: I think that in general the biggest pressure for metropolitan consolidation has come from voters in central cities that are in financial trouble. If a central city is relatively sound fiscally, there isn't that much demand for consolidation. But if you consider a central city which has serious fiscal problems and very high tax rates and which faces the prospect of serious future problems in providing public services at socially accepted levels of quality, then pressure will come from central city voters to consolidate in order to strengthen their tax base.

G. Cook: The situation in Toronto is different. The Toronto central city is very strong, and was so even at the time of federation in 1954. I think it's interesting in this connection to notice what sort of different results you would obtain, depending on what sort of index you use to redistribute. In the case of Toronto, they used the assessment base in the proportion that your assessment bore to the assessment of the metropolitan area. The use of this procedure was more costly to the city of Toronto than a procedure that, for example, would have employed median family income as an index. In that case Toronto would have been more favorably disposed toward federation.

Becker: Then in that particular instance, where you have a healthy central city, the pressure would seem to come from the suburbs.

G. Cook: That's correct.

Another issue I'd like to raise is that the political leaders in a consolidated system are unlikely to support the reverse process of deconsolidation. This was indeed the case in Toronto, and the opinions of these leaders were used to support the argument that the metropolitan system was an effective form of organization. Municipalities that were formerly opposed to any form of centralization now support the current degree of centralization, but, interestingly enough, don't support further centralization.

Vickrey: You didn't talk to any of the former mayors of small municipalities?

G. Cook: There was some opposition to consolidation expressed in one case. But that could simply have represented a bargaining tactic employed in the hope of obtaining a more favorable fiscal formula.

Pollakowski: Given the concerns about metropolitan consolidation being expressed here, would anyone like to comment on other policy alternatives for achieving some of the traditionally expressed goals of consolidation?

G. Cook: There is, of course, the Lakewood Plan.[1] But that wouldn't work in the case of Toronto because of the lack of a governmental body equivalent to a county which was already providing services.

Shoup: In Los Angeles County the county government was loath to see

---

1. The Lakewood Plan represents the most extreme example of the use of contractual arrangements to provide local public services. In the Lakewood Plan cities in Los Angeles County, cities negotiate with the county, other cities, special districts, and private producers to purchase all of the usual local public services. See Bish (1971).

any area incorporate and provide its own services. And the county government was able to maintain its role as a large bureaucracy serving any municipality that wished to incorporate. The problem that has developed is that the county tends to underprice any service it sells to a Lakewood Plan city in order to make sure that every one of these cities contracts with the county government for provision of its services. This has led the "independent cities," which provide their own services, to sue the county government, alleging that the county government is selling services below cost. And, of course, to the extent that this allegation is true, the county residents who do not live in municipalities that purchase services from the county finance this subsidy through the county property taxes they pay. Unfortunately, there is no good way to determine the proper price to charge for these services.

Larry D. Schroeder: Thus any deficits that ensue are made up through countywide taxes on those services.

Shoup: That's correct.

Schwartz: Presumably something can be said about the appropriateness of the pricing of services if you can identify marginal costs.

Shoup: This was done for police services, and the price being charged by the county turned out to be well below marginal cost. After many court cases and independent audits, the independent cities forced the county to raise the price it charged for many of its public services. Interestingly enough, the county sheriff is now providing more services free to these independent cities. He thus makes up for charging a higher price for what he does sell to them by correspondingly giving them more free services. The result is that their total payment hasn't increased— it's a very difficult system to monitor.

G. Cook: Has there been any shift of municipalities to the Lakewood Plan type from the independent type?

Shoup: This is another case where you have to look at the bureaucratic aspects. Although every city that has incorporated since the Lakewood Plan came into existence has contracted with the county sheriff for police services, only one independent city ever tried to dispense with its police department and contract with the county sheriff. And there was a recall election soon after—largely arranged, I think, by the police officers who were fired. In fact, aside from the financing aspects, one of the explanations usually given for the attractiveness of the Lakewood Plan is that participation in it means that these contract cities do not have a local police chief to deal with. I think among public administrators there is a maxim that in any dispute between a police chief and a mayor or a city administrator, the mayor or city administrator always loses; and a lot of the pressure for increased police budgets comes not from the citizens, but from the police department. Contracting for your police services tends to reduce this particular demand for the service.

References

Becker, Arthur P. 1974. "Property Tax Reform: An Analysis of a Proposal for Milwaukee." In *Proceedings of the Sixty-Seventh Annual Conference on Taxation, 1974,* ed. Stanley J. Bowers, pp. 93-128. Columbus, Ohio: National Tax Association–Tax Institute of America.
Bish, Robert L. 1971. *The Public Economy of Metropolitan Areas.* Chicago: Markham.
Cook, Bill. 1972. *A Statistical Analysis of Tax Burden Shifts Resulting from Removing the Tax on Improvements and Placing it Totally on Land.* Washington, D.C.: District of Columbia Department of Finance and Revenue.
Schwartz, Eli. 1958. *An Analysis of the Potential Effects of a Movement Toward a Land Value Based Property Tax.* Albany: Economic Education League.

Index

Ability to pay, 250, 251
Advisory Commission on Intergovernmental Relations (ACIR), 14, 15, 16
Ahmedabad, India, 155, 158, 161, 163, 164
Albuquerque, New Mexico, 71
American Telephone and Telegraph, 223
Annual value: assessment based on, 158, 163–64
Assessment, 302; of classes of property, 7, 220, 256; variations in, 8; of EFU land in Oregon, 44; of forest land in Oregon, 45; of farmland, 57–58; of buildings, 114, 305; in relation to income, 163; preferential, 164; in less developed countries, 171; uniformity in, 195–96, 211; of residential property, 196, 219n, 256; of commercial property, 196, 232; of vacant land, 196; public records of, 211; raising of, 211; as part of market value, 226, 228; in Boston, 228; as basis of property tax burden, 230n; freeze on, 303, 304, 305; in Milwaukee, 309; in Toronto, 315
—procedures: 8; by full market value, 9, 195–240 passim; in Oregon, 36, 44; by use value, 59; by land value, 114, 158–59, 161, 165, 220, 303, 307–8; in less developed countries, 157–60; by capital value, 158, 161, 163, 164; by annual value, 158, 163, 164; by improvement value, 158–59, 161, 165, 220, 307–8; role of public in, 211
—sales ratio (ASR): in commercial property, 205, 220; and full value assessment, 207, 208; dispersion of, 209; in residential property, 209, 210; defined and applied, 226
Association of Oregon Industries, 47
Atlanta, Georgia, 245; homestead exemption in, 8, 175–93 passim; tax burden in, 180

Auckland, New Zealand, 107
Austin, J. S., 183n
Australia: property tax in, 107, 119n

Bahl, Roy W., 7–8, 252n
Bailey, M. J., 82
Baltimore, Maryland, 61, 61n, 63–65, 66, 69, 245; development in, 52, 62–63
Baltimore County, Maryland, 71, 72, 73, 77
Beaton, Charles R., 19
Becker, Arthur P., 9, 114n
Berger, Jay, 125, 127, 127n, 128
Bethlehem, Pennsylvania, 309
Bishop, Robert L., 110n
Bogotá, Colombia: property tax in, 154, 155, 159, 167; valorization scheme in, 168–70
Bombay, India, 155, 158, 160, 163, 164; housing renovation in, 165–66
Bombay Municipal Corporation, 165, 166
Boston, Massachusetts, 9, 16, 195–240 passim, 218n, 245, 309; public services in, 26; SMSA in, 26; revenue sources for, 212–20
Boston Assessors Office, 227
Boston Edison, 223
Boston Gas, 223
Boston Redevelopment Authority (BRA), 207, 208, 222n, 223, 224, 224n, 240
Boston Urban Observatory, 219, 224, 240
Boyd, J. H., 82, 83
Break, George, 176n
Bronx, New York, 313
Buchanan, James M., 97
Bucks County, Pennsylvania, 59
Buildings: assessment of, 114, 305; life of, 125, 127; construction of, 126, 127; rental of, 128, 129; finance of, 129
—height of: optimum, 109, 121–25 passim,

319

—assessment: 57–58, 259; by market vs. use value, 59, 74, 75; preferential, 59, 75; by use value, 74n, 75, 76
—conversion: 52–77 passim; sequencing of, 52
—preservation: 55, 56, 75, 76; in Oregon, 37; affected by estate tax burden, 74
Farmowners: liquid assets of, 73, effect of land tax on, 306
Farm use: defined, 43
Federal Land Bank, 44
Federal revenue sharing, 243
Fire protection: cost of, 304–5
First iteration, 234, 237
Fischel, William A., 24–26, 28
Flagg, Ernest, 112n
Flatters, F. V., 98
Florida: land use planning in, 41
Forests: in Oregon, 45, 47
Fox, William F., 20
Full value assessment, 235, 237, 239; distributive impact of, 232. *See also* Market value

Gaffney, Mason, 118n, 119n
Ganz, Alex, 22n
General equilibrium model: of industrial location, 5; in homestead exemption study, 8, 191; in tax incidence study, 176–82, 183, 184; demand equations in, 178, 180
George, Henry, 307
Georgia, 175. *See also* Atlanta
Georgia Coastal Marshland Protection Act, 42
Goetz, Charles J., 98
Goods: property tax effect on, 183, 184; price of, 183, 184, 254; "import" and "export" of, 254, 256, 267
—private: consumption of, 24, 25; production of, 98
—public: consumption of, 24, 25, 95–96; demand for, 87, 96; finance of, 88, 259
Government: role of, in population control, 6, 98, 101; expenditures, 19; fragmented nature of, 102–3, 133, 135; housing programs of, 106; alternative forms of, 133, 245; efficiency and equity studies of, 245–46; general and special

purpose, 253, 257
—consolidation; 7, 138–51, 310–13; in Toronto, 135–51; burdens and benefits of, 147; redistributive effects of, 149, 150, 151; fiscal considerations of, 310–17; motivation for, 313–17; politicians in, 315; Lakewood Plan of, 315n, 315–17
—federal: 4, 5; aid to cities from, 215; property of, 217; responsibility of, for welfare, 243; finance of public services by, 249–52
—intervention: in locational decisions, 101; in agriculture, 103; in communications, 103; in transportation, 103
—local: 4; and property tax, 24, 106; revenue of, 166, 247; receiving state aid, 218n, 218–19; and public services, 244–53
—metropolitan: in less developed countries, 164; in Toronto, 310, 311, 313
—rural: expenses of, 306
—state: 4; authority of, in Oregon, 38, 40; tax policy and land sale, 59; in urban planning, 102–3; control of public services, 218, 219, 244–53; aiding local governments, 218n, 218–19; aid to schools, 265; finance of correctional services, 284–87

Hamer, Andrew N., 16
Hamilton, Bruce, 86, 87, 89, 92, 97
Harberger, Arnold C., 8, 176, 191
Harriss, C. Lowell, 119n
Harvard Law School International Tax Program, 222n
Hawaii: land use control in, 40–41; land development in, 41; property tax base shift in Oahu, 119; property tax law of, 119; Honolulu, 129n
Health, 247, 249, 250, 252; state responsibility for, 219; as state and federal concern, 250; state income vs. local property tax finance of, 277–80; tax burden from, 296, 297
Henderson, J. V., 98
Hicks, Ursula K., 114n
High-rise. *See* Buildings
Highways, 247
Holland, Daniel M., 8–9, 220, 230, 230n, 309

Responsibility ratio: in public services, 296

Revenue, 249, 257, 302, 307; tax, 24, 302; production function, 121, 129n; annual net, 125, 127, 130; sources of, 212–20, 244; of local governments, 247

Rhode Island Coastal Wetlands Act, 42

Richman, Raymond L., 107

Rights: in property, 83, 84, 102; of state vs. out-of-state residents, 103; in development, 303

Robinson, Joan, 110n

Rockefeller, Nelson, 307

Roxbury, Massachusetts, 214

Rural sector: effect of urban population planning on, 102

Rural-urban land conversion, 52, 69

Sales tax, 157, 218

Sander, Barbara A., 71

San Diego, California, 245

San Francisco, California, 101

San José, California, 102

Schmenner, Roger W., 21, 22, 23

School, public: in Oregon, 31; allowed in EFU zone, 43; property of, 265

School Board of the City of Milwaukee, 244, 247, 265

Schroeder, Larry D., 8, 183

Scott, Anthony D., 98

Seoul, Korea, 155, 158, 159, 161, 164, 165; land adjustment scheme in, 167–68

Seoul Special City (SSC), 167

Sewerage Commission of City of Milwaukee, 247

Shoup, Donald C., 6, 118n

Singapore, China, 155, 158, 160, 163, 164

Sjoquist, David L., 8, 183

Skyscrapers. *See* Buildings

Smith, Theodore R., 222n

SMSA, 21, 22, 23; in Kentucky, 21; in Boston, 26; in Atlanta, 176, 177

Social security: income from, 252

State Building Repairs and Reconstruction Board, 165

Stevens Valuation Quarterly, 222n

Stigler, George, 16

Subdivision: in Oregon, 33, 38, 40, 44; in Baltimore, 61, 62, 64; as alternative in land sales, 71; pattern of, 76

Suburbanization, 13–14, 90; of employ-ment, 13–14; effect of, on industry, 14; effect of, on property tax, 14; effect of, on urban poor, 14; forces of, 14, 15, 20; in Oregon, 36, 46; and urban financial burdens, 243

Suburbs, 306, 315; restrictions of, 55–56; homogeneous, 89; housing in, 89, 90, 91; stratified, 89, 91, 92, 97; public services in, 91; zoning in, 91; population restrictions in, 101; of Toronto, 135, 136, 313

Sudbury, Massachusetts, 196n

Survey of Consumer Expenditures, 184

Survey of Current Business, 181

Tax: revenue, 24, 302; base, 27; policy, 51, 52, 57, 304; effects of, on urban development, 52; exemptions, 59, 224; relief, 90; used to modify environment, 90; advantages, 113; in Toronto, 136, 137, 138; credits, by family size, 264, 267, 268; reductions, 276, 297–98; incidence, differential, 287–95; in city vs. state, 295–96; compensation for burdens, 303, 304; on capital, 305, 306; price effect of, 310

Tax burden, 302; redistribution of, 119, 228; change in, 230, 232, 249, 250, 252, 253, 276, 291, 292; "initial impact" method of estimating, 232; "steady state" method of estimating, 235, 237–39; reduction in, 246, 247; aggregate, 252, 253, 271, 277, 280, 282, 291, 295, 296, 297; from shift from local to state finance of public services, 252–87; by income and family size, 264, 267, 268, 270–72, 275–76, 277–80, 287–95, 296–98; incidence of, 265; impact of property vs. city tax on, 287–95

Taxpayers: attitudes of, 210; political influence of, 210; tax burden on, 252; classes of, 253; local, 254; liquidity problems of, 303

Tax Reform Act of 1976, 74

Texas, 313

Toronto, Canada, 310, 311, 313, 314–15; federation in, 7, 135–51; population planning in, 101; suburbs of, 135, 136; municipalities of, 135, 136, 137, 143, 150, 151; property tax in, 138, 147–48, 150–51; public services in, 138–47